IDEAS IN CONTEXT 48

EARLY MODERN LIBERALISM

Early modern liberalism rediscovers an important phase in the development of liberal thought. Despite the fact that "liberalism" as a term was not applied to political thought or political parties in England until late in the eighteenth century, Annabel Patterson argues that its central ideas were formulated by seventeenth-century English writers in defiance of their society's norms, and then transmitted to the American colonies. The author is particularly concerned with the means and agents of transmission, with those who ensured that the liberal canon would be preserved, expanded, republished and dispersed; for example, the eighteenth-century philanthropist Thomas Hollis, among whose heroes were Milton, Marvell, Locke and Algernon Sidney. Important recipients of this tradition were Thomas Jefferson and John Adams. Framed by chapters on Hollis and Adams, this book shows what early modern liberals had in common and thereby reopens, with a contemporary twist, the transatlantic conversation that began in the seventeenth century.

IDEAS IN CONTEXT

Edited by QUENTIN SKINNER *(General Editor)*,
LORRAINE DATSON, WOLF LEPENIES,
J. B. SCHNEEWIND and JAMES TULLY

The books in this series will discuss the emergence of intellectual traditions and of related new disciplines. The procedures, aims and vocabularies that were generated will be set in the context of the alternatives available within the contemporary frameworks of ideas and institutions. Through detailed studies of the evolution of such traditions, and their modification by different audiences, it is hoped that a new picture will form of the development of ideas in their concrete contexts. By this means, artificial distinctions between the history of philosophy, of the various sciences, of society and politics, and of literature may be seen to dissolve.

The series is published with the support of the Exxon Foundation.

A list of books in the series will be found at the end of the volume.

EARLY MODERN LIBERALISM

ANNABEL PATTERSON

Yale University

CAMBRIDGE
UNIVERSITY PRESS

PUBLISHED BY THE PRESS SYNDICATE OF THE UNIVERSITY OF CAMBRIDGE
The Pitt Building, Trumpington Street, Cambridge CB2 1RP, United Kingdom

CAMBRIDGE UNIVERSITY PRESS
The Edinburgh Building, Cambridge CB2 1RP, United Kingdom
40 West 20th Street, New York, NY 10011–4211, USA
10 Stamford Road, Oakleigh, Melbourne 3166, Australia

© Annabel Patterson 1997

First published 1997

Printed in the United Kingdom at the University Press, Cambridge

Typeset in Baskerville no. 2 11/12½ [CE]

A catalogue record for this book is available from the British library

Library of Congress cataloguing in publication data
Patterson, Annabel M.
Early modern liberalism / Annabel Patterson.
p.   cm. – (Ideas in context 48)
Includes index.
ISBN 0 521 59260 7
1. Liberalism – History – 17th century.   I. Title.   II. Series.
JC574.P37   1997
320.51′2 – dc21   96–18733   CIP

ISBN 0 521 59260 7 hardback

Contents

Illustrations

Acknowledgments

This book was written in the flush of energy released by a late-life move to Yale University, the intellectual stimulus provided by new colleagues, and the extraordinary resources of the Stirling, Beinecke and Mudd libraries. I am particularly grateful to Alexander Welsh for triggering a proper encounter with Locke; to John Demos for reading kindly the chapter on John Adams; and to David Quint and Larry Manley for their unfailing courtesy and encouragement. Nobody, however, could be a better listener than April London, of the University of Ottawa, whose knowledge of the eighteenth century I was able to tap for the secret histories of that period; and Nicholas Van Maltzahn, from the same university, shared with me at a crucial stage his work on Milton's posthumous reception. David Norbrook and David Wootton have been consistently generous in similar academic exchanges.

Thanks to Owen Fiss and Bruce Ackermann of the Yale Law School and their Legal Theory Workshop, I was not only at once exposed to the most rigorous forms of interdisciplinary thought, but also given the opportunity to sit next to Quentin Skinner at dinner – a meeting of much consequence for the development of this book. And I am especially in the debt of the two readers for Cambridge University Press, one an intellectual historian as generous as he is shrewd, and the other Nigel Smith of Keble College, Oxford, whose knowledge of the literary-historical axis in early modern England is encyclopedic. Both engaged with my arguments so strenuously that they are, I hope, considerably better fortified now. If not, I have no one to blame but myself.

Lastly, I take this opportunity to thank all my friends in other universities on both sides of the Atlantic for the proofs they have given that there really is a republic of letters – which in the now closely-related fields of early modern English studies seems to be growing as exponentially as my family. In both arenas, if we disagree on details, we share a common project; or, as Milton actually put it, "out of many moderat varieties and brotherly dissimilitudes that are not vastly disproportionall arises the goodly and the gracefull symmetry."

Introduction

Principles

This book is not a disinterested academic investigation. Though nobody familiar with what I have written elsewhere will be surprised to find me once again in the missionary position, candor requires that I explain why this topic – the origins of liberalism – deserves reconsideration at the end of the twentieth century. By "liberalism" I mean primarily the political thoughts that flow from the claim that all human beings are naturally equal, and have therefore equal rights, within their own political community, to a broad range of shared advantages: ownership of one's own body, in the sense of freedom from arbitrary imprisonment, torture or slavery; the right to own property; the right to some voice, be it only through the ballot box, as to how one shall be governed and taxed; the right to equal treatment before the law; the right to express one's opinions in public; the right to practice the religion of one's choice, or to practice none; the right to education and to information.

By "origins," I imply an arbitrary decision to start somewhere, in what is now referred to as early modern England – a period generously interpreted here as beginning with the Reformation and continuing through much of the eighteenth century. It is always possible, of course, to trace the genes of political ideas as far back as classical antiquity, and particularly tempting to do so for liberalism, since one of its more important branches was classical republicanism, as derived from Cicero, Livy, Tacitus and some remarks by Aristotle. But in this project I am particularly concerned with the original transmission of liberalism from England to the United

States of America, which narrows the evolutionary period to two rather than twenty centuries.

All of the above-listed "rights," which have come to be known as "human rights," were explicitly defined in England in the seventeenth century and even earlier, in an environment in which few, if any, of such now commonplace ideas were publicly discussed or remotely possible of acceptance. Their conception was therefore extraordinary and perilous. All of them travelled to the American colonies, either in the heads of the earliest colonists or between the covers of books acquired by the later ones. All of them reappeared during the American Revolution, to be rearticulated in the Declaration of Independence and the Bill of Rights. Thanks to American dominance of the world economy during the early twentieth century, all have subsequently spread abroad to the point where, as Ruth Grant put it in introducing John Locke's liberalism, "the basic principle of human freedom and equality is now part of the universal ideology of our times; even the worst of modern tyrannies pays lip service to it."[1]

Why, then, should the story of liberalism's origins need telling *again*? In part because of the gap between ideology and experience, which responsible scholars and citizens should constantly report. All of these principles continue to be given lip service, while in practice they are undermined by intransigent poverty, greed, religious enthusiasm, expedience, ignorance, ennui. In the United States itself conservative politicians have threatened to make "liberalism" barren as a term not only by attacking its legacy in political, social and educational life, but also by ignorantly or deliberately misconstruing the term itself and divorcing it from its roots in the revolutionary and constitutionalist periods. Liberalism was *not* invented during the New Deal or the 1960s. Nor is "invented" a helpful term, since its principles were wrung out of bitter experience that none of us, if we could really understand what it was like *before* liberalism became accepted as more or less synonymous with enlightened government, would wish to return to. But the correction this book offers is not intended only for American readers. We can everywhere benefit from reminders of what it was like in supposedly civilized countries before liberal principles were anything more than minority opinion; and such reminders are particularly necessary in

---

[1] Ruth Grant, *John Locke's Liberalism* (Chicago and London, 1987), p. 1.

the academy, where it is customary to build new reputations by sneering at earlier idealisms and accomplishments as philosophically blinkered or politically oversimplified.

Terminology

In the 1990s "republicanism" has begun to appear as the umbrella term of choice, especially for British historians, for the range of ideas that in this book are gathered instead under "liberalism." In David Wootton's *Republicanism, Liberty and Commercial Society, 1649–1776*, for example, four magnificent essays by Blair Worden resurrect the political thought of Marchamont Nedham, James Harrington, Algernon Sidney and Henry Neville, and present it as a coherent tradition, *despite* their considerable disagreements.[2] For Worden, these four were practically the only republican thinkers of their era. But for an attempt to expand republican thought considerably (and to backdate it), one can turn in contrast to Markku Peltonen, who argues for an unbroken tradition of civic responsibility carried by humanist thought from the mid-sixteenth century through to the civil war period.[3] The Wootton volume opens with the problem of terminology, citing John Adams, second president of the United States, to the effect that "there is not a more unintelligible word in the English language than republicanism", (p. 1). Today's political historians and philosophers evidently disagree as to how loosely or precisely the term "republicanism" can most fruitfully be applied; whether it must refer only to political theorists of or agitators for a headless commonwealth, or whether it can serve as a grab-bag for ideas of civic virtue and disinterestedness.

"Whig," on the other hand, often used as a synonym for either "liberal" or "republican," has the disadvantage, in addition to archaism, of requiring constant qualification. As the party system developed in England at the end of the seventeenth century and during the eighteenth, shifting alignments produced the same ambiguities as today inhere in the names of political parties all over the world. More precisely, under Walpole's ministry in the 1720s the Whigs not only became a corrupt oligarchy, they could legitimately

---

[2] See *Republicanism, Liberty, and Commercial Society, 1649–1776*, ed. David Wootton (Stanford, 1994), pp. 45–193.

[3] Markku Peltonen, *Classical Humanism and Republicanism in English Political Thought 1570–1640* (Cambridge, 1995).

be accused (and were) of betraying the principles of the Revolution in order to remain in power.[4] In certain argumentative contexts, therefore, to make "Whig" a useful term calls for the addition of "Real," "Old," "Calves Head," "Roman," "Court," "Common-wealth," "Rockingham," or some such modifier.[5] This expedient tends to subdivide people into ever smaller and sadder clubs and cells; while the weird etymology of the word "Whig" (from the Scottish "whiggamore") appropriately inhibits its transfer to any modern political vocabulary.

The advantages of "liberalism" as a term are precisely its non-existence as a party label in England until the nineteenth century; its obvious etymological connections with the term "liberty," which was then ubiquitous; and its subsequent emergence, in contradistinction to "republicanism," as a term *not* restricted to political theory or systems of government, headless, bicameral, or otherwise, but more broadly conceived so as to include religious, legal and economic issues, past and present.

It is, I should add, misleading to cry "anachronism" – on the grounds either that liberalism as a *term* did not exist in the seventeenth century, or that it did not exist as a mental construct prior to the nineteenth century. In their excellent introduction to *The Liberal Tradition from Fox to Keynes*, Alan Bullock and Maurice Schock insisted, first, on the intellectual incoherence of the tradition they saw nevertheless embracing Fox and Bentham, Richard Cobden and Lord John Russell, John Stuart Mill and Maynard Keynes; and secondly on the origins of this tradition in the "17th-century struggle for freedom of conscience and the resistance of Parliament to the arbitrary authority of the King." They emphasized the necessity of understanding liberalism historically, and of joining as well as distinguishing its different roots and branches:

It owes much to the Dissenters with their strong belief in individualism, the place of the conscience in politics and their democratic tradition of self-government, but something also to the Whigs with their aristocratic tradition of civil and religious liberty and their dislike of arbitrary

---

[4] For a detailed account of how Whig corruption and reactionary legislation – the Riot Act, the Septennial Act, the Black Act, etc. – led to a reconfiguration of loyalties and political language during Walpole's ministry, see Kathleen Wilson, *The Sense of the People: Politics, Culture and Imperialism in England, 1715–1785* (Cambridge, 1995), pp. 84–136.

[5] "Whig" is unfortunate as a term not only because it is archaic, but because of the internecine struggles within modern history as a discipline, in which Herbert Butterfield's anachronistic *The Whig Interpretation of History* (1931) has served as dogma.

government. It inherits a belief in natural law and natural rights only to see these scornfully repudiated by Bentham and the Philosophical Radicals in favour of the principle of utility. From the Classical Economists and the Manchester School it derives the orthodoxy of free trade and *laissez-faire*, yet at the end of the 19th century embraces the heretical view of working-class radicalism that something ought to be done for the poor.[6]

My book will end, more or less, where their anthology began, and will have, as theirs did not, a transatlantic focus. But of mine it could equally be said, I trust, that "it establishes the continuity between 19th-century Liberalism and that older tradition which reaches back to Milton and Locke" (p. xxi).

In fact, if one wants to see how early modern liberalism was conceived by one of its pioneers (at one of the most inventive because desperate stages of his thinking), one can hardly do better than turn to the final pages of John Milton's appeal, in the spring of 1660, to the English nation to remain a republic of sorts, by refusing to accept the house of Stuart back at the head of their government. Although Milton's alternative proposal for a permanent unicameral senate has subsequently been perceived, including by John Adams, as wildly illiberal, his concluding definition of what most needed to be preserved of the ideals of the revolution is instructively broad and importantly bifurcated, the "whole freedom of man" consisting, as he insists, "either in spiritual or civil libertie." His first priority is "this liberty of conscience which above all other things ought to be to all men dearest and most precious." Then "the other part of our freedom consists in the civil rights and advancements of every person according to his merit." For fulfilling the second priority what is required is a massive decentralization of the law and the fiscal apparatus:

so they shall have justice in their own hands, law executed fully and finally in thir own counties and precincts, long wishd, and spoken of, but never yet obtain'd; . . . publick accounts under our own inspection, general laws and taxes with thir causes in our own domestic suffrages . . . all distinction of lords and commoners, that may any way divide or sever the publick interest, remov'd.[7]

And, as another of liberalism's central concerns, Milton fastens on

---

[6] *The Liberal Tradition from Fox to Keynes*, ed. Alan Bullock and Maurice Schock (New York, 1957), pp. xix–xx.
[7] Milton, *The Readie and Easie Way to Establish a Free Commonwealth* (London, 1660), in *Complete Prose Works*, ed. D. M. Wolfe *et al*, 8 vols. (New Haven, 1953–82), 7:456–61.

education, in a way that, as we shall later see, would have pleased
John Adams in his young and ferociously liberal stage:

They should have heer also schools and academies at thir own choice,
wherin thir children may be bred up in thir own sight to all learning and
noble education not in grammar only, but in all *liberal* arts and exercises
. . . communicating the natural heat of government and culture more
distributively to all extreme parts, which now lie numm and neglected.
(7:460; italics added)

Despite the remarkable fit between these recommendations and
much liberal thought today, the term Milton himself chooses to
govern this linked set of goals is not "liberalism" but something in
1660 rather more courageous:

What I have spoken, is the language of that which is not call'd amiss *the good
Old Cause*: if it seem strange to any, it will not seem more strange, I hope,
then convincing to backsliders. (7:462; italics original)

Milton's "Good old cause" was also a good umbrella for the
advanced ideas he was attempting to rescue from the forces of
reaction in 1659; but unlike "liberalism" it was even then nostalgic,
and is now merely archaic. In his time it could embrace, without
obscuring, the differences between himself and Andrew Marvell,
Edmund Ludlow and Algernon Sidney – differences that were then
crystallized in their attitudes to Oliver Cromwell. Subsequently it
fails by its incapacity to address more complicated variants: the
differences of opinion and allegiance between Fox and Burke, John
Adams and Thomas Jefferson, Lord John Russell and his friend
Thomas Moore.

"A moment of distress produces enquiry"

To leap, then, from almost the beginning of my chronological period
to its end – the moment when "liberalism" as a term entered both
the language and the political landscape – it will be instructive to
look briefly at why both Russell and Moore could and did claim that
label, despite significant ideological and intellectual disagreements.
The English peer and the Irish poet contradicted each other, for a
start, on the value of the Revolution of 1688: Russell seeing it, in his
Essay on the History of the English Government and Constitution, as both the
definitive turning-point from arbitrary to constitutional government
and the sea-mark against which to measure his own political

environment; Moore attacking it (in *Corruption and Intolerance*) as a set of empty formulae.[8] They held virtually opposite opinions also on the value of party politics, on the merits of the Whigs, on the Napoleonic wars, on the achievements of the Reform Bill, and (reversing their natural class alliances) on the character of the aristocracy. These disagreements can readily be discovered by comparing Russell's *Essay* with his edition of Moore's *Memoirs, Journal, and Correspondence*, not least because Russell occasionally marks them in its footnotes. We will return to them in more detail at the conclusion of chapter 7, in relation to the *Secret History* in which both may have been involved as a joint project supported by liberals of different kidney.

Yet both Russell and Moore cut their teeth and nourished their liberalism on its early modern canonical expressions. Moore mockingly described his personal library, before his successes as a writer, as consisting of Milton, Shakespeare, one volume of the *Iliad*, one of Blair's poems, "One, somewhat damag'd, of Voltaire;/A part of Locke, and of Rousseau."[9] His satirical essay on Irish history, *Memoirs of Captain Rock*, published in 1824, cites Milton's late and obscure pamphlet, *Considerations touching the Likeliest Means to Remove Hirelings out of the Church*, in support of the Irish agitation against tithes! And his early squib, *Corruption and Intolerance*, had invoked the authority of Locke's first *Letter concerning Toleration* for an argument for the separation of church and state: "The boundaries on both sides are fixed and immutable. He jumbles heaven and earth together, the things most remote and opposite, who mixes these two societies" (p. 51). It had also, significantly, called aloud, in a society riddled still with corruption and intolerance, for a writer as tough and versatile as Andrew Marvell: "Can *no* light be found, no genuine spark/Of former fire to warm us? Is there none/To act a Marvell's part? I fear, not one." And Moore's footnote explains, for those less well-read than he:

---

[8] Moore, *Corruption and Intolerance . . . Addressed to an Englishman by an Irishman* (London, 1809, 2nd edn), pp. 4–5: "It never seems to occur to those orators and adressers who round off so many sentences and paragraphs with the Bill of Rights, the Act of Settlement, &c. that all the provisions which these Acts contained for the preservation of parliamentary independence have been long laid aside as romantic and troublesome. The Revolution, as its greatest admirers acknowledge, was little more than a recognition of ancient privileges, a restoration of that old Gothic structure . . . "

[9] Moore, *Replies to the Letters of the Fudge Family in Paris* (London, 1818), p. 143.

Andrew Marvell, the honest opposer of the court during the reign of
Charles the second, and the last Member of Parliament who, according to
the ancient mode, took wages from his constituents. How very much the
Commons have changed their pay-masters! See the State-Poems for some
rude but spirited effusions of Andrew Marvell. (p. 27)

Russell's *Essay* will seem more familiar territory to historians of
political thought than the squibs (Moore's word) of an angry young
Irish poet. It was originally published in 1825 as the intellectual
context for his reform agendas, and in the belief that England had
lost much of what had been gained at the Revolution and was in
danger of losing more. It was republished in 1865 from the perspective of what had since been achieved. It constitutes the early
nineteenth-century equivalent, in genre and principle, of Sidney's
Discourses or Locke's *Two Treatises*; and Russell evidently saw its
original historical and motivational context as almost as dark as that
of the 1680s. He enunciates both a canny theory of progress – the
idea that reactionary government can, by generating critique, lead
to further advances (one step backward leads to two steps forward)
only to dismiss it as likely in the 1820s:

Thus we read in history, that after the means of patronage have enabled
the ministry to trench one by one upon the best privileges of freedom, a
moment of distress produces enquiry, and, by an unexpected blow, the
nation wins a triumph which is equivalent to all that has been gained by
the Court. But this advantage is at present entirely lost. Our enquiry on the
subject of the influence of the Crown [by which Russell meant the entire
system of government ministry and its financial costs] leads us to the
conclusion that it is increasing rapidly and continually, and that the
murmurs which it excites from time to time serve only to produce new
restrictions upon liberty.[10]

The 1865 edition appeared, however, with a long and optimistic
quotation from Milton on its title-page:[11]

Methinks I see in my mind a noble and puissant nation rousing herself like
a strong man after sleep, and shaking her invincible locks; methinks I see
her as an eagle renewing her mighty youth, and kindling her undazzled
eyes at the full midday beam . . .

---

[10] Russell, *An Essay on the History of the English Government and Constitution* (London, 1865), p. 334.

[11] In 1823 the title-page epigram had been taken instead from Lucan's *Pharsalia*, 1:137–41.
This famous passage describing Pompey as an aged oak, decayed but still firm-standing and
venerated, subsequently deployed by Andrew Marvell in his elegy for Oliver Cromwell, was
no longer, Russell acknowledged, an appropriate metaphor for the Victorian state. For
Lucan's simile and Marvell's application of it to the Protectorate, see my *Marvell and the Civic
Crown* (Princeton, 1978), pp. 91–93.

A well-read Victorian would have been able to identify the quotation as derived from Milton's most inarguably liberal pamphlet, *Areopagitica: A Speech for the Liberty of Unlicens'd Printing*,[12] now to be understood, by deliberate anachronism, in relation to Victorian theories of nation and empire. Milton's narrowly conceived, mid-seventeenth-century idea of reform as the removal of pre-publication licensing (for Protestants only) has expanded in Russell's secular program to cover a huge list of "improvements" in domestic and foreign affairs, from "Slavery abolished" and "Unity of Italy recognized" to "Roman Catholic disabilities repealed" and "Taxes on glass, soap, coals, candles, paper, newspaper stamps and many other articles, repealed" (p. xciii). We do not have to share Russell's Victorian complacency[13] to grasp the fact that he saw Milton's principles as capable of almost indefinite extension.

Russell's epigrams to individual chapters continue this message of continuity with the past as that which enables progress or reverses once again the reverses of reaction. His chapter on Stuart history from Cromwell through the Restoration opens with a citation from Edmund Ludlow's *Memoirs*: "But certainly it can never be worth the scratch of a finger to remove a single person, acting by an arbitrary power, in order to set up another with the same unlimited authority" (p. 80). His chapter on "Definitions of Liberty" opens with a quotation from Algernon Sidney's *Discourses*: "The liberties of nations are from God and nature, not from kings" (p. 91). That on "Personal Liberty," which had originally prepared for Russell's assaults on the Test and Corporation Acts and the Catholic Relief Bill, repeats the Miltonic quotation from *Areopagitica* (p. 105). The late chapter on "Influence of the Crown," towards which warning the rest of the *Essay* was geared, returned to Sidney's *Discourses* for the dark premise that "Men are naturally propense to corruption; and if he, whose will and interest it is to corrupt them, be furnisht with the means, he will never fail to do it . . . It is hard to find a tyranny in the world that has not been introduced in this way." And the final chapter, on the liberty of the press as a security to the English constitution, introduces, in the context of proposed new censorship legislation, another superb passage from *Areopagitica*,

---

[12] See Milton, *Complete Prose*, 2:557–58,
[13] The term "complacency" may seem unkind to Russell, who was a liberal all his life; but in 1865 he expressed the doubt that "there are models of government, still untried, promising a cup of felicity and of freedom which England has not yet tasted" (p. lii).

converting Milton's reproach to the parliament of 1643 to Russell's to the parliament of 1825:

If it be desired to know the immediate cause of all this free writing and free speaking, there cannot be assigned a truer than your own mild, free, and humane government . . .We can grow ignorant again, brutish, formal, and slavish, as ye found us; but you then must first become that which ye cannot be, oppressive, arbitrary, and tyrannous as they were from whom ye have freed us. That our hearts are now more capacious, our thoughts now more excited to the search and expectation of greatest and exactest things, is the issue of your own virtue propagated in us. Give me the liberty to know, to utter, and argue freely, according to conscience, above all liberties. (p. 336)

"I would fain believe," wrote Russell in 1825 as the last sentence of his *Essay*, and allowed it to stand in 1865, "that all ranks and classes of this country have still impressed upon their minds the sentiment of her immortal Milton – 'Let not England forget her precedence of teaching nations how to live'" (p. 350). In this, remarkably, Russell was quoting from the address to parliament that preceded Milton's *Doctrine and Discipline of Divorce* in 1644,[14] a pamphlet that appealed to parliament to listen to proposals for reform of the laws on marriage coming from men "of what liberall profession soever" (2:230).

Predecessors

This book has many predecessors, some quite recent, most of which will be acknowledged later in this Introduction, as I record both my debts to and my procedural differences from them. But one of the oldest will help to set the tone and delimit the project. In 1860 the New England historian John Wingate Thornton published an anthology of the political sermons delivered in the American colonies prior to the Revolution, in order to explain to mid-nineteenth-century readers the role that the church had played in developing the principles which fuelled the colonists' resistance to English control of both church and state. Entitled *The Pulpit of the American Revolution*, Thornton's collection opened with Jonathan Mayhew's famous "Discourse concerning Unlimited Submission and Non-Resistance to the Higher Powers," which was defiantly preached in Boston on January 30, 1750, the official day of remembrance of the execution of Charles I; and it ends with the election

---

[14] Milton, *Complete Prose*, 2:232.

sermon of Ezra Stiles, president of Yale, a sermon preached before the Connecticut General Assembly on May 8, 1783, and whose running-title was "The future glory of the United States." These sermons, and the well-informed introductions that Thornton provided for them, constitute a polemical history of the Revolution and its provocations (the Stamp Act of 1765, the Tea Act of 1767, the affair of the judges' salaries). But Thornton's anthology did far more than preserve these documents for the future, and explain their connection to historical events. It is packed with editorial reminders of where Mayhew and Stiles and the other ministers (who included Samuel Langdon, president of Harvard) learned their principles.

In Benjamin Franklin's library, Thornton pointed out, were "Locke, Hoadley, Sydney, Montesquieu, Priestley, Milton, Price, Gordon's Tacitus" (p. xxxiv). Of these, the English seventeenth-century authors, John Milton, Algernon Sidney, John Locke, were particularly Thornton's heroes, and he used every opportunity to insert their names and quotations from their work into his notes and introductions. Another hero, however, was John Adams, not least because he had educated himself in early modern English political thought and history. In annotating Mayhew's *Discourse*, for example, Thornton cites parallels from Milton's regicide tracts, and then continues the tradition onward, through Mayhew, to Adams:

This lesson was well conned: hear one of Dr. Mayhew's disciples, John Adams, twenty-five years afterward, in 1775, in defence of resistance to the despotism of the British Parliament: . . . 'Hampden, Russell, Sydney, Somers, Holt, Tillotson, Burnet, Hoadley, etc., were no tyrants nor rebels, although some of them were in arms, and the others undoubtedly excited resistance against the tories.'[15] (p. 75)

Occasionally Thornton pushed the story of liberalism, or as he would have put it, of liberty, further back. In reproaching Phillips Payson for saying in his sermon of 1778 that the colonists need look for their moral ancestry no further back than the first settlers, he wrote:

It is a mistaken pride and a fallacy which would lead us not to look for our origin beyond the Atlantic. We cannot know ourselves or our history without this . . . Liberty was not born here; and we cannot learn her lineage, nor that of our Puritan ancestors, – her devotees, – nor appreciate the cost and wealth of our inheritance, without the study of English history, and civilization, and of the Reformation; for the fruits of this were simply

---

[15] Thornton was here quoting from Adams's *Novanglus* papers, published in the *Boston Gazette* in 1774. See Adams, *Works*, ed. Charles Francis Adams, 10 vols. (Boston, 1851), 4:57–58.

transplanted to our shores by the *children* of those who wrought it. Alfred is ours, and Runnemede, and Edward VI., and Elizabeth; Raleigh, Bacon, and Shakspeare; Hampden, Milton, Cromwell, Sydney, yes, and "King Charles the martyr," are ours; and it is our glory that we continue the roll with the magnificent names of Washington, Franklin, and Edwards, – an earnest, may we hope, of our future. (pp. 333–34)

This evangelical historicism is unpopular today, even in the academy. But one of Thornton's strongest points is that American nationalism was made by discovering the *alternative* history of England – the minority tradition of critique and reformism – and appropriating it to local purpose. Appropriating it and disseminating it, in the popular press:

There are extant American reprints of these authors, or of portions of their works, issued prior to and during the Revolution, in a cheap form, for popular circulation, addressing, not passion, but reason, diffusing sound principles, and begetting right feeling. There could hardly be found a more impressive, though silent, proof of the exalted nature of the contest on the part of the Americans, than a complete collection of their publications of that period.

Who can limit the influences exerted over the common mind by these volumes of silent thought, eloquent for the rights of man and the blessings of liberty? . . . These books and libraries were the nurseries of "sedition;" they were as secret emissaries propagating in every household, in every breast, at morning, in the noonday rest, by the evening light, in the pulpit, the forum, and the shop, principles, convictions, resolves, which sophistry could not overthrow, nor force extinguish. This was the secret of the strength of our fathers. (pp. xxxiv–xxxv)

Orotund and excessive as it is, Thornton's belief in the secret ministry of books is a faith worth recalling in the television era, when the emissaries propagating in every household monopolize, if the surveys are accurate, an astonishing portion of our waking attention. And for someone in my profession, even more heartening is his faith in the role of higher education. None of his liberal heroes receives more praise from Thornton than the man who is the subject of my own first chapter, Thomas Hollis, the eighteenth-century philanthropist who made friends with Jonathan Mayhew, and through him sent to Harvard a magnificent collection of books "especially on government" for its fledgling library.[16]

In our own century, enormous amounts of scholarly energy have

---

[16] See Thornton, *Pulpit*, p. xxxii.

been devoted to early modern liberalism and its transatlantic inheritance; though with less overtly polemical motives and usually by dividing up into separate projects the elements that Thornton had deliberately scrambled – political thought, the role of the pulpit, the reading of the colonists, seventeenth-century and eighteenth-century history. In 1959 Caroline Robbins, in *The Eighteenth-Century Commonwealthman*, solidly documented the existence and activities of eighteenth-century liberals (whom she called the "Real Whigs") who emerged just a few years after the Williamite Revolution of 1688, and deployed an eclectic mixture of natural rights theory, ancient constitutionalism and classical republicanism to argue that the Revolution had not gone far enough, or that its principles had been betrayed, first by William himself, and much more alarmingly by George III and IV. Robbins stressed that the Commonwealthmen "were only a fraction of politically conscious Britons in the Augustan Age, and formed a small minority among the many Whigs," and, more darkly, that "no achievements in England of any consequence can be credited to them":

Their continued existence and activity, albeit of a limited kind, served to maintain a revolutionary tradition and to link the histories of English struggles against tyranny in one century with those of American efforts for independence in another. The American constitution employs many of the devices which the Real Whigs vainly besought Englishmen to adopt and in it must be found their abiding memorial.

But despite this somewhat melancholy assessment, Robbins chronicled the way in which the commonwealthmen anticipated Thornton in their attitude to publication. It was thanks to them, and to interesting collaborations between intellectuals and publishers, that the now classic texts of Milton and Sidney (as also those of James Harrington, Edmund Ludlow, and Henry Neville) were published or republished, first between 1697 and 1701, and in coordinated stages thereafter.[17]

---

[17] Caroline Robbins, *The Eighteenth-Century Commonwealthman: Studies in the Transmission, Development and Circumstance of English Liberal Thought from the Restoration of Charles II until the War with the Thirteen Colonies* (Cambridge, Mass., 1959), pp. 3–6. See also M. M. Goldsmith, "Liberty, Virtue, and the Rule of Law, 1689–1770," in *Republicanism, Liberty and Commercial Society*, pp. 197–232. Goldsmith not only deftly summarizes the construction of what he calls the "republican" canon, but adds to Robbins's list of canonizers the figure of Francis Hutcheson, who from the University of Glasgow transmitted Molesworth's agenda to Robert Foulis, Richard Baron and Thomas Brand, close friend and eventual heir of Thomas Hollis.

Partly as a result of the foregrounding of this eighteenth-century tradition, and a new understanding of the importance of such figures as Robert Molesworth and John Trenchard, the intellectual origins of the American Revolution, always a topic of major importance to historians, became contested. From the 1960s onwards, for example, Bernard Bailyn, Gordon Wood, John Pocock and Steven Dvoretz have argued against and for the centrality of John Locke's thought, a dispute to which we shall return in chapter 8.[18] Trevor Colbourn's *The Lamp of Experience* took a more humanist tack, focusing on what and how Adams, Franklin and Jefferson actually read, and on the contents of the colonists' libraries, public and private.[19] More recently, the claims of the seventeenth-century liberals have been restated with the same thoroughness that Robbins devoted to the next two or three generations, extending her interest in the political and historical *context* of ideas to the previous generation of dissidents and reformers. Typical of this new focus, in part a countermovement against the British "revisionist" historiography of the 1960s and 1970s, are the essays on *Milton and Republicanism* emerging from a 1992 colloquium in Paris, which opens with a study of Milton's intellectual debts to Aristotle and Cicero, passes through John Lilburne and Thomas Streater, and concludes with the influence of Milton on Thomas Jefferson.[20] Intellectual biography has also been transformed by the belief that political thought is essentially a product of its political environment; for instance, in Jonathan Scott's epic portrait of Algernon Sidney, which places his *Discourses concerning Government* firmly in the history of the later Restoration, and alongside the work of Locke, Neville, William Penn, Slingsby Bethel, George Savile, marquess of Halifax,

---

[18] See Bernard Bailyn, *The Ideological Origins of the American Revolution* (Cambridge, Mass.,1967); Gordon S. Wood, *The Creation of the American Republic, 1776–1787* (Chapel Hill, 1969); J. G. A. Pocock, *The Machiavellian Moment: Florentine Thought and the Atlantic Republican Tradition* (Princeton, 1975); and Steven Dvoretz, *The Unvarnished Doctrine: Locke, Liberalism and the American Revolution* (Durham, 1990). For "Locke in America" as seen from a specifically post-colonialist perspective, see Barbara Arneil, *John Locke and America: The Defence of English Colonialism* (Oxford, 1996).

[19] H. Trevor Colbourn, *The Lamp of Experience: Whig History and the Intellectual Origins of the American Revolution* (Chapel Hill, 1965). I am grateful to Janelle Greenberg for bringing this intelligent study, and its library lists, to my attention.

[20] See the essays by Martin Dzelzainis, Nigel Smith and Tony Davies in *Milton and Republicanism*, ed. David Armitage, Armand Himy and Quentin Skinner (Cambridge, 1995), pp. 3–24, 137–55, 254–71. Of particular importance in relation to my project is, in addition, Nicholas von Maltzahn's "The Whig Milton, 1667–1700," pp. 229–53.

and Andrew Marvell.[21] And between the model of Robbins and the younger generation of contextualists stands the giant figure of Richard Ashcraft, whose *Revolutionary Politics and Locke's Two Treatises of Government* is, in spirit if not in method, the genius of my shore.[22]

Procedures

In the light of these predecessors, distant or recent, I can explain better what this book is not. It is not about political theory *tout court.* I shall not reengage the hoary old question of whether such "rights" as I listed earlier are "really" rights (according to some law of nature) and hence "inalienable," or whether they are merely claims that have come over time to seem stronger than their counterclaims. Nor shall I redo the work that has been done in scrupulously explicating and *differentiating* the thought of seventeenth-century liberals and their eighteenth-century promoters. My project is less that of intellectual history, as traditionally practiced, and more a story of ways and means. I am interested in how and why liberal claims came to be made in the first place, seemingly against all the odds, and made with such persistence that they gradually came to seem reasonable. The task is to recuperate a cultural history of liberal thought that is inseparable from both its historical conditions and its forms of expression, to retell the story of "how we got liberalism" as the belated victory of eloquence and personality over intolerance. The role that eloquence plays in the story is crucial, for I wish to show that "literature," another contested category, and sometimes also treated as an "L-word," was one of the important media by which liberal ideas were transmitted. This argument evidently runs parallel to my earlier claim that the problem of "how we got literature" can partially be approached by seeing the idea of

---

[21] Jonathan Scott, *Algernon Sidney and the Restoration Crisis 1677–1683* (Cambridge, 1991). This follow-up to Scott's preceding *Algernon Sidney and the English Republic, 1623–1677* (Cambridge, 1988) is in its own way revisionary, since it seeks to replace the "Exclusion crisis" as a cause of the 1688 Revolution by a more deeply seated ideological division in the country, on which Sidney stood to the far left. For a more cautious study of Sidney's career, one that occasionally corrects Scott in points of detail, see Alan Houston, *Algernon Sidney and the Republican Heritage in England and America* (Princeton, 1991).

[22] See Richard Ashcraft, *Revolutionary Politics and Locke's Two Treatises of Government* (Princeton, 1986). Ashcraft's revisionary preface is an excellent statement of the methodological limitations that have beset political philosophy hitherto. It is worth noting, however, his own footnote: "For reasons of space, I have not attempted to incorporate literary sources into my discussion of political theory in this study" (p. 7).

the literary as the privileged space carved out for independent thought by unspoken agreement between writers and rulers, from Augustan Rome onwards.[23] But the story of "how we got liberalism" begins later and is finally more heroic, because of its dependence on personality: without the inventiveness, irrepressibility, sheer human courage, entrepreneurial skills, sense of humor and (dare we say it) occasional genius of the men who figure in this book, the narrative of how we got liberalism might not have been a success story.

I do not intend to engage directly with the question of what has happened to liberalism since the nineteenth century, and whether it remains a viable set of claims and principles for late twentieth-century societies. This issue has been confused by noise not only from the right of the political spectrum, but also from the left, and the past has been distorted in the image of the present. I refer, of course, to C. B. MacPherson's Marxist definition of liberalism as "possessive individualism," and hence responsible for what ails us. Considering the political thought of seventeenth-century England from the perspective of post-war Canada, MacPherson concluded that "[our] central difficulty" originated in early modern individualism, "the conception of the individual as essentially the proprietor of his own person or capacities, owing nothing to society for them."[24] As "propriety" emerged in the course of struggles between monarchical prerogative and the defensive "rights" of subjects, and as taxation was often the battle-ground, it merged, in MacPherson's thinking, completely with "property," a merger made explicit in John Locke's *Two Treatises of Government*. This property-centered and entrepreneurial definition of liberalism required MacPherson to set up Thomas Hobbes and Locke as parallel father-figures of the liberalism so defined,[25] whereas in the political circumstances of their time they represented polar opposition, Hobbes writing *Leviathan* from the royalist sanctuary of France during the English revolution of the 1640s, Locke writing the *Two Treatises* as a friend and supporter of

---

[23] In *Censorship and Interpretation* (Madison, Wis., 1984, repr. 1990).
[24] See C. B. MacPherson, *The Political Theory of Possessive Individualism: Hobbes to Locke* (Oxford, 1962), p. 3.
[25] MacPherson also includes, as progenitors, the Leveller movement of the 1640s, but his interest was in dismissing any notion that the Levellers were genuinely interested in social welfare, by emphasizing the inconsistency between different versions of the *Agreement of the People*, as to whether the franchise should be extended to general manhood suffrage or whether it should exclude all wage-workers and those on poor relief. See *Political Theory*, pp. 107–59; and David Wootton, "The Levellers," in *Democracy*, ed. J. Dunn (Oxford, 1992), pp. 71–89.

Shaftesbury and the Whigs in the context of the Exclusion crisis, and himself taking shelter from the Restoration government in Holland. On other traditionally liberal themes – freedom of conscience, freedom of speech, the educability of all, the concept of the person in whom can inhere "rights," equality before the law, some voice for all, men *and* women, in the system of government – Hobbes and Locke are not even in the same ballpark.[26]

Within the terrain of political philosophy, there are signs that contemporary liberal theory has broken the confines of the Mac-Pherson paradigm.[27] Thus, for example, in *Liberalism and Republicanism in the Historical Imagination,* Joyce Appleby negotiates a partial retreat from her own earlier views, and begins to speak less in the language of the Marxist economic historian and more in that of the cultural historian. She offers a canny account of American cultural history, of how the nineteenth century constructed a doctrine of progress to justify explosive entrepreneurialism, which required partial suppression of the intellectual traditions that had made the American Revolution possible. Earlier resistance theory, which implied the promise of *political* change, was transformed into the promise of endless *economic* change for the better; the result was "the West's mixed legacy of wealth-making and empowerment, exploitation and manipulation" (p. 32). Neverthless, trace memories remained, in the form of allusions to the "dangers of priestcraft and aristocrats, of seventeenth-century enthusiasm and Laudian oppression, of Roman tyrants and Athenian mobs." To a modern reader, these can seem inappropriate and puzzling unless, Appleby suggests, "we can think our way back to a world that took its soundings about what could happen from what had already done so."[28] The nineteenth-century version of liberalism had so many limitations (its

---

[26] Whereas Locke wrote the *Letter concerning Toleration* and later argued against the return of press licensing, Hobbes favored state control of education and the press. "There was never any thing so deerly bought, as these Western parts have bought the learning of the Greek and Latine tongues," because "by reading of these Greek, and Latine Authors [e.g. Aristotle's *Politics* and the works of Cicero], men from their childhood have gotten a habit (under a false shew of Liberty,) of favouring tumults, and of licentious controlling the actions of their Soveraigns." See *Leviathan* (1651), Part II, Chapter 21. In Chapter 29 he repeated this attack, and added: "I cannot imagine, how anything can be more prejudiciall to a Monarchy, than the allowing of such books to be publikely read, without present applying such correctives of discreet Masters, as are fit to take away their Venime."

[27] See, for example, James Tully, *An Approach to Political Philosophy: Locke in Contexts* (Cambridge, 1993), pp. 76–77; Alan Houston, *Algernon Sidney and the Republican Heritage,* pp. 5–9.

[28] Joyce Appleby, *Liberalism and Republicanism in the Historical Imagination* (Cambridge, Mass., 1992), p. 29.

seemingly blind preoccupation with progress in the face of evidence for the contrary, its masculine heroes, its middle-class and northern European bias, its claiming to represent universal norms while merely rationalizing American practices) that many have assumed or wished it exhausted. Yet "it would be a mistake," she suggests, "to minimize the capacity of liberalism to cross racial and ethnic boundaries to win adherents to its *personal* characteristics" (pp. 30–31), using a term, "personal," which implies all those other liberal themes I named above. Appleby proposes refertilizing liberalism with republican notions of civic humanism such as those recuperated from the seventeenth and eighteenth centuries by John Pocock. And she offers a tentative new credo, wherein are foregrounded two ideas or procedural correctives central to my own project, memory and imagination. The questions of what a richer liberalism would look like, she concludes, "pull us back to the foundational sites of our history, where memory and imagination play a part in the closing and opening of the American mind" (pp. 32–33). I will not presume to say what precisely Appleby means by memory and imagination, nor do I worry only about "the American mind," whatever that might be;[29] but the work I want these terms to do in this argument seems not incompatible with her program, especially with the injunction that we "think our way back to a world that took its soundings about what could happen from what had already done so." By memory I mean, simply, as informed a knowledge of the past as historical inquiry can provide; not the cultic memory sometimes opposed to conventional historiography and certainly not a conservative nostalgia. By imagination I mean the capacity to project a better future by analyzing the defects of the present. These activities are triggered especially when any society staggers. As Lord John Russell noted, "A moment's distress produces inquiry."

A second political philosopher now reaching for a rejuvenated account of liberalism through the agency of memory is John Rawls. Rawls's *Political Liberalism* (1993) recasts in the aftermath of the Reagan era his earlier *Theory of Justice*, which was produced in the wake (in both senses) of the 1960s. As is well known, Rawlsian liberalism is founded on the notion of justice as fairness, an idea to which he believes all reasonable people can be brought to assent,

---

[29] It is not by coincidence that Appleby alludes here to Allan Bloom's *The Closing of the American Mind*, the best-selling hammer of liberalism that derives from political Straussianism.

and which could roughly be defined, in his own modest and practical phrasing, as "fair social cooperation . . . on a footing of mutual respect" (p. 157). Justice as fairness is founded, in Rawls's theory, on a deep consensus about the "basic liberties"; and although he is coy about actually stating which they are, the freedom of political speech and the press is clearly one of the most basic, along with liberty of conscience, freedom of association, and the liberty and integrity of the person – to travel, to earn a living, not to be imprisoned without cause. Rawls makes the interesting move of combining, even in a single sentence, philosophical essentialism and commonsense pragmatism: the idealist premise that what makes us human is the capacity and opportunity for moral choice, and the attractions of workability:

If free political speech is guaranteed . . . serious grievances do not go unrecognized or suddenly become highly dangerous. They are publicly voiced; and in a moderately well-governed regime they are at least to some degree taken into account. Moreover, the theory of how democratic institutions work must agree with Locke that persons are capable of a certain natural political virtue and do not engage in resistance and revolution unless their social position in the basic structure is seriously unjust and this condition has persisted over some period of time and seems to be removable by no other means. (p. 347)

The phrase "natural political virtue" belongs, of course, to the abstract definition of liberalism, and Rawls usually proceeds by way of logic alone. Likewise, his allusion here to Locke's *Second Treatise* might seem to operate simply on the level of political theory in the abstract. But at least in its preface, *Political Liberalism* glances back to early modern Europe, identifying two developments that for ever after made unanimity impossible: the Reformation, with its consequences in the religious wars of the sixteenth and seventeenth centuries; and the emergence of centralized states "ruled by monarchs with enormous if not absolute powers" (p. xxii) which forced the aristocracy or the rising middle classes to argue and occasionally fight for more reasonable arrangements. This perception Rawls could have found already articulated in the Locke of the first great *Letter concerning Toleration*. Of the two transformations, the Reformation, Rawls thinks, had the greatest consequences for political philosophy, for it introduced a problem unknown to the ancient world:

How is it possible that there may exist over time a stable and just society of free and equal citizens profoundly divided by reasonable religious, philosophical, and moral doctrines? . . . What are the fair terms of social cooperation between citizens characterized as free and equal [classical republicanism] yet divided by profound doctrinal conflict? (pp. xxv–xxvi)

Thus, he argued, "the historical origin of political liberalism . . . is the Reformation and its aftermath, with the long controversies over religious toleration in the sixteenth and seventeenth centuries. Something like the modern understanding of liberty of conscience and freedom of thought began then" (p. xxiv).

My own view of this early phase of liberal thinking shares much with both Rawls and Appleby, but goes further than either in shifting the terms of understanding away from political theory in the abstract and towards cultural history, particularly as this focuses our attention on the most intractable of problems in the history of thought – where new thoughts come from, and why. What circumstances enable people to conceive of the existence of "rights" they or others currently do not have, that are nowhere recognized within the legal and political structures into which they are born? My third and fourth chapters on "unjust tribunals" give salient examples of how this happened in early modern England in the context of the treason trial: one from the middle of the sixteenth century and the center of the counter-Reformation, one from the middle of the seventeenth century and the center of the first English revolution, and two from the counter-revolution more usually known as the Restoration. Reading again the accounts of these trials reminds us that "inalienable" rights were barely imaginable in the past. Two of these four trials resulted in the execution of the defendant, as a direct result of the manner in which the trial was conducted, in what would now be regarded as a kangaroo court, but was then standard practice. How then did standard practice come to be seen as manifest injustice? How is it possible to arrive at a situation where legal rights that never previously existed (the right to legal counsel, for example) can come, just a few centuries later, to be called "fundamental"?

In the United States this problem is sometimes posed as whether there can be, constitutionally, "unenumerated rights." As debated, for example, between Ronald Dworkin and Richard Posner, the question is stated as one that theory alone can solve.[30] That is to say,

---

[30] See Ronald Dworkin, "Unenumerated Rights: Whether and How *Roe* should be Overruled," *University of Chicago Law Review* 59 (1992), 381–432; Richard Posner, "Legal Reasoning from the Top Down and from the Bottom Up: the Question of Unenumerated Constitutional Rights," *University of Chicago Law Review* 59 (1992), 433–50.

it is framed as a dispute over whether the level of generality or abstraction in the Bill of Rights and subsequent amendments permits us to take the widest view, or requires us to take the narrowest, as to what those documents mean by such terms as "liberty" and "equality." But few would deny that when those documents were framed, the meaning of their abstractions carried for the framers a particular historical imperative: the need to mark the separation from England by the construction of markedly different legal and sociopolitical norms. While "liberty" and "equality" themselves had been around almost from time immemorial as ideological vessels, the American Amendments Four to Eight signified their break with the past by grounding both abstractions in certain specific provisions – all of which illustrated equality in the abstract by concrete provisions for improving equality before the law.

My own theory of how people reason toward rights they do not possess has less of a legal ring to it than the concept of unenumerated rights, but at bottom they are in sympathy. The evidence surveyed here suggests that people reason from experience of felt injustice to principles of fairness: finding oneself in a legal predicament (such as one's own trial for treason) where the cards are stacked against one throws the justice of the system into question. When such thoughts pass from the intuitive stage to the analytical, people will turn for assistance to whatever models of protest or imagined alternatives their society contains in its repertoire. This repertoire includes, along with the high-intellectual tradition of politico-legal and utopian critique over time, both the folkloric or popular cultural tradition with its victim-heroes, engaging the hindsight of complaint and the foresight of millenarianism, and (somewhere between the high and the low traditions) the testimony of "history" as the written story of the society in question.

At the third (rationalist-essentialist) stage of analysis, what has happened to oneself and what has happened to others can be merged with ideas of what should and should not happen to anyone – that is to say, the discovery of principles. I suggest, moreover, that people can reason from "rights" *already* established in their system to broader principles underlying them, which in turn are then asked to authorize new ("unenumerated") rights. This is reasoning from the bottom up, what Dworkin calls "the best conceptions," and which Frank Easterbrook complains of as "boosting the level of generality."[31] Thus in early modern England the long-established right to trial by a jury of one's peers was capable of rational extension, and three of my four defendants so extended it, to the principle that the jury should be entitled, as themselves rational if unexpert persons, to interpret the law, discern injustice, and protect the isolated citizen against the power of the monarch and her or his administration. And in the late 1820s Lord John Russell and his fellow liberals explicitly extended the thinking of Milton and Locke on toleration to the repeal of the Test and Corporation Acts and the bill for Catholic Relief.

Such a theory does not discard the notion of tradition so dear to intellectual history, but transforms it by making it more personal. It qualifies the dogma (which is also the dilemma) of the intellectual historian, that ideas can only have precedents in other ideas, which makes them infinitely recessive. It expands the liberal archive, usually restricted to the treatises of professional philosophers such as Locke, which Richard Ashcraft wittily downgraded as "secondary literature" (secondary in its relation to social consciousness), to include the primary materials of cultural history: newspapers, polemical pamphlets, broadsides, plays, poems, historiography, personal correspondence, translations.[32] Instead of an airless academic channel through which books produce only more books, prophetic empiricism recognizes a chain of complex individuals who, in response to something shocking or alarming in their own historical and sometimes personal circumstances, engaged with those circumstances in innovative and courageous proposals for change.

But books – what Thornton called "volumes of silent thought" – are truly an important part of the story as well, especially in their material dimension, their price, their availability, their changing identity as things that get made, remade, destroyed, edited, reedited, packed in boxes and mailed across the Atlantic. It has become fashionable when discussing, say, the effect of the printing press on the first English revolution to cite out of context Milton's metaphor in *Areopagitica*, of books as dragon's teeth sown in the earth that spring up armed men; but not enough work has been done on what processes are implied by such sowing and how long they take. The episode of the dragon's teeth in the legendary history of Thebes was

---

[31] Frank Easterbrook, "Abstraction and Authority," *University of Chicago Law Review* 59 (1992), 349–80.
[32] Ashcraft, *Revolutionary Politics and Locke's Two Treatises of Government*, pp. 6–7.

retold in Ovid's *Metamorphoses*, and, given Ovid's preoccupation with the role and dangers of the artist in imperial Rome, may well have been metaphorical before Milton acquired it. It is thanks to Milton's brilliant formulation of the metaphor, and the elliptical claims thereby made for literature, that the phrase "dragon's teeth" has acquired the force of a mantra. But Milton's defence of the book might itself not have survived, to become a classic of modern liberalism, without the intervention of those who resowed it, to be harvested again and again by much later readers: John Toland, indefatigable deist and tolerationist, who produced the first complete edition of Milton's prose works in 1698; the poet James Thomson, who wrote an eloquent introduction for *Areopagitica* in 1738; Richard Baron, radical cleric, who produced the magnificent two-volume edition of 1753, along with a polemic claiming that Milton should be read for the eloquence of his prose, not for his verse; and Thomas Hollis, Whig philanthropist, who sent Baron's edition of the prose to Harvard College, and persuaded his friends in the colonies that much of pertinence to their own situation was contained therein.

And instead of the notion that thought can do its work best when most insulated from personal vibrations, its secret ministry is mysteriously carried to fulfilment by the vagaries of style. "It is style," wrote J. Robert Oppenheimer in an essay entitled "The Open Mind," "which complements affirmation with limitation and with humility":

it is style which makes it possible to act effectively, but not absolutely; it is style which enables us to find a harmony between the pursuit of ends essential to us, and a regard for the views, the sensibilities, the aspirations of those to whom the problem may appear in another light; it is style which is the deference that action pays to uncertainty; it is above all style through which power defers to reason.[33]

This book is at many stages about style, and the ways in which speaking to people, in writing, on the printed page, can result in a

---

[33] J. Robert Oppenheimer, *The Open Mind* (New York, 1955), p. 54. The title essay for which the book was named was delivered as a talk in 1948 before a joint session of the Rochester Association for the United Nations and the Rochester Foreign Policy Association. In 1954, during the McCarthy era, and in revenge for Oppenheimer's role in the Vista Project, which resulted in the deployment of tactical nuclear weapons in Europe instead of a military build-up for total retaliation, senior officers in the U.S. Force succeeded in persuading President Eisenhower to deny Oppenheimer security clearance, on the grounds of his long-standing friendships with members of the Communist Party. The following year *The Open Mind* was published as a book, its warnings about Cold War policies newly relevant to his own situation.

liberal or an illiberal exchange, depending on the style chosen. Some
of the style in question has formerly been classed as "literature," or
on literature's margins. Most has not, but perhaps it deserves to be
so classified; unless we were to do away, for the purposes of thinking
about political thought, with that hopelessly permeable frontier. For
that reason, this book features what some may regard as exception-
ally or excessively long quotations. They are long in order to permit
their original authors to speak in their own words, and so that
today's readers can appreciate the role of eloquence in deferring to
reason. Usually, it appears, though there are highly interesting
exceptions, a liberal exchange in the early modern period was
forwarded by simplicity, accessibility, and a sense of humor. I have
tried to put this discovery to practical use myself.

One final caveat: nobody's perfect; or, as Lord John Russell put it
in defending a free press, "Even the worst men love virtue in their
studies" (p. 342). That is to say, there is often a visible gap between
the political ideals expressed and the lives lived, not because the
ideals are expressed hypocritically, but because the lives are erratic
and stressful. The story of liberalism's origins in early modern
England is not only, for corrective purposes, necessarily oversimplified in what follows; it is inevitably tarnished by the inconsistencies
and eruptions of bias that can always be cited by cynics to put
liberalism on the defensive. Let us glance back for a moment to
Milton's theory of a liberal education, with all the ambiguities
attached to that phrase, both then as now:

They should have heer also schools and academies at thir own choice,
wherin thir children may be bred up in thir own sight to all learning and
noble education not in grammar only, but in all *liberal* arts and exercises
. . . communicating the natural heat of government and culture more
distributively to all extreme parts, which now lie numm and neglected.
(7:460; italics added)

A sympathetic reader can see that Milton, just like Locke and Rawls,
is here talking about how "persons are capable of a certain natural
political virtue"; but because he writes in the vitalist idiom of the
revolutionary moment which he was then attempting to prolong,[34]
he communicates perhaps rather better than they how we might
actually achieve a just and civil society. Unlike Rawls, Milton

---

[34] For Milton and vitalism, see John Rogers, *The Matter of Revolution: Science, Poetry, and Politics in the Age of Milton* (Ithaca, 1996).

explains the connection between natural capacity and its systemic encouragement. But *The Readie and Easie Way* is *also* the pamphlet in which Milton notoriously restricted elections to those of a "better breeding," "not committing all to the noise and shouting of a rude multitude" (7:442–43), thereby undermining the educational vision he was groping for. By similar token, Milton is only one of a series of early modern liberals who campaigned for freedom of the press and liberty of conscience, but not for everyone. Anticatholicism, especially in its pan-European, Francophobic aspects, occasionally spoils the tone and narrows the insights not only of Milton, but also of Marvell, Sidney, and even, in the next century, Thomas Hollis, fighting to keep episcopacy out of New England; as indeed the Anglo-American academy remains unconsciously biased in favor of Protestant thought today. In the arena of legal justice, three of my four defendants in the "unjust tribunals" of the era, Sir Nicholas Throckmorton, Sir Henry Vane and Algernon Sidney, had distinguished themselves either before or after their own trials by their ruthlessness against their own ideological adversaries and, in the cases of Vane and Sidney, their willingness to see the juridical cards stacked against them. Even Locke, who grasped the nettle of historical irony sown in the Reformation, that it is those out of power who "desire to live upon fair terms, and preach up Toleration," and drew from it the logic of the complete separation of church and state, nevertheless retained the right of the magistrate to interfere with Roman Catholics as potential dangers to civil society; for what does the doctrine that "faith is not to be kept with heretics" signify, he asked, "but that they may, and are ready upon any occasion to seize the government, and possess themselves of the estates and fortunes of their fellow-subjects; and that they only ask leave to be tolerated by the magistrate so long, until they find themselves strong enought to effect it."[35]

Nevertheless, Locke's understanding of the need for toleration was broader and deeper than Milton's. In the history of liberalism, advances are made sometimes purely in response to circumstances, sometimes by logical expansion of the claims of one's predecessors, expanded in the hindsight that subsequent history and personal experience provides. And when Thomas Jefferson sat down in 1776 to prepare his speeches in connection with the disestablishment of

---

[35] Locke, *Letters concerning Toleration*, ed. Thomas Hollis (London, 1765), p. 59.

the church in Virginia, he used Locke's *Letter concerning Toleration* as a stepping-stone for another advance in the theory of toleration. Jefferson's notes mark the leap of logic succinctly. "It was a great thing to go so far (as he himself sais of the parl. who framed the act of tolern.) *but where he stopped short, we may go on.*"[36]

---

[36] *Papers of Thomas Jefferson*, ed. Julian P. Boyd *et al.*, 19 vols. (Princeton, 1950), 1:548; italics added.

CHAPTER I

Deeds of peace: Thomas Hollis's republic of letters

This Mr. Hollis . . . was a bigotted Whig, or Republican; one who mispent an ample fortune in paving the way for sedition and revolt in this and the neighboring kingdoms, by dispersing democratical works . . . This Hollis, indeed, might be said even to have laid the first train of combustibles for the American explosion.
The Reverend Baptist-Noel Turner, Letter to the Editor, *New Monthly Magazine*, October 17, 1818

We begin not at the beginning, but almost at the end of the story, in the middle of the eighteenth century in England. The purpose of this chapter is to redescribe one of the major routes by which early modern liberalism travelled to the American colonies, and thereby to reopen the much debated question of its influence on the founding period of the United States. The reasons for beginning the story of liberalism at the wrong end of the early modern period will, it is to be hoped, become fully evident in subsequent chapters, as ideas, arguments and persons introduced here under the generous auspices of Thomas Hollis reappear and intersect in ways that would otherwise, were we working chronologically, have been harder to perceive.

Although the shape of this argument is preeminently humanist biography, describing what Thomas Hollis accomplished and why it mattered, it will perhaps make better sense to a reader unfamiliar with English politics in the second half of the eighteenth century if placed in a rudimentary historical framework. Hollis began his career as an entrepreneur in the world of publishing in the last years of George II and the Newcastle-Pitt ministry. When George III succeeded his father in October 1760, he was initially welcomed as the first Hanoverian born on English soil, until he made the mistake of replacing Newcastle and the Whigs with Lord Bute, his Scottish tutor, a high Tory with no political experience and not even a seat in the House of Commons. The short-lived Bute ministry became the bait of the famously savage *Letters of Junius*, and Bute resigned in 1763. The Grenville ministry which followed (1763–5) created further trouble by its legislation affecting the American colonies, especially the Stamp Act of 1765, and its attack on John Wilkes for his publication of the *North Briton*, an event so mishandled that it transformed Wilkes into a hero of the Radicals. A huge National Debt as the result of the Seven Years War, major trouble in Ireland, suspicions that George, whatever minister was actually in power, still consulted Bute "behind the curtain," and was engaged in a campaign to recover aspects of the royal prerogative that had been bargained away at the Revolution – all these constituted a dark side of the era that for some historians and most literary scholars was the Age of Reason. And in the church – for this was more important to Hollis even than the disastrous war with the colonies – there remained on the books the Test and Corporation Acts passed under Charles II, whereby both Roman Catholics and Dissenters were excluded from all offices civil or military, and, as Lord John Russell remarked in 1814, surveying the current situation, "even the doors of the Houses of Lords and Commons were [still] shut against them."[1]

So who was Thomas Hollis, and why should we still care about him? W. H. Bond discovered that he was actually the fifth Thomas Hollis, the heir of "a tribe of wealthy and successful manufacturers and merchants, Dissenters in religion and Old Whigs in politics."[2] The second Thomas Hollis had become involved with America in the 1680s via Increase Mather, and specifically with Harvard College, for which Mather was attempting to secure a new charter. Thomas Hollis III was a huge benefactor to Harvard, and established the Hollis professorships in Divinity and Natural Philosophy, the oldest chairs in the country. He had also presented the college with "a new & fair Edicion of Milton's Poetical works," along with a request for a catalogue of the library's holdings, so that he might know what to send them in the future.[3] With this incentive, Harvard proceeded to catalogue its books, and to print the catalogue in 1723, "to transmitt to friends abroad," whereby we today have an invalu-

[1] Russell, *Essay on the History of the English Government and Constitution* (London, 1865), p. 118.
[2] W. H. Bond, *Thomas Hollis of Lincoln's Inn: A Whig and his Books*, (Cambridge, 1990), p. 6.
[3] This must have been the two-volume edition of Milton's poetry published in 1720 by Jacob Tonson, a copy of which is still at Harvard.

able record of what *was* available to readers in the first quarter of the eighteenth century.[4]

Our Thomas Hollis was great-nephew to Thomas Hollis III. He was born in 1720; and partly because of the disadvantaged situation of Dissenters at Oxford and Cambridge, he was privately educated. He was educated, moreover, precisely on the principles of Milton's *Of Education*, perhaps because his great-uncle, from whom he inherited much of his wealth, had been an ardent Miltonist.[5] But the *Memoirs* record that he entered in his diary on August 24, 1759 a sign of his personal encounter with *Of Education*, in which, he noted, Milton had exhausted the subject in a single sheet – that being how the first edition of Milton's pamphlet was published. And the almost forty-year-old Hollis added a personal credo, taken from Milton's famous Sonnet 7, "How soon hath time":

> Yet be it less or more, or soon or slow,
> It shall be still in strictest measure even
> To that same lot, however mean or high,
> Tow'rd which time leads me, and the will of heaven.

In Hollis's *Memoirs*, to which we shall return, the second volume opens with an engraving Hollis had made of Milton at a much younger age of decision-making, with the entire sonnet beneath the portrait; and we should notice that Hollis had calmly arranged for I. B. Cipriani, the engraver, to alter the sonnet's internal dating, from Milton's twenty-third year to his twenty-first, the more conventional threshold of maturity (Figure 1). Perhaps even more characteristically, in appropriating Milton's statement of vocational confidence for his own use, Hollis constrained it with modesty. "At least," wrote Hollis, "I will attempt it" (1:84). It appears, therefore, that Hollis constructed his own personality and Weberian idea of *arbeit*, vocation, on the basis of a reading of Milton's; a reading, it is best to admit from the start, that belongs in the hagiography of dissent.

---

[4] See Thomas Godard Wright, *Literary Culture in Early New England 1620–1730* (New Haven, 1920), pp. 181–83. Goddard notes that "the Library grew so rapidly after the publication of the 1723 Catalogue that the Corporation saw fit to order, at the meeting of June 2, 1725, the printing of three hundred supplements . . . one hundred of which were to be sent to Thomas Hollis, for distribution in England" (p. 183).

[5] After the death of his father in 1735, Hollis was brought up in his cousin's house under the guardianship of John Hollister, Treasurer of Guy's Hospital, who, "*to give him a liberal education*, suitable to the ample fortune he was to inherit, put him under the tuition of Professor Ward." See J. G. Nichols, *Literary Anecdotes of the Eighteenth Century*, 6 vols. (London, 1812), 3:20.

IOHN   MILTON

DRAWN AND ETCHED MDCCLX BY I.B. CIPRIANI A TVSCAN AT THE DE SIRE
OF THOMAS HOLLIS F.R. AND A.SS. FROM A PICTVRE IN THE COLLECTION OF THE
RIGHT HON. ARTHVR ONSLOW SPEAKER OF THE COMMONS HOVSE OF PARLIAMENT

HOW SOON HATH TIME THE SVTTLE THEEF OF YOVTH
STOLN ON HIS WING MY *ONE* AND TWENTIETH YEER
MY HASTING DAYES FLIE ON WITH FVLL CAREER
BVT MY LATE SPRING NO BVD OR BLOSSOM SHEW'TH
PERHAPS MY SEMBLANCE MIGHT DECEIVE THE TRVTH
THAT I TO MANHOOD AM ARRIV'D SO NEAR
AND INWARD RIPENESS DOTH MVCH LESS APPEAR
THAT SOM MORE TIMELY-HAPPY SPIRITS INDV'TH
YET BE IT LESS OR MORE OR SOON OR SLOW
IT SHALL BE STILL IN STRICTEST MEASVRE EEV'N
TO THAT SAME LOT HOWEVER MEAN OR HIGH
TOWARD WHICH TIME LEADS ME AND THE WILL OF HEAV'N
ALL IS IF I HAVE GRACE TO VSE IT SO
AS EVER IN MY GREAT TASK MASTERS EYE

Figure 1   The "Onslow" portrait of John Milton as a young man; engraved by
I. B. Cipriani. From *The Memoirs of Thomas Hollis* (London, 1780), Vol. 2, frontispiece.
Yale Center for British Art.

The vocation was, perhaps, formally initiated in 1758, when Hollis sent his first parcel of books to Harvard College, including that impressive repackaging of Milton's prose mentioned in my Introduction: the two-volume large Quarto edition produced by the radical Whig cleric and editor Richard Baron. Of course this was not how Milton *first* got to America. As George Sensabaugh pointed out thirty years ago, as early as 1664 Increase Mather owned *An Apology for Smectymnuus*, *The Reason of Church Government*, and the first *Defence of the English People*. At the turn of the century what would become the New York Public Library acquired *The Doctrine and Discipline of Divorce, Pro se defensio*, and the 1669 edition of *Paradise Lost*; while by 1714 Yale possessed *Paradise Lost and all Poetical Works* and the three-volume edition of his prose produced by John Toland in 1698.[6] But Sensabaugh's seemingly exhaustive study of Milton's reception in early America did not concern itself with "lines of inter-Atlantic communion," as he put it. Wishing to focus on the patterns of American response to Milton as he gradually became a household word, and how that reception was shaped by growing national self-consciousness, Sensabaugh restricted himself to American imprints. "During such a derivative period," he explained, "an American imprint was enough to declare an American interest."[7]

For those who do see the importance of "inter-Atlantic" communications, especially in liberal education, Thomas Hollis was an early model of what such conversations could be and what might motivate them. Hollis, and the group to which he belonged and which he helped to consolidate – eighteenth-century liberals on both sides of the Atlantic – created (without benefit of technology) an internet of ideas and information which could, they believed, help to change their world for the better. The ideas could be seen as a

---

[6] George Sensabaugh, *Milton in Early America* (Princeton, 1964), p. 34. Sensabaugh was himself drawing on Leon Howard, "Early American Copies of Milton," *Huntington Library Bulletin* 7 (1935), 169–79; and Thomas Godard Wright, *Literary Culture in Early New England 1620–1730* (New Haven, 1920), pp. 180–86.

[7] Sensabaugh, *Milton in Early America*, p. x. This systematic study should be a starting point for anyone interested in Milton's reception in America. Beyond the self-imposed limitation of focusing on American imprints, however, the breadth of the coverage, with one or two notable exceptions, tends to flatten out the interpretive possibilities – that is, the possibility of our understanding Milton better by seeing how he was understood by others; and it is never quite clear to what extent a specifically *political* understanding of Milton was available (as compared to his citation in belettristic contexts, or as an advocate for married love, or as a symbol of general high-mindedness). My differences from Sensabaugh, as well as my debts, will be several times noted below.

minority tradition, even underground and subversive, of political, religious and social thought; or they could be seen as an *avant-garde* movement. The information consisted in the history, including the personal history, of those who had first forged such controversial propositions.

In other words, Hollis and his friends inherited from John Toland and the Whigs of the Williamite era a commitment to rescue and preserve for posterity the earlier canon of European liberal reformism. Toland's work, which itself had to be rediscovered by Blair Worden, Caroline Robbins and others, had already done a great deal for the survival of John Milton, Edmund Ludlow, James Harrington and Algernon Sidney (if Toland were indeed responsible for the 1698 edition of Sidney's *Discourses concerning Government*).[8] But Hollis went far beyond Toland in the range of his intellectual embrace. From the seventeenth century he promoted not only Milton, Ludlow, and Sidney (Harrington was marginally less important in his pantheon) but also Andrew Marvell, Thomas May, Marchamont Nedham, John Locke, Lord Russell, James Tyrrell, Sir William Temple, Robert Molesworth, and Toland himself; and from the sixteenth-century figures like John Ponet, George Buchanan, Christopher Goodman, François Hotman, and the anonymous author of the *Vindiciae contra tyrannos*. Unlike most political theorists of our own time, Hollis regarded the similarities between these writers and thinkers as far more significant than their differences, since all of them conceived of a more egalitarian and tolerationist polity, in church or state or both, than they had ever experienced. And he also regarded the literary, aesthetic or otherwise cultural aspects of the *way* these writers had worked and were subsequently disseminated as of almost equal significance, strategically, as the intellectual bones of their arguments.

It was perhaps for this reason that Hollis was particularly obsessed by Milton, who became his ideal of the scholar-activist and the principle of energy at the heart of this growing liberal canon. Hollis and his friends were more ambitious than Toland had been with respect to Milton. They not only saw to it that Milton's polemical prose should remain accessible; they defended its permanent value against those who, while admiring *Paradise Lost*, consigned his

[8] This is Blair Worden's proposal, in "Republicanism and the Restoration," in *Republicanism, Liberty, and Commercial Society, 1649–1776*, ed. David Wootton (Stanford, 1994), p. 177. See also Edmund Ludlow, *A Voyce from the Watch Tower*, ed. Blair Worden (London, 1978), pp. 17–30.

pamphlets to the territory, at best, of a mistaken (left-handed) radicalism of which their author had, or should have, repented. They insisted that the Milton of the antiprelatical and regicide tracts was the *same* – in conviction and in courage – as the Milton of the Restoration poems; and Hollis ensured that that complex image would be, if not respectable, at least unavoidable.

With the exception of one surprising venture into literary criticism on behalf of "the divine Milton" Hollis himself wrote nothing polemical. He preferred to speak vicariously through others. Nevertheless, this chapter claims for him and for what he represents a special niche in the history of liberalism, as the books he sent to Harvard were originally shelved in a special alcove. I am not the first to make such a claim. W. H. Bond, whose attraction to Hollis was that of a bibliographer and bibliophile, wrote an elegant monograph, which, while primarily concerned with the beautiful bindings and other decorations that Hollis designed for his books, also contains important biographical information. Bond was preceded by Caroline Robbins, who discovered Hollis in the 1950s when working on *The Eighteenth-Century Commonwealthman* (1959). She not only defined his principles but sought out and catalogued his extraordinary benefactions in terms of books to Harvard and other American libraries;[9] But Robbins, and Bond, and I, could all rely on the remarkable late eighteenth-century *Memoirs* of Hollis written by the radical Archdeacon Francis Blackburne at the request of Brand Hollis, Hollis's adopted heir. The two-volume *Memoirs*, privately and beautifully printed in folio in 1780, are a crucial, if chaotic, archive of Hollis documents, which transmit the contents of Hollis's own diary and much of his correspondence.[10] The *Memoirs* also constitute an independent monument to a late eighteenth-century political

---

9 Caroline Robbins: "The Strenuous Whig, Thomas Hollis of Lincoln's Inn," *William and Mary Quarterly* 7 (1950), 405–53; "Library of Liberty – Assembled for Harvard College by Thomas Hollis of Lincoln's Inn," *Harvard Library Bulletin* 5 (1951), 5–22. Paradoxically, her larger work seems to have muddied the waters by enabling the "republican revisionism" of American colonial history, subsequently acquiring credal status in the work of Bernard Bailyn, Gordon Wood and John Pocock, by which Locke was displaced from the "good" liberal canon. See David Wootton, "The Republican Tradition: From Commonwealth to Common Sense," in *Republicanism*, ed. Wootton, p. 8.

10 The impact of the *Memoirs* was both described and extended by Nichols, *Literary Anecdotes*, 3:15–22. Nichols also included his own brief biography of Hollis, which includes some details not found in the *Memoirs* (3:61–66), and a long note on his association with the bookseller William Bowyer, including the abortive plans for a new edition of Marvell's works (2:448–51).

controversy, in which Milton featured as a symbol of the difference between Whig and Tory political thought, conducted at the level of ethics and taste.

Blackburne himself was an interesting fellow, whose genial truculence seems perfectly legible in his portrait (Figure 2). An anecdote from his own autobiography tells that, on the threshold of a university education, he was approached by "a worthy old lay gentleman," who commanded: "Young man, let the first book thou readest at Cambridge be Locke on government." Blackburne took this advice, so thoroughly that he was refused a fellowship at Cambridge.[11] By 1750 he had abandoned all hope of advancement in the church, and refused to subscribe to the 39 Articles. In 1752 he published anonymously *A Serious Inquiry into the Use and Importance of External Religion*, an attack on the Anglican establishment, which was reprinted in 1768 under Blackburne's name in the second edition of *The Pillars of Priestcraft Shaken*, a collection of dissenting tracts published by Richard Baron. Blackburne professed and practiced religious toleration, inclusive of Jews. In the late 1760s he had become indebted to Hollis, who had been instrumental in getting Andrew Millar to publish another of his controversial works.[12] By the time that Brand Hollis asked him to write his friend's *Memoirs*, Blackburne was an old man in his seventies with nothing further to lose. The *Memoirs* therefore became a work of considerably more than personal loyalty. Written in a feisty and often brilliantly sardonic style, they carried out Blackburne's agenda alongside that of Hollis as Blackburne understood it. And central to Blackburne's agenda was the securing of Milton's reputation, as a weapon against the church establishment that had managed to "church-out" Milton and prevent Blackburne's advancement.

But there was also an immediate provocation. In 1779, while the *Memoirs* were in press, Dr. Samuel Johnson published the first volumes of his *Lives of the Poets*, containing his largely derogatory account of Milton's work. This provocation was enough to stop the press. Blackburne wrote a flaming defence of Milton that was also an attack on Johnson and the Tory politics then being offered as objective literary criticism and a refined modern sense of taste. Fifty-four pages were inserted in the middle of the second volume of the

---

[11] Francis Blackburne, *Works*, 7 vols. (Cambridge, 1804), 1:iv.

[12] Blackburne, *The Confessional, or A Full and Free Inquiry into the Right of . . . Establishing Systematical Confessions* (London, 1766).

Painted by G.Cuit.   Engraved by James Fittler

FRANCIS BLACKBURNE, M.A.

Archdeacon of Cleveland.

Figure 2 Portrait of Francis Blackburne. From Blackburne, *Collected Works* (v.p., 1748), Vol. 1, frontispiece. Beinecke Rare Book and Manuscript Library, Yale University.

Memoirs, with bibliographical signposts (repeated and starred pagination) to make the insertion obvious;[13] and in the same year (1780) Blackburne's *Remarks* were also printed separately in a small octavo, along with Milton's *Of Education* and the *Areopagitica*, preceded by the poet James Thomson's famous preface to that tract. When the first American edition of Milton's prose works was published in Boston in 1826, Francis Jenks, the editor, registered the importance of this phase of the transmission at the end of his Introduction:

> With regard to [Milton's] character, I am aware there are prejudices against it, which it is desirable should be removed. Johnson's Life of Milton is the source, from which most readers in this country, I suspect, receive their impressions respecting him. But there never was a greater disgrace to a man who professed to be guided by principle, than that Life is to its author. The admirers of Milton in this country, owe it to the injured shade of that great man, to enlighten the public mind on this subject . . . The biographer's motives are sufficiently clear, and his mere malignity stands out in tangible and bold relief on every page. They are both most ably and acutely exposed in Archdeacon Blackburne's "Remarks upon Johnson's Life of Milton," which were written in extreme old age with all the animation and strength of early manhood, and which ought to be in the hands of every one that reads or possesses the "great critic's" pages.[14]

But at least some Americans already knew of Blackburne's defence. Brand Hollis sent a copy of the *Memoirs* to Benjamin Franklin, Thomas Jefferson and John Adams, and may have been the source of the copies presently at Harvard, Yale and Princeton. He also sent Franklin Blackburne's separately published defence of Milton against Dr. Johnson. And Franklin wrote back, in 1784:

> These volumes are a Proof of what I have sometimes had occasion to say, in encouraging People to undertake difficult Public Service, that it is prodigious the quantity of Good that may be done by one Man, *if he will make a business of it*. It is equally surprising to think of the very little that is done by many . . .[15]

A year earlier Hollis had begun his export of Milton and the other writers whom, he believed, were equally important for the rest of the world to encounter, to persons and educational institutions in the colonies and elsewhere. Hollis bought the bed upon which Milton

---

[13] Bond, *Thomas Hollis*, p. 2.

[14] *A Selection from the English Prose Works of John Milton*, ed. Francis Jenks, 2 vols. (Boston, 1826), p. lxvi.

[15] See A. H. Smith, ed., *The Writings of B. Franklin*, 10 vols. (New York, 1906), 9:103–5. Cited in Robbins, "The Strenuous Whig," p. 408.

had died, and gave it as a tribute to Mark Akenside.[16] He named several of his farms – his inherited agricultural estates – after his cultural heroes and icons: Milton, Harrington, Sidney, Ludlow, Neville, Locke, Marvell, Buchanan, Russell, and Harvard and Liberty! But his devotion was not merely sentimental and eccentric. Either he personally (though anonymously) prepared new editions of the seventeenth-century liberals, as was the case with Toland's *Life of Milton* (1761),[17] Neville's *Plato redivivus* (1763),[18] Algernon Sidney's *Discourses concerning Government* (1763), Locke's *Two Treatises of Government* (1764), and Locke's *Letters concerning Toleration* (1765); or he bought older and by then rare editions of such works and sprinkled them like rain on thirsty intellectual and political soil abroad. His benefactions were not exclusively centrifugal, however. Milton's college, Christ's College, Cambridge, received copies of the first three editions of *Paradise Lost* and a copy of the 1645 *Poems of Mr. John Milton*, "elegantly bound." Having obtained Locke's own copy of the 1698 edition of the *Two Treatises*, with Locke's and Pierre Coste's manuscript corrections, and having based his own 1764 edition upon it, Hollis donated the original to English higher education; significantly not to Locke's own Oxford college which had been complaisant enough to the monarchy to expel him, but to Milton's college at Cambridge, where two centuries later it could be used by Peter Laslett for his definitive edition of the *Two Treatises*. But for Hollis's selflessness this precious evidence of Locke's concern for his unacknowledged text might have disappeared into private hands.

It looks as though Hollis's career as an exporter of liberal doctrine began in the 1750s, when he became friends with Richard Baron,

---

[16] Blackburne explains that he had hoped for an ode to Milton in return; but Akenside never even thanked him, and "an encomium to Milton, as an assertor of British liberty, at that time of the day, was not the thing" (*Memoirs*, 1:111–12).

[17] Hollis's edition of Toland's *Life of Milton* (orig. 1698) contains large numbers of notes, some of which correspond to his commonplace book notes in his copy of *Eikonoklastes*. e.g. "Speaking of government, he cited the Arcadia." See *Memoirs*, p. 756. Some, however, are oral tradition: 'The late Reverend Mr.Thomas Bradbury, an eminent dissenting minister, used to say, that Jer. White, who had been Chaplain to Oliver Cromwell',' and whom he personally knew, had often told him, "That Milton was allowed by the Parliament a weekly table for the entertainment of foreign ministers, and persons of learning, such especially as came from Protestant states; which allowance was also continued by Cromwell," (p. 110).

[18] Henry Neville, *Plato redivivus or a Dialogue concerning government* (London: A. Millar, 1763). This was the fourth edition of Neville's tract, first published in 1680. Hollis's edition includes a biography of Neville, with a description of the Rota and a detailed account of its membership and procedures. Hollis explains that Neville began in the council of state as a favorite of Cromwell's, but became disillusioned to the point of hostility.

whom Blackburne describes as "a dissenting minister, and a high-spirited republican, an adorer of Milton, Sydney, and Locke" (1:61). Baron had discovered a copy of the second edition of *Eikonoklastes*, which he republished in 1756,[19] afterwards donating the rare original to Hollis for his collection. Baron's edition of *Eikonoklastes* contained an eloquent defence of Milton's prose, subsequently incorporated by Blackburne in the *Memoirs* as part of his own attack on Johnson. But Baron had also "corrected" the 1751 editions of Sidney's *Discourses on Government* and Ludlow's *Memoirs*. He had donated to Harvard the manuscript of Trenchard's essays, annotated by himself.[20] In 1753 he had acted as the textual editor of the new two-volume edition of Milton's prose which, as I have mentioned, Hollis sent to Harvard in 1758.[21] Later Baron would republish Marchamont Nedham's *Excellency of a Free State*, with a preface, in 1767.

By the 1760s Hollis was anonymously collaborating with Baron, whom he commissioned to proofread another of his darling projects, Locke's *Letters concerning Toleration*, and tried to involve in a major new edition of Marvell's works, a plan that unfortunately came to nothing at that time. The *Memoirs* include some telling details about this failed project, which was to have included all of Marvell's polemical prose. The new edition was planned as one handsome quarto (the same format subsequently used for the works of Algernon Sidney), with Baron as the editor of the prose and William Bowyer the bookseller for "the poetical and Latin parts." After long discussion, however, Bowyer withdrew, and Baron, "not thinking himself equal to the task, for want of anecdotes, did not seem inclined to undertake it" (1:361–62). John Nichols, who wrote a longer version of this episode for his biography of Bowyer,[22] surmised that Baron felt unable to provide adequate annotation for the prose – an editorial feat that remains incomplete even today. The project was taken over by Captain Edward Thompson just after

---

[19] Milton, *Eikonoklastes, Now first published from the author's second edition, printed in 1650: with many enlargements; by R. Baron. With a preface showing the transcendent excellency of Milton's prose works* (London: A. Millar, 1756).

[20] See Robbins, *Eighteenth-Century Commonwealthman*, p. 428, n. 65.

[21] *The Works of John Milton, historical, political, and miscellaneous. Now more correctly printed from the originals, than in any former edition, and many passages restored, which have been hitherto omitted* (London: A. Millar, 1753). Blackburne explains that Baron had wanted to write his own life of Milton to replace that by Thomas Birch in the 1738 edition, but was prevented: "We are told, indeed, in a note found among Mr. Hollis's papers, that Millar would not suffer Baron to write Milton's Life anew . . . lest offence should be given to Dr. Birch" (p. 529).

[22] Nichols, *Literary Anecdotes*, 2:449.

Hollis's death, when Brand Hollis passed over to him all of Hollis's Marvell materials.[23] But Nichols also felt obliged to defend Bowyer, one of his own cultural heroes in the book trade, from the imputation of political cowardice:

What were Mr. Bowyer's reasons for this refusal does not appear. We may venture to say, that party considerations had no share in his reluctance; for this worthy and learned printer made no scruple to print other works, published about this time, which were, in their contents, no less obnoxious to the Ruling Powers than the revival of Marvell's principles and strictures would have been. (p. 449)

Hollis's anonymity in all these projects was a mixture of modesty and caution. But, wrote Bond,

despite all precautions, the scale of his operations was so extensive and they went on so long that he clearly became notorious. Almost certainly he was an object of suspicion to the Tory government, from his association with radical politicians like [John] Wilkes and incendiary publishers like John Almon and George Kearsley, from the nature of the texts that he caused to be reprinted, and from their wide distribution. (p. 30).

But the export of books is only part of the story. Equally important to Hollis, and hence eventually to us, was his friendship and collaboration with Jonathan Mayhew, who had himself held a Hollis fellowship at Harvard,[24] and was the main channel by which our Thomas Hollis communicated with American intellectuals and political activists – although this too had something to do with Baron. In one of his own books, Hollis had written himself a note, dated 1758, to the effect that the first edition of Baron's *Pillars of Priestcraft and Orthodoxy Shaken*[25] had included what he (Hollis) recognized as the first formal statement of liberal political theory produced in America. This was Jonathan Mayhew's famous *Discourse concerning Unlimited Submission and Non-Resistance to the Higher Powers*, an act of defiance against the requirement that the colonies and their

---

23 See Edward Thompson, ed., *The Works of Andrew Marvell, Esq. Poetical, Controversial, and Political*, 3 vols. (London, 1776). In his preface Thompson remarked: "The late Mr. Thomas Hollis, of honourable memory, had once a design of making a collection of his compositions and advertisements were published for that purpose by the late Andrew Millar; and all the manuscripts and scarce tracts, collected for that purpose, were afterwards given me by his ingenious friend" (p. i). Among the subscribers to this edition were John Wilkes, Samuel Adams, Edmund Burke, Catherine Macaulay, Brand Hollis and Blackburne himself.

24 See John Langdon Sibley, *Biographical Sketches of Graduates of Harvard University* (Cambridge, Mass., 1873), Class of 1744, p. 443.

25 [R. Baron, ed.], *The Pillars of Priestcraft and Orthodoxy Shaken*, 2 vols. (London: R. Griffiths, 1752).

preachers observe the anniversary of the execution of Charles I.
Mayhew's sermon, later designated "the morning gun of the revolution,"[26] was based on that classic text of monarchist political
thought, Romans 13, but from an oppositional standpoint that may
owe something to Milton's regicide tracts.[27] The last section, which
deals with the history of Charles I's reign, could be seen as Mayhew's
own version of *Eikonoklastes*, to which, however, he acknowledged no
overt debt.[28] There is no doubt that Mayhew was well read in the
seventeenth-century liberal tradition; but at this stage of his career
he evidently preferred not to name his authorities. After Hollis and
Mayhew established their correspondence, however, Mayhew
preached another famous sermon in which that reserve was breached.
In *The Snare Broken* (1766), delivered in the context of the repeal of
the Stamp Act, and dedicated to William Pitt the elder, to whom
Hollis sent a copy, Mayhew named his authorities:

Having been initiated, in youth, in the doctrines of civil liberty, as they
were taught by such men as Plato, Demosthenes, Cicero . . . among the
ancients; and such as Sidney and Milton, Locke and Hoadley, among the
moderns; I liked them; they seemed rational.[29]

In style and content, this passage is reminiscent of Milton's autobiographical statements; and between the two sermons lies a truly
Miltonic friendship between Mayhew and Hollis, conducted in both
terms of apposite quotations, and of serious political-theoretical
discussion.

On August 27, 1760 Hollis had written to Mayhew about his gift to

---

[26] See John Wingate Thornton, ed., *The Pulpit of the American Revolution: or, the Political Sermons of the Period of 1776* (Boston, 1860; repr. New York, 1970), p. 43.

[27] Sensabaugh was convinced that part of this sermon, the part that actually confronts the biblical injunction to obedience, was closely based on Milton's first *Defence*, and he published parallel passages in demonstration; see *Milton in Early America*, pp. 61–66. This is the most convincing part of Sensabaugh's argument that Mayhew's earlier sermons contained passages of careful paraphrase, as distinct from quotation, from Milton's republican tracts. Sensabaugh also, but less successfully, aligned with *Areopagitica* Mayhew's *The Right and Duty of Private Judgement Asserted* and its sequel, *Objections Considered* (pp. 55–60), and found borrowings from *The Tenure of Kings and Magistrates* and *The Ready and Easy Way* in *Unlimited Submission*.

[28] There is some similarity in Mayhew's topics to those that Milton raised in *Eikonoklastes* (e.g. "Upon his going to the House of Commons," "Upon the Rebellion in Ireland," which begins with "The Rebellion and horrid massacer of English Protestants in Ireland to the number of 154000"); but that Mayhew was using Thomas May's *History of the Parliament* (1647), 2:4, is indicated by the fact that he accepts May's figure for the massacre of "above two hundred thousand men, women, and children."

[29] *The Snare Broken. A Thanksgiving-Discourse Preached at the Desire of the West Church in Boston . . . May 23, 1766. Occasioned by the Repeal of the Stamp-Act* (Boston, 1766), p. 35.

Harvard of Milton's prose works, and shared with him President Holyoke's grudging acceptance of the gift. "We have just now received from your bountiful hand a most beautiful as well as a most valuable present of Milton's prose works," Holyoke had written, on December 18, 1759; "valuable to us, as we have a very high regard for that great man, whom (his political works not at all withstanding) we esteem a great honour to the British name" (*Memoirs*, 1:74). With scathing elegance, Blackburne glossed this exchange as revealing the current state of Milton's reputation in the colonies:

Mr. Hollis seems to have understood from this parenthesis, that Mr. Holyoke and his associates approved of Milton's political principles with some reserve. And indeed, from the President's manner of expressing himself, one would imagine they had *real* objections to those principles. Be that as it may, Mr. Hollis in the same letter to Dr. Mayhew, after citing Mr. Holyoke's restriction, thought proper to deliver his sentiments of Milton's political principles in the following detail.

And here is Hollis's defence of those principles, which also contains an ironic coda suggesting that President Holyoke had greatly misunderstood the extent of what his gratitude should be:

If I understand Milton's political principles, they are these; that government, at least our government, is by compact. That, a king becoming a tyrant, and the compact thereby broken, the power reverts again to the constituents, the people, who may punish such tyrant as they see fit, and constitute such new form of government as shall then appear to them to be most expedient . . . It is true, indeed, that that form of government, which he and many other able honest men inclined to on the death and punishment of the tyrant Charles, was a commonwealth, which the army, that Hydra-beast, prevented; forcing the nation thereby, aginst its bent, after numberless vexations, to call back that riot-prince Charles the Second. But Milton, or the warmest common-wealth man, never thought of altering the antient form of government, till Charles the First had sinned flagrantly and repeatedly against it, and had destroyed it by his violences.

On the contrary, there are several and very fine passages in his prose works, where he commends that antient form exceedingly, and with highest justice; and it is undoubted truth, that we owe the most noble, the most happy Revolution [of 1688], to his principles, and to those of his friends . . . You see, dear Sir, if I have explained myself clearly, that it is to Milton, the divine Milton, and such as he, in the struggles of the civil war, and the Revolution, that we are beholden for all the manifold and unexampled blessings which we now every where enjoy; *and Mr. President Holyoke for liberty and his college* . . . (*Memoirs*, 1:92–93; italics added)

In other words, it was crucial to Hollis's agenda of sending Milton "and such as he" across the Atlantic to inform the colonists that his idol be defined, at least for strategic purposes, as a constitutional monarchist, of a recognizably Lockean flavor. And on January 19, 1761, Hollis sent two copies of his new edition of Toland's *Life of Milton* to Mayhew, who gave one to Thomas Hutchinson, the Lieutenant Governor of Massachusetts, to whom, we are told, "it was very acceptable."[30]

Hollis was, unsurprisingly for a Dissenter, committed to religious toleration (with, as was also the case for Milton, the exception of politically active Roman Catholicism). As Nichols was to write, for the next generation:

The suspicious eye with which both Mr. Thomas Hollis and his Biographer beheld the Roman Catholicks, and the restrictions under which they contended that Roman Catholicks should continue to be bound, constitute the only error of importance . . . And this was more the error of the times in which they lived, than of the men; – men who, had they lived some few years later, would have survived these prejudices (for such I must call them), and, consistently with the privileges which each of them claimed for himself, and indeed for all other Religionists, would have been the advocates of full, equal, and perfect religious liberty, and for extending the participation of all civil rights to the subjects of civil government.[31]

Given this prejudice, Hollis's relations with America were focused on Archbishop Secker's campaign to enforce episcopacy there, and the attempt to set up a rival Society for the Propagation of the Gospel in Foreign Parts, which was making puritan New England extremely nervous. So there is his letter of 1766 to Mayhew on Mayhew's religious controversy with East Apthorpe,[32] in which he advised him to use irony on his opponent, "with finest innuendo to his having been bred a dissenter . . . You will find he will feel like Satan to Ithuriel's spear" (*Memoirs*, 1:365). When Mayhew died in 1766, at the premature age of forty-six, Hollis transferred his energies as the English correspondent to the colonies to Andrew Eliot. In May 25, 1768 he sent more books on civil and religious liberty to Harvard via Eliot, noting in the accompanying letter that "the matchless John Milton was intended for the church, but would not enter it, on perceiving he must first subscribe slave" (*Memoirs*, 1:396).

---

[30] See *Memoirs*, 1:107.   [31] Nichols, *Literary Anecdotes*, 3:20–21.
[32] Hollis arranged to have all of Mayhew's pamphlets in his controversy with Apthorpe published by Andrew Millar in 1763.

And although the scheme for imposing episcopacy on New England had been temporarily dropped, Hollis urged the colonists to continue the opposition against Archbishop Secker, with Milton's antiprelatical pamphlets open in front of them:

and as the truth will be wholly with them, and ridicule is a test of truth, I could wish myself the writers would mix a little irony and banter at times among their graver compositions. Milton, the great forerunner of the sons of liberty *here and in North America*, used both in his prose-works successfully and gloriously.[33]

The year before Hollis had evidently sent Eliot a parcel of books for himself, for Eliot had written back:

Harrington, Sydney, Locke, almost any man may study his whole life to advantage. I am particularly obliged to you for Milton's prose works. They who consider that very great man only as a poet of the first rank, know less than half his character. He was every thing. I have often read detached pieces of his, and shall never be weary of his *Defensio Populi Anglicani* . . . I blush to own that I have never gone through the whole of these prose works. I have lost a great deal. Perhaps my pleasure is the greater now. Milton wrote Latin so well, that it seems a pity he should be read in any other language. But his sentiments are so just, and his attachment to liberty so firm, that he ought to be open to every Englishman.[34]

Both the Mayhew and the Eliot correspondence make it clear that they were swimming against the stream; that even by the late 1760s, or perhaps especially as the tension between Britain and the colonies heightened, it was politically incorrect to admit one's admiration of Milton's prose, or to identify his principles as one's own.

THE DEEDS OF PEACE

Bond discovered that one of the mottoes most frequently inscribed in the books that Hollis sent to Europe and the New World was "By deeds of peace." This phrase derives from Milton's *Paradise Regained*, and is part of the last temptation of Christ, expressive of the Messiah's rejection of military conquest and imperialism:

---

[33] Memoirs, 1:402; letter of July 1, 1768.

[34] *Letters from Andrew Eliot to Thomas Hollis*, in *Massachusetts Historical Society Collections*, 4th series, 4 (Boston, 1858), pp. 412–13. These letters date from November 1766 to June 1771, and contain much information about the religious controversy and the growing resistance of the colonists to the British government. See especially Eliot's letter of January 29, 1769, pp. 434–41.

> But if there be in glory aught of good,
> It may by means far different be attain'd,
> Without ambition, war, or violence;
> By deeds of peace . . .   (3:88–9)

By inscribing this Miltonic concept in books by other authors, Hollis was sending a quiet but complex message about his own mission, its strengths and limitations, and also, perhaps, a warning against misreading Milton's apparently renunciative and passive ethos in the Restoration poems. For the Miltonic quotation, unidentifed, continued to be one of Hollis's own most effective instruments for intervention in the politics of his time. On the title-page of his 1765 edition of Locke's *Letters concerning Toleration* there appear the following lines of blank verse, unexplained:

> For on Earth,
> Who against Faith and Conscience can be heard
> Infallible? yet many will presume:
> Whence heavy persecution will arise.

These lines too derive from Milton, and they conclude the passage in Book xii of *Paradise Lost* (ll.529–31) where the archangel Michael is prophesying the later history of the church militant as a time of a demonic alliance between church and state, marked by the rise of a persecuting society. For Hollis, the last two books of the poem were the site of Milton's most explicit comments on the culture of the Restoration; by attaching these lines to Locke's *Letters*, published after the Williamite Revolution, he was making a subtle historical point. If Milton's archangelic intelligence could intimate the history of religious persecution from its origins to the 1660s, Locke's cool logic (in the first *Letter concerning Toleration*) could extend that history through the 1680s and 90s; while Hollis himself, by editing Locke's letters for *his* generation, could reveal still larger continuities, both in the problem and the "means" of its solution.

But Hollis's most significant act of making Milton the fulcrum of the liberal canon was, paradoxically, his edition of Algernon Sidney's *Discourses concerning Government*, published in 1763 along with Sidney's correspondence (his letters to his father and to Henry Savile), an account of his trial, his "Apology" and the introductory biography written by Richard Baron for the 1751 edition. Facing the title-page of this oversize quarto volume was placed a fine engraved portrait of

Sidney (Figure 5),[35] and beneath the portrait was the full text of an anecdote about Sidney, which soon, as we shall see in chapter 5, acquired a history of its own.

Facing Sidney *on* the title-page, however, is another quotation: "Or to the unjust tribunals under change of times." Presumably most of the intended readers of this new edition, of which several copies were sent to New England, knew that they were looking at a line from *Samson Agonistes*. They may or may not have known that this line could be read as an allusion to the trials of the regicides in 1660–62, especially that of Sir Henry Vane; but they could certainly grasp the fact that Milton had prophesied also Sidney's trial and execution.

In this text, however, Hollis did not rely on a single Miltonic allusion. Baron's memoir of Sidney is made three times as long as its own narrative warranted by Hollis's insertion of *contextual* notes – a virtual commonplace book compiled from a large range of historical, legal and polemical sources, such as Ludlow, Clarendon, royalist sermons, Marvell's Restoration satires, Temple's *Observations on the Dutch Provinces*, John Trenchard's *Short History of Standing Armies*, and others more obscure; but no one is featured more frequently than Milton. There are quotations from Milton's *First Defence* and the *History of Britain*, none of which seems particularly called for. A sentence from a letter Sidney supposedly wrote to Rochester explaining his flight from England at the Restoration as ideological ("in short, where Vane, Lambert, Haselrigge cannot live in safety, I cannot live at all") inspired Hollis, who did not know that this letter was a forgery produced after the Revolution, not only to insert an account of Vane's trial, but also to include the whole of Milton's commonwealth sonnet in praise of and addressed to Vane (pp. 25–26). As a gloss on a single sentence describing Sidney's movements when in exile, Hollis remarks:

The Reader will forgive the following digression, if it be a digression, respecting good and bad ministers, which makes part of Milton's inimitable prayer, in his first prose tract, intitled "Of Reformation": "Then amidst the hymns and halleluiahs of Saints, some one may perhaps bee heard offering at high strains in new and lofty measures . . . "

---

[35] Hidden away in a footnote much later in the volume, in ostensible relation to one of Sidney's letters to his father, Robert, earl of Leicester, was Hollis's key to his own editorial and promotional role. "There is likewise extant a proof impression of a seal of the head of A. Sydney, now in the possession of Thomas Hollis, F. R. and A.SS. which seal was engraved during the civil wars, by that celebrated English artist Thomas Simon" (p. 38).

and then proceeds to quote at length from Milton's attack on episcopacy. If the reader *does* forgive the digression, at least sufficiently to read it, she may identify the innovative "one" with either Milton or Sidney. Burnet's statement, that Sidney "had studied the history of government in all its branches, beyond any man I ever knew," provokes Hollis to quote a long passage from the peroration of *Areopagitica*, reminding his readers that Milton too, along with Sidney, was one of the earlier inhabitants of "*the mansion house of liberty*", and one of the "pens and heads there, sitting by their studious lamps, musing, searching, revolving new notions and ideas . . . " (p. 43). And as the "Memoir" of Sidney draws to an end with the statement that his *Discourses on Government* are "one of the *noblest* books that ever the mind of man produced," this evaluation too is glossed, remarkably, by Hollis's insertion of Baron's defence of *Milton*'s prose writings, extracted from his preface to the 1756 edition of *Eikonoklastes* (p. 45).

The *Discourses* themselves were left with the annotation that Baron had supplied, that is, expanded and corrected references to Sidney's sources; but when Hollis introduced Sidney's letters to Henry Savile, ambassador to France in the 1670s, he returned to his strategy of placing Milton at the wellspring of all of Sidney's ideas. Thus Sidney's reference in 1679 to the efforts of Shaftesbury and Halifax "in pleading for indulgence to tender-conscienced protestants" (p. 67) provokes a spate of commentary on the subject of religious toleration from Harrington's *Commonwealth of Oceana*, from Marvell's *Account of the Growth of Popery and Arbitrary Government*, and, it need hardly be said, from Milton's *Areopagitica*:

Yet if all cannot be of one mind, as who looks they should be? This doubtless is more wholesome, more prudent, and more christian, that many be tolerated, rather than all compelled. I mean not tolerated popery, and open superstition, which as it extirpats all religious and civill supremacies, so itself should be extirpat, provided first, that all charitable and compassionate meanes be used to win and regain the weak and the misled. (p. 68)

Lastly, in connection with a letter of 1682 in which Sidney comments to Savile on the increasing power of France in the English court, Hollis took, or created, the opportunity to reintroduce "honest Andrew Marvell, and the matchless John Milton" as figures who had ostentatiously refused the role of courtier and sycophant: the first represented by an anti-French satire attributed to Marvell in the

Poems on Affairs of State, and the second by twenty-six lines from *Paradise Regained* – those very lines which end with Hollis's favorite reference to the "means far different" and the "deeds of peace" (pp. 102–03). By these means, inarguably different from the ways of politicians, Hollis continued to sprinkle Milton abroad, as it were, as part of a liberal network.

On March 31, 1762, Hollis's diary recorded the completion of the new edition of Sidney's works; and Blackburne subsequently recorded *its* reception in England:

> Many were the reflections thrown obliquely upon Mr. Hollis for this most valuable and seasonable publication; and it was from his patronizing this edition with so many additional quotations from British writers on the subject of constitutional liberty, that purchased him the name and reputation of a republican. And indeed no wonder. The book was published at that critical period when it began to be visible that the management of our public affairs was consigned into the hands of men notoriously known to have entertained principles unfavourable to liberty, the principles upon which those men acted who sacrificed Sydney without law or justice, to the tyranny of a profligate court and ministry.[36]

A perfect example of the kind of reader Hollis had in mind in creating his network on the other side of the Atlantic where the political soil was more fertile was Thomas Jefferson. Jefferson owned a copy of Hollis's edition of Sidney,[37] and in 1804 he corresponded with the Reverend Mason Locke Weems on the subject of a projected American edition of the *Discourses*:

> It is probably the best elementary book of the principles of government, as founded in natural right, which has ever been published in any language: and it is much to be desired in such a government as ours that it should be put into the hands of our youth as soon as their minds are sufficiently matured for that branch of study. (Cat. 3. 13)

Jefferson recommended that the projected edition, to which he agreed to subscribe, should have a two-volume format, with the trial, life and letters in one and the more important *Discourses* in the other, for "many purses can reach one volume which would not conveniently extend to the other." His own purse, however, being of marvellous extension where books were concerned, he also owned (as only a part of his huge collection) everything Hollis had

---

[36] *Memoirs*, 1:186–87.
[37] *The Library Catalogue of Thomas Jefferson*, ed. Millicent Sowerby, 5 vols. (Washington, D.C., 1952), 3.12.

recommended as a "library of liberty": Richard Baron's 1753 edition of Milton's prose (5:168) and Hollis's 1767 edition of Marchamont Nedham's *Excellencie of a Free State* (3:12), and first editions of Harrington's *Oceana* (3:15), of Ludlow's *Memoirs* as edited by John Toland in 1698 (1:154), of Locke's *Letter concerning Toleration* as translated by William Popple (1690; Cat. 2:44), and of Burnet's *History of His Own Time* (1:161). Jefferson also owned William Hakewell's edition of the *Modus tenendi parliamentum* (3:182), Thomas Atkins's 1689 *Defence of the Lord Russel's innocency* (3:187), the *Works* (1750) of Sir William Temple, (1:155), Catharine Macaulay's *History of England* (1:164), *Cato's Letters* (3:133) and a volume of William Rastell's *Collection of Statutes* (1611) containing Milton's signature. The overlap between Jefferson's interests, as recorded in his 1815 catalogue, and those of Thomas Hollis was probably not coincidental. On April 17, 1787 he was sent a copy of Blackburne's *Memoirs*, with a letter from Brand Hollis accompanying it:

I request the favor of your benevolent acceptance of the memoirs of the late excellent Thomas Hollis, who was friend to the rights of America & of mankind in general. How would he have rejoiced to have seen these days Tyranny defeated and the seeds of freedom planted in another world for which he could scarcely have hoped tho to which he was in no small degree instrumental by dispersing the best of books on the most interesting subjects . . . an encouragement for others to do the like. (*Cat.* 1:166)

LITERARY CRITICISM

But in addition to weaving the web of liberalism so broadly, Hollis had also engaged in his own more direct defence and interpretation of Milton, as the ethical heart of his own endeavor. Is literary criticism, including criticism of those with whom one disagrees, one of the deeds of peace? It depends, of course, on the style of disagreement. In 1764, Hollis had taken upon himself the public defence of *Paradise Lost* against the charge that Milton had therein abandoned the Good Old Cause. As Blackburne put it, "the tory scribblers" were anxious to ingratiate themselves with George III by attacking Milton, and one of them, "who was dull enough to be earnest," proposed in the *London Chronicle* that Milton had used *Paradise Lost* as an apology for his regicide tracts, "by giving the same characters to the apostate angels that belonged to his rebellious brethren" (*Memoirs*, 1:226). Hollis replied in the same journal. On

April 28, 1764 he opened a two-pronged defence, half political, half literary. He began by denying that the Whigs in the Glorious Revolution were in any sense rebels (conveniently overlooking the fact that the "rebel-brethren" in question were not the Williamite Whigs but the Caroline Independents); but then proceeded to tackle his opponent on a procedural matter – how to interpret Milton's poem correctly. Hollis did not question his adversary's assumption that *Paradise Lost* was a political allegory. Instead, he found support in an odd place – John Upton's *Critical Observations on Shakespeare* – for a counter-allegory.[38] For Upton, if one wanted to allegorize the poem, and to imagine that Milton "frequently hinted at those times, in which he himself had so great a share," the identifications would be reversed. The poet himself would be the faithful angel Abdiel, confronting in Satan "the Tyrant's plea" of necessity. The heavenly battle of the sixth book would be an image of the civil wars;

> nor would any solution have been found, had not Cromwell, putting on celestial armour (for this was Milton's opinion)[39] like the Messiah all armed in heavenly panoply, and ascending his fiery chariot, driven over the malignant heads of those who would maintain tyrannic sway. (1:622–23)

And Hollis, still following Upton, then produced *Samson Agonistes* as further evidence of where Milton's sympathies were to be found after the Restoration:

> Let us consider his tragedy in this allegorical view. Samson imprisoned and blind, and the captive state of Israel, lively represents our blind poet, with the republican party after the Restoration, afflicted and persecuted. But these revelling idolators will soon pull an old house on their heads; and God will send his people a deliverer. How would it have rejoiced the heart of the blind seer, had he lived to have seen with his mind's eye the accomplishment of his prophetic predictions! when a deliverer [William] came and rescued us from the Philistine oppressors. And had he known the sobriety, the toleration, and decency of the church, with a Tillotson at its head, our laws, our liberties, and our constitution ascertained, and had considered too the wildness of fanaticism and enthusiasm, doubtless he would never have been an enemy to such a church, and such a king.

---

[38] John Upton, *Critical Observations on Shakespeare* (London: G. Hawkins, 1746), pp. 156–61.

[39] At this parenthesis, the *Critical Observations* remarked in a footnote that Milton had explicitly used allegory in the *Apology for Smectymnuus*, where, after asking for "leave to soare awhile as the poets use" he introduced the figure of "the invincible warriour Zeal shaking loosely the slack reins drives over the heads of scarlet prelats and such as are insolent to maintain traditions, brusing their stiff necks under his flaming wheels" (*Complete Prose*, 1:900). This note reveals Upton to be an acute critic, one who recognized that Milton's imagination *in the prose tracts* was insistently allegorical.

This first sally was both anonymous and, by its use of Upton, only at second hand. But having gotten his first letter printed apparently emboldened Hollis. In a second letter, dated June 7, 1764, he now rose to Milton's defence in his own words, though still anonymously: " . . . your correspondent," he wrote, has tried to invalidate "free maxims of government . . . and the authority of Milton in particular . . . by imputing Whig principles to the chief devil." But he has failed as a *reader* of poetry:

He has, at least, omitted the only regular method of proof, which was, first to define Whiggism, then to shew its correspondence with the character of Satan, and so draw an inevitable consequence. To be sure, he has had the sagacity to perceive, that, according to Milton, the devil used specious pretences to convert inferior spirits to his party; but this is taken from an improper part; he has omitted the true motive of the infernal serpent, which was not to level but controul, not to create a democracy in heaven, (which however would have proved him a Republican and no Whig) but to set himself highest on the eternal throne. This appears from his private meditation . . . and this is therefore to be depended on.

Having made the point that his adversary has not learned the elementary rules of literary exegesis, Hollis then turned to the logic whereby a political allegory convenient to the Tories has been claimed:

Does this [Satanic behavior] approach nearer to the system of the Tories or of the Whigs? For if indeed to be innovators, disturbers of the peace of heaven, contumelious dictators of right and wrong, created them Whigs; we may, by the same reasoning, honour the new ministry of queen Anne, the rebel Jacobites, and the present abettors of toryism, by that respectable name.

Hollis was here making the inarguable point that all political conflict renders the party out of power the "diabolical party" to their opponents, particularly if there is any danger that the balance will swing back again. "The sense of Milton," he concludes, "was widely different," and he referred, as the clinching argument with respect to authorial intention, to "the passage relating to Nimrod . . . which has always been supposed to allude to his own times."[40] This was a

---

[40] For the political symbolism of Nimrod in *Paradise Lost* and in seventeenth-century polemic, see my *Reading between the Lines* (Madison, 1993), pp. 252–56. Compare also Edmund Ludlow, *A Voyce from the Watch Tower*, ed. Worden, p. 309: "it being the great designe of our adversaryes to keep up their Nimrodian power by dividing the languages of the people of God." Ludlow's *Voyce* (the 1662 section of his *Memoirs*) was evidently designed to restore a common purpose among those opposed to the Restoration.

masterly rhetorical move, since the "always" implies a timeless authority that topical allusion knowingly sacrifices.

But procedurally, in terms of the notoriously unstable science of interpretation and of allegory's particular dubiety,[41] it is telling that Hollis was not prepared to rely exclusively on "the text" of *Paradise Lost* for his theory of authorial intention. He turned for the *coup de grace* to historical context, to biography: "if Milton was a tory in his heart, and wrote his poem to calumniate his own party . . . as this writer vainly surmises, why did he suffer contempt and persecution after the Restoration, and not rather pull off the mask?" (*Memoirs*, 1:624–26). In the still unsettled arena of validity in interpretation, the question remains a good one.

THE POWER OF THE VISUAL

Usually Hollis liked to work behind the scenes: unnamed and, as with free-floating quotations, half-mysteriously; as an *agent provocateur*, as when he attempted through Mayhew and Eliot to set the colonists on the right intellectual paths; and also (although this is harder to understand nowadays, when the culture of the book is disintegrating before our eyes) subliminally. Among the means for the deeds of peace in which Hollis believed was the image: he was convinced of the suasive effect of beautiful bindings, symbolic devices like acorns and liberty caps, and dignified or otherwise emotionally stirring representations. In today's materialist study of the book and the publishing trade there is sometimes a more or less conscious prejudice in favor of the cheap imprint with its broader capacities for outreach, and even a suspicion of the aesthetically pleasing edition as elitist. But Hollis recognized the capacity of fine books to convey an aura of reflectiveness and respectability; the beautiful leather bindings said to the prospective reader: "There is something precious in here, and it will last!" Caroline Robbins discovered a letter in which Hollis made this explicit: "The bindings of Books," he wrote in June 1765:

are little regarded by me for my own proper library; but by long experience I have found it necessary to attend to them for other libraries; having thereby often drawn notice, with preservation, on many excellent books or

---

[41] For a shrewd summary of the problems caused in Milton criticism by allegory's shifting reputation, see Sharon Achinstein, *Milton and the Revolutionary Reader* (Princeton, 1994), 177–82.

curious, which it is probable, would else have passed unheeded or neglected.[42]

On July 9, 1766 President Holyoke of Harvard College wrote to Hollis about the appearance of the first major bequest: "Having reserved one of the alcoves in our Library, of which there are ten in all, for your books, we have now placed them, and a most beautiful appearance they make: we have some other alcoves that look very well, but not as the Hollis" (*Memoirs*, p. 603).

Blackburne was eloquent on the extraordinary care Hollis expended in making his large-quarto edition of Locke's *Letters* not only as accurate as they could be (by basing each one on its first edition), but also visually an ideal of *consideration* that the eye could intuit before it read. Blackburne explains how Hollis first engaged Baron "to correct the press," i. e. to read proof, and then sent him to engage a printer, the younger Strahan. Baron then, "at Mr. Hollis request . . . called upon Mr. Strahan, to let him know that this edition was to be printed in the simplest, that is, the most elegant manner." Hollis also persuaded Millar, who owned the press, to have the *Letters* printed on royal quarto paper; and, added Blackburne:

> The pains that Mr. Hollis took to have the new edition of these letters are incredible; he may be said to have watched over them with the care and anxiety of a parent. (*Memoirs*, 1:224.)

Unmarried and childless – his relationship with the younger and subsequently adopted Brand is discreetly handled in all the literature – Hollis had evidently sublimated his ideas of lineage and patrimony in the spirit of the *Areopagitica*.

But beautiful books are one thing; the remembrance of human personalities, through their faces, is quite another; and in his commitment to the human face Hollis was unusual, even for that portrait-conscious era. On December 22, 1761 he recorded in his diary that he had just bought "a very fine original drawing of Oliver Cromwell, as large as the life, by Cooper, in a black ebony frame, for three guineas." But he did not keep it to himself. Five years later he sent it to Cromwell's College, Sidney Sussex, Cambridge, where it still resides, probably the favorite image of Cromwell for modern reproduction. Under his private memorandum of this gift, Hollis inscribed these lines:

---

[42] Robbins, p. 426, citing Hollis letters at Harvard, U.A. I. 15, 512x. But see also *Memoirs*, p. 603.

I freely declare, I am for old Noll,
Though his government did a tyrant resemble,
He made England great, and her enemies tremble.
(*Memoirs*, 1:298)[43]

Thus Marvell's *Dialogue between the Two Horses*, a Restoration satire against both Charles II and James II, becomes part of speaking with the dead, in Hollis's generous and impersonal version of that art.

In 1763 Hollis bought from Ralph Thoresby a portrait of Marvell himself (now known, unsurprisingly, as the Hollis portrait), and had I. B. Cipriani create an etching from it, for distribution to his friends at home and abroad. "If Marvell's picture," he wrote, "does not look so lively and witty as you might expect, it is from the chagrin and awe he had of the Restoration then just effected. Marvell's picture was painted when he was forty-one, that is, in the year 1661 . . . in all the sobriety and decency of the then departed Commonwealth."[44] This portrait is reproduced in the *Memoirs*; and the same applies to engraved portraits of Ludlow, Sidney, Locke and, more surprisingly, Hubert Languet, the sixteenth-century Huguenot political theorist and probable author of the *Vindiciae contra tyrannos*. Hollis arranged for extra copies of the portraits to be printed independently, and dispatched them abroad, where if framed and hung they would reach a wider audience than the books alone could conceivably command.

But nobody's face was more important to Hollis than that of Milton. The *Memoirs* contain no less than five engraved portraits of Milton, all drawn and etched by Cipriani on Hollis's commission: Milton as a boy of ten, taken from a 1618 portrait by Cornelius Johnson that Hollis had owned (opposite p. 95);[45] a representation of the bust of Milton that Hollis also owned,[46] here set on a monument as the defender of the English people (opposite p. 383); on the

---

[43] See Andrew Marvell, *Poems and Letters*, ed. H. M. Margoliouth, rev. Pierre Legouis, 2 vols. (Oxford, 1971), 1:208–13. The poem was printed in *Poems on Affairs of State* (1689), where it was ascribed to Marvell.

[44] See Thompson, *The Works of Andrew Marvell*, 1:lvii.

[45] The *Memoirs* record that Hollis bought this portrait on June 3, 1760, "at the sale of the effects of the late Charles Stanhope, Esq. who purchased it of the executors of the widow of Milton." Nichols added a splendid anecdote: "A fire happening at his lodgings in Bedford-street, Jan. 23, he calmly walked out, taking the picture only in his hand," *Literary Anecdotes*, 3:63. The original is now in the Pierpont Morgan Library, New York.

[46] The *Memoirs* describe it as having been "executed soon after Milton had written his 'Defensio pro Populo Anglicano,' as some think, by one Pierce, a sculptor of good reputation in those times, or by Abraham or Thomas Simon." George Vertue had previously owned this bust for many years, as he told Hollis about two years before he died.

frontispiece of the second volume the "Onslow" portrait of Milton in his twenties[47] (see Figure 1), accompanied by the sonnet that Hollis had quoted in his diary to stand for his own moment of vocational commitment; another portrait based on the bust, emphasizing Milton's blind eyes (Figure 3) (opposite p. 513), and under this image the sonnet "To Mr.Cyriack Skinner upon his Blindness," one of the four "commonwealth" sonnets excluded from the 1673 edition of Milton's works. The sequence is completed by a portrait of Milton in a pose of confidence and vision (Figure 4) (opposite p. 529) and under it a crucial quotation from *Paradise Lost*, 7:24–28:

> I Sing with mortal voice unchang'd
> To hoarce or mute though fall'n on evil dayes,
> On evil dayes though fall'n and evil tongues
> In darkness and with dangers compast round,
> And solitude.

The source of this last and most powerful portrait was a print by William Faithorne, as prefixed to the 1670 edition of Milton's *History of Britain*, where it was identified as "Joannis Miltoni Effigies Ætat:62." And behind it lay an important crayon drawing, also by Faithorne, that Hollis had seen in the possession of Messrs. Tonson the bookseller.[48] In commissioning Cipriani's engraving, Hollis evidently wished to stress the interaction between the words, especially that crucial "Unchanged," and the human face fixed at a certain age. The emphasis on evil days and evil tongues is appropriate also to Hollis's own mission in times that had not significantly improved; but if Hollis had been content to simply reproduce the Faithorne portrait the face would, like Marvell's in the "Hollis" portrait, have seemed older and more pessimistic than his series required. So Cipriani re-engraved the Faithorne image with a brilliance of line that defies the subject's chronological age, and placed Milton's face in an aureole of fine lines raying outwards. This visual strategy for representing inspiration – what Walter Benjamin calls an aura – suggests with some precision how memory and imagination can cooperate in the hagiography of dissent. And if one places this portrait *beside* Cipriani's version of the Onslow portrait, one can indeed see in what sense Milton remained "unchanged" over his lifetime; at least as that was construed by Hollis (with the

---

[47] The original is now in the National Portrait Gallery, London.
[48] The original crayon drawing is now at Princeton.

IOHN   MILTON

DRAWN AND ETCHED MDCCLX BY I.B.CIPRIANI A TVSCAN FROM A BVST IN PLAISTER
MODELLED FROM THE LIFE NOW IN THE POSSESSION OF THOMAS HOLLIS F.R.AND A.SS.

CYRIAC THIS THREE YEARS DAY THESE EYES THOVGH CLEAR
TO OVTWARD VIEW OF BLEMISH OR OF SPOT
BEREFT OF LIGHT THEIR SEEING HAVE FORGOT
NOR TO THEIR IDLE ORBS DOTH SIGHT APPEAR
OF SVN OR MOON OR STAR THROVGHOVT THE YEAR
OR MAN OR WOMAN YET I ARGVE NOT
AGAINST HEAV'N'S HAND OR WILL NOR BATE ONE IOT
OF HEART OR HOPE BVT STILL BEAR VP AND STEER
RIGHT ONWARD WHAT SVPPORTS ME DOST THOV ASK
THE CONSCIENCE FRIEND TO HAVE LOST THEM OVER-PLY'D
IN LIBERTIES DEFENCE MY NOBLE TASK
OF WHICH ALL EVROPE RINGS FROM SIDE TO SIDE
THIS THOVGHT MIGHT LEAD ME THROVGH THIS WORLDS VAIN MASK
CONTENT THOVGH BLIND HAD I NO OTHER GVIDE

Figure 3 Bust of John Milton, as engraved by I. B. Cipriani. From *The Memoirs of Thomas Hollis*, opposite p. 513. Yale Center for British Art

IOHN MILTON

DRAWN AND ETCHED MDCCLX BY I.B. CIPRIANI A TVSCAN
AT THE DESIRE OF THOMAS HOLLIS F.R. AND A.SS. FROM
A PORTRAIT IN CRAYONS NOW IN THE POSSESSION OF
MESS.TONSON BOOKSELLERS IN THE STRAND LONDON

——————— I SING WITH MORTAL VOICE *VNCHANG'D*
TO HOARCE OR MVTE THOVGH FALL'N *ON EVIL DAYES*
ON EVIL DAYES THOVGH FALL'N AND EVIL TONGVES
IN DARKNESS AND *WITH DANGERS COMPAST ROVND*
AND SOLITVDE ———————

Figure 4 The "Faithorne" portrait of John Milton at 62; engraved by I. B. Cipriani. From *The Memoirs of Thomas Hollis*, opposite p. 529. Yale Center for British Art.

help of Sonnet 7) to stretch from his early moment of self-dedication to that when he fulfilled that promise by writing *Paradise Lost.* The young man, surrounded by a naturalistic and flourishing laurel wreath, and the old one whose wreath has been recast in stone, are clearly the same person. Beneath them both floats the tiny liberty cap that was Hollis's favorite signature.

In his journal records of Milton's portraits, Hollis remarked that "some are of an opinion, that all other effigies are copied from them, wholly or in part, or else are spurious" (*Memoirs*, 1:619–20). On this matter of authenticity, the *Memoirs* include an anecdote about the Faithorne drawing that Hollis had heard by way of his friendship with George Vertue:

About the year 1725 Mr. George Vertue, a worthy and eminent British Antiquary, went on purpose to see Mrs. Deborah Clark, Milton's youngest and favourite daughter, and some time his ammanuensis, who then lodged in a mean little street near Moorfields, where she kept a school for children for her support. He took this drawing with him, and divers paintings said to be of Milton; all which were brought into the room, by his contrivance, as by accident, whilst he conversed with her. She took no notice of the paintings; but when she perceived the drawing, she cried out, "O Lord! that is the picture of my father: how came you by it?" and, stroaking the hair of her forehead, added, "Just so my father wore his hair." This daughter resembled Milton greatly.

This daughter was Deborah Clarke, who died in 1727, at the age of seventy-six. The conversation between Hollis and Vertue, from which this anecdote derives, took place, according to Blackburne, in 1755. So a form of oral history, whose own authenticity will constitute one of the theoretical problems of my fifth chapter, is used to authenticate a portrait whose truth-content was essential to the Hollis project. We cannot, in fact, decide whether it was Hollis, or Vertue, or Blackburne, who was responsible for the narrative shape of this anecdote; we can be sure that its narrative shape is essential to its historiographical purpose.[49]

"This daughter resembled Milton greatly." So, we might say, did Thomas Hollis – except for his greater personal modesty. When he retired to the country, exhausted, he wrote to a friend on October 28, 1772, "Had I stayed in London, I should have adled. O it was a terrible magnanimity with which I lived there! *With dangers compassed*

---

[49] There is another version of the story related by Vertue in a 1730 letter to a Mr. Christian. See Nichols, *Literary Anecdotes*, 2:248.

round and solitude!" (*Memoirs*, 1:457; italics added). This last echo of *Paradise Lost* is possibly the most revealing of the strains of his secret advocacy, and of the rigorous idealism that held him to it. Hollis died suddenly in 1774, at the premature age of fifty-four, while walking through one of his farms; in one of which, according to Nichols, "he [had] ordered his corpse to be deposited, in a grave ten feet deep, and that the field should be immediately plowed over, that no trace of his burial-place might remain."[50]

But in the *London Chronicle* for February 8 (appropriately the same paper in which he had championed Milton) there appeared an obituary for Hollis, signed only "Lycidas." The writer spoke particularly of how hard Hollis had worked for his causes, "like his own admired Milton (justly admired)," and inserted a pertinent quotation from Milton's own vocational doubts as to why, indeed, one should live laborious days:

> Were it not better don as others use,
> To sport with Amaryllis in the shade,
> Or with the tangles of Neaera's hair.
> (*Memoirs*, 1:469–70).

After his death Brand Hollis continued his adoptive father's mission to America; and in particular he established a long-distance friendship with John Adams, second president of the new United States. In 1786 Adams visited England, and dined with Brand Hollis. He wrote in his *Diary*:

In Hollis mead Mr. Hollis was buried ten feet deep and then ploughed over; a whim to be sure; but singularity was his characteristic.[51]

THE LEGACY

When Blackburne was writing the Hollis *Memoirs*, he had, as I have said, his own agenda, to discredit Dr. Johnson's opinions of Milton as anything but objective literary criticism. Nevertheless, Blackburne's testimony as to the success of Hollis's campaign is worth considering, since a biographer is more likely to exaggerate than diminish the accomplishments of his subject. And as far as Milton was concerned, Blackburne believed that Hollis had failed. Hollis had distributed

---

[50] Nichols, *Literary Anecdotes*, 3:65.
[51] John Adams, *Diary*, in *Works*, ed. Charles Francis Adams, 10 vols. (Boston, 1851), 3:403.

Milton's prose, in Baron's edition, along with copies of Toland's *Life*, to Leipzig, Stockholm, Upsala, Hamburg, Gottingen, Basle, Geneva and Groningen. But Blackburne's eyes were fixed on the English reception, which he saw as not only not improved since the seventeenth century, but actually on the decline:

> The readers of Milton's prose works in these days I believe are very few; and few of those that read them, it is probable, take the pains to understand them. He is seldom quoted in our present political squabbles. (p. 93)

Blackburne attributed much of the problem to Milton's eighteenth-century critics and biographers, especially bishops Newton and Atterbury, and Addison's issues on Milton in *The Spectator*. Without their emphases and exclusions, he remarked, "it would not have been a secret (as I believe it is even now to many persons not wholly illiterate) that Milton ever wrote anything but the Poem called Paradise Lost" (1:140).

And he added in a footnote, to illustrate the benighted intellectual climate in which he and Hollis had operated, another anecdote, whose sardonic style is certainly his own:

> An astonishing instance of which happened in this present month of January, 1777. A gentleman of fine parts, and many excellent accomplishments, and among the rest, an elegant scholar, coming into a friend's room, and opening the first quarto volume of Milton's prose works, which was lying upon the table, asked, "What have you got here?" Being answered, "Some of Milton's prose-tracts;" the visitor cried out, with surprize, "Bless me! Did Milton write all this in prose?"

Blackburne, of course, excepted from his criticism of Milton's critics the ardent Richard Baron, whose preface to his edition of *Eikonoklastes* had gone rather overboard in praising the prose, even to the extent of depreciating the poetry; although, Blackburne added, "in that judgement, as he respects the practical uses of human life, he might not be far wrong" (1:143). Baron had, significantly, attributed to Milton's prose all the qualities that Andrew Marvell had defined as characteristic of and unique to *Paradise Lost*, and that Milton's admirers in England and America followed each other in praising, to the point of empty iteration. For Marvell, in the poem that introduced the epic in the 1674 edition, Milton was a Prometheus without recklessness, a sacred pioneer:

> That Majesty which through thy Work doth Reign
> Draws the Devout, deterring the Profane.

And things divine thou treat'st of in such state
As them preserves, and thee, inviolate.
At once delight and horror on us seize,
Thou sing'st with so much gravity and ease;
. . .
Where couldst thou words of such a compass find?
Whence furnish such a vast expense of mind?
. . .
Thy Verse created like thy Theme sublime.
In Number, Weight, and Measure, needs not Rime.[52]

For Baron, it was not the "Verse" but the *prose* which was sublime. In his polemical tracts, he claimed, "the great Milton has a stile of his own; one fit to express the astonishing sublimity of his thoughts, the mighty vigour of his spirt, and that *copia* of invention, that redundancy of imagination, which no writer before or since hath equalled" (*Memoirs*, 1:145). But while Blackburne was tolerant of Baron's enthusiasm, he wished to record his own less utopian vision: "We who have outlived the jubilee then current [in 1756]," he lamented, "have seen Milton's doctrines on religion and government in lower reputation than ever; nor, it may be feared, has Mr. Hollis's patriotic efforts to disperse, and by that means to recommend them, had all the success that he, and such as he, earnestly wished" (1:146).

On the other hand, Blackburne retained his own prophecy of better readers elsewhere. Dr. Johnson had called Milton "fantastical" for "thinking to compose the confusions of his country" by writing *The Readie and Easie Way*. "But the Dr. should have considered," Blackburne replied tartly, "that he may not live to see the end of the world; and Milton's tract may fall into the hands of a generous posterity, exasperated by despotic oppression, beyond the bounds of submission, when this plan of government may point out to them the salutary means of redress and deliverance" (*Memoirs*, vii).

At the end of his own analysis of "The Legacy" of seventeenth-century republicanism, Blair Worden makes a claim that is in no way demolished by what I have here demonstrated. "The Enlightenment," he writes, "never swallows seventeenth-century republicanism whole":

It dilutes it, refines it, debates with it, sometimes dissents from it; but it does not break free of it. The same is true of the anti-monarchical thinking of eighteenth-century Europe and, on a larger scale, of the eighteenth-century

---

[52] Marvell, *Poems and Letters.*

American colonies . . . It was through the creation of the canon by Toland and his friends in 1698–1700 that the republicanism of the seventeenth century, whose hopes had been so repeatedly blighted and whose fears so repeatedly confirmed, acquired a vigorous posthumous life.[53]

If one adds that it was *also* through the enlargement, defence and dissemination of the canon by Thomas Hollis and *his* friends, at a time when they were actually able to influence changes abroad that were impossible in England, one has only made that posthumous life more vigorous and valuable still.

[53] Worden, "Republicanism and the Restoration," pp. 192–93.

CHAPTER 2

"Prejudice . . . sways a world of people":
Milton's sonnets

In the Introduction I used John Milton as an example of an early modern liberal, without suppressing the limitations of his thinking. In *Of Education* Milton wrote to Samuel Hartlib, that all-round practical reformer, about how to "enflame" young common-wealthmen with the love of learning, and teach them to "delight in manly, and liberall exercises." If "liberall exercises" in Milton's society had come to mean "pursuits or occupations becoming to a gentleman," as Milton's modern editor (following the OED) informs us, it was in the 1640s, and especially in the Hartlib circle, perhaps regaining more than a shadow of its medieval semantics: "worthy a free man," as opposed to "servile" or "mechanical."[1] Anyone as alert as Milton to latinate etymology, and as obsessed with the semantics of "liberty,"[2] must have recognized that a liberal educa-tion in 1644 could be designed only in a free society, politically speaking. That it could only be designed for citizens spared the necessity of earning their bread in the sweat of their brow was one of the contradictions that Milton himself never fully resolved.[3]

Despite this confusion on class issues, he undoubtedly grew clearer on how the different aspects of liberal thought could become

---

[1] Milton, *Of Education*, in *Complete Prose Works*, ed. D. M. Wolfe *et al.*, 8 vols. (New Haven, 1953–82), 2:385.

[2] The poem he published as his earliest was a metaphrase, produced at age fifteen, of Psalm 114, which began:

> When the blest seed of Terah's faithful Son,
> After long toil their *liberty* had won.

The King James version reads, in contrast: "When Israel went out of Egypt, the house of Jacob from a people of strange language."

[3] In the famous autobiographical digression in *The Reason of Church Government*, Milton described how God's "Secretary conscience," in an imaginary dialogue, reproached him for dilatoriness in entering the debates about ecclesiastical polity: "When time was, thou couldst not find a syllable of all that thou hadst read, or studied, to utter in [the church's] behalfe. Yet ease and leasure was given thee for thy retired thoughts out of the sweat of other men." See *Complete Prose*, 1:804; and for the phrase "Secretary conscience," 1:822.

part of a single program. Almost a decade after *Of Education*, Milton addressed Cromwell on the need for such a program, in his *Second Defence of the English People*, published at the end of May 1654. Precisely in order to qualify his apparent celebration of Cromwell's supremacy, Milton advised him, first, always to consult with the other revolutionary leaders, including those who had disagreed with his policy or whose reputation was for moderation: Whalley, Overton, Whitelocke and Algernon Sidney. Second, he declared that the new regime should "leave the church to the church"; that is to say, initiate that legal and financial separation of church and state on which John Locke put so much seemingly inventive emphasis. For Milton, the Erastianism of the Stuart era permitted "two powers, utterly diverse" to "make harlots of each other" (4.i.678). Third, in the terrain of civil liberties, Cromwell was advised to engage in law reform by abolishing bad old laws and refraining from making new: "For . . . nothing can so effectively mould and create virtue as liberty" (4.k.678–79).

Immediately after these broad structural imperatives come the needs, for Milton, of education and freedom of speech. "Would that you might take more thought," he wrote to Cromwell, "for the education and morality of the young than has yet been done, nor feel it right for the teachable and the unteachable, the diligent and the slothful to be instructed side by side at public expense" (p. 679). In this seldom quoted sentence, we can see how his earlier restriction of education to the gentry has been modified both by an idea of state education and by the principle of merit, to be determined, presumably, by examination. And lastly, he turned to the large question of ideological toleration, the question of how big the Protectorate tent should be:

may you permit those who wish to engage in free inquiry to publish their findings at their own peril without the private inspection of any petty magistrate . . . May you always take the side of those who think that not just their own party or faction, but *all citizens equally have an equal right to freedom in the state.* (4.i.679; italics added)

It may be only coincidence that this section of the *Second Defence* was *omitted* from one of the most popular teaching editions of Milton's works, Merritt Hughes's *Complete Poems and Major Prose*; but one could wish that it was at least as well known as his smaller-minded sentences.

For the remainder of the early modern era Milton was a preeminent example of liberalism in the broad political sense I defined in the Introduction, and as that mixed brew of principles was gradually bottled and labelled. He was certainly promoted as such at the end of the seventeenth century by Edward Phillips and John Toland, a program repeated and expanded in the mid-eighteenth century, as we have seen, by Richard Baron and Thomas Hollis. For all of these the liberal Milton was first and foremost the Milton of the prose tracts, but also the author of *Paradise Lost* and *Paradise Regained*, of *Samson Agonistes* and the sonnets. Out of these texts, seventeenth- and eighteenth-century readers carved a story of commitment to liberal ideas that they could use and reuse for inspiration and solidarity whenever political history showed signs of repeating itself in the bad old ways.

For many modern readers, Milton either has or has not counted as a liberal primarily in the arena of freedom of the press. Although several of Milton's contemporaries, Roger Williams, William Walwyn, John Saltmarsh, Henry Robinson, John Lilburne,[4] and in the next generation John Owen, Andrew Marvell and John Locke, entered this debate, it was the *Areopagitica*, rather than Walwyn's *Compassionate Samaritane* or Marvell's *Rehearsal Transpros'd*, or even Milton's own *Of True Religion*, the last work he published, that became a canonical text of modern liberalism. The *Areopagitica* achieved its preeminence primarily on the basis of its eloquence. But there are always those who proclaim that Milton must not count as a liberal, that in fact he was deeply *illiberal*, not only on the grounds that he acted briefly as licenser of *Mercurius Politicus* for the Council of State in 1651 and was therefore a hypocrite, but also because of the exceptions he granted to the ideal of toleration towards the end of *Areopagitica*: "I mean not tolerated Popery, and open superstition."[5] Thus Anthony Lewis, in his affirmative study of First Amendment history, remarked that "Milton is revered as a voice of freedom, but on matters of religious opinion he allowed only one truth: the Protestant";[6] and from the opposite camp Stanley Fish, in the much reprinted essay, "There's No Such Thing as Free Speech

---

[4] For reminders how far from unique was Milton in the development of tolerationist arguments during the revolutionary period, see Ernest Sirluck, ed., *Complete Prose*, 2:73–92; Nigel Smith, *Literature and Revolution in England, 1640–1660* (New Haven and London, 1994), pp. 121–24.

[5] Milton, *Complete Prose*, 2:565.

[6] Anthony Lewis, *Make No Law: The Sullivan Case and the First Amendment* (New York, 1991), p. 53.

and a Good Thing Too," uses Milton's exception as the deconstructive lever in his misguided attempt to rid the United States of its "First Amendment pieties."[7]

For George Sensabaugh Milton was "that Grand Whig," despite the fact that the term "whig" was not coined until after Milton's death; and Sensabaugh was reading backwards through the various appropriations of Milton by the Whigs that began with Charles Blount's *Just Vindication of Learning* in 1679 and William Denton's *An Apology for the Liberty of the Press* in 1681, "two unlike but unmistakable adaptations of *Areopagitica*."[8] An even more misleading term for Milton, however, is "radical," which seems to have entered the conversation via Christopher Hill's neo-marxist history from below;[9] but it remains a problematic designation for a thinker whose few brief concessions to the idea of a popular politics were overshadowed, even at his most explicitly republican moment, by his deeper distaste for and suspicion of "the inconsiderate multitude."[10]

Some of the disputes in Milton studies have been caused, evidently, by our making inappropriate decisions not about what Milton thought and said, but about what to call him. The advantages of designating Milton an early modern liberal are many. Not least among them is the opportunity it gives for reducing the disagreements among Milton's readers, and even for expanding their number. Not all issues can, of course, be defused. Conservative literary critics, from Dr. Johnson through T. S. Eliot and beyond, must deplore the Milton of the regicide tracts, and, as happened in the eighteenth century, attempt to divorce him from the author of *Paradise Lost*. But a liberal Milton can own more of his own works, with fewer self-contradictions, than can a radical Milton, or even a retroactive Whig. The seemingly disparate stages of his career come together under this aegis to form an intelligible human profile, especially if that profile is understood in the light of the *programs* outlined in the *Second Defence* and the *Readie and Easie Way*. The right

---

[7] Stanley Fish, *There's No Such Thing as Free Speech and a Good Thing Too* (New York and Oxford, 1994), pp. 102–19; Paul M. Dowling's attempt to undermine the influence of the *Areopagitica* by giving it a Straussian (ironic) reading against its own grain suggests, by another kind of irony, that the old tract is still potent. See Dowling, "*Areopagitica* and *Areopagiticus*: The Significance of the Isocratic Precedent," *Milton Studies* 21 (1985), 49–69.

[8] George Sensabaugh, *That Grand Whig Milton* (Stanford, 1952), p. 55.

[9] See, for example, Michael Wilding, "Milton's Early Radicalism," and "Regaining the Radical Milton," in his *Dragon's Teeth: Literature in the English Revolution* (Oxford, 1987), pp. 7–27, 232–58.

[10] Milton, *The Readie and Easie Way to Establish a Free Commonwealth*, in *Complete Prose*, 7:375.

to express one's opinions in public is asserted implicitly in every one of his tracts merely by their appearance; but Milton also explored that right explicitly in several of his sonnets. The right to practice the religion of one's choice (though the right to practice none would have been inconceivable to him) drives *Lycidas* and the sonnet on the Piedmont massacre as much as it informs the prospectus of church history at the end of *Paradise Lost*. And as for the right to education and information, there are few writers who have so consistently demonstrated their belief in its importance, its value to the state as well as to the individual, its genetic relation to probity and productivity. Perhaps the profoundest of Milton's beliefs, because the simplest, the right to know not only produced *Of Education* and the *Areopagitica*, but also the debates on intellectual inquiry (and its limitations) conducted in *Paradise Lost* and *Paradise Regained*, and frequently intimated in those condensed moments of autobiography, the sonnets.

By no coincidence Milton's sonnets have appeared three times in this broader definition of his liberalism, for they are the subject of this chapter. The choice may seem perverse, for what can be more unequivocally literary than a sonnet? What further from the eighteenth-century ideal of Milton as heroic defender of political freedoms? And yet, as I have shown, Thomas Hollis arranged for Sonnet 7, "How soon hath time," to be engraved by Cipriani beneath his portrait of Milton as a very young man, and quoted it in his diary as an empowering if demanding call to duty. And one of the most revealing (though least discussed) aspects of Milton's own political behavior and its subsequent interpretation is the fact that he suppressed his four "commonwealth" sonnets, which (with one remarkable exception) never appeared in his lifetime, but which were carefully retrieved by his admirers.

To Milton scholars, Milton's sonnets have for some time posed a problem at the intersection of literature and history. Two books, appearing when the demise of New Criticism had made possible a return to historical criticism, recognized the unusual status of Milton's sonnets in his *œuvre* as a whole. The first was Mary Ann Radzinowicz's *Toward Samson Agonistes* (1978), a literary biography with a teleological imperative: that is to say, Radzinowicz was committed to answering the question of how the Milton of the regicide pamphlets became the advocate of "calm of mind, all passion spent." The second was Anna Nardo's *Milton's Sonnets and the*

Ideal Community (1979). Each assumed that Milton's sonnets, which had previously been dismissed as a random collection of occasional poems, told a complex and continuous story about his life, his thought, and their causal interrelationship. Neither went quite as far as this chapter proposes to go in seeing the sonnets as a key, once almost lost or at least pocketed, to Milton's understanding of himself as an early modern liberal.

Though returning defiantly to the biographical model of understanding that New Criticism had outlawed, Radzinowicz was committed to the view that when Milton gathered his sonnets together for publication he created that object of New Critical esteem, a unified structure. She believed that, retroactively and quite deliberately, Milton had created a sonnet "sequence" composed of individual "clusters," which together stood for the major phases of his own experience:

Milton intended each sonnet to bear its individual meaning; he grouped the sonnets by interlinked cross-reference and wrote them at distinct periods, often several years apart, so that a thematic meaning emerges within subgroups. He then printed them retrospectively, breaking chronology for other effects, and brought them together so that a final polyphonic harmony would be apparent in them.[11]

Radzinowicz saw the final structure as a narrative of maturation: from Milton's "youthful confident sense of the irresistibility of virtue and the certainty of election" (1–7), to studies of the "ethics of purity" (8–10), to those of Milton's "most revolutionary period" that consider the consequences of writing the divorce tracts (11–14), to those in which Milton "labored to prevent the revolution from failure" (15–18), to the last and most purely autobiographical group, which "as a whole records calm of mind and assent to the temporal circumstances of the period" (pp. 131–42).

Anna Nardo's agenda was ostensibly quite different. She approached the sonnets as exhibits in the history of a genre, in which Milton's might by others have been judged unimportant by virtue of their *lack* of sequential structure. Compared to Petrarch's or Shakespeare's sequences, sustained analyses of a single if multifoliate ethical problem, Milton's were undeniably a hodgepodge of poems written over a quarter of a century, often in response to specific

---

[11] Mary Ann Radzinowicz, *Toward Samson Agonistes* (Princeton, 1978), p. 129.

frustrations. For Nardo, what bound these fragments together was the notion of an "ideal community" of heroic or at least high-minded figures past and present. "Each sonnet," she claimed, "details a unique engagement with a person, event, or partisan issue of the day, but each also asks its readers to consider this one moment in the light of man's ongoing fight against barbarity":

> At the center [of the ideal community] is an individual – free and virtuous, with a calm and humble faith. Surrounding this "upright heart and pure" are the groups of significant "others" that form the society that Milton envisioned: a beloved woman, the home, friends male and female, the nation, and Protestant Europe. Embracing all, of course, is a totally provident and beneficent God.[12]

These ways of talking about Milton are too thoughtful to be dismissed, but neither can they now, I believe, completely serve our turn. Almost at the turn of the millennium, the difficulty in distinguishing between what is timeless and what time-bound appears still more intractable. An earlier version of this chapter was written to honor a venerable Miltonist who desired that his own Festschrift should focus on the *literary* Milton. Rewriting it in the context of what appears to be a crisis of vocational identity in the late twentieth-century university, the question of how, and still more why, we should still be reading Milton's sonnets seems to deserve a larger scrutiny; especially since the questions such a reading throws up are pertinent in theoretical discussions of the life of the mind and whether it requires special protections. Why are there different versions of Milton's sonnets available for our consideration today – the private versions recorded in his "Cambridge" manuscript, and the public versions registered first in *Poems of Mr. John Milton* (1645) and then, with additional sonnets, in the 1673 edition of his collected works? Why, paradoxically, do the published versions offer a more privatized, even secretive, account of the relation between "life" and "works" than does the personal manuscript? And why, above all, did the 1673 edition of Milton's works, published just a year before his death, *still* omit the sonnets written in the 1650s to Cromwell, Vane and Fairfax, and the poem on his blindness addressed to Cyriack Skinner, which ends with Milton's triumphant statement that he does not regret his blinded eyes:

---

[12] Anna Nardo, *Milton's Sonnets and the Ideal Community* (Lincoln, Nebr., 1979), p. 18.

Cyriack, this three years day these eys, though clear
To outward view, of blemish or of spot;
Bereft of light thir seeing have forgot,
. . . Yet I argue not
Against heavns hand or will, nor bate a jot
Of heart or hope; but still bear up and steer
Right onward. What supports me dost thou ask?
The conscience, Friend, to have lost them overply'd
In liberties defence, my noble task,
Of which all Europe talks from side to side.

These four sonnets had to be recovered for the public canon of Milton's works by Edward Phillips, by John Toland, and by Thomas Hollis, who characteristically chose the sonnet to Cyriack Skinner, with its emphasis on the human organism "overply'd," rather than the now more famous "When I consider how my light is spent" to resonate with his portrait of Milton as the blinded bard.

If Milton is to stand as a pioneering figure in the creation of early modern liberalism, as Toland, Baron, Hollis, Blackburne, Mayhew, Eliot, Jefferson and Adams believed he should, we need to find unsentimental answers to the questions I have just posed. Rather than superimposing on the conflicting evidence that Milton left behind patterns derived half-consciously from religion or individualism, from ideals of community or personal maturation, we have to read both scrupulously and unflinchingly, in the hope that a shrewd grasp of Milton's intentions will translate into better understanding of what "Liberties defence" could then and might still mean in practical terms, in terms of the long haul.

Milton's sonnets, like much of his mid-century pamphleteering, are full of disingenuities and repressions, whose centrifugal pressure makes their small shells always on the verge of explosion. With Radzinowicz I share the conviction that Milton's sonnets came retroactively to tell the story of his life and political career, not least in the history of their printing; but the process by which this narrative was created was more disingenuous and of longer duration than she acknowledged, the shape of the life and career more embattled and less harmonious than the one proposed by her five clusters. I share with Nardo the conviction that Milton in his sonnets created the community with which he wished to be identified; but its most important members were dead, some very long dead indeed, and some did not really fit the honorific portraits he drew of them.

The story that Milton made his sonnets tell was indeed that of the "ongoing fight against barbarity," but we learn of the defeats in that campaign as much or more than the victories. As Milton wrote in his last pamphlet, *Of True Religion, Heresy, Schism and Toleration* (1673), in which, incidentally, he *strengthened* his exclusion of Roman Catholics from the freedoms to be extended to others, "It is a humane frailty to err, and no man is infallible here on earth."[13]

And in the course of constructing a "life" and a community, Milton seems to offer historical knowledge and political commitment as simultaneously a bait and a delusion. He constructs a sonnet *sequence*, peppered with signs that autobiography and chronology are its very themes; but he ensures that it will remain impossible for his readers to date its ingredients with any certainty. I take this provocative behavior to constitute a poetics, not of the timeless, but of sequentiality itself: of what it means, philosophically, to be timebound, bound by what one has said and done, written and published, previously; and bound to follow, belatedly, those who have gone before.

Since not all my readers (I trust) are professional Miltonists, it may be helpful to display in a user-friendly format the rather confusing evidence that Milton left behind. First, the numbers now assigned to the sonnets, 1 through 23, are those of modern editions, a fact which obscures the four remarkable suppressions of 1673. Second, in the *Poems of Mr. John Milton*, published in January 1646 at the height of the civil war, Milton included only ten sonnets, as follows:

1. O Nightingale, that on yon bloomy Spray
2–6. Five sonnets in Italian, all but one conventional love poems, the exception being addressed to his friend Charles Diodati, who had died in 1638
7. How soon hath time the suttle theef of youth
8. Captain or Colonel, or Knight in Arms
9. Lady that in the prime of earliest youth
10. Daughter to that good Earl, once President.

In the 1673 edition of his *Works*, Milton added almost as many sonnets again:

11. A Book was writ of late call'd *Tetrachordon*
12. I did but prompt the age to quit their cloggs
13. Harry whose tuneful and well-measur'd Song
14. When Faith and Love which parted from thee never

---

[13] Milton, *Complete Prose*, 8:423.

18.   Avenge O Lord thy slaughter'd Saints, whose bones
19.   When I consider how my light is spent
20.   Lawrence of vertuous Father vertuous Son
21.   Cyriack, whose Grandsire on the Royal Bench
23.   Methought I saw my late espoused Saint.

Without the four missing sonnets, it would hardly be necessary to read this as a sequence, and if so read, as only autobiographical in the loosest and most conventional sense. Beginning with love and early friendship, it moves in Sonnet 7, "How soon hath Time," to a moment of religious and self-dedication. Sonnet 8 seems a light-hearted, even playful appeal for the survival of poetry in time of war; Sonnet 9 a biblical praise of some young and pious woman; Sonnet 10 another, more complex praise of a woman for being her father's daughter.

The second half of the sequence begins far less conventionally. Sonnets 11 and 12 introduce a discordant note, in that they clearly register the unpleasant reception of at least one of Milton's polemical pamphlets, *Tetrachordon*. We have entered the arena of political engagement. But Sonnet 13 backs off into a praise of Henry Lawes and his music, and hence harks back to the 1634 production of their joint composition, the *Masque at Ludlow*. Sonnet 14 echoes 9 in its religious praise of an unidentified woman (though this one is evidently dead). Sonnet 18 appeals to the God of the Old Testament to avenge the Piedmontese martyrs, a topic that requires some historical explanation but remains well inside the territory of acceptable piety. Sonnet 19 echoes 7 in its emphasis on vocational patience, in its expressed desire to "serve . . . my Maker, and present/My true account." Both 20 and 21 return to the theme of male friendship, in addition to that of virtuous ancestry; and 23 to the praise of a dead woman, but now in a far more personal and elegiac register: "*My* late espoused Saint," an unnamed wife. But there is hardly anything in these nineteen poems to indicate that they were occasional, in the sense of being written at historically unique and significant moments; nothing to disturb the hypothesis that writing sonnets is a harmless literary activity, and if not timeless, aspiring to that condition. To this extent the public presentation of the sonnets supports Thomas Corns's contention that in the 1646 volume Milton was aiming above all for respectability.[14]

---

[14] Thomas Corns, "Milton's Quest for Respectability," *Modern Language Review* 77 (1982), 769–79.

From what source, then, derives the belief that Milton arranged his sonnets in strict chronological order based on the moment of composition? From Milton's personal ("Cambridge") manuscript, in which Sonnets 8, 11/12, 13, 14, 15 and 16 all carried at some stage in his thinking manuscript titles that stated or implied a precise dating, one that appears to match or at least does not conflict with the poem's position in the sequence. Thus Sonnet 8 carried in the manuscript two versions of the same title: "On his dore *when* ye Citty expected an assault," in the hand of a copyist, subsequently deleted, and below it in Milton's own hand, "*When* the assault was intended to ye Citty." Both versions contain not just a sign of time but a sign of *the times*. The precise formulation must have been important to Milton, or he would not have corrected it. The effect of the correction, while de-literalizing the poem's talismanic function, is to give the "when" more prominence. Yet (whether or not at the same time) Milton *deleted* the manuscript's marginal dating of 1642 – a change of mind that inspired E. A. J. Honigmann to posit another occasion altogether, not the Royalist assault on London expected on November 13, 1642, but another alarm in May 1641.[15]

But for readers in 1645 the question was moot, since the sonnet appeared before them *almost* stripped of its uneasy ricochet between local wartime news and the claims, from time *almost* immemorial, for poetry's protective function:

> Captain or Colonel, or Knight in Arms,
> Whose chance on these defenceless dores may sease,
> If deed of honour did thee ever please,
> Guard them, and him within protect from harms,
> . . .
> Lift not thy spear against the Muses Bowre,
> The great Emathian Conqueror bid spare
> The house of Pindarus, when Temple and Towre
> Went to the ground: And the repeated air
> Of sad Electra's Poet had the power
> To save th'Athenian Walls from ruine bare.

I say "almost," because, with the title gone, the poem's challenge to the reader becomes better balanced. Knowledge of ancient history is required to answer the question: who was "the great Emathian Conqueror?" (Alexander), and when did he spare the house of Pindar? (during the destruction of Thebes in 335 B.C.) I

---

[15] E. A. J. Honigmann, ed., *Milton's Sonnets* (New York, 1966), pp. 102–3.

submit that this act of historical reconstruction, which has to be repeated for "sad Electra's poet,"[16] generates more interesting questions about the contemporary situation and the reticence with which it, too, is described (whose "defenceless dores" are they, and why is history repeating itself?) than the question debated by Honigmann and the *Milton Variorum*,[17] of when precisely Milton would have reason to fear Royalist retribution for statements made in his pamphlets. And, as Thomas Warton intelligently noted, this question would still be pertinent after the Restoration. Warton assumed that by reprinting his sonnet in the 1673 edition of his poems, Milton appealed to Charles II for the same immunity as in 1642 he had asked from Charles I through his military agents:

> As a poet, Milton had as good right to expect this favour as Pindar. Nor was the English monarch less a protector of the arts, and a lover of poetry, than Alexander. As a subject, Milton was too conscious that his situation was precarious, and that his seditious tracts had forfeited all pretensions to his sovereign's mercy.[18]

The distinction between "as a poet" and "as a subject" is well taken.

From his own late eighteenth-century Tory position, Warton made sure, however, to indicate his firm disapproval of Milton's politics whenever his role as annotator permitted. In his note on *Il Penseroso*, for example, he enforced a distinction between the early and the commonwealth Milton, the poet and the politician, to the disadvantage of the latter:

> No man was ever so disqualified to turn puritan as Milton . . . What very repugnant and unpoetical principles did he afterwards adopt! He helped to subvert monarchy, to destroy subordination, and to level all distinctions of rank. But this scheme was totally inconsistent with the splendours of society [and religion] . . . The delights arising from these . . . were to be sacrificed to the cold and philosophical spirit of calvinism, which furnished no pleasures to the imagination. (p. 95)

---

[16] Thomas Warton supplied the information in 1785: "Plutarch relates, that when the Lacedemonian general Lysander took Athens, it was proposed in a council of war intirely to rase the city, and convert its site into a desert. But during the debate, at a banquet of the chief officers, a certain Phocian sung some fine anastrophics from a chorus of the *Electra* of Euripides; which so affected the hearers, that they declared it an unworthy act, to reduce a place, so celebrated for the production of illustrious men, to total ruin and desolation." See Warton, ed., *Poems upon Several Occasions . . . by John Milton* (London: James Dodsley, 1785), p. 340.

[17] A. S. P. Woodhouse and Douglas Bush, *A Variorum Commentary on The Poems of John Milton*, Vol. 2, Part 2 (New York, 1972), pp. 374–75.

[18] *Poems upon Several Occasions*, p. 340, n. 10.

But perhaps Milton himself had given him grounds for this behavior. Removing the historically specific title from Sonnet 8 has a complex effect indeed.

Sonnet 12 (number 11 in the Cambridge manuscript) also carried an occasionalist title, "On the detraction wch follow'd on my writing certain treatises." But here the clear indication of sequentiality (the sonnet follows the detraction which followed the treatises) is accompanied by vagueness as to which treatises they were. Since Sonnet 11 (numbered 12 in the manuscript, and there carrying the title "On the same") mentions by name *Tetrachordon*, published March 4, 1645, we assume that "certain treatises" referred to the four divorce pamphlets as a group; but why was Milton not more helpful, and why was even that limited helpfulness reduced when Sonnet 12 appeared in the 1673 edition without even this partial explanation?

The title gone, one can see more clearly how Milton withheld, in the text of the sonnet itself, any clear indication of his own views:

> A Book was writ of late call'd *Tetrachordon*;
> And wov'n close, both matter, form and stile;
> The Subject new: it walk'd the Town a while,
> Numbring good intellects; now seldom por'd on.

Without the reference to "my writing," the passive construction of the event ("A Book *was writ* of late") focuses on broader cultural issues. Instead of a temporary need for self-defence, the opening lines instead pose the problem of cultural innovation and the difficulty of placing a "Subject new" before a receptive audience. Moreover, there is a smaller temporal sequence invoked within the frame of the up-to-the-moment opening: a book "was writ *of late*," "it walk'd the Town a while," but "now" already it is "seldom por'd on," topical no longer. In the chaotic press world of the mid-1640s the fate of most polemic is instant obsolescence; or, to put the issue more philosophically, how short a time it takes for present occasion to become recent past – a troublesome concept that must inflect with slight irony the temporal marker in the opening line: "of late." That word "late", as we shall see, will acquire both irony and pathos as it reappears in the sequence as a whole in a number of odd formations.

But after the temporal markers, the argument shifts to the *quality* of the book's reception. The sonnet complains that the "stall-reader" complained that "Tetrachordon" was too learned for pronunciation, and parodies this philistinism by the use of comic rhymes. And then, in the last five lines, the point becomes one of linguistic history:

> Those rugged names to our like mouths grow sleek
> That would have made Quintilian stare and gasp.
> Thy age, like ours, O Soul of Sir John Cheek,
> Hated not Learning wors then Toad or Asp;
> When thou taught'st Cambridge, and King Edward Greek.

These last three lines are an epitome of Milton's troublemaking for his readers. Not only do they require one to know *when* it was that Sir John Cheke tutored the young King Edward VI and the intellectual controversy generated by his changing the pronunciation of Greek at St. John's College, Cambridge, an innovation suppressed by bishop Gardiner in 1542. They provoke one to ask why Cheke is chosen as mentor. Was it for the sake of invoking an earlier scholar and humanist educator? Was it for the sake of remembering Edward VI, a hero to English Protestantism? It is also unclear what the sonnet's conclusion actually asserts about the relationship between the recent past and an earlier era, with respect to the climate for intellectual innovation. On the one hand Milton asserts a symmetry between the 1540s and the 1640s ("Thy age, *like* ours") and on the other his negative syntax ("Thy age . . . Hated *not* Learning") seems to require a contrast between them. The *Milton Variorum* dutifully studies this crux and the scholars who have wrestled with it (pp. 391–92); but it passes lightly over what is perhaps the most puzzling aspect of Milton's implied comparison of himself to Cheke – the fact that Cheke's reactionary pamphlet, *The Hurt of Sedicion*, berating the Norfolk followers of Robert Kett in 1549, had in 1641 been reissued by the Royalist Gerard Langbaine as *The True Subject to the Rebell*, with clear application now to the Long Parliamentarians.[19]

These inferences from the Cambridge manuscript of a gap between Milton's original intentions in *writing* the sonnets and his intentions in publishing them can only by strengthened by considering the commonwealth sonnets. Two of these originally carried autograph datings, in titles that never made it into print: "On ye Lord General Fairfax at ye seige of Colchester," that is to say, the

---

[19] This was first pointed out by H. Schultz, "A book was writ of late," *Modern Language Notes* 69 (1954), 495–97. Schultz remarked that it "may too easily be taken for granted that the poet intended compliments where he intended none," a warning that I would extend to Cheke's political afterlife rather than, as did Schultz, merely to the question of whether his educational program was benign.

summer of 1648;[20] and, the most occasionalist of all, "To the Lord Generall Cromwell May 1652/On the proposals of certaine ministers at ye Commtee for Propagation of the Gospel," that is, the parliamentary committee established on February 18, 1652, of which Cromwell was a member. Both titles were deleted in the manuscript, suggesting that Milton himself had in fact planned to publish these sonnets, and had begun by softening their historical specificity. Only later, perhaps, was it recognized that a more radical suppression was advisable.

The testimony of the Cambridge manuscript, then, produced the mainstay of the argument for a strictly chronological sequence: Sonnet 8, dated 1642, and inviting a tighter dating of November of that year; Sonnets 11 and 12, with an implied dating of 1645; Sonnet 13, dated February 1646; Sonnet 14, dated December 1646; Sonnet 15, with an implied dating of summer 1648; Sonnet 16, firmly dated May 1652. And it would be relatively simple to argue that Milton's decision to withhold this information from public inspection was prudential, and part of his decision to keep a low profile during the Stuart Restoration.

The poetics of historicity

I now want to argue, however, that whatever the motive for removing the overt signs of his political life during the civil war and inter-regnum, the *results* of this strategy are actually more complex than so far suggested. While on a superficial inspection (and that is what the sonnets of a blind old republican at the end of his life would likely receive) the effect was to move the sequence towards the private, the pious, and the bland, the suppression of temporal markers in the central sonnets can also create, as it were, interpretive pressure going in the other direction. Once the contrast between the vaguely autobiographical and the chronologically precise is no longer marked, vagueness begins to attract attention to itself. Surrounding the central group of sonnets in which "signs of the times" had once

---

[20] Milton's great biographer, David Masson, saw the significance: "This Sonnet is usually headed now 'To the Lord General Fairfax'; but it is better to restore the original title from Milton's own MS. Draft, though the pen is there drawn through the title in sign of deletion. For one thing this fixes the date of the sonnet. The siege of Colchester in Essex lasted from the 15th of June to the 28th of August 1648, and was one of the most memorable incidents of what is called 'The Second Civil War.'" See Masson, *The Poetical Works of John Milton*, 3 vols. (London, 1890), 1:220.

predominated are two clusters of sonnets in which the personal, the introspective, and the autobiographical are the manifest themes, but in which Milton (since he did not apparently revise them) must have *started* with a decision to mystify chronology. These sonnets abound with mythical (I am tempted to say false) datings – hints of a time scheme against which the poet is measuring himself; yet they have all proved virtually impossible to date with any certainty. And what also becomes visible when the entire sequence is in place is an anxiety spreading from the ambiguous semantics of "late," as Milton deploys the word in different ambiences.

Let us reconsider Sonnet 7, which locates itself in relation to his "three and twentieth year" (and which Thomas Hollis calmly rewrote to make it a marker of Milton's attaining his majority):

> How soon hath Time the suttle theef of youth,
> Stoln on his wing my three and twentieth yeer!
> My hasting dayes flie on with full career,
> But *my late spring* no bud or blossom shew'th.
> Perhaps my semblance might deceive the truth,
> That I to manhood am arriv'd so near,
> And inward ripenes doth much less appear,
> That som more timely-happy spirits indu'th.
> Yet be it less or more, or soon or slow,
> It shall be still in strictest measure eev'n,
> To that same lot, however mean or high,
> Toward which Time leads me, and the will of Heav'n;
> All is, if I have grace to use it so,
> As ever in my great task Masters eye.

Nobody doubts that Milton was here recording a chronological moment of great vocational import. The odd timing (adjusted by Hollis) was explained by William Hunter on the grounds that "the age of twenty-three had been appointed by the Canons of 1604 as the earliest date for one's ordination as a deacon," and, while fifteen of his twenty classmates had already been ordained, Milton was still hesitating over his decision.[21] But we don't know for certain whether that "three and twentieth year" is 1631, at the end of which he *became* twenty-three, or 1632, during most of which he *was* twenty-three.[22]

---

[21] William B. Hunter, "The Date of Milton's Sonnet 7," *English Language Notes* 13 (1975), 10–14.

[22] W. R. Parker argued for the latter by analogy with Milton's use of the Latin phrase *anno aetatis*. See "Some Problems in the Chronology of Milton's Early Poems," *Review of English Studies* 11 (1935), 276–83; but compare Ernest Sirluck, "Milton's Idle Right Hand," *Journal of English and Germanic Studies* 60 (1961), 781–84.

Nor do we know for certain whether Sonnet 7 followed or preceded in its order of *composition* the opening sonnet of the sequence, with its characteristically Miltonic appeal to the nightingale, bird of love, and its own emphasis on retardation:

> Now timely sing, ere the rude Bird of Hate
> Foretell my hopeles doom in som Grove ny:
> As thou from year to year hast sung *too late*
> For my relief . . .

Both these poems suggest, without defining it, a standard of achievement and a timetable that needs to be renegotiated; and similar prevarications occur in the famous autobiographical Sonnet 19, "When I consider how my light is spent,/Ere half my days," which constitutes, as it were, the other half of the vocational problem posed by Sonnet 7. Given its infuriating imprecision as to *when* it was written (was it 1642, 1644, 1651 or late 1655?) Sonnet 19 has even been seen as a warning *against* historical criticism, an encouragement to deconstructive undecidability.[23]

But against such a temptation Milton had himself constructed Sonnet 10, the last of the sequence created in the *Poems* of 1645. In the longer sequence created in 1673, this poem operates as a fulcrum between the early and the later Milton, and the two types of sonnets he produced: on the one hand, those that narrate, however evasively, the events that he thought of as symbolic or threshold moments of his personal life or his life conceived as a vocation; on the other, those that, while still in a sense autobiographical, broaden the narrative to engage the political history of his day. Sonnet 10 is the fulcrum of my theory that in constructing this sequence Milton articulated a specialized poetics, a theory of literature appropriate not only to his own personality but to his own historical moment and perhaps to ours also; that is to say, a theory of how literature cannot be understood *except* in the perspective of history, which in turn cannot be understood *except* by absorbing and understanding literary evidence:

> Daughter to *that good Earl*, once President
> Of Englands Council and her Treasury,
> Who liv'd in both, unstain'd with gold or fee,

---

[23] For a longer discussion of this issue, and bibliography, see my essay, "That Old Man Eloquent," in *Literary Milton*, ed. Diana Treviño Benet and Michael Lieb (Pittsburgh, 1994), pp. 33–36.

And left them both, more in himself content,
Till the sad breaking of *that Parlament*
 Broke him, as *that dishonest victory*
At Chaeronea, fatal to liberty,
Kill'd with report *that Old man eloquent,*
Though later born, then to have known the dayes
Wherin your Father flourisht, yet by you
Madam, me thinks I see him living yet;
So well your words his noble vertues praise,
That all both judge you to relate them true
And to possess them, Honour'd Margaret.

Here details that are inarguably literary – syntactical repetition and pointing, and the formal structure of the italianate sonnet – collaborate to reveal a failure of revelation: we learn from the closest of readings that "the text itself" is insufficient for the task of signification – that it points beyond itself to historical facts that the reader must go out and bring back if any cognitive event is to occur. This sonnet continues the theme of belatedness installed in Sonnets 1 and 7, but translates it into the register invoked by Sonnets 11 and 18, in which "late" points to a verifiable historical event. More precisely, the octave constructs the problem of historical knowledge as a set of interrelated questions for which there are certain answers. Like the question provoked by "my late espoused Saint" – "Which one?" – those provoked by Milton's markedly repeated "that" is also "which one?" Which good earl? (a question rendered more difficult of solution when the manuscript title, "To ye Lady Margaret Ley" was dropped). Which parliament was it whose breaking broke him? And to which old man eloquent from ancient history is Milton's good earl compared? But unlike Sonnet 23, where the autobiographical question, "Which wife?" remains insoluble, Sonnet 10 operates in the confidence that the fit reader will know what needs to be known.

Obviously, the answer to the first question is the readiest to hand, even today: James Ley, earl of Marlborough, father of the Lady Margaret to whom the sonnet is addressed. And the fact that he died on March 10, 1629 permits the certain recognition of "that Parliament" as the last of the Caroline parliaments, dissolved on March 4, 1629 by Charles I, after the demonstration, famous or notorious depending on one's own political inclinations, when the Speaker Sir John Finch was forcibly prevented from reading the royal order to adjourn until the Commons had passed resolutions against tonnage and poundage and innovations in religion. The dissolution inaugurated the period referred to either as the eleven years of Personal Rule or the Eleven Years' Tyranny, again depending on one's ideological take on these events. That Milton called it a "sad breaking" is not surprising, but the phrase admits the constitutional disaster without explicitly assigning blame to either the king or the party of Eliot, Coke, Selden and others. It *is* surprising, given how clearly his republican political theory had already developed, that Milton does not mention the Petition of Right; but the milder position was obviously more appropriate to a sonnet honoring Ley, who had made a career in the service of James I and Charles I.

Nevertheless, the third "that," requiring another historical solution from the far more distant past, adds a republican gloss. The dissolution of 1629 is the equivalent in political theory of the battle of Chaeronea in 338 B.C., when the Athenian democracy succumbed to Philip of Macedon, news of which is said to have caused the death of Isocrates, "that Old man eloquent" with whom Milton aligned (or contrasted) himself in 1644 in the writing (and naming) of *Areopagitica*.

The rewards that accrue from restoring these facts to the spaces held open by those deictic substitutions ("that good Earl, that Parliament, that dishonest victory, that Old man eloquent") are, however, fallacious.[24] At least, the further one goes towards filling out the historical profiles this sonnet sketches so lightly, the more uncomfortable grows that knowledge. James Ley, born in the reign of Edward VI, had apparently been an able municipal lawyer who had first acquired a political reputation at the beginning of James's reign. This was as commissioner of the great seal for Dublin, where he became generally hated for his severity against Catholic recusants. When James brought him back from Ireland to serve as attorney to the court of wards and liveries, Ley entered the profitable world of legal patronage. When Sir Francis Bacon vacated the attorney-generalship in 1617, Ley was reported by Buckingham to have offered ten thousand pounds for the vacant post, which, however, he failed to receive. At sixty-nine years of age, and according to D'Ewes already "a decrepit old man,"[25] he married as his third wife Jane Butler, Buckingham's niece,[26] and so put himself in line for prefer-

---

[24] As they may, by reading an annotated edition of the sonnets, be too easily won.

[25] Sir Symonds D'Ewes, *Autobiography and Correspondence*, ed. J. O. Halliwell, , 2 vols.(London, 1845), 1:160.

[26] Buckingham himself was twenty-nine in 1621 when the marriage took place; his niece would therefore have been still in her teens.

ment from the favorite, resulting in his appointment as lord chief justice of the King's Bench in January 1621. In that capacity he presided at Bacon's trial in the House of Lords for financial corruption. In 1624 Ley retired from the bench to become lord high treasurer and a privy councillor, also under Buckingham's auspices, despite the fact that Ley had no financial experience and showed no aptitude for it.[27] He resigned the post four years later to his assistant, Sir Richard Weston, and Charles I thereupon made him president of the council. Six months later, according to Clarendon, he "was removed under pretence of his age and disability for the work."[28] He died, at seventy-nine years of age, in the following spring. It is only on the basis of Milton's sonnet, and the coincidence between the date of his death, on March 14, 1629, that it has been attributed to political disappointment rather than simple decrepitude.

The *Dictionary of National Biography* sums up Ley's career as follows:

Ley, although a feeble statesman, was an able, erudite, and impartial judge . . . On the other hand, Sir James Whitelocke denounces him as "an old dissembler," who was "wont to be called 'Vulpone'" and says that he borrowed money of the judges when lord chief justice (*Liber Famelicus*, p. 108).[29]

In the ellipsis between these two contrary evaluations, the *Dictionary* inserts, unconscious of any irony, the first four lines of Milton's sonnet, with its apparent dissociation of Ley ("unstained with gold or fee") from such venality as Bacon had been charged with in 1622, and that led to his disgrace.

This hole opening up in the fabric of the ideal community under the pressure of historical inquiry is likely only to gape wider if we also pursue "that Old man eloquent" a little further. For Isocrates' legendary suicide after the battle of Chaeronea could not have been, as Milton's sonnet implied, motivated by its fatality to Athenian liberty, since his *Philippus*, written in 346 after an earlier round of

---

27 On the scramble for Buckingham's patronage during the summer of 1624, as it became apparent that the favorite's star was still rising and would carry him over into the next reign, see Thomas Cogswell, *The Blessed Revolution: English Politics and the Coming of War, 1621–1624* (Cambridge, 1989), pp. 271–74. On Ley's eagerness "to try his hand at finance," Cogswell cites John Chamberlain's letters to Dudley Carleton, *The Letters of John Chamberlain*, ed. N. E. McLure, 2 vols. (Philadelphia, 1939), 2:568, 572, 576.

28 Henry Hyde, earl of Clarendon, *History of the Rebellion and Civil Wars in England*, ed. W. Dunn Macray, 6 vols. (1888; repr. edn Oxford, 1969), 1:59.

29 In fact Whitelocke made this remark in 1627, close to the time of Ley's death, adding that though "wont" to be called Volpone "I think he as well deservethe it now as ever."

hostilities between Philip of Macedon and Athens, initiated his campaign to have Philip assume rule over a united Greece; and, as the *Oxford Companion to Classical Literature* observes, this placed him in absolute contradistinction to that other eloquent old man who indeed lamented Chaeronea, Demosthenes. The reason for that suicide, if truly historical, would have been, therefore, "not that Philip had been victorious – thus rendering practicable the chief hope of Isocrates – but that Athens was still determined to resist him." Again, a citation of Milton's sonnet, innocent of any irony, appears at the end of this account. The *Milton Variorum* acknowledges the problem in Milton's invocation of Isocrates, but resolves it in the most high-minded manner possible:

> If this aspect of the matter were present to Milton, the implication would be quite different, namely, that the Earl's policy was to reconcile the King and Parliament (as his loyal and rewarded service of the crown would indeed suggest) and that his hopes, like those of Isocrates, were shattered. This seems better to fit the facts, while the condemnation of Charles by the implied comparison of him to Philip seems better to suit Milton's own principles (and prejudices).

The *Variorum* editors therefore chose to believe that Milton believed in the earl's idealism and integrity while disagreeing with his allegiances; the closest they came to imagining that Milton's sonnet might have been disingenuous was to wonder: "Is it possible that Milton wrote the lines in one sense and allowed Lady Margaret to read them in the other?" (p. 386). As for Thomas Warton in 1785, he reopened the issue by remarking that "A republic brought under the dominion of a king, was a part of the Grecian history which Milton was likely to remember."[30]

But what of Milton's relationship to Lady Margaret herself? Introduced by a wonderfully intricate turn from the octave, which ends with "that Old man eloquent," into the sestet, which begins with a phrase of which we should by now have learned to be suspicious, "Though *later* born . . . " the relationship is itself a figure of syntactical obscurantism. Of whose belated birth are we here informed?[31] Of the daughter to whom the entire sonnet is addressed, and to the definition of whose filial excellence, by way of an account of her parent, it is, in one long sentence, dedicated? Or to the writer

---

[30] Warton, ed., *Poems upon Several Occasions*, p. 342.

[31] In fact, Milton's own punctuation, with only a comma at the octave, permits the momentary false assumption that we are still dealing with that "old man eloquent."

of the sonnet who suddenly emerges in the first person in the ninth line, in charge of the only main verb:

> Though later born, then to have known the dayes
> Wherein your Father flourisht, yet by you
> Madam, methinks I see him living yet.

In fact, one need scarcely decide which of the two is "later born," since Milton (born in 1608) and Margaret, born when her father was about sixty, were almost the same age. That being the case, and if we take the term "flourished" conventionally, implying a man at the height of his powers and reputation, we can take the idea of belatedness more literally (and more critically) than an idealistic reading of the sonnet would suppose.[32]

To me, the centrality of Sonnet 10 (numerically central, when the commonwealth sonnets are missing) is a case worth making. But to make it requires a conception of the split subject that only a historically invested literary method is peculiarly equipped to accommodate. In that conception, we try to tell the truth while putting our best foot forward; an objective which requires, or ought to require, continual retrospection and stock-taking. Milton took stock, publicly, more often than most. When Milton wrote Sonnet 10, probably, he was busy reconstructing his life in defiance of the mistakes he admitted in the *Doctrine and Discipline of Divorce*; when he came to publish it, as the last of the sonnets in the 1645/6 *Poems of Mr. John Milton*, a volume that Louis Martz has persuasively described as Milton's leave-taking of his moral and intellectual apprenticeship,[33] he must have been at least partly conscious that irony had accrued to his relationship with the Lady Margaret, now that his wife had returned. When he republished it in 1673, other ironies must have attached themselves to "the sad breaking of that Parlament," and the "dishonest victory . . . fatal to liberty" whose later versions Milton had tried unsuccessfully to prevent in 1559/60. As history moved on, the *words* of the sonnet, its disingenuities notwithstanding, were capable of carrying the message to the Restoration that Milton claimed he had never stopped proclaiming, "though fall'n on evil days." If he was not, as he also proclaimed, "unchang'd" over time,

---

[32] This is not the place to discuss the ambiguity of Milton's personal relationship to Lady Margaret. For the struggles of Miltonists with this issue, see "That Old Man Eloquent," pp. 41–43.

[33] Louis Martz, *Poet of Exile: A Study of Milton's Poetry* (New Haven and London, 1980), pp. 31–59.

he registered his changes with a subtlety that deserves our continued attention.

THE COMMONWEALTH SONNETS

But Sonnet 10 was written at a stage in Milton's career – somewhere between 1642 and 1645 – when he was ambivalent about the drive towards change in his society as a whole. Not so the four "commonwealth" sonnets, whose very existence drastically alters the character of Milton's sonneteering, rendering it, for the purposes of literary history, exceptional. Whereas Petrarch had included attacks on the Avignon papacy in his sonnet sequence, and others had followed his lead, Milton was unusual in deploying for political comment a medium conventionally dedicated to the description of love affairs, and unique in stretching it to topics conventionally rendered by the Pindaric ode. And while part of the conjuring trick of the sonnets as published was to produce, as it were, a meditation on political life past and present in the guise of largely sentimental or pious concerns, there was no such indirection in the case of the sonnets to or about Cromwell, Vane and Fairfax, whose weight as historical personalities, whose *names* as metrically inscribed in their sonnets, would have easily outweighed the anonymous pious women and ordinary male friends of the surrounding units – *had the sequence been published as a whole.*

The later publication history of the commonwealth sonnets now lurks in the notes of scholarly editions, where far too many non-specialists have no idea of its significance. Much of the color of the story is, in any case, bleached out by such professional habits. Some of it was restored by Thomas Warton, who thought about Milton always in terms of reception history and politics. In his notes on the sonnet to Fairfax, he wrote:

For obvious political reasons this Sonnet, the two following, and the twenty second, were not inserted in the edition of 1673. They were first printed at the end of Philips's Life of Milton prefixed to the English version of his public Letters, 1694. They are quoted by Toland in his Life of Milton, 1698. Tonson omitted them in his editions of 1695, 1705. But *growing less offensive by time*, they appear in his edition of 1713. The Cambridge manuscript happily corrects many of their vitiated readings. They were the favourites of the republicans long after the restoration: *it was some consolation to an exterminated party, to have such good poetry remaining on their side of the question.* (p. 351; italics added)

In other words, these four sonnets have the same status in literary history as do Marvell's three poems on Cromwell, which were omitted for prudential reasons from his posthumous *Miscellaneous Poems* of 1681, published in the context of the Exclusion crisis. But "growing less offensive by time," they were absorbed back into the canon. There the protocols of modern editing are likely to distract attention from the very real dangers involved in their early publication, dangers to which Warton, while disapproving of these sonnets in principle, was more alert than one might have expected of him.

But Warton was apparently unaware of a much earlier publication of Milton's sonnet on Vane, although he included in his notes on that poem a mini-biography and assessment of Vane as statesman and thinker, and proposed that Milton had alluded to Vane's execution in 1662 in *Samson Agonistes*, when the Chorus complains how God apparently forgets his heroes:

> Oft leav'st them to the hostile sword
> Of heathen and profane, their carcasses
> To dogs and fowls a prey, or else captiv'd:
> Or to th'unjust tribunals, under change of times,
> And condemnation of th'ingrateful multitude.[34]

For in 1662 the otherwise unknown George Sikes published an elaborate account of Vane's trial, from papers prepared by Vane himself and secreted from his gaolers, and a tract of his own, half biography, half advertisement of Vane's opinions and beliefs. In *The Life and Death of Sir Henry Vane, Kt.*, tucked away in the middle of the religious polemic which forms the bulk of this work, is a piece of political defiance, which also constitutes the first formal "reading" of a Milton sonnet:

Would you know his Title in reference to his countrey? He was A Common-Wealths-Man. That's a dangerous Name to the Peace and Interest of Tyranny . . . The Character of this deceased Statesman . . . I shall exhibit to you in a paper of Verses, composed by a learned Gentleman and sent him, July 3, 1652. (p. 93)

Sikes then reproduced the text of this anonymous sonnet, which he had obviously received from Vane himself, along with the other materials relating to Vane's defence and justification. He then proceeded to explain to his readers the relationship between octave

---

[34] *Poems upon Several Occasions*, pp. 355–56.

and sestet. Thus "in the former part of these verses, notice is taken of a kind of angelical intuitiveness and sagacity [Vane] was furnished with, for spying out and unridling the subdolous intentions of hollow-hearted States," that is to say, the sonnet begins by praising Vane's diplomatic skills abroad (p. 94); but "the latter part of this Sufferers Elogy in the 'bove-mentioned Verses, concerns his skill in distinguishing the two Swords or Powers, Civil and Spiritual, and the setting right bounds to each" (p. 98); that is to say, Vane's important definition of the two branches of the Good Old Cause, religious toleration and civil liberties. But because Milton's sonnet is now being seen in the context of the Restoration and the trials of the regicides, it has acquired meanings that Milton could not have anticipated. The sonnet ends by assuring Vane that "on thy firm hand religion leans/In peace, and reckons thee her eldest son"; a decade later Sikes (and Milton himself) have witnessed the opposite:

by an over-ruling stroke of abused Prerogative, a majority in Parliament can be procured, that will pull up all the antient Laws Rights and Liberties of the Nation by the Roots and establish mischief by a new Law (make Reason and Duty Treason, and that *post factum* too). (p. 98)

After Sikes's intervention, the suppressed party waited for the times to change again. And change they did. After the Revolution of 1688, Edward Phillips, Milton's nephew, was the first to get the four sonnets into print. He did not do so, however, until 1694, in his *Letters of State, Written by Mr. John Milton, To Most of the Sovereign Princes and Republicks of Europe* (1694); and even then the epistle "To the Reader" begins with a defensive disclaimer:

Prejudice overrules and sways a World of People, and there is no question but this Collection will meet with a great deal . . . [but] after the exactest Scrutiny that can be made there is nothing to be met with in the following Sheets, not wrested by Tyrannical Innuendo, that can give the least offence. (A2r)

No explanation is given for the presence of the four commonwealth sonnets in the preliminaries to the state correspondence.[35] And in the following year Tonson's edition again omitted them, suggesting that, if they were, in Warton's words, "growing less offensive by time," *some* offence was still capable of being taken.

As for John Toland: he too hedged his bets. His *Life of Milton* is presented as a letter to a friend (Thomas Raulins of Kilreag in

---

[35] They are printed on pp. xlvi–xlvii.

Herefordshire); its author is identified only as I.T., and hopes to be protected by the impartiality of historiography, ideally understood. The *Life* ends by citing Sir Francis Bacon, to the effect that "a forbidden Writing is thought to be a certain Spark of Truth that flies up in the faces of them that seek to tread it out."[36] And within the *Life*, the four sonnets are introduced separately, as if they were merely documents of Milton's career: first, the sonnets to Fairfax and Vane, in entirety (1:24); and a few pages later, the sonnets to Cyriack Skinner and Cromwell, also in their entirety, but with the following explanation for the latter:

Our Author was now Latin Secretary to the Protector Oliver Cromwell, who, he confidently hop'd, would imploy his Trust and Power to extinguish the numerous Factions of the State, and to settle such a perfect Form of Free Government, wherin no single Person should injoy any Power over or beside the Laws; but he particularly expected his establishing an impartial Liberty of Conscience, to which he incourages him by these Lines, never printed among his Poems. (p. 35)

For Toland, who either did not know or suppressed the fact of the poem's date and occasion, the sonnet to Cromwell was a Protectorate work, matching in intention the address to the chief executive/new dictator in Milton's *Second Defence*. It was, therefore, a braver intervention than it would have seemed in 1652.

Toland's mission was, as we have seen, continued by Thomas Hollis, who was especially invested in Milton's Sonnets 7 and 22. But he evidently felt that the other commonwealth sonnets were not sufficiently known or understood in the second half of the eighteenth century. Or so we can infer from two of his polemical footnotes in his 1763 edition of Algernon Sidney's works. In his opening *Memoir* of Sidney Hollis added a long note on Vane's behavior at his trial, a quotation from Sikes's edition of it, and Milton's sonnet to Vane (pp. 25–26). In so doing, he explained to posterity the deeper meaning of Sidney's supposed complaint (however textually inauthentic) that "where Vane, Lambert, Haselrigge cannot live in safety, I cannot live at all" (p. 24); that is, the continuity of political persecution from one generation to the next.

In annotating Sidney's own trial, Hollis's attention was caught by Sidney's reference therein to Cromwell as someone who "though he was a tyrant, and a violent one," drew the line at the argument that

---

[36] Milton, *A Complete Collection*, 3 vols. ("Amsterdam," 1698), 1:47.

"possession was the only right to power" (p. 135). Sidney had observed that Cromwell objected strenuously to this argument when proposed by Thomas White, in *The Grounds of Obedience and Government* (1655). And Hollis seized this opportunity to reprint Milton's sonnet to Cromwell in his notes, as testimony to Milton's liberal sentiments. In it, he claimed, Milton had "held out the Beacon" of civil and religious liberties to Cromwell, "*before* he destroyed the Parliament, and . . . set up Tyrant, for himself." This fixing of the sonnet's occasion (as prior, if not to the Instrument of Government, at least to Cromwell's dissolution of the first Protectorate parliament) is worth a moment's notice; for without access to the Cambridge manuscript, Hollis could not have known that the sonnet was written in May 1652, especially since Toland had presented it as a Protectorate poem. Hollis's dating was an inspired guess, perhaps; but truer to the tone of the poem than other later commentary.

In 1785, for example, Thomas Warton gave this poem a very mixed review:

The prostitution of Milton's Muse to the celebration of Cromwell, was as inconsistent and unworthy, as that this enemy to kings, to antient magnificence, and to all that is venerable and majestic, should have been buried in the Chapel of Henry the Seventh. But there is great dignity both of sentiment and expression in this Sonnet. Unfortunately, the close is an anticlimax to both. After a long flow of perspicuous and nervous language, the unexpected pause at "Worcester's laurel wreath," is very emphatical, and has a striking effect . . .

Milton's praise of Cromwell may be thought inconsistent with that zeal which he professed for liberty: for Cromwell's assumption of the Protectorate, even if we allow the lawfulness of the Rebellion, was palpably a violent usurpation of Power over the rights of the nation, and was reprobated even by the republican party. (pp. 353–54)

Warton was in many ways a good reader. That account of the octave as "a long flow of perspicuous and nervous language" and his sense of the meaning of Milton's striking enjambement is unrivalled in its own perspicuity. But Warton, who *did* have access to the Cambridge manuscript, nevertheless chose himself to suppress the subtitle, "To the Lord Generall Cromwell May 1652/On the proposals of certaine ministers at ye Commtee for Propagation of the Gospel," which *requires* the earlier dating. This permitted the historical slippage which makes the sonnet *follow* "Cromwell's assumption of the Protectorate," and therefore, to Warton, inconsistent with Milton's liberalism. Even more revelatory of Warton's values, however, is his praise for the militarist octave, with its unexpected metrical spillover:

> Cromwell, our cheif of men, who through a cloud
> Not of warr onely, but detractions rude,
> Guided by faith & matchless Fortitude
> To peace & truth thy glorious way hast plough't,
> And on the neck of crowned Fortune proud
> Hast reard Gods Trophies, & his work pursu'd,
> While Darwen stream with bloud of Scotts imbru'd,
> And Dunbar feild resounds thy praises loud,
> And Worsters laureat wreath; . . .

and his contempt for the sestet, in which Milton offered Cromwell in brief the message that Thomas Hollis had read out both his epics: the superiority of the deeds of peace and religious toleration:

> . . . *yet much remaines*
> To conquer still; peace hath her victories
> No less renownd then warr, new foes arise
> Threatning to bind our soules with secular chaines:
> Helpe us to save free Conscience from the paw
> Of hireling wolves whose Gospell is their maw.

In conclusion: it makes all the difference, when reading Milton's sonnets, that we bring to their elucidation and evaluation a strong sense of historical context. Included in this context is, of course, Milton's own biography; but equally or more important is the detailed history of the sonnets' publication or non-publication, and the deployment of chronology, known or invented, by Milton and others. If my first chapter may have seemed one-sided in its recelebration of Hollis's celebration of Milton, this one has replaced the single-minded hagiography of dissent by the skepticism of contemporary textual exegesis. Yet Hollis and Warton were reading the *same* short poems. If their political biases permitted them to describe them in such astonishingly different terms, it may have been Milton's own ambivalences, I have tried to suggest, that gave predilection its mandate.

CHAPTER 3

Unjust tribunals 1: "Read this trial"

> . . . such as thou hast solemnly elected,
> With gifts and graces eminently adorn'd
> To some great work, thy glory,
> And people's safety, which in part they effect:
> Yet toward these, thus dignifi'd, thou oft,
> Amidst thir height of noon,
> Changest thy count'nance . . .
> . . .
> Oft leav'st them to the hostile sword
> Of Heathen and profane, thir carcases
> To dogs and fowls a prey, or else captiv'd:
> Or to th'unjust tribunals, under change of times.
>
> John Milton, *Samson Agonistes*

In 1671 John Milton published a closet drama on the story of Samson, during which his Hebrew Chorus meditate, in the lines cited above, on the uneven progress of progress. The reference to "unjust tribunals, under change of times," was, as we have seen, interpreted in the eighteenth century as a topical allusion to the trials of the regicides, but one that could have wider extension.[1] These words came to stand for the type of "justice" available during the reigns of the second two Stuarts for those in the defeated party. These perils also attended those on the outskirts of the reestablished Anglican church, whether Catholic or nonconformist Protestants. In the 1670s, when Charles II was posing as the defender of religious toleration in order to protect Catholics and win the support of Dissenters, conformity suddenly became a political card in the hands of the House of Commons, who passed "tests" to catch papists and acts against conventicles, while from different motives high-church

---

[1] See p. 45 above; and also Thomas Warton, ed., *Poems upon Several Occasions* (London, 1785), p. 356.

figures like Samuel Parker were calling for greater severities. In this tricky situation, imaginative strategies were needed to define a character and a stance for the disempowered. Milton's Samson, blinded and toiling in the mill with slaves, yet capable of a miraculous return of strength, was one rather threatening possibility. Andrew Marvell, in *The Rehearsal Transpros'd* (1672), developed within the metaphor of the Restoration "play" the weapon of mock-heroic to discredit Samuel Parker; and John Bunyan, who spent twelve years in gaol for his intransigence as an itinerant preacher, wrote his great allegorical novel, *The Pilgrim's Progress* (1678), to provide the dissenting churches and sects with an inspirational myth of patience and perseverance.

In the center of the *Progress* Bunyan placed his most graphic account of what Dissenters, in particular, could continue to expect from the Restoration government: the story of the trial of Christian and Faithful in the city of Vanity Fair. Despite its spiritual referent, the account is given in realistic and recognizable legal detail. The two pilgrims have created a hubbub in the city by refusing to participate in its trade. Therefore:

word [was] presently brought to the great one of the fair, who quickly came down, and deputed some of his most trusty friends to take these men into examination, about whom the Fair was almost overturned . . . But they that were appointed to examine them, did not believe them to be any other than Bedlams and Mad, or else such as came to put all things into a confusion at the Fair . . . So they beat them pitifully, and hanged Irons upon them, and led them in Chaines up and down the fair, for an example and terror to others, lest any should further speak on their behalf, or joyn themselves unto them. But Christian and Faithful behaved themselves yet more wisely; and received the ignominy and shame that was cast upon them, with so much meekness and patience, that it won to their side (though but few in comparison to the rest) several of the men in the fair. This put the other party yet into a greater rage, in so much that they concluded the death of these two men.[2]

The results of the trial having been decided in advance, "they were brought forth before their Enemies and Arraigned." The indictment charged them with having made commotions and divisions in the town, and of having "won a party to their own most dangerous Opinions, in contempt of the Law of their Prince" (p. 93). Since the

---

[2] Bunyan, *The Pilgrim's Progress*, ed. J. B. Wharey, rev. Roger Sharrock (Oxford, 1960), pp. 90–92.

judge is Lord Hategood, it is no surprise to find three witnesses
volunteering to give testimony whose names are Envy, Superstition
and Pickthank, and who lie enthusiastically under oath. Of Faithful,
whose case is heard first, it is said that he not only decries the town's
religion, but has libelled its magnates, saying "that if all men were of
his mind . . . there is not one of these Noble-men should have any
longer a being in this town" (p. 94). When Faithful asks to speak a
few words in his own defence, the Judge replies, "Sirrah, Sirrah,
thou deservest to live no longer, but to be slain immediately upon
the place; yet that all men may see our gentleness towards thee, let
us hear what thou hast to say." Oddly, although the charge of
libelling the aristocracy was false, Faithful refuses to deny it, insisting
that "the Prince of this Town, with all the Rablement his Attendants
. . . are more fit for a being in Hell, than in this Town and
Countrey" (p. 95). And so, having only now defined the statutes
under which Faithful is indicted – three persecuting laws enforcing
idolatry, made respectively by Pharaoh, Nebuchadnezzar and Darius
– Lord Hategood declares that Faithful has broken their substance
"not only in thought (which is not to be born) but also in word and
deed"; and, in addition, "for the *Treason* he hath *confessed*, he
deserveth to die the death" (italics added). We scarcely need the roll-
call of the jury, "whose names were Mr. Blind-man, Mr. No-good,
Mr. Malice, Mr. Love-lust, Mr. Live-loose, Mr. Heady, Mr. High-
mind, Mr. Enmity, Mr. Lyar, Mr. Cruelty, Mr. Hate-light, and
Mr. Implacable," to recognize that in such a system a jury of one's
peers is no guarantee of impartiality. The trial of Faithful is therefore
clearly brought within the history of treason trials in early modern
England, a history which liberalism made every effort to record, to
preserve and to disseminate. And in the fifth (1680) edition of the
Progress, a new woodcut representing Faithful's martyrdom appears
on the title-page beneath the portrait of the sleeping Bunyan, with
these four lines of verse underneath, which stress the legal aspect of
the central episode:

> Brave Faithful, Bravely done in word and deed,
> Judge, Witnesses and Jury have insteed
> Of overcoming thee, but shewn their rage,
> When they are dead thou'lt live from age to age.

The juridical practice of early modern England was even more
outrageous, at least in the arena of the treason trial, than Bunyan

here represented. If judged by standards now taken for granted in Western Europe and North America the law itself was seriously defective. It was, after all, precisely those clauses in the original American Bill of Rights that deal with trial procedure and what leads up to it – the requirement of a search warrant (Fourth Amendment), the provision that no one shall be compelled in a criminal case to be a witness against himself (Fifth Amendment), the right to a speedy and public trial, to be informed of the nature and cause of the accusations, to confront the witnesses for the prosecution and to be able to obtain witnesses in his favor (Sixth Amendment), and the embargo against excessive bail, excessive fines, and "cruel and unusual punishment" (Eighth Amendment) – that were deemed necessary in 1791 because English common law practice gave no secure or comprehensive protection in these areas even at the end of the eighteenth century. Just after the Williamite Revolution, Sir John Hawles published a commentary on some of the more notorious state trials of the reign of Charles II, explaining the Revolution partly in terms of "undue Prosecutions in criminal, but more especially in capital matters," which had so undermined the public trust.

Hawles's *Remarks upon the Tryals of Edward Fitzharris, Stephen College . . . the Lord Russel, Collonel Sidney,* published in 1689, was one of the many books on the interface between law and government owned by Thomas Jefferson.[3] In his commentary on the trial of Stephen College, the joiner executed in 1681 for insulting the king and the duke of York in conversation and cartoons at the time of the Oxford parliament, Hawles paused to sum up what he called the legal "practise of late times," *late* implying, as it did for Milton and would do for Locke, recent and very topical. Hawles, who became William's solicitor-general in 1695, deserves quotation at some length, not least because his account of late Stuart juridical practice in trials for treason reads today like something out of Kafka:

It is so very much like, or rather worse than the practise of the inquisition, as I have read it, that I sometimes think it was in order to introduce popery, and make the inquisition, which is the most terrible thing in that religion, and which all nations dread, seem easy in respect of it. I will therefore recount some undeniable circumstances of *the late practice*: a man is by a messenger, without any indictment precedent, which by the common law

---

[3] *The Library Catalogue of Thomas Jefferson*, ed. Millicent Sowerby, 5 vols. (Washington, D.C., 1952), 3:186.

ought to precede, or any accuser or accusation that he knows of, clapt up in close prison, and neither friend nor relation must come to him, he must have neither pen, ink or paper, or know of what, or by whom he is accused . . . If any person advise or solicit for him, unless assigned by the court by which he is tried, they are punishable: he is tried as soon as he comes into the court, and therefore of a solicitor there is no occasion or use . . . The prisoner indeed hath liberty to except to thirty-five of the jury peremptorily, and as many more as he hath cause to except to, but he must not know beforehand who the jury are; but the king's counsel must have a copy of them . . . there is a proclamation to call in all persons to swear against him, none is permitted to swear for him; all the impertinent evidence that can be given is permitted against him, none for him; as many counsel as can be hired are allowed against him, none for him. Let any person consider these circumstances, and it is a wonder how any person escapes: it is downright tying a man's hands behind him, and baiting him to death, as in truth was practised in all these cases. The trial of Ordeal, of walking between hot iron bars blindfold, which was abolished for the unreasonableness of it, though it had its [biblical] saying for it too, that God would lead the blind so as not to be burnt if he were innocent, was a much more advantageous trial for the suspected than what was *of late practised*, where it was ten to one that the accused did not escape.[4]

I cite Hawles from the great collection of *State Trials*, yet another strategy in liberalism's long campaign to render such practice not only unacceptable, but almost incredible, a Kafkaesque nightmare. When Thomas Salmon brought out (anonymously) the first edition of *State Trials* in 1719, documents clearly designed to support a "Whig" agenda, he compared Scots civil law procedures favorably to what still pertained in England. "It must be admitted, that the Party accused has in Scotland all the fair play imaginable: he has what Counsel he thinks fit; he has a Copy of his Charge in his own language; his Counsel are permitted to inspect the very Depositions against him before he is brought to Trial; and they are in so little haste to dispatch a State-Prisoner, that the Trial often lasts some months."[5] It is clearly to be inferred from Salmon's "in Scotland" that, despite Hawles's consignment of the ordeals he described to "the late times" and even despite the new Treasons Trial Act of

---

[4] *A Complete Collection of State Trials*, ed. T. B. Howell, 21 vols. (London, 1816), 8:733–34; italics added.

[5] *A Complete Collection of State Trials*, ed. Thomas Salmon, 4 vols. (London, 1719), 1:2. For an account of the various editions of *State Trials* and the agendas they served, see Donald Thomas, *State Trials*, 4 vols. (London and Boston, 1972), 1:4–8.

1696, the concept of "fair play" for the accused in an English treason trial was still embryonic.[6]

Hawles included in his remarks on College's trial a specific attack on the denial of counsel. The practice was archaic in two senses; first, that to defend a person accused of treason was held to be speaking against the monarch; and second, that the accused was required to speak for himself, in the full expectation that he *would* incriminate himself; in other words, self-defence was expected to serve, in the traditions of the residually magic political rituals of the early modern state, as a form of confession. Yet what was not fully grasped by the legal institution was the rebarbative force of this compulsion to bear witness, a force increasingly understood and manipulated by the dissenting and liberal communities. When accused men defended themselves with intelligence and passion, their trials became (like Milton's actual drama, Marvell's pseudo-drama and Bunyan's novel) dramatic representations of issues that, if left to lawyers, might have been rendered safely professional and obscure. And when accused men defended themselves, others of similar views would be taking notes in the courtroom, and could (by flouting the press laws) make the drama of the treason trial available in print to a larger audience.

The result was the creation, as it were, of an alternative legal canon: the records, most often produced surreptitiously and printed illegally, of what were seen as unusually unjust trials, which could then serve a purpose related to that of Bunyan's, of providing ethical and emotional support to any temporarily disadvantaged party or actively persecuted minority. But in addition, as we shall see, this alternative legal literature (of which the *State Trials* served as a canonizing and legitimating mechanism) could actually serve a practical legal purpose: of providing instruction in the ways of courts and the strategies of self-defence which could literally be passed on from one defendant to another. In the rare (one in ten) case suggested by Hawles, this educative process allowed the defendant to escape conviction. In the last case we shall examine, however, that of Algernon Sidney, this strategic use of the precedent trials became,

---

[6] The Treasons Act (2 & 8 Will. 3, c. 3) permitted all defendants to have a copy of the indictment five days before trial, to employ counsel to make their defence in court, and to subpoena their own witnesses. See G. C. Gibbs, "Press and Public Opinion: Prospective," in *Liberty Secured? Britain Before and After 1688*, ed. J. R. Jones (Stanford, 1992), p. 244.

precisely because the "law" was itself unstable and liable to judicial manipulation, a snare and a delusion.

This "trial" literature, which had by the Restoration become a significant genre with well-defined conventions, made its first appearance in the middle of the sixteenth century, in a case that laid down both some effective strategies of self-defence and the importance of making such trials available to a broad reading public. This was the trial of Sir Nicholas Throckmorton in 1553,[7] for complicity in the uprising led by Sir Thomas Wyatt the younger against Mary Tudor, who had just assumed the throne in defiance of the rival Protestant faction who asserted the claims to the succession of Lady Jane Grey. The motives for the rebellion combined religion and politics, in that Mary was not only herself a Roman Catholic, for some an unwelcome change back from the Edwardian Reformation, but planned to marry Philip II of Spain, which portended foreign domination. Throckmorton was accused of helping to design the rebellion, which was patently an exaggeration. Most of the evidence for the prosecution consisted of depositions of conversations the accused was supposed to have had, with men who were not brought in to confront him. The prosecution produced only one witness, and he was known to be bargaining for his life by turning state's evidence; whereas a witness for the defence who was already in court was not allowed to testify. The case turned on some precise wording in treason legislation, which had for the previous two decades been in a state of constant and contradictory revision; but when Throckmorton asked that the relevant statutes be read aloud to the members of the jury, his request was denied. Nevertheless, he managed to conduct his defence with such a mixture of legal sophistication and moral superiority, spiced with wit and the common touch, that the jury acquitted him. Its members were thereupon themselves thrown into prison, and fined so exorbitantly that the case became something of a skeleton in the cupboard of British legal historians.[8]

---

[7] I repeat here material included in *Reading Holinshed's Chronicles* (Chicago, 1994), pp. 154–83, on the grounds that the Throckmorton trial and its recording in the *Chronicles* initiated and set the protocols for the genre discussed in this and the following chapter.

[8] Modern historians of the jury trial have downplayed the case, treating it as an exception to a system that worked (within its own legal terms) with reasonable integrity. Compare Thomas Andrew Green, *Verdict According to Conscience: Perspectives on the English Criminal Trial Jury 1200–1800* (Chicago, 1985), p. 141, where Throckmorton's case appears in a single footnote; J. S. Cockburn, *History of English Assizes: 1558–1714* (Cambridge, 1972; repr. 1986), where, again, Throckmorton's case appears in a single footnote, p. 123.

In the different cupboard of libertarian thought, this case became, conversely, an inspiration – at least for the man who features as my second exhibit, John Lilburne, who was tried for treason almost exactly a century later, ironically by those very parliamentarians who had established themselves as the defenders of "liberty" against monarchical prerogative. Lilburne was not merely the intellectual leader of the Levellers but the most inspired publicist of that miscellaneous group of religious activists partly based on the army who attemped to push the mid-century revolution further in the direction of social reorganization than its leaders in the Long Parliament had ever intended. By the time he was charged with treason in 1649, specifically for his revised version of the *Agreement of the People* and his publication of *England's New Chains*, Lilburne had published more than eighty pamphlets, and had earned himself the folklore title of "Freeborn John." In *England's New Chains* he disputed the legality of the Long Parliament in highly insulting terms. His trial in 1649 has been ably analyzed by Sharon Achinstein as her opening exhibit of the "revolution in print" that characterized the 1640s;[9] but there were aspects of Lilburne's strategy in making his defence that become even more interesting when we know that he learned them by *reading* the trial of Throckmorton. Lilburne too defended himself so brilliantly, and with such theatrical panache, that the jury acquitted him, to the enormous enthusiasm of the London citizenry; his case thereby became itself part of a long-standing dispute as to who, finally, represented the Law in England: the learned judges or the "twelve men," the symbolic representatives of the people.

The other trial considered in this chapter, however, had the tragic structure symbolically captured in Bunyan's Vanity Fair episode, in that the defendant lost his case, as it was clear from the outset he would, and was subsequently executed. In 1662 Sir Henry Vane was tried for treason by the newly established Restoration government, and treated as a scapegoat for the entire commonwealth and Protectorate experiment. Considering that the judge who presided over Vane's trial was John Kelynge, who in January 1661 had sentenced Bunyan to Bedford Gaol, Vane was probably one of the historical referents for Bunyan's martyr Faithful, sentenced to die for

---

[9] Sharon Achinstein, *Milton and the Revolutionary Reader* (Princeton, 1994), pp. 42–58.

treason by the court of Vanity Fair.[10] A very different account of Vane's trial, preceded by a biography, was surreptitiously published in 1662, a feat now attributed to the otherwise unknown George Sikes, who (playing a role not unlike that of Raphael Holinshed) explained his editorial procedure:

The necessity of this course for thy information, as to the truth of his Case, be pleased to consider on these following accounts. He was much over-ruled, diverted, interrupted, and cut short in his Plea (as to a free and full delivery of his mind upon the whole matter at the Bar) by the Judges of the Kings-Bench, and by the Kings Counsel. He was also denied the benefit of any Counsel to speak on his behalf.

And what he did speak at the Bar and on the Scaffold, was so disgustful to some, that the Books of those that took Notes of what passed all along in both places, were carefully called in and suppressed. It is therefore altogether unpossible to give thee a full Narrative of all he said, or was said to him, either in Westminster-Hall, or on Tower-Hill.

The Defendant foreseeing this, did most carefully set down in writing, the substance of what he intended to enlarge upon, the three dayes of his appearance at the Kings-Bench Bar, and the day of his Execution. Upon these considerations, I doubt not, it will appear undispensably necessary, to have given this faithful Transcript of such Papers of his, as do contain the most substantial and pleadable grounds of his publick actings, any time this twenty years and more, as the only means left of giving any tolerable account of the whole matter, to thy satisfaction. Yet such Information as could be picked up from those that did preserve any Notes, taken in Court or at the Scaffold, are here also recorded for thy use, and that, faithfully, word for word.[11]

It was, to repeat, Vane's experience of "unjust tribunals, under change of times" to which Milton was probably alluding in those lines from *Samson Agonistes*, along with the insults given to the bodies of Cromwell, Ireton and Bradshaw, whose corpses were exhumed and posthumously treated like traitors – hanged on a gallows in

---

[10] Compare Bunyan's strategy in *The Holy War*, published in 1682, in which he brings Christian allegory up to date in terms of the Exclusion crisis and Charles's determination to take back control of the law courts by imposing new charters on the corporate towns. See Roger Sharrock, *John Bunyan* (London, 1968), pp. 127–28. "Bedford, like London, received its new charter in 1684, after it had been packed with new burgesses whose votes could be trusted." Accordingly, Bunyan represents the city of Mansoul as being taken over by Diabolus, who arranges for the creation of new aldermen, Mayor and Recorder, and imposes a loyalty oath to himself as a condition of public service.

[11] *The Tryal of Sir Henry Vane, Kt. at the Kings Bench, Westminster, June the 2d. and 6th, 1662. Together With what he intended to have Spoken the Day of his Sentence, (June 11.) for Arrest of Judgement, (had he not been interrupted and over-ruled by the Court) and his Bill of Exceptions. Printed in the Year, 1662*, (pp. 5–6).

Tyburn. But in the eighteenth century this Miltonic complaint was also applied (by Thomas Hollis) to yet another definitive treason trial, that of Algernon Sidney in 1683, an event that Milton's Chorus might have anticipated, given their melancholy premises. Sidney was tried for complicity in a plot against Charles II, to whom he had promised obedience on being allowed to return to England in 1677. Only one witness could be produced against Sidney, Lord William Howard, a co-conspirator who was evidently embroidering his tale to enhance his own chances of survival; and the Crown therefore had to improvise, producing as the second "witness" to the charge of imagining the death of the king the manuscript of Sidney's republican answer to Filmer's *Patriarcha*. And whereas Vane gave no explicit sign of having consulted his predecessors in such a predicament (although he did cite a number of legal authorities) Sidney inarguably did. As Jonathan Scott discovered, his letters to his co-conspirator John Hampden show that he carefully instructed himself in both Lilburne's trial and Vane's;[12] and during the trial he referred, unsuccessfully, to "Throgmorton's case," an allusion that links all four trials as a series in Sidney's understanding at the time. Sidney thereby had both comic and tragic models for his own behavior, but it was Vane's trial and its outcome to which he finally committed himself. The result was, ironically, a "confession" of principles that exceeded all three of its precedents in finding an audience in liberal history. And because it thereby became the interpretive frame for Sidney's *Discourses on Government*, which in turn became a canonical text of early American liberalism, the Sidney trial requires more space than its three predecessors, and will be treated separately in the next chapter.

SIR NICHOLAS THROCKMORTON

In Francis Blackburne's *Memoirs* of Thomas Hollis, there is reference to Hollis's knowledge of "Throgmorton's long trial, as a conspirator with Wyat." It is not surprising, perhaps, that Hollis possessed a detailed knowledge of the trial, which allowed him to ascertain that John Ponet was not involved in Wyatt's conspiracy, because the trial

---

[12] See Jonathan Scott, *Algernon Sidney and the Restoration Crisis, 1677–1683* (Cambridge, 1991), pp. 303–16; the letters were found in the East Sussex Record Office, Lewes, Glynde Place Archives No. 794.

contains "not the least hint" of such complicity.[13] He was, however, only one of a series of careful readers of this trial, which he probably found in "Holinshed's" *Chronicles*,[14] despite the fact that by 1716 it was also available in the first edition of *State Trials* edited by Thomas Salmon. Had it not been for Raphael Holinshed, however, the account of Throckmorton's trial might never have survived. Like Thomas Hollis himself, Holinshed was one of liberalism's transmitters, as well, perhaps, as one of its inventors; and from the earliest stages of his work on English history, he was profoundly concerned with the history, philosophy and practice of law.

In describing the Norman Conquest of England by William I, Holinshed focused on the new legal code that the Conqueror established, and its disadvantages for the subject nation:

abrogating in maner all the ancient lawes used in times past, and instituted by the former kings for the good order and quietnes of the people, he made new, *nothing so equall* or easie to be kept, which neverthelesse those that came after (not without their great harme) were constreined to observe: as though it had beene an high offense against God to abolish those evill lawes, which king William (a prince nothing friendly to the English nation) had first ordeined, and to bring in other and more tollerable. (2:13; italics added)

And, Holinshed continued:

Here by the waie I give you to note a great absurditie; namelie, that those lawes which touched all, and ought to be knowne of all, were notwithstanding written in the Norman toong, which the Englishmen understood not; so that even at the beginning you should have great numbers, partlie by the iniquitie of the lawes, and partlie by ignorance in misconstruing the same, to be wrongfully condemned. (4:31)

These themes, of the skepticism that changes in the law can produce, that rulers do not necessarily have the interests of their subjects in mind when the laws are established, that there will be ideological pressure (inflected with religion) against reform, and that the "lawes ought to be knowne of all," constituted Holinshed's personal brand

---

[13] Francis Blackburne, *Memoirs of Thomas Hollis* (London, 1780), p. 560.

[14] *Holinshed's Chronicles of England, Scotland, and Ireland* (London, 1808; repr. New York, 1965). The *Chronicles* were first published in 1577 and were then largely the work of Holinshed, though with the assistance of William Harrison and Richard Stanyhurst. After Holinshed's death, a new edition was produced in 1587 by a group of five antiquaries, with Abraham Fleming as chief editor. For Hollis's knowledge of the 1587 *Chronicles*, from which he cited Harrison's new chapter on parliament, see *Reading Holinshed's Chronicles*, pp. 274–75.

of ancient constitutionalism, in which, it is no coincidence, the idea of "equall" law is paramount.

These principles could have resurfaced in the minds of Elizabethan readers when, hundreds of pages later, they came across an account of Throckmorton's trial,[15] with the following introduction:

But now forsomuch as a copie of the order of Sir Nicholas Throckmorton's arreignement hath come to my hands, and that the same may give light to the historie of that dangerous rebellion, I have thought it not impertinent to insert the same: not wishing that it should be offensive to anie, sith it is in every mans libertie to weie his words uttered in his owne defense, and likewise the dooings of the quest [jury] in acquitting him, as maie seeme good to their discretions, sith I have delivered the same as I have found it, without prejudicing anie mans opinion . . .

When Holinshed inserted his long report of the trial, which is many pages longer than his accounts of the trials of the principals, Lady Jane, Northumberland, and Wyatt himself, the reader might well wonder why such emphasis was to be placed on this conveniently "found" text, and put more than two and two together. Indeed, the readers of the *Chronicles* were really being invited to themselves take on the responsibility of jury duty, along with the injunction to independent judgment that the role ideally implies.

This is the only instance in the *Chronicles* of a major political trial in which both prosecution and defence are fully represented, so fully, indeed, that we are given what appears to be a verbatim transcript of the entire proceedings. The question of whether it could have been in fact a verbatim transcript, and if so, by whom, will be considered shortly. But as Holinshed inserted it, it appears also to be a reprinting. Its presentation in the *Chronicles* typographically mimics the title-page of a pamphlet; and in other instances where the *Chronicles*'s typography does the same thing, the original pamphlet has survived. Finally, not only does the fullness of the account suggest evenhandedness; the trial is presented in what we would now recognize as dramatic form, complete with speech prefixes and occasional stage directions. The "title-page" itself calls the text a "Dialogue," a provocative term in the circumstances, and adds that this form was chosen "for the better understanding of every man's

---

[15] For a detailed argument as to how far this "transcript" can be taken as representing what was actually said during the trial, see my "'For Words Only': From Treason Trial to Liberal Legend in Early Modern England," *Yale Journal of Law and the Humanities* 5 (1993), pp. 397–400.

part," an even more interesting suggestion; but that the idea of drama was formally in the minds of those who produced this text is also suggested by the fact that Throckmorton speaks of his trial as a "pageant" and a "woeful tragedy," and reminds the "lookers-on" that such spectacles have been common enough on the juridical stage in recent years.

How did this text "come into" Raphael Holinshed's hands? The chronicler does not tell us, but we can make an educated guess. John Bellamy, one of the few historians who have recognized its significance, assumed that the account of the trial was probably compiled by Throckmorton himself after Mary's death, though "based on notes taken at the time."[16] But it does not read like the protagonist's reconstruction several years after the event, nor is it told in the first person, as we would expect from personal reconstruction. Rather, the vraisemblance of the dialogue and its air of completeness demands one of three possibilities: very extensive notes made at the time, by another interested party or parties, since Throckmorton could scarcely have been scribbling while he spoke; subsequent fabrication by someone with a great ear for dialogue and a lively political imagination – a political playwright, as it were; or some combination of the two. Any of these three could have been followed by pamphlet publication; though the non-survival of an original suggests that it was published surreptitiously during Mary's reign, rather than after her death, when such material could have been licensed.

Some skepticism about the "transcript's" accuracy as a verbatim account, or even its truth-content more generally, has been expressed, on the grounds that official transcripts of trials were not produced until the eighteenth century, and shorthand was not used until late in the seventeenth. Kitson Clark, who challenged Sir Leslie Stephen's *naïveté* in the *Dictionary of National Biography* on this matter, nevertheless admitted that Throckmorton's trial "certainly reads as if it were taken down verbatim," and, as one of the possible explanations for its existence, that "it may very well have been reconstructed from the memories of people who had actually been present in the Guildhall at the time of trial, possibly assisted by their notes, possibly assisted by the recollections of Sir Nicholas himself."[17] This sounds like an excellent compromise between too

---

[16] John Bellamy, *The Tudor Law of Treason* (London, 1979), p. 246.
[17] G. Kitson Clark, *The Critical Historian* (New York, 1967), p. 95.

much skepticism of the document and too little, and whenever I use the term "transcript," this is the compromise sense I wish it to bear. With regard to its truth-content, the likelihood that Throckmorton did conduct his defence precisely as recorded in the *Chronicles* is supported both by his otherwise astonishing acquittal, and the fact that he subsequently had an important (if unpopular) career as a diplomat under Elizabeth.

It is clear from the start that Throckmorton planned his trial as an appeal to broader principles that might be thought to inhere in the trial by jury as it had evolved since the Conquest, principles that included impartiality and access to the necessary information to reach an impartial verdict. A large part of Throckmorton's strategy in the opening moments of the trial consisted in a struggle for control over procedure, implying that the accepted formalities were stacked against the defendant, and including the suggestion that "due process" meant taking enough time: "My lords I praie you," he said, when his judges expressed impatience, "Make not too much hast with me, neither thinke not long for your dinner, for my case requireth leasure, and you have well dined when you have doone justice trulie. Christ said, Blessed are they that hunger and thirst for righteousnesse." And this citation from Matthew 5:6 was only the first of a series of brilliantly chosen biblical allusions. This was not only to claim the moral high ground, but also a strategy likely to appeal to a jury of London merchants, so many of whom, as Susan Brigden has demonstrated, were the resilient and resourceful core of Protestantism at this time.[18]

Throckmorton particularly invoked those passages, such as Mark's account of the unjust trial of Christ by the Pharisees or Paul's epistle to the Ephesians, which stressed the relation between the persecution of a religion, solidarity in the face of it, and that religion's subsequent validation and triumph. Mark's elliptical description of the illegal night-time examination of Christ, the production of the false witnesses, and Pilate's washing of his hands provided one telling analogy. And when at the end of the trial Throckmorton bade farewell to his jury by citing Paul's farewell to the Ephesians, he surely expected them to remember Paul's request that "utterance may be given unto me, that I may open my mouth boldly, to make known the mystery of the gospel; For which I am an ambassador in

[18] Susan Brigden, *London and the Reformation* (Oxford, 1989).

bonds." Sir Nicholas Throckmorton, another ambassador in bonds, was an equally gifted communicator.

Throckmorton was far from naive about the media aspect of a large political trial, and evidently capable of exploiting its theatrical possibilities, as well as bringing them to consciousness (which theorists of the drama call *verfremdungen*, breaking the illusion). While the jury were being called and challenged, Throckmorton remarked:

> I trust you have not provided for me this daie, as in times past I knew another gentleman occupieng this wofull place was provided for. It chanced one of the justices upon gelousie of the prisoners acquitall, for the goodnesse of his cause, said to an other of his companions a justice, when the jurie did appeare; I like not this jurie for our purpose, they seeme to be too pitifull and too charitable to condemne the prisoner. No no, said the other judge (to wit Cholmeleie) I warrant you, they be picked fellowes for the nonce, he shall drinke of the same cup his fellowes have doone. I was then a looker on of the pageant as others be now here: but now wo is me, I am a plaier in that woful tragedie. (4:33)

By the use of a highly pertinent and well-told anecdote Throckmorton was able to warn the "others" in the audience that what they were watching, though it may have been rehearsed, was more serious than public entertainment. That brilliant parenthesis ("to wit Cholmeleie") establishes the anecdote's relevance to the day's proceedings, since Sir Roger Cholmley was one of the crown's commissioners; and the vulgarity of the reported conversation punctured the aura of sobriety on which the Law as an institution depends.

Concordant with this strategy was a set of guidelines that Throckmorton conveyed to the jury about what to expect in the realm of legal hermeneutics. This came in the form of a hortatory appeal to the commissioners who were about to try him:

> I praie you remember I am not alienate from you, but that I am your christian brother; neither you so charged, but you ought to consider equitie; nor yet so privileged, but that you have a dutie of God appointed you how you shall doo your office; which if you exceed, will be greevouslie required at your hands. It is lawfull for you to use your gifts which I know God hath largelie given you, as your learning, art, and eloquence, so as thereby you doo not seduce the minds of the simple and unlearned jurie, to credit matters otherwise than they be. For master sergeant, I know how by persuasions, inforcements, presumptions, applieng, implieng, inferring, conjecturing, deducing of argument, wresting and exceeding the law, the circumstances, the depositions and confessions, that unlearned men may be

inchanted to thinke and judge those that be things indifferent, or at the woorst but oversights to be great treasons; such power orators have, and such ignorance the unlearned have . . . Notwithstanding, you and the justices excuse alwaies such erronious dooings, when they be after called in question, by the verdict of the twelve men: but I assure you, the purgation serveth you as it did Pilat, and you wash your hands of the bloudshed, as Pilat did of Christs. (4:33–34)

Athough this speech was formally addressed to the commissioners, its true intended audience was the jury of "the twelve men," who were thereby instructed in the hermeneutics of suspicion, in the *style* of the early modern treason trial ("applieng, implieng, inferring, conjecturing . . . wresting and exceeding the law"), and warned to be on their guard against them.

To understand what Throckmorton meant by "wresting and exceeding the law," however, we need to go beyond the hermeneutics of suspicion to the intricacies of Tudor treason law. John Bellamy has shown how from Henry VIII through Elizabeth I the law changed its mind dramatically several times as to what could count as treason.[19] What we mean by the law changing its mind, of course, is the instability introduced by political or religious agendas, or, in the case of Henry VIII, sexual agendas. The Henrician Treason Act of November 1534 (26 Hen. VIII, c. 13), which was produced in the inflammatory circumstances of Henry's divorce from Katherine of Aragon to marry Anne Boleyn and the break from Rome that these actions appeared to necessitate, was clearly designed to suppress all criticism of the monarch. To that end it calmly introduced three brand-new treasons, including treasonable words that were merely speaking. It was now treason to call the king, even in speech, a heretic, a schismatic, a tyrant or an infidel, any of which terms might have reasonably been used by a devout Roman Catholic at the time. In 1547 the king's heir, now Edward VI, openly repudiated this definition in a new treason statute (1 Edw. VI, c.12), which opened by describing the 1534 act as "verie streighte, sore, extreme and terrible." Edward's act claimed to be a return to the ancient definition of the medieval Edward III's treason statute of 1352 (25 Edw. III, st. 5,c. 2), which required "overt act," but in fact it retained certain provisions of the 1534 act, with respect to challenging the royal supremacy over the church. When Mary came to the throne, the rival defeated faction was tried under the treason acts of

---

[19] Bellamy, *Tudor Law of Treason*, pp. 9–35.

both Edward III and Edward VI; but before Throckmorton was indicted she had produced a treason act of her own. In particular, the preamble to her statute focused on the fact that many of the nobility and gentry "have of late (for words only, without other opinion, fact or deed) suffered shameful death not accustomed to nobles," and "that the severity of such like extreme, dangerous and painful laws" was to be abandoned, as against the queen's will and character. It was this confusing situation that Sir Nicholas Throckmorton and his judges inherited; and it was Throckmorton, rather than his judges, who was able to turn to his advantage the self-contradictions – indeed, the political expediency – of the law as exposed by its recent history.

One of the central points that Throckmorton made was that under the new Marian statute, by which treason law reverted to that of Edward III, mere conversations, which were all that could be proven against him as to the charge of complicity (or worse, of masterminding the whole conspiracy) were no longer treason. He had effectively been indicted under a statute no longer in force. Conspiring or "devising" to levy war, as distinct from actually levying it, was not even treason by the medieval definition. The crown's lawyers inexplicably failed to make full use of the fairly flexible concept of "imagining the queen's death," and thus opened themselves to the charge of illegal procedure.

Evidently Raphael Holinshed, always interested in the law, regarded this statutory instability as particularly worthy of his readers' attention. At the point in the trial where Throckmorton was pressing his advantage on the basis of the Marian statute, Holinshed remarked in the margin: "Happy for Throckmorton that those statutes stood then repealed." And at the end of the "transcript," he added his own summary:

Thus much for Sir Nicholas Throckmorton's arraignment, wherein is to be considered, that the repealing of certain statutes in the last parliament was the chief matter he had for his advantage; whereas the repealing of the same statutes was meant notwithstanding for another purpose (as before you have partly heard), which statutes or the effect of the chief branches of them have been since that time again revived, as by the books of the statutes it may better appear, to the which I refer the reader. (4:55)

It would be possible to read this comment as a warning against any enjoyment of Throckmorton's escape, a reminder that he was able, and perhaps improperly, to take advantage of a loophole in the law that had now, under Elizabeth, been properly closed. It would be equally possible to read it as an ironic reflection on the severity of the Elizabethan treason statute of 1572, a severity that even her sister of the persecuting reputation had publicly (if briefly) repudiated.[20]

Aware that these recent changes in the law should work in his favor, Throckmorton requested a courtroom reading of both the Marian statute repealing all previous treason laws except that of Edward III, and that ancient Edwardian statute itself. This request was refused; "No sir, there shall be no bookes brought at your desire, we doo all know the law sufficientlie without booke," said Sir Thomas Bromley, the lord chief justice (4:45); whereupon, despite the fact that he had earlier made much of his ignorance of the law, Throckmorton produced from his memory the precise *wording* of the relevant statutes. "Now I praie you of my jurie which have my life in triall," he continued, "note well what things *at this daie* be treasons, and how these treasons must be tried and decerned; that is to say, by open deed, which the lawes dooth at some time terme (Overt act)" (4:46; italics added). The surprise that he had sprung on the queen's lawyers is dramatically indicated in Bromley's irate question: "Why doo not you of the queenes learned councell answer him? Me thinke, Throckmorton, you need not have the statutes, for you have them meetlie perfectlie."

In addition, Throckmorton deftly applied his experience as a member of parliament, where he had recently worked alongside the very men who were now serving as commissioners in his trial. He reminded them sharply of their own role in constructing Mary's new treason act, with its preamble declaring that the laws of her father and brother had been unjust:

To what purpose serveth the statute of repeale the last parlement, where I heard some of you here present, and diverse other of the queenes learned councell, grievouslie inveie against the cruell and bloudie lawes of King Henrie the eight, and against some lawes made in my late sovereigne lord and masters time, king Edward the sixt. Some termed them Dracos lawes, which were written in bloud: some said they were more intollerable than anie laws that Dionysius or anie other tyrant made. In conclusion, as manie men, so manie bitter tearmes and names those lawes had. And moreover,

---

[20] Immediately after Throckmorton's acquittal, in November 1554, however, Mary issued a new and more severe treason act (1 & 2 Philip and Mary, c. 9), which returned mere words against her or King Philip, including prayers, to the category of treason.

the preface of the same [Marian] statute doth recite, that for words onelie, manie great personages, and other of good behaviour, have beene most cruellie cast awaie by these former sanguinolent thirstie lawes, with manie other suggestions for the repeale of the same. (4:52)

He thereby managed to cast his judges in the role of time-servers who had chosen to forget their own reformist statements of the very recent past. And, turning to the jury, he concluded: "honest men which are to trie my life, consider these opinions of my life, judges be rather agreable to the time, than to the truth: for their judgements be repugnant to their own principle, repugnant to their godlie and best learned predecessors opinions, repugnant I saie to the proviso in the statute of repeale made in the last parlement." His final appeal was both to religion and to the civil society: "And in that you all be citizens, I will take my leave of you with St. Paules farewell to the Ephesians, citizens also you be" (4:53). It was a masterly blend of the three categories of reasoning outlined in my Introduction: rationalist-essentialist (the appeal to principles), historical-traditional (the appeal to "learned predecessors") and experiential-determinist (it was *his* life that, being in such danger, had sharpened Throckmorton's wits and his memory). Especially his memory. As commissioner Southwell put it with grudging admiration: "You have a very good memorie" (4:49). If the law is to justify itself by its long memory, it would be well, Holinshed's record implies, if we all had memories as good as Throckmorton's.

It took the jury about three hours to bring in a verdict of "Not Guilty," to the fury and embarrassment of the commissioners and also Queen Mary. As Holinshed had stated in his own preamble to the trial, "with which verdict the judges and councillors there present were so much offended, that they bound the jurie in the summe of five hundred pounds apeece," to appear before the Star Chamber. On April 21, they appeared before the Star Chamber judges, and then, remaining intransigent, were sent to prison, Emanual Lucar and Thomas Whetston to the Tower, and the rest to the Fleet (4:31). Four of them, under this pressure, submitted and confessed they had erred in their verdict, and Holinshed published their names. Later he also transferred from John Foxe's *Acts and Monuments* (1563) the follow-up to the story of "those honest men" who stayed firm. They were recalled before the Star Chamber, where Lucar "said openlie before all the lords that they had doone in the matter like honest men, and true and faithfull subjects" (4:64).

The Star Chamber judges, "taking their words in marvellous evill part, judged them worthie to paie excessive fines," Whetson and Lucar £2000 apiece, and the other six 1000 marks apiece. In December of the following year, since the still-imprisoned jurors complained that the fines amounted to more than their net worth, they were commuted to more realistic amounts.[21]

We can learn a considerable amount about the way the Throckmorton trial functioned as a "text" in at least one circle of contemporary readers by way of the *Remarks* upon it written by John Bradford, the Protestant martyr, in 1555.[22] These remarks, which appear to be intended as a preface to a published edition of the trial, imply that it had *not* been published by the spring of 1555, when Bradford was in prison in London awaiting execution for heresy. If it was published later in that year, after his burning on June 30, it must have been quickly and effectively suppressed. In the *Remarks*, Bradford explains that he has been "lent" a manuscript copy of the "book," and has evidently written his preface to the Throckmorton trial in the manuscript itself. When he was first imprisoned in the Tower, in February 1554, he shared a room with Cranmer, Latimer and Ridley, since the prison was overcrowded owing to Wyatt's rebellion. The interest of his *Remarks* resides in Bradford's concern to extend the trial's readership, beyond the radical Protestant community of which he was a member to the entire educated class, "the nobility and gentlemen of England." His repeated injunction, "Read this book," and his analysis of Throckmorton's own education in scripture and "the statutes, laws, and chronicles," closely matches the educational agenda of Holinshed's *Chronicles*. It deserves our own careful attention, not least for the injunctions it contains as to *how* to read this kind of material.

---

[21] In Elizabeth's reign, Sir Thomas Smith clearly alluded to Throckmorton's trial without mentioning it by name. In his *De Republica Anglorum*, Smith wrote that he had seen in his time (carefully adding in parenthesis "not in the reigne of the Queene nowe") "an enquest for pronouncing one not guiltie of treason contrarie to such evidence as was brought in . . . not onely imprisoned for a space but an houge fine set upon their heads, which they were faine to pay"; and he further recorded the public response to this episode: "those doinges were even then of many accounted verie violent, and tyrannical, and contrarie to the libertie and custome of the realme of England." Sir Thomas Smith, *De Republica Anglorum*, ed. Mary Dewar (Cambridge, 1982), p. 121.

[22] John Bradford, *Remarks on a Memorable Trial*; from Emmanuel College Library, Cambridge, Ms. 2.2.15, no. 98; reprinted in *The Writings of John Bradford . . . Martyr, 1555*, ed. Aubrey Townsend, 2 vols. (Cambridge, 1848), 1:405–07.

To the reader John Bradford wisheth grace, mercy, peace, and increase of all godly knowledge and life.

After this book came to my hands, as I was in prison for the testimony of the Lord, I could not but read the same to see how the Lord assisted his servant that put his trust in him: which thing I thank God I did so see, that I could not but think myself bound to help what I could by my testimony, to allure all others by this book thereunto. And therefore I, being a poor man of vile state and condition concerning this world, and of learning unmeet of place in any book for my name, have presumed by a godly presumption, tending to do good to all men and hurt to no man, to write thus much in behalf of this book, that it is worthy to be had in print, and diligently read of all men, but especially of the nobility and gentlemen of England: whose houses and names could not but continue, if that yet now they would begin to take this gentleman a sampler to ensue, and a pattern to press after. For here thou, good reader, shalt perceive a gentleman in deed, and not in name only: his trust was in the Lord, and not in man, and therefore he was not confounded: he honoured God, and therefore God hath honoured him accordingly. His study was in God's word, and therefore found he comfort: by it he found more wisdom and had more knowledge than all his enemies, which were not few nor foolish to the judgement of the world. They came to him as Goliath the mighty giant, harnessed and armed cap-a-pie: he came as a little David with his sling, and had the victory. In this weak man thou mayest see God's power, presence, wisdom, and goodness, to occasion thee to put thy trust in the Lord, and to hang altogether upon him, who in the evil day will deliver them that fear him. What wisdom, what grace, what audacity, did God give to him in his need! What could all the learned lawyers, which better might be termed lewd losels of the realm, do against him? What could all the power of the queen's highness prevail? Such a thing it is to trust in the Lord, to fear him, and to be a godly student of his word, as doubtless it appeareth this good man was. Who would not serve such a God, as can in despite of all his enemies triumph over them by his simple servant?

Read the book, and thou shalt see what knowledge this gentleman had in the statutes, laws, and chronicles of the realm, to teach the nobility and gentlemen, which are and would be magistrates and rulers of the realm, to spend more time to attain wisdom and knowledge to execute their offices than they now do. Read this book, and thou shalt see what false packing there is against the simple and plain truth. Read this book, and thou shalt see how unrighteousness sitteth in place of justice. Read this book, and thou shalt see how truth is defaced, and falsehood maintained. Read this book, and thou shalt see how perilous a thing it is to testify the truth.

The good men empanelled of the quest shall tell the same. A greater honour never came to the city of London than by those twelve men. What said I, to the city of London? Nay, to the whole realm of England: for, alas!

if they had not more conscience and truth than king, queen, lords, counsellors, judges, sergeants, attornies, solicitors, lawyers, &c., England had been guilty of innocent blood; as alas, alas! it is to be feared too much thereof crieth for vengeance. Lord, spare us, and have mercy upon us.

But what reward had this good jury? Well, I pass over that: a papistical reward. What is that? Forsooth, such as Julianus Apostata gave to the faithful Christians. God our Father look better on this gear in his good time, which in respect of his enemies is at hand; "for they have scattered abroad his law." O that amongst us, who pretend to be God's friends, were true repentance! Then might we say: *Tempus est ut miserearis, Domine*: It is time, O Lord, to show mercy upon us." God do so for his holy name's sake! Amen.

Thus much I was so bold to scribble in this book, being lent unto me, because I would occasion some men of authority and learning to commend it, as it is most worthy.

E carcere,
JOHN BRADFORD.

Thus a proper reading of the Throckmorton trial will provide, according to Bradford, the following benefits: religious consolation; pragmatic and state-worthy instruction in the laws and statutes; skeptical awareness of the brute fact that "false packing" exists and that often "unrighteousness sitteth in the place of justice"; and a reminder of the importance of the jury system.

The mistreatment of the Throckmorton jurors, in particular, became part of the legal theory of jury rights and obligations in the next century. While Lilburne would, as we shall see, focus on Throckmorton's strategies for survival, William Walwyn, another Leveller leader in prison at the same time, alluded to the Throckmorton affair as a model of the principle by which the trial by jury was essential to justice as fairness. "Neither I nor my partners in suffering are any whit doubtful of a full and clear vindication, upon a legal trial," wrote Walwyn:

For in my observation of trials I have generally found juries and jurymen to be full of conscience, care, and circumspection, and tenderness in cases of life and death; and I have read very remarkable passages in our Histories; amongst which the case and trial of Throckmorton, in Queen Mary's time, is most remarkable; the consciences of the jury being proof against the opinion of the judges, the rhetoric of the counsel who were great and learned, nay, against the threats of the court, which was then absolute in power and tyranny, and quit the gentleman like true-hearted, well-resolved Englishmen, that valued their consciences above their lives; and I cannot think but these times will afford as much good conscience, as that time of gross ignorance and superstition did.[23]

The treatment of the Throckmorton jurors was also cited in the *State Trials* in connection with the case of the Quakers William Penn and William Mead, and its direct consequence, the important Bushell's case. Penn and Mead were acquitted in September 1670 of the charge of causing a riotous assembly, against the insistence of the London Recorder that they bring in a guilty verdict. Again the jurors were fined, and the foreman, Edward Bushell, imprisoned, which resulted in his successfully bringing a habeas corpus action.[24] The original case, of the two Quakers who had refused to remove their hats, with its attendant bad publicity for the regime, was one of the subjects on which Andrew Marvell wrote to his nephew William Popple, on November 28, 1670:

[At] the Tryal of Pen and Mead, Quakers, at the old Baily, the Jury not finding them guilty, as the Recorder and Mayor would have had them, they were kept without Meat or Drink some Days, till almost starved, but would not alter their Verdict; so fined and imprisoned. *There is a Book out* which relates all the Passages, which were very pertinent, of the Prisoners, but prodigiously barbarous by the Mayor and the Recorder. The Recorder, among the rest, commended the Spanish Inquisition, saying it would never be well until we had something like it.[25]

There exists a remarkable verse biography of Throckmorton, first published by the Whig Francis Peck in 1736. Peck remarked in his preface that "the trials of Sir Nicholas Throckmorton & John Lilburn, are (for the prisoners excellent defence of themselves) the two most remarkable, I think, of any we have yet extant."[26] The pairing was intelligent; for it turns out that Lilburne had access to Holinshed's record of the Throckmorton trial, and applied it to very good effect.

[23] William Walwyn, *The Fountain of Slaunder Discovered* (1649), in *The Writings of William Walwyn*, ed. Jack R. McMichael and Barbara Taft (Athens, Ga., 1989), pp. 374–75. See also Walwyn's defence of the jury system, *Juries Justified* (1651), pp. 433–45.

[24] See *A Complete Collection of State Trials*, ed. T. B. Howell, 21 vols. (London, 1816), 4:951–1015, which includes the report of Bushell's case. For the reference to "Throgmorton's Case," see p. 967.

[25] Andrew Marvell, *Poems and Letters*, ed. H. M. Margoliouth, rev. Pierre Legouis, 2 vols. (Oxford, 1971), 2:318 (italics added).

[26] Francis Peck, ed., *The Legend of Sir Nicholas Throckmorton, Kt. Chief Butler of England & Chamberlain of the Exchecquer; who Died of Poison, A.D. 1570, an Historical Poem: By (his Nephew) Sir Thomas Throckmorton of Littleton* . . . (London, 1736), p. 32.

JOHN LILBURNE

An equally detailed, apparently verbatim, and even longer account of Lilburne's trial was published in London[27] almost instantly after his acquittal. The agent-editor of this pamphlet was "Theodorus Verax," the pseudonym of the radical Clement Walker, who was himself engaged in a publishing campaign against the Long Parliament.[28] It too was presented as though in dramatic form, with speech prefixes and occasional stage directions, some of which have real theatrical flavor. Halfway through the pamphlet, Lilburne himself made an allusion to:

Throgmorton, in queen Mary's time, who was impeached of higher Treason than now I am; and that in the days of the commonly accounted bloodiest and cruellest prince that this many hundred of years hath reigned in England: . . . Throgmorton was in this place arraigned as a Traitor, and enjoyed as much, if not more [procedural] favour, than I have now enjoyed, although his then judges and prosecutor were bent to take away his life.[29]

And Walker's pamphlet carried at this point a telling marginal annotation: "Whose remarkable and excellent Defence you may at large read in Hollingshead's Chronicle, in the Life of Queen Mary, *which discourse is excellently well worth the speedily reprinting, especially seeing men are made traitors for words*" (p. 21; italics added). That men were indeed still being made traitors for words in 1649 is demonstrated by Walker's own fate. Thanks to the appearance of the second part of his *History of Independency*, and also, no doubt, to his determination to enter Lilburne's trial in the public record, on November 13, 1649, Walker himself was arraigned on a charge of treason, and placed in the Tower, where he died, never having come to trial, in 1651.

The significance of Lilburne's trial in a cultural history of early modern liberalism is that, though the charge was treason, the basis

---

27 *The Triall of Lieut. Collonel J. Lilburne . . . Unto which is annexed a necessary Appendix. Published by Theodorus Verax* (Southwark, 1949).

28 Clement Walker is best known as the author of the *History of Independency* (1648–49), which is hostile to the Independents. Although at the beginning of the civil war he joined the parliamentary side, by 1647 he was suspected of being one of the instigators of the London riots, and in 1648 he voted in favor of an agreement with Charles I, and was consequently expelled from the House of Commons in Pride's Purge. Like Lilburne himself, Walker was an indefatigable publicist, and from 1643 to 1651 he used the press to promote and defend his opinions.

29 I cite from *A Complete Collection of State Trials*, ed. T. B. Howell, 21 vols. (London, 1816), 4:1288.

for the charge was no actual or alleged conspiracy against the government of the day, but merely the writing and publication of pamphlets critical of that government. Much of Lilburne's defence, therefore, focused on whether he could be proven to be the author of those pamphlets; but supposing he were – and here the logic of early modern jurisprudence sometimes seems perverse – then Lilburne challenged the indictment on the question of whether writing and publication of political criticism were indeed an "overt act." There seems little doubt that Lilburne, who was also tried under 25 Edward III, found this strategy in Throckmorton's trial, and applied it to an even better test of the concept, with which (under the legal doctrine of fighting words) we are still wrestling. The most certain proof of what Lilburne learned from Throckmorton must surely be his strategic appeal to the preamble of the Marian statute as evidence that even the arbitrary monarchs of previous generations "abhorred and detested the making of words or writing to be treason; which is such a bondage and snare, that no man knows how to say or do, or behave himself" (4:1401). So what was a revolutionary and reformist government doing in returning to such a reactionary interpretation?

But apart from these central arguments, many of the psychological tricks that Lilburne used in his own self-defence he clearly learned from Throckmorton: namely, his constant procedural challenges, especially in the important opening moves, challenges which Lilburne himself presented as part of a larger argument that legal formalism is designed to confuse the ordinary defendant (4:1294–95); his insistence on the importance of two witnesses; and his sense of the value of humor in winning over the jury. Lilburne in fact managed to squeeze in a long speech at the beginning, craving "no more but that which is properly and singly the liberty of every free-born Englishman, viz. The benefit of the Laws and Liberties thereof, which by my birth-right and inheritance is due unto me." He challenged the legality of a commission of *oyer* and *terminer*, which he failed to find authorized in the Petition of Right and Magna Carta, he refused to hold up his hand to identify himself, and he demanded counsel, of course unsuccessfully, all this before adding his own gloss, like Throckmorton, to the formal question, "By whom wilt thou be tried?" Lilburne answered,"By the known laws of England, I mean, by the liberties and privileges of the laws of England, and a jury of my equals legally chosen" (4:1270–1, 1275, 1294). There was one particularly comedic moment, when Lilburne declared he could proceed no further without access to a chamber pot, which was brought into the courtroom and filled accordingly. Whether or not Lilburne intended it, this episode, presented as if by a stage direction ["Whilst it was fetching, Mr. Lilburne followeth his papers and books close; and when the pot came, he made water, and gave it to the foreman"][30] is, as it were, the essence of the common touch.

Another unenumerated right articulated in both these trials is the layman's right of access to the law, which is obviously connected to but exceeds the right to legal counsel. It had been Throckmorton's strategy to pretend ignorance of the law all the better to surprise his judges with his memory of it when his request for a reading of the statutes was refused. But the effect of this strategy was that he was able to stage, for the jury's benefit, an encounter with his judges over the *public*'s access to the law in more general terms, by emphasizing the importance of the published statutes, which being in English were in theory legible by all citizens. On the judges' part it was made very clear that knowledge of the law by laymen was undesirable altogether, a dangerous impropriety. "You know it were indifferent [fair]," said Throckmorton, "that I should know and heare the law whereby I am adjudged, and forasmuch as the statute is in English, men of meaner learning than the justices can understand it, or else how should we know when we offend." "What would you doo with the statute booke?" said Hare. "The jurie doth not require it, they have heard the evidence, and they must upon their conscience trie whether you be guiltie or no, so as the booke needeth not" (4:45–46).

Lilburne grasped both the tactical and theoretical advantages of this position. Throughout his two-day trial, he explicitly thematized the problem of the layman's access to the law. He constantly referred to his own reading of such "good old English laws" as were written in English. In accordance with his charge that the Long Parliamentarians were a reincarnation of the Norman Yoke, Lilburne complained:

you come to ensnare and entrap me with unknown niceties and formalities that are locked up in the French and Latin tongue, and cannot be read in English books, they being not expressed in any law of the kingdom, published in our own English tongue: it is not fair play according to the

---

[30] *State Trials*, 4:1379.

Law of England, plainly in English expressed in the Petition of Right, and
other the good old statute laws of the land." (4:1294)

Lilburne was evidently not possessed of Throckmorton's mnemonic
powers, and he was in this respect treated with greater latitude, for
he was allowed to bring with him into the court bundles of notes, a
copy of Coke's *Institutes*, and a statute-book, from which he read to
the jury the statutes of Edward VI on the need for two witnesses,
which he interpreted as meaning two witnesses for each offence.
"Here is the statute-book, let the Jury hear it read," cried Lilburne
(4:1396). In contrast, the attorney-general warned the rest of the
commissioners that to grant Lilburne's demand for legal counsel and
for a copy of the indictment in English "would be a precedent for all
future times; by means of which there would never be an end of
trials in criminal cases" (4:1309).

Behind this strategy lay the following ideas: that ancient constitutionalist call for the law to be conducted in English; proto-Enlightenment theories of the individual's educability and responsibility for
himself; and an "equalization" of the law which stood for a yet
larger idea of democratization. But Lilburne rendered their connection visible – by his constant references to Magna Carta and the
Petition of Right of 1628, and by his claim that "due process" was as
much "the common right of all or any of the people of England, as
well as parliament men" (4:1393). In his summation of his defence he
reiterated his claim that denial of counsel and of witnesses for the
defence meant that his judges "go about to murder" him, "without
law and against law" (a charge which Stephen College, who would
later instruct himself in Lilburne's trial, repeated, but with grimmer
consequences).[31]

Lilburne therefore commended himself to the protection of his
"honest jury and fellow-citizens," who "are the conservators and
sole judges of my life, having in them alone the judicial power of the
law, as well as fact"; whereas his judges, he extravagantly asserted,
were "but cyphers to pronounce the sentence," as well as "the
Norman Conqueror's intruders" (4:1395). And, according to
Clement Walker, "The People with a loud voice cried, *Amen, Amen,*

---

[31] See *State Trials*, 8:573. When College requested council, he said, "My Lord Coke says, it is
the birth-right of every Englishman to have counsel in matters of law, and Lilburne had it
upon solemn argument in his Trial." And when the court refused to return to him the
papers he had prepared for his defence, he asked specifically to be allowed the one "that
has in the margin of it, the cases of Lilburne and Stafford" (8:586).

and gave an extraordinary great hum," causing such unease in the Guildhall that the attending military officer sent for "more fresh companies of foot-soldiers." Huge demonstrations of joy were to follow the verdict of "not Guilty"; "And yet for all his acquittal by the law, his adversaries kept him afterwards so long in prison, that the people wondered, and began to grumble that he was not discharged" (4:1405).

In 1648 the Leveller *Agreement of the People* had included law reforms in its utopian constitution, including access to the law in English, the right of the accused to call witnesses on his own behalf, and to avoid self-incrimination, and the restriction of capital punishment to cases of murder or violent insurrection.[32] Yet the section that contains these provisions is bracketed as somewhat futuristic: "These following Particulars were offered to be inserted in the Agreement, but judged fit, as the most eminent grievances, to be redressed by the next Representative." The "next Representative" concerned with reform of the treason law would not appear until after the Glorious Revolution, which in many ways was still a juridical disappointment.[33]

Lilburne (and presumably Walwyn also) learned about Throckmorton through Raphael Holinshed, who ensured that an otherwise ephemeral pamphlet, produced surreptitiously, should permanently enter the national archives. From there this record passed into the *State Trials*, as also (thanks to Clement Walker) did the record of Lilburne's trial. Then political history experienced another revolution (in the older sense of the term), and Sir Henry Vane, a leading figure in that same Long Parliament that had attempted to rid themselves of Lilburne's importunities, now found himself in Lilburne's extremity.

SIR HENRY VANE

There was an even more symbolic turning of the tables involved, however. Violet Rowe, Vane's modern biographer, did not shrink from the evidence of Vane's ruthlessness toward his political opponents when they engaged in conspiracy against the Long

---

[32] See *Leveller Manifestoes of the Puritan Revolution*, ed. D. M. Wolfe (New York, 1944), pp. 301–02.

[33] For the limitations of the Williamite *Declaration of Rights* in January 1689 with relation to treason law (and in general) see Lois Schwoerer, *The Declaration of Rights 1689* (Baltimore, 1981), especially pp. 194, 288–89.

Parliament.[34] More symmetrically, perhaps, Vane had been instrumental in the parliamentary impeachment of Charles I's minister, Thomas Wentworth, earl of Strafford. Thomas May, whose *History of the Parliament of England* (1647) is unquestionably sympathetic to the parliamentary cause, nevertheless included one of the most striking, as well as chilling, anecdotes that we have about this early phase of the revolution. The anecdote reveals those characteristics which made Vane disliked and untrusted. John Lilburne called him one of "those foure sons of Machiavel"[35] and this anecdote supports the stigma:

After all this long Triall, the House of Commons fell into debate about a Bill of Attainder against the Earle of Strafford; and voted him guilty of high Treason in divers particulars of that Accusation, in which they had proceeded against him; and in more particular he was voted guilty of High Treason, for his opinion given before the King, at a secret Councell, which was discovered by some notes of Sir Henry Vane, who was also a Privy Councellor, and present at that time; in which notes it was found that the Earle of Strafford had said to the King, That he had an Army in Ireland, which his Majesty might imploy to reduce this Kingdome to obedience. These notes Sir Henry Vane, eldest Sonne to the before named Sir Henry had found (as he alleadged to the House) in his Fathers Cabinet, and produced before the House without his Fathers knowledge; who seemed extreme angry with his Sonne for it.[36]

As Rowe pointed out, Strafford's defence included the fact that the parliamentarians could only produce a single witness to the charge of his having raised a regiment of Irish Roman Catholics to support the king; but when Pym produced the notes that Vane had given him, they were taken to constitute another form of witness.

This anecdote has the opulent texture of secret history, as defined in chapter 5. Rowe asks the pertinent question: "How had the younger Vane obtained the notes?":

He explained that he had been searching through his father's black velvet cabinet (or red, so Clarendon thought), for papers in connexion with his own marriage settlement in September 1640, when he saw the Council notes. Out of concern for the public interest, he made his copy. (p. 11)

---

[34] Violet A. Rowe, *Sir Henry Vane the Younger: A Study in Political and Administrative History* (London, 1970). See, for example, Vane's insistence on the execution of the conspirators in Waller's plot in 1643 and of Christopher Love for complicity in a royalist plot in 1646 (pp. 19, 155–57).

[35] Rowe, *Sir Henry Vane*, p. 96.

[36] Thomas May, *The History of the Parliament of England* (London, Moses Bell, for George Thomason, 1647), Book 1, p. 92.

The story, as she rightly remarks, "is very odd, for his father's secretary had not seen the letter which authorized Vane to open the cabinet, nor the key (which his secretary presumably normally kept in his own possession when his master was away), which Vane had used." In any case, Vane was the indirect second witness who brought Strafford to the scaffold. And here he was, twelve years later, facing the same kind of deadly interrogation.

Of course, Vane was not the only scapegoat for the revolutionary experiment. Edmund Ludlow, who himself managed to escape to Switzerland, recorded in his *Memoirs* fourteen days after his arrival in Geneva in 1660:

I finde in the Gazet the execution of Major Generall Harrison, Mr. John Carew, Cheife Justice Cooke and Mr. Hugh Peters; the first upon the 13 October, the second upon the 15th, and the two last upon the 16th, at the place where Charing Cross stood (as well to revenge the wrong done to that secret relique, as to gratify Nero with the sight of that tragedy, the shedding the blood of those eminent servants of the Lord).[37]

Thus Ludlow opened his own martyrology, on the model of John Foxe's *Acts and Monuments*, and proceeded to recount in considerable detail the trials not only of these three regicides, but also of Thomas Scott, Gregory Clement, Adrian Scroope, and of the colonels John Jones, Francis Hacker and Daniel Axtell. Twelve more trials resulting in execution, including that of Colonel Henry Martyn, preceded that of Vane, who with Major General Lambert had been incarcerated for two years while the government, in "cool blood," as Vane himself put it, built its case against them. Perhaps it was also felt that the symbolic effects of Vane's trial would be lessened if he had merely been one of the earlier crowd.

It is evident that Vane, for all his intellectual resources, made a relatively ineffective defence,[38] especially compared with those described, or rather redescribed by Ludlow, of which Cooke's was a model of legal and logical acumen.[39] Ludlow made use of contempo-

---

[37] Edmund Ludlow, *A Voyce from the Watch Tower: Part Five: 1660–1662*, ed. Blair Worden (London: Royal Historical Society, Camden 4th series, Vol. 21, 1978), p. 199.

[38] Rowe disagrees: "From the first to the last he defended himself with astonishing legal acumen, considering that he was not a laywer by profession" (p. 238).

[39] Ludlow, *Voyce*, pp. 229–33. Ludlow makes the claim that John Cooke had been appointed Chief Justice of Munster by Cromwell, had been exemplary in this role, and that he had constantly pressed for law reform (p. 230), which resulted in several members of his own profession now testifying against him.

rary pamphlets issuing from the underground press: *An Exact and most Impartial Accompt of the . . . Trial . . . of Nine and Twenty Regicides* (1660) and *The Speeches and Prayers of Some of the Late King's Judges* (1660), for the latter of which the printer Twynne was himself tried for treason and executed.[40] Vane could have saved himself a good deal of frustration had he had access to the former. But no doubt one of the reasons for keeping him and Lambert in the Scilly Isles, and for excluding them from an appeal to habeas corpus, was to tighten security against such information. Vane's lawyers had been denied access to him throughout his incarceration.

But what made Vane's trial stand out from those of 1660, apart from its postponement, was the surprise the crown's lawyers sprung on him between the arraignment and the trial itself. When he was arraigned before the Middlesex Grand Jury in April, they were persuaded to bring in a true bill against him for treason, on the grounds that he had levied war against the king. It was not until his actual trial in June that he heard for the first time that the king in question was not Charles I, but Charles II, so that all the material he had prepared for his defence (an account of his actions from 1642 onwards) was rendered irrelevant. He had not, of course, been allowed at the arraignment a copy of the indictment, nor counsel as to how to respond to it, and so, unsurprisingly, he asked for it to be read again, which was granted, and then to have it read in Latin, which was not – an interesting irony in view of Lilburne's insistence that all legal proceedings should be in English. If this were not merely another device to buy time, his request reflects both a suspicion that the Latin version might differ from the English, and the class difference between Lilburne and himself.

In fact, not content with what Vane himself said on this issue, Sikes added a better narrative "from another hand . . . as followeth":

The Prisoner did much press for Counsel to be allowed him, to advise with about any further Exceptions to the Indictment, besides those by him exhibited, and to put all in to form, according to the customary proceedings and language of the Law, as also to speak to them at the Bar, on his behalf, he not being vers'd in the punctilio's of Law-writings and Pleas. He further said, That the Indictment, which so nearly concern'd his

---

[40] For Twynne's trial, see Joseph P. Loewenstein, "Legal Proofs and Corrected Readings: Press Agency and the New Bibliography," in *The Production of English Culture*, ed. David Lee Miller, Sharon O'Dair, and Harold Weber (Ithaca and London, 1994), pp. 111–18.

Life, being long, and his memory short, it could not well be imagined that he should upon the bare hearing it read, be able in an instant to find out every material Exception against it, in form or matter. He pleaded a good while on this account, but Counsel was finally denied him till he should plead *guilty* or *not guilty*, unto which, being a third time urged, he pleaded *Not guilty*; The Court having assured him beforehand, that after pleading, Counsel should be assigned him, *which yet was never performed.* (pp. 20–21, final italics added)

The issue here was whether Vane could successfully argue that there was something faulty in the indictment itself, which is defined as pleading over, or pre-pleading. Without legal advice, Vane moved several exceptions to the indictment, "as that the 25 Ed.3 is not pursued; that he had levied no such force as amounted to a levying of War; . . . and the particular acts of levying War, being not set forth, he thought therefore the Indictment was insufficient"; and, as a piece of unpremeditated folly, he said "that it had not been proved that he was the same Sir Henry Vane who was excepted from the pardon."

But the King's Counsel said, If he would plead that Plea, they would joyn that Issue with him, if he pleased, which if it should be found against him, it would be too late to plead, *not guilty*. (p. 20)

Much more substantial, however, was Vane's insistence that he had acted throughout as an agent of parliament, and so to call his actions treason was in effect to indict the entire parliament, indeed, the entire nation. Unfortunately, what he actually said was this: "I acted as a Member in the sovereign Court of Parliament, and if any thing concerns the Jurisdiction of that Court, I ought not to be judged here; at which the Court and King's Counsel took great offence." That is to say, the case became fatally focused on the constitutional issue, of whether "parliament" at all times was in fact the supreme court that Vane claimed, and whether Charles II were *de facto* or only *de jure* king between 1649 and 1660. As the earlier trials had shown, there was no way that Vane could have won this argument in 1662. This early moment, before Vane had even pleaded, set the tone of the trial, even though its outcome was already decided. In his *Reasons for Arrest of Judgement*, which the court refused to receive, but which was subsequently published in the *Tryal*, Vane told another anecdote that echoes in its structure and purpose Throckmorton's anecdote about Sir Roger Cholmley:

On the day of my Arraignment, an eminent person was heard to say, I had forfeited my head, by what I said that day, before ever I came to my Defence: what that should be, I know not, except my saying in open Court, *Soveraign Power of Parliament*, which the Attorney-General writ down, after he had promised at my request, no exception should be taken at words. And whole volumes of Lawyers Books pass up and down the Nation with that Title, *Soveraign Power of Parliaments*. (p. 72)

There could scarcely be a better example of what can happen when a prisoner is not protected against accidental self-incrimination. As Vane complained in this appeal, "as no Counsel was allowed, so neither were the Judges Counsel to me, as they said themselves, they would, and ought to be, but rather suffered me to go wrong and prejudice my self, some of them saying, *Let him go on, the worst will be his own at last.*"

But in addition, if we compare his actual trial with that of both Lilburne and Throckmorton, we can see that, where his predecessors had been able to score points about legal formalism, Vane was forced to capitulate on procedure from the start, so that he lost the moral initiative. And though like Throckmorton Vane had evidently managed to have someone smuggle lawbooks into his hands when in prison,[41] he was bullied and harassed by his judges in a way that made a coherent defence impossible, even had he known for longer than four days (the time allotted him to prepare a defence) what the charges would be. Vane cited Sir Edward Coke and Fortescue primarily, but also Hooker, Selden, and Lambarde on the Saxon laws (p. 42); but his citations were primarily on the constitutional issue of the rights of parliaments. On the *de jure* and *de facto* definition of monarchy, he cited (presumably unaware that Cooke had done so unsuccessfully the previous year)[42] 11 Hen. 7, enacted to protect the subject from endless reprisals during the the Wars of the Roses. "Otherwise, if he be loyal to the King *de jure*, he shall be hanged by the King *de facto*; and if he be faithful to the King *de facto*, he shall die by the King *de jure*, when he recovers possession" (p. 58). The wit of this formulation, however, was outfaced by the judges' refusal to admit that Charles's exile had interrupted his rule. Vane put great stress on the unprecedented nature of his case, which he claimed required it to be heard by Parliament (pp. 59–62). He was, however, reading from his notes (like Lilburne, he was not possessed of

---

[41] See Rowe, *Sir Henry Vane*, p. 235n.   [42] See Ludlow, *Voyce*, p. 233.

Throckmorton's excellent memory, and needed the support of his papers). As Sikes remarked editorially:

The main substance of these Papers was read and enlarged upon by the Prisoner, the day of his Tryal. He was often interrupted, but his memory was still relieved by his Papers, so as after whatever diversions caused by the Court or the Counsel, he could recover himself again, and proceed. Yet the edge and force of his Plea, as to the influencing of the Jurors Consciences, may appear to have been much abated by such interruptions, as doubtless was intended, and will more at large appear, when it shall please God to afford us a full Narrative of the Proceedings of the King's Judges, Counsel and Jurors about him, and of all that he occasionally said, upon the digressions by them caused. (p. 51)[43]

And finally Vane, unlike Throckmorton and Lilburne, was not allowed to make a last address to the jurors after the prosecution had completed its case.

What Sikes accomplished, in effect, was to render Vane's defence as coherent as it could be *without* rewriting it. Sikes had begun his "Life" of Vane with his own account of the protections afforded the subject by Magna Carta and its subsequent ratifications, and an account of liberal constitutional theory that calmly blends ancient constitutionalism with natural law. Thus he cites "Edward the Confessor's Laws," Lambarde, and Coke, on "the ancient fundamental Laws, Rights and Liberties of this Nation," but he also declares that "all this stir about the great Charter, some conceive very needless, seeing that therein are contained those fundamental Laws or Liberties of the Nation, which are so undeniably consonant to the Law of Nature, or Light of Reason, that Parliaments themselves ought not to abrogate, but preserve them" (pp. 7–8).

But Sikes could also rely on what Vane himself had written after his defence had failed, and he awaited the hanging, drawing and quartering pronounced (which in the event were replaced by simple beheading). Vane's "Reasons for an Arrest of Judgement," which were smuggled out of prison and published in the *Tryal*, reinstated the ethical appeal that his predecessors had managed to articulate in court, and that, under duress, he had sacrificed for constitutional defiance. Indeed, the "Reasons" echo Throckmorton's trial in ways that may not be coincidental. Like Throckmorton, Vane com-

---

[43] This rather supports than disconfirms the hostile report of the *Kingdomes Intelligencer*, that he appeared "amazed and speechless, complaining often of his broken memory and long imprisonment." See Rowe, *Sir Henry Vane*, p. 238n.

plained that the jury were tampered with. Someone had informed him that:

> six moderate men, that were like to consider what they did, before they would throw away my Life, were summoned to be of my Petty Jury, which the King's Counsel hearing, writ a Letter to one of the Sheriffs, to unsummon them; and a new List was made, the night immediately before the day of Verdict, on purpose that the Prisoner might not have any knowledge of them, till presented to his view and choice in Westminster-Hall. (pp. 72–73)

This retroactive account makes up for the fact that Vane evidently muffed the phase of challenging the jury; but it also enables the reader to retain her ideals of jury trial despite stark evidence of its systemic imperfections.

Again, where Throckmorton had preempted the authorities' desire for speed ("I praie you make not too much hast with me, neither thinke not long for your dinner, for my case requireth leasure, and you have well dined when you have doone justice trulie," p. 32) Vane complained after the event that his life had been sacrificed to appetite: "The Jury (as was told me) must not eat or drink, till they had done their work; . . . but why such haste and precipitancy for a man's Life, that's more than Meat or Estate, when you can let Civil Causes about mens Estates depend many years?" (p. 67). And beyond that material intimidation, one of the king's counsel, he complained, was:

> seen to speak privately with the Foreman of the Jury, immediately before the Jurors went from the Bar, after he had spoken openly, *That the Prisoner was to be made a publick Sacrifice, in reference to the Actions done against his Majesty that now is.* All this is very far from that Indifferency in Tryal, and from that Equality which the Law requires. (p. 55)

As Vane's "indifferency" may echo Throckmorton, so his description of how his jury was actually manipulated matches in its language the speech in which Throckmorton had preempted such manipulation, including an appeal to Christian fairness:

> What worse circumstances can a Prisoner be in, than to stand at a Bar of Justice to be tryed, and there hear his professed Accuser and Adversary, misrepresenting, miscalling, and aggravating the actions he is questioned for, pressing all upon the Jurors consciences with the greatest edge and flourish of all the Art, Wit and Eloquence, he is furnished with (as Tertullus served Paul) and then be deprived of all possible defence against his

slanderous and injurious suggestions? Paul was not so served; he had the last word to his Jury, when Tertullus had done, Acts 24. (p. 76)

So, by having his "Reasons" published by Sikes, Vane had the last word after all.

Following this model, Edmund Ludlow constructed his own more extensive hagiography, in which Vane is featured as the last and perhaps the most significant of the commonwealth martyrs. This scene is introduced in Ludlow's *Memoirs* with preliminaries that stress how crucial was this whole process of saving and disseminating trial records:

What Sir Henry Vane said at his tryall on behalfe of the publique, and his owne particular, was so rationall and convincing that his adversaryes . . . unwilling to have their workes of darkness discovered, supprest the notes which were taken of what he sayd in his justification; wherein he so highly owned the authority of the Parliament, that some of his freinds thereupon told him he had cast away his life; whereunto he replyed, I as little vallew my life *in a good cause*, as the King doth his promise; Sir Henry perceiving, *notwithstanding the engagement for his life*, by all the circumstances of his tryall, that they intended nothing more than to butcher him. Though what he said be supprest, yet, the heades of what he would have sayd being published at large, I shall forbeare to particcularize it, save only what was sent in the generall in a publique manuscript from London to Geneva, dated the 22 June 1662, whereby may be seene the sense men had of that affaire. (p. 311; italics Ludlow's)

Ludlow thus combined a free-speech polemic, legal critique, an attack on Charles for perfidy, and an acknowledgment of the problem of how one assesses the public response to such events ("the sense that men had of that affaire") into a single statement, one that obviously bears on the writing of his *Memoirs* as a whole. It is surely no coincidence that Ludlow's account of Vane's trial immediately follows his explanation, in Part 5 of the *Memoirs*, of what his metaphor of the Watch Tower means: the alertness that will ensure that, while lying low in the bad times, "when the Lord's tyme is come we may up and be doing, and the Lord may appeare to be with us and to owne us" (pp. 309–10). Given the sophistication of this strategy, it is odd that Blair Worden regarded Ludlow's decision to "reproduce material from the martyrological tracts" as "either naive or disingenuous" (p. 84). When John Toland edited the *Memoirs*, and arranged for them to be published in 1698 in Vevey, Switzerland, he was following the models of Sikes and Ludlow (though, as Worden has shown, with his own agenda intertwined) as to what should be reproduced and why.[44]

That "why" needs still further extrapolation. The import of Vane's last words as so rescued for posterity was not merely an extended complaint that he had received the form of justice and not its substance, and that he might better "have cast lots on a Drumhead for his Life, as a Prisoner of War, than to be so tryed in a time of Peace" (p. 76). Vane was described by royalist historians as defiant throughout his trial, and possibly he was, though defiance is hard to square with official reports of his lack of presence. Thomas Hollis, in his notes to his edition of Sidney, cited his old enemy Archdeacon Echard and Bishop Kennett, to the effect that Vane's "whole behaviour was so assuming and insolent, that the Court and King's Counsel told him, that his own defence was a fresh charge against him."[45] But Vane went down in the alternative canon as defiant in a more complex way. Vane had been the first to outline the dual structure of the Good Old Cause as both political and religious, "just natural rights in civil things, and true freedom in matters of conscience."[46] He now, in his "Reasons for Arrest of Judgement," presented himself, like Milton in 1667, as "unchang'd/To hoarse or mute, though fall'n on evil days." "As for that glorious Cause," he wrote, knowing that a genuinely humble submission to Charles might still save him:

which God hath owned in these Nations, and will own, in which so many Righteous souls have lost their lives, and so many have been engaged by my countenance and encouragement, shall I now give it up, and so declare them all Rebels and Murderers? No, I will never do it: That precious Blood shall never lie at my door. (p. 80)

And in yet another document included by Sikes, "Meditations concerning Man's Life, &c. Penned by this Sufferer in his Prison State," there appears a surprisingly political statement "concerning Government":

---

[44] So too was Richard Baron, when he "corrected" the 1751 edition of the *Memoirs*, and Thomas Hollis, when he sent a copy of Toland's edition to Harvard, where it was found by Caroline Robbins.

[45] [Thomas Hollis, ed.], Algernon Sidney, *Discourses concerning Government* (London: A. Millar, 1763), p. 25. Hollis included this section from *The Historical Register* in order to show that Vane was further betrayed, since the Cavalier Parliament had petitioned Charles that Vane should not lose his life, and Charles had apparently accepted the petition. This section of Echard and Kennet's report was italicized by Hollis.

[46] Vane, *A Healing Question Propounded and Resolved* (1656), in *Somers Tracts*, ed. Sir W. Scott, 13 vols. (London, 1809–15), 6:603.

He that gives up his Will to the Rule and Government of another, becomes subject to that other. Men that are born equal, come to be made subject two wayes; either by the free giving up of themselves to others, or by others violent assuming and exercising power over them, becaue they are strangers, as Nimrod the mighty hunter of men, served his fellow mortals. Government is either Royal, or Seignioral and Tyranical, as the Turks. 'Tis then properly Royal, be it administered by one, by many, or by all their Representatives, when he or that that have Soveraign Power, obey the Laws of Nature, preserve the natural Liberty and propriety of the Goods and Persons of the Subjects, which no reasonable men, acted by sound judgement, will ever absolutely give away, but secure their right in, and power over, by fundamental Contracts and Agreements with their Governor. (p. 123)

The story of Vane's trial thus concludes with a clearer statement of liberal constitutional theory than he could possibly have presented, on his feet, to a hostile audience. And perhaps more interestingly still, given the debates in our own time as to whether the culture of the disempowered in the Restoration was also a culture of defeat, Vane left that question undecided:

Under the cross Accidents," he wrote, "issuing from such Contests, to which man is subject through others arbitrary Domination, he may carry himself well, two wayes:

1. By a strong and vigorous resistance thereof, to the last, for diverting or blunting the point of it, so as either to escape or force it.

2. The other way, and perhaps the surest, is to take and receive these Accidents at the worst, let them prove what they will, though to the loss of Life and all that's dear to him in this World . . . He that takes the first course, labours to escape; he that takes the latter is content rather to suffer. *This many times proves the better bargain.* (p. 124; italics added)

Despite my italicization, it seems possible to argue that Vane in fact chose the first option by way of the second, transforming his defeat into yet another motive for resistance by the next generation.

But although I have placed this trial on the tragic side of the theatrical spectrum (a metaphor that Vane himself invoked, as had Throckmorton), it is worth noticing that Sikes availed himself of the advantages of humor at the moment where it might seem least appropriate. On the scaffold – where the theatrical metaphor works best – Vane began to speak of the Cause:

Upon this the Trumpets sounded, the Sheriff catched at the Paper in his hand, and Sir John Robinson, who at first had acknowledged that he had nothing to do there, wishing the Sheriff to see to it, yet found himself something to do now, furiously calling for the Writers-Books, and saying, *he treats of Rebellion, and you write it.* Hereupon six Note Books were delivered up. The Prisoner was very patient and composed under all these injuries and soundings of the Trumpets several times in his face, only saying, *'Twas hard he might not be suffered to speak*; but, sayes he, *my usage from man is no harder than was my Lord and Masters; and all that will live his life this day, must expect hard dealing from the worldly spirit* – The Trumpets sounded again, to hinder his being heard. Then again Robinson and two or three others, endeavoured to snatch the Paper out of sir Henry's hand, but he kept it for a while, now and then reading part of it; afterwards, tearing it in pieces, he delivered it to a Friend behind him, who was presently forced to deliver it to the Sheriff. Then they put their hands into his pockets for Papers (as was pretended) which bred great confusion and dissatisfaction to the Spectators, seeing a Prisoner so strangely handled in his dying words. (pp. 88–89)

This comic skirmish was all for show, since Vane had already made copies of these papers and committed them "to a safe hand." It speaks volumes about what early modern liberals had learned, in practical terms, about the survival of their message, even when, or especially when, they themselves could not survive; and Sikes's dramatic presentation here is an instance of what they had learned. In its capacity to set the stage, its ironic treatment of Sir John Robinson, who "found himself something to do" by confiscating notebooks, its witty stylistic details (the sardonic parenthesis "as was pretended"), and its value-laden cadence ("so strangely handled in his dying words"), Sikes's account of Vane's execution is a perfect example of the claims by Robert Oppenheimer cited in my introduction:

it is style which makes it possible to act effectively, but not absolutely; . . . it is style which is the deference that action pays to uncertainty; it is above all style through which power defers to reason.[47]

Except that, in this instance, one might rephrase the last claim to read "it is above all style by which reason refuses to defer to power."

[47] J. Robert Oppenheimer, *The Open Mind* (New York, 1955), p. 54.

CHAPTER 4

Unjust tribunals II: Algernon Sidney

Algernon Sidney,
Of Common-wealth Kidney,
Composed a damn'd Libel (ay marry was it)
Writ to occasion
Ill blood in the Nation,
And therefore dispers'd it all over his Closet.
It was not the writing
Was prov'd, or indicting;
Tho' he urged Statutes, what was it but fooling,
Since a new Trust is
Plac'd in the Chief Justice,
To damn Law and Reason too by over-ruling.

"A New Song of the Times, 1683," *State Poems*, 1697

It might seem unnecessary to provide another account of the most notorious of all seventeenth-century trials, that of Colonel Algernon Sidney, so ably has it been analyzed by Jonathan Scott, and placed in the context of Sidney's life-long commitment to republicanism.[1] My own focus, however, is less on the trial as the "reckoning" to which Sidney's energetic and complex life had brought him, and more on its production and reproduction in the canon of early modern liberalism; and by further exploring how Sidney placed himself in that canon, and as an extension of the series Throckmorton–Lilburne–Vane, it is possible to understand aspects of his defence that might otherwise seem merely erratic or failures of concentration, signs that Sidney was showing his age. In fact, they might still be the latter, but, precisely because Sidney was so well prepared for his ordeal, even over-prepared, by his reading of the predecessor cases, the story of his mistakes is more complicated.

[1] Jonathan Scott, *Algernon Sidney and the Restoration Crisis, 1677–1683* (Cambridge, 1991), especially pp. 317–66. My admiration for this book remains intact, despite the several demurrals entered against it in this chapter.

In addition, the importance of Sidney's trial and its dissemination was and is enormously increased by its imbrication with his *Discourses concerning Government*. Unlike Throckmorton, who never articulated his political theory except in his testimony, or Lilburne, who scattered his thought in so many pamphlets that none acquired canonical status, or Vane, whose political *writings* were not at issue in his trial, Sidney could not have been executed without the existence of his *Discourses*, and without his execution his *Discourses* would not have become a lever of early modern liberalism, both in England in the eighteenth century and in colonial and revolutionary America. For reasons which had everything to do with publicity, Sidney must be seen as having won as much in the failure of his defence for the future of liberal thought as Throckmorton and Lilburne did in the success of theirs. Scott cites the various commentators, including the conservative Evelyn and the French ambassador Barillon, who felt that the injustice of the trial had seriously damaged the government's reputation.[2] As Scott put it, "Sidney's trial and execution established, and slightly exceeded, the limits of public tolerance. Consequently, it was to be the last of this series." From Scott's perspective, the series in question was that of the Popish Plot and its retributive aftermath, the Protestant Plot. This book extends the series backwards in time. But there is no doubt that the years 1680 to 1683 were crucial to the consolidation of the trial transcript as a new cultural-political genre. The correspondence between John Locke and his friend David Thomas during 1681 provides a mini-bibliography of the genre, since Locke in London was acquiring for Thomas the trials of those indicted as conspirators in the Popish Plot and the various published testimonies.[3] Significantly, Locke's letters do not record similar transactions with respect to the trials of Lord Russell and Sidney himself, the first of which appeared in print before he fled the country in early September 1683. Russell's scaffold speech was published by the radical printer, John Darby, Senior. The tract was on sale in the streets "within an hour" of Russell's death on July 21, 1683, and went through three editions within the year.[4] But Locke owned Sir George Treby's *Truth Vindicated concerning [Edward*

---

[2] Scott, *Algernon Sidney and the Restoration Crisis*, pp. 340–41.

[3] John Locke, *Correspondence*, ed. E. S. de Beer, 8 vols. (Oxford, 1976–89), 2:323, 337, 377.

[4] On Lord Russell's speech, see Lois Schwoerer, "Liberty of the Press and Public Opinion: 1660–1695," in *Liberty Secured Britain Before and After 1688*, ed. J. R. Jones (Stanford, 1992), p. 219.

Fitzharris's] Confession (1681) and L. Braddon's *Essex's Innocency and Honour Vindicated* (1690).[5] Locke's notebooks indicate that he sent Thomas a tract on the trial of Stephen College, a premonition of what was to come.[6]

Scott makes the important moral point that there was nothing unique about Sidney's trial in terms of early modern jurisprudence, in which the "unjust tribunal" was never confined to one side of the political spectrum. Precisely because this was so, I would argue, ideas of legal reform were theoretically more likely to spread through the legally literate community, especially in America, and to acquire an aura of common sense in an era of common danger. In the denial of counsel and of a copy of the indictment, at least to commoners, Sidney's trial ran true to form, including the precedents of the trials of those accused during the Popish Plot, when Slingsby Bethel, the London sheriff, and Attorney-General Jones had managed manifestly unjust trials with Sidney's oversight and approval. Along with the cases of Throckmorton, Lilburne and Vane, Sidney had informed himself of the precedents in the attainder of Strafford, whom Vane had helped to destroy, and Stafford, for whom Sidney had done the same. Sidney was incarcerated for months without knowing what the charges were against him, and in this he was preceded by many others, including, as we have seen, Throckmorton, Lilburne and Vane. And like Throckmorton, the chief witness to the conspiracy for which he was indicted was a man bent on obtaining a pardon for himself.

Yet we need to account for the fact that Sidney's "thought in context" proved more powerful than any of its predecessors. As Scott observed, both Sidney and Locke, through the accident of their encounter with Sir Robert Filmer's *Patriarcha* in the context of the 1681 Exclusion crisis, eventually changed our intellectual environment. They "proved the most important lightning-rods by which a sixteenth- and early seventeenth-century political view of the world was transmitted intact to the eighteenth century, where it proved all-conquering" (p. 210). The transmission process itself is my focus also; but by recognizing how the trial and the *Discourses* became inseparable in the liberal tradition, it becomes possible to see what even Scott's analysis has omitted; not least the way in

---

5 John Harrison and Peter Laslett, *The Library of John Locke* (Oxford, 1965), nos. 1136, 1069.
6 See Richard Ashcraft, *Revolutionary Politics and Locke's Two Treatises of Government* (Princeton, 1986), p. 347, n.37, citing Locke MS.c.1, fols. 124, 167.

which Sidney's obsession with the law and its abuses pervades the *Discourses*, and was revealed in his trial as a self-fulfilling prophecy.

Sidney was arrested on June 26, 1683, a week before the government had anything other than hearsay evidence against him, technically an illegal arrest. On the same day his papers, including the manuscript of the *Discourses*, were confiscated. Direct evidence of a plot in which Sidney was one of the six designers would follow on July 9 when Lord Howard was taken, who, according to Burnet, "at his first examination . . . told, as he said, all he knew."[7] Later he would tell a good deal more than he knew. Sidney was then held in the Tower until early November, while the government attempted to build its case on firmer ground. In late October Sidney and Hampden filed a habeas corpus; and the government responded by moving ahead with his trial, having come up with the expedient of using the *Discourses* in place of a second human witness. The charge of "imagining the king's death" was to be supported by Sidney's own words in an unpublished manuscript. In the meantime Lord Russell, with two material witnesses against him, had been successfully prosecuted under Justice Pemberton, and executed on July 21. Sidney included those proceedings in his material for study.

In this instance, in contrast to the cases of Russell (and of Throckmorton, Lilburne and Vane), the transcript of Sidney's trial was published by the government early in 1684, to preempt surreptitious editions with their editorial coloring, as also, presumably, to show to the world the weakness of Sidney's defence.[8] Judge Jeffreys himself ordered its assignment to Benjamin Tooke "and that no other Person presume to Print the same." It was, however, reprinted in Dublin by Joseph Ray, who also reprinted, as had Mary Crooke before him, *The Very Copy of a Paper Delivered to the Sheriff*, that is to say, Sidney's scaffold speech, which Sidney, no doubt with Vane's experience in mind, had made no attempt to deliver *as* a speech, but handed one copy to the sheriff, advising him that another resided in safe hands. Its publication was promptly prohibited, but a Dutch edition appeared almost immediately, spawning so many manuscript

[7] Gilbert Burnet, *The History of My Own Time*, ed. Osmund Airy, 2 vols. (Oxford, 1907), 2:369.
[8] *The Arraignment, Tryal & Condemnation of Algernon Sidney, Esq. for High-Treason. For Conspiring the Death of the King and Intending to raise a Rebellion in this Kingdom. Before the Right Honourable Sir George Jeffreys . . . at . . . King's Bench at Westminster, on the 7th, 12th, and 17th of November, 1683* (London: Benjamin Tooke, 1684).

copies that the government threw in the towel and permitted a London edition.[9]

Six years later, in the milder climate of the Williamite Revolution, John Darby published the first edition of the *Discourses*, with a brief preface by John Toland. Darby and Toland thereby began the gradual process of accretion and consolidation whereby the Sidney legend became monumental. In 1705, John Darby Jr. published a second edition of the *Discourses*, with a portrait of Sidney and his famous motto, Toland's preface, and the *Last Paper*. This volume also added an excellent if highly tendentious index, in which, for example, the subheadings under "Absolute power and Monarchy" include "Burdensome and dangerous," "The sad effects of it," "Encourages venality and corruption," and "Few or none long subsist under it."

Half a century later, in 1751, Andrew Millar published a third and new edition by Richard Baron, the friend of Thomas Hollis. This volume included Toland's preface, Baron's "Memoirs" of Sidney's life (into which was inserted his *Last Paper*), and his much longer *Apology*, which was actually his vindication. Sidney's manuscript of the *Apology* (no longer extant) had been secreted by Sidney's servant Joseph Ducasse, himself a Huguenot refugee from France, until after the Revolution, when he produced it for the inspection by a committee of the House of Lords.[10] Its addition to the *Discourses* meant that, with the exception of his *Court Maxims*, all of Sidney's works were now available together. And Baron had put considerable scholarly work into this new edition of the *Discourses*, checking, expanding and correcting the marginal and footnote references: adding, for example, the Spanish text of citations from Los Casas; book and line references for Sidney's frequent quotations from Lucan and Juvenal (his favorite classical poets); and on more than one occasion correcting Sidney's understanding of Tacitus.

Baron's edition represented, as I suggested earlier, the second phase of liberal canon-building, whereby he and Thomas Hollis and a few others assumed the mission begun by the Williamite Whigs. That mission had expanded; its growth is economically registered by comparing the printer's advertisements at the back of the 1705 and 1751 editions. Where John Darby could list as of interest to Sidney's

---

[9] See Scott, *Algernon Sidney and the Restoration Crisis*, pp. 311–12.
[10] See *Journal of the House of Lords* (1689), p. 390.

readers his editions of Harrington's *Oceana* and John de Witt's *The True Interest of the Republick of Holland*, the like-minded "Books printed for and sold by A. Millar" included, along with the works of Harrington, those of Boyle, Ludlow and Locke, Thuanus' *Historia sui temporis*, the *Complete Collection* of Milton's prose edited by Baron, and *An Historical and Political Discourse of the Laws and Government of England . . . With a Vindication of the Antient Way of Parliaments in England*, edited from notes of John Selden by Nathaniel Bacon.

But the best expression of this project, at once commemorative, aggregative and collaborative, was undoubtedly Thomas Hollis's 1763 edition of Sidney's works, of which something has already been said in Chapter 2. But perhaps it bears repeating. Hollis took over the Baron text of the *Discourses* and the *Apology*, along with Baron's biography. He added a new portrait of Sidney; as compared to the romantic image of 1705, this was a severe Roman bust in profile, engraved by Cipriani after J. Basire. A flag over his shoulder identified his ruling passion as patriotism, while a famous anecdote beneath him brought Lord Molesworth's testimony to ennoble his image. And opposite that image, on the title-page, stands that other motto from Milton's *Samson Agonistes*, "Or to the unjust tribunals under change of times," which pointed to Hollis's most substantial addition to the Sidney legend; not the letters to his father and Henry Savile, but the transcript of the trial itself, which had now been transformed, by its proximity to the *Apology*, from government propaganda into testimony for Sidney. As the *Discourses* had been defined by Jeffreys as the missing second witness for the prosecution, so the *Trial* was now transformed by Hollis into a witness for the defence.

Hollis's application of Milton's "unjust tribunals" to the trials of 1683 was not only shrewd in its grasp of liberal historiography, but prompted, surely, by his own careful reading of the *Discourses*. For whereas Scott and Alan Houston have analyzed most of their salient characteristics, neither focused on their obsession with "unjust tribunals," a worry that unites the *Discourses* internally and prophetically links them to Sidney's own trial. Houston focused on the great themes of freedom and slavery, virtue and corruption, constitutionalism and revolution, the ethico-political poles of Sidney's conceptual universe;[11] Scott identified the *Discourses'* inconsistent mixture of

---

[11] Alan Craig Houston, *Algernon Sidney and the Republican Heritage in England and America* (Princeton, 1991).

natural law, ancient constitutionalism and historical example, their "unqualified bellicosity" (p. 236), and their commitment to political relativism and the inevitability of change. But Sidney's concern with the legal *system* and its corruption under Charles II was more urgent than can be explained by any generalized theory of government according to Law and resistance (as authorized by Grotius) to magistrates who exceed its mandate.

Sidney's concern with unjust tribunals surfaces explicitly in his account of Restoration political culture:

These men having neither will nor knowledge to do good, as soon as they come to be in power, justice is perverted, military discipline neglected, the public treasures exhausted, new projects invented to raise more; and the prince's wants daily increasing, through their ignorance, negligence, or deceit, there is no end of their devices and tricks to gain supplies. To this end, swarms of spies, informers, and false witnesses, are sent out to circumvent the richest and most eminent men: *the tribunals are filled with court-parasites of profligate consciences, fortunes, and reputation, that no man may escape who is brought before them. If crimes are wanting, the diligence of well-chosen officers and prosecutors, with the favour of the judges, supply all defects; the law is made a snare.*[12]

Conversely, when Sidney encourages his reader to look back to the heroic era of the English commonwealth (*before* Cromwell's ascendancy), he includes a praise of republican justice alongside that of its military success:

I could give yet more pregnant testimonies of the difference between men fighting for their own interests in the offices to which they had been advanced by the votes of numerous assemblies, and such as serve for pay, and get preferments by corruption and favor, if I were not unwilling to stir the spleen of some men by obliging them to reflect upon what has passed in our own age and country; to compare *the justice of our tribunals within the time of our memory*, and the integrity of those who[*] for a while managed the public treasure; the discipline, valour, and strength, of our armies and fleets; the increase of our riches and trade; the success of our wars in Scotland, Ireland, and at sea, the glory and reputation not long since gained, with that condition into which we are of late fallen. (Section 28, p. 220; marginal note.[*] The parliament of 1641)

In a less polemical context not even Sidney would have been able to maintain so clear a distinction between Commonwealth justice and

---

[12] Sidney, *Discourses concerning Government*, ed. Thomas Hollis (London, 1763), p. 214 (Chapter II, Section 27). All subsequent quotations will be from this edition; but for the convenience of those using 1772 or other editions, chapter and section references are given.

Restoration injustice. His own attitude during the Popish Plot trials presided over by his Whig allies goes unregistered here, but we have to suspect inconsistency, if not absolute hypocrisy. In his own trial Sidney was to be caught by Jeffreys in that trap. But like the blind spots of Milton and Thomas Hollis with respect to toleration, and even those of Locke (to be discussed in chapter 8), Sidney's intense biases were part of the tough weave of thought in context that kept the design intact.

Indeed, by turning the lens slightly, it would be possible to argue that the structure of the *Discourses* resembles that of Locke's *Two Treatises*, not least because they share the same agenda. Both begin with a devastating logical attack on Filmer's patriarchal theory in its own terms, largely those of scriptural citation. Both move to a reassertion of the theoretical bases of the English constitution; and both lead inexorably in the last sections to the conclusion that, since the constitution has been subverted by the present government, armed resistance to it is justified. (Both, as Scott observed, offer a new-old definition of the Latin "rebellare" in the course of that justification.) In Sidney's case that move is not, as in Locke, through natural law contract theory, but through an increasingly broad definition of "law" as the English legal system, which includes constitutional law and history, and decrees, in Sidney's argument, that the king is subject to the law, not above it. Most of his third Chapter is devoted to this theme, and his ancient constitutionalism and insistence on parliament's sovereignty are only one aspect of the larger point. Filmer had conceded the standard position articulated by James I: "a king, governing in a settle kingdom, leaves to be a king, and degenerates into a tyrant, so soon as he ceases to rule according unto his laws"; but he had added a dangerous qualification: "yet where he sees them rigorous or doubtful, he may mitigate or interpret." This provocation inspired perhaps Sidney's most eloquent declaration, made famous by John Adams's subsequent quotation of it in an actual and highly politicized legal case (see chapter 8, p. 296 below) at an inflammatory moment in colonial history. But Adams's application of Sidney's eloquence to the unpopular defence of Captain Preston almost a century later only rendered visible the prophetic and progressive nature of the claims that Sidney was making; by appealing to the past he accomplished the very opposite of conservativism:

Fortescue says plainly, the king cannot change any law: magna charta casts all upon the laws of the land, and customs of England: but to say, that the king can by his will make that to be a custom, or an antient law, which is not, or that not to be so, which is, is most absurd. He must therefore take the laws and customs, as he finds them, and can neither detract from nor add anything to them. The ways are prescribed as well as the end. Judgments are given by equals, "per pares." The judges, who may be assisting to those, are sworn to proceed according to law, and not to regard the king's letters or commands. The doubtful cases are reserved, and to be referred to the parliament, as in the statute of 35 [*sic*] Edw. III. concerning treasons, but never to the king. The law intending that these parliaments should be annual, and leaving to the king a power of calling them more often, if occasion require, takes away all pretence of a necessity, that there should be any other power to interpret or mitigate laws . . . That rule must always be uncertain, and subject to be distorted, which depends upon the fancy of such a man. He always fluctuates, and every passion that arises in his mind, or is infused by others, disorders him. The good of a people ought to be established upon a more solid foundation. For this reason, the law is established, which no passion can disturb. It is void of desire and fear, lust and anger. It is "mens sine affectu," written reason retaining some measure of the divine perfection. It does not injoin that which pleases a weak, frail man; but, without any regard to persons, commands that which is good, and punishes evil in all, whether rich or poor, high or low. It is deaf, inexorable, inflexible. (Chapter III, Section 15, pp. 315–16).

The concept of law as "mens sine affectu," passionless and above interest, is strongly reminiscent of Throckmorton's appeal to the literal understanding of the treason statutes, and his allusion to Sergeant Stanford's own earlier rationale for limiting just such "interpretation" and "mitigation" as Filmer seemed to allow: "You said, considering the private affections manie times both of princes and ministers within this realme, for that they were men, and would and could erre, it should be no securitie, but verie dangerous to the subject, to refer the construction and extending of penall statutes to anie judges equitie."[13] And Sidney's reference here to the ancient Edwardian treason law (although he, or his editors, made the mistake of calling it 35 Edw. III) would seem to confirm that the Throckmorton trial was part of his library during his writing of the *Discourses*, as well as during his imprisonment.

In fact, Sidney signalled his interest in law in the opening pages of the *Discourses*, when, in refuting Filmer's claim that subjects

---

[13] *Holinshed's Chronicles of England, Scotland, and Ireland*, 6 vols. (London: J. Johnson *et al.*, 1808), 4:48.

ought to place an implicit trust in princes, as they do in any other professionals, he remarked dryly (and topically): "I do not send for Lower or Micklethwait when I am sick, nor ask the advice of Mainard or Jones in a suit of law, because the first are physicians, and the other lawyers; but because I think them wise, diligent, and faithful, there being a multitude of others who go under the same name, whose opinion I would never ask" (Chapter 1, Section 3, p. 9). In this list, it was Sir William Jones, even more than Sergeant Maynard, whose name carried the ideological flag.[14] As Attorney-General he had directed the prosecution of the accused in the Popish Plot in 1678, a task that eventually turned his stomach and led to his resignation in November 1679. His disgust was, however, not strong enough to keep him away from trials conducted by the opposition. Joining the House of Commons in November 1680, he took over the management of the trial for treason of Lord Stafford, for which, as Scott observes, the king swore revenge and accomplished it, with a special irony, when at the beginning of his trial Sidney asked unsuccessfully for a copy of his indictment, on the grounds that "my lord Strafford had a copy, and my lord Stafford."[15] And when later West was sworn as a witness in order to give a general account of the Rye House Plot, and Sidney objected, Jeffreys' riposte was as follows:

Mr. Sydney, you remember in all the tryals about the late popish plot, how there was first a general account given of the plot in Coleman's tryal, and so in Plunket's, and others; I don't doubt but you remember it. And Sir William Jones, against whose judgement, I believe, you won't object, was attorney at that time.[16]

To repeat: that the tit-for-tat structure of partisan jurisprudence was here acknowledged by both sides does not invalidate, but rather

---

[14] Sergeant Maynard, who had helped to try Strafford, was also active for the Whigs during the Exclusion debates. But Sidney apparently chose his physicians as well as his lawyers for their political principles. Sir John Micklethwaite had been recommended by the Long Parliament in 1644 to replace William Harvey "who hath withdrawn himself from his charge and retired to the party in arms against the Parliament" (*DNB*); and Richard Lower, according to Anthony à Wood, "closed with the Whigs" during the Popish Plot, "supposing that that party would carry all before them; but being mistaken, he lost much of his practice at or near the court." See Wood, *Athenae Oxonienses*, ed. Bliss, Vol 4., Col. 298. Since Micklethwaite died on July 29, 1682, we can infer that Sidney wrote this passage, and probably the whole treatise, before that date.

[15] *The Arraignment, Trial, and Condemnation of Algernon Sydney*, in *Discourses*, ed. Hollis, p. 113; subsequently cited as *Trial*.

[16] Sidney, *Trial*, p. 116. Scott mistakenly stated that Jeffreys referred here to Stafford's trial.

vindicates, the theoretical idealism of Sidney's call for the law to rise above politics.

But there are other, equally farsighted, explorations of legal theory in the *Discourses*. One, that recalls both Throckmorton and Lilburne, is the argument that the symbolic representation of an ideal of impersonal justice resides in the jury system, and that (a more radical proposal than even Lilburne had made) "the law has put all judgments into the hands of the people. This power is executed by them in grand or petty juries, *and the judges are assistants to them*, in explaining the difficult points of the law . . . The strength of every judgment consists in the verdict of these juries, which the judges do not give, but pronounce or declare" (Chapter III, Section 26, p. 371).[17] For this assertion Sidney cited Bracton, who in Chapter III competes with Grotius and Machiavelli as a primary authority.

Another legal issue was Filmer's claim that proclamations could replace laws, to whose refutation Sidney devotes the long late Section 43, inserting into it one of his two clear indications[18] that this is, after all, an Exclusion pamphlet as well as a broader "Account of the Growth of Popery and Arbitrary Government"; or perhaps it would be more accurate to say that it is the latter rewritten in the light of 1681:

Let proclamations obtain the power of laws, and the business is done. They may be so ingeniously contrived, that the antient laws, which we and our fathers have highly valued, shall be abolished, or made a snare to all those that dare remember they are Englishmen, and are guilty of the unpardonable crime of loving their country, or have the courage, conduct, and reputation required to defend it. This is the sum of Filmer's philosophy, and this is the legacy he has left to testify his affection to the nation; which having for a long time lain unregarded, has been lately brought into the

---

[17] Compare also Chapter III, Section 22.

[18] Compare Chapter II, Section 27, p. 211: "If [the reader] be not convinced of this, he may soon see a man in the throne, who had rather be a tributary to France than a lawful king of England, whilst either parliament or people shall dare to dispute his commands, insist upon their own rights, or defend a religion inconsistent with that which he has espoused." Compare also Chapter III, Section 43, where Sidney states that Filmer's argument in effect proposes that "we should waive the bill of exclusion, and not only admit [James] to reign as other kings have done, but resign the whole power into his hands" (p. 449). These passages must cast doubt on Scott's campaign to undo the connection between the *Discourses* and the Exclusion debates. See *Algernon Sidney and the Restoration Crisis*, pp. 9–21, and especially the misleading statement that Locke, in never mentioning exclusion in the *Two Treatises* was, "*like Sidney* . . . not an exception but the rule. The same is true of . . . Penn, Marvell, Bethel, Neville, Tyrell, and Halifax" (p. 15). Marvell, incidentally, was unlikely to mention it, since he was already dead by the time of the debates.

light again, as an introduction of a popish successor, who is to be established, as we ought to believe, for the security of the protestant religion, and our English liberties. (p. 448)

And then there is a little flurry of topical legal allusions in the last sections of the *Discourses*, allusions that substantially change its flavor, while completely undermining Sidney's claim in his defence that his answer to Filmer was pure theory, "not calculated to any particular government in the world" (*Trial*, p. 134). In Section 42, Sidney amusingly convicts Filmer of having been misled by the use of the king's title in juridical language, and explains that while a man is to be tried "coram rege," he is nevertheless to be tried "secundum legem terrae, according to the law of the land," not by the king's version of the law. And here he entered the only veritable anecdote in the *Discourses*, one that required some readerly investigation for its point to be fully made:

For this reason a noble lord, who was irregularly detained in prison in 1681, being by habeas corpus brought to the bar of the king's bench, where he sued to be released upon bail; and an ignorant judge telling him he must apply to the king, he replied, that he came thither for that end; that the king might eat, drink, or sleep, where he pleased; but when he rendered justice, he was always in that place. (pp. 442–43)

The author of this witticism cannot now be traced through the records of King's Bench;[19] but a few paragraphs later Sidney engaged in a couple of topical ripostes directly at Charles II's expense. To demonstrate the limits of the king's power to pardon, he noted that "the waterman who had been pardoned by his majesty in the year 1680. for a murder he had committed, was condemned, and hanged, at the assizes upon an appeal" (p. 444). And still nearer to home, he turned to the example of Danby, languishing in the Tower since his impeachment in 1679 for complicity in the secret treaty of Dover:

Nay, in cases of treason, which some men think relate most particularly to the person of the king, he cannot always do it [pardon]. Gaveston, the two Spencers, Tresilian, Empson, Dudley, and others, have been executed as traitors for things done by the king's command; and it is not doubted they would have bene saved, if the king's power had extended so far. I might add

---

[19] It cannot have been Shaftesbury, who applied for a writ of habeas corpus three times, unsuccessfully, in 1681; but he applied to the sessions at the Old Bailey, whereupon Chief Justice Pemberton stated that that court did not have jurisdiction over the Tower, and referred Sidney *to* the king's bench.

the cases of the earls of Strafford and Danby; for, tho' the king [Charles I] signed a warrant for the execution of the first, no man doubts he would have saved him, if it had been in his power. *The other continues in prison, notwithstanding his pardon; and that will not be more to his satisfaction, unless he be found innocent, or something all out more to his advantage than his majesty's approbation of what he has done.*[20]

Seen through the lens of Sidney's obsession with law, then, it now appears that the structural goal of the *Discourses*, however prolix and unrevised, was remarkably clear. Sidney may have been following the structure of the *Patriarcha*, section by section, but his own thought was not dictated by it. His agenda was to move the reader gradually to understand that the only guarantor against partisan jurisprudence was *shared* jurisprudence. There was safety in numbers. "Two eyes see more than one, and human judgement is subject to errors" (Chapter III, Section 46, p. 459). It was crucial to ensure that parliament was the highest court in the land, with authority over the king. Not that Sidney was naive about parliament's integrity or institutional viability. Some of the most interesting passages late in the treatise register the influence of Andrew Marvell's *Account of the Growth of Popery and Arbitrary Government*, particularly in its lengthy account of how the long-lived Cavalier Parliament became so corrupted, in Marvell's words, that "by being so throughly acquainted, they understand their number and party, so that the use of so publick a counsel is frustrated, there is no place for deliberation, no perswading by reason, but they can see one another's votes through both throats and cravats before they hear them."[21] Sidney's version of this argument focuses specifically on the way political corruption leads to the passing of bad statutes; which does not mean that the parliamentary system is intrinsically bad, but only in need of a clean-up:

[20] *Discourses*, Chapter III, Section 42, p. 444; Thomas Osborne, earl of Danby, imprisoned in April 1679, had been pardoned by Charles prior to a vote on the articles of impeachment by the Commons. Charles then prorogued the parliament before the procedural impasse could be resolved. In August 1682 Danby sought a writ of habeas corpus in King's Bench, but his judges deferred to parliament as the higher court. He was not granted bail until February 1684, when the credibility of Oates had failed, and Jeffreys had become lord chief justice. Sidney's statement that Danby "continues in prison" therefore provides another set of chronological boundaries for the composition of the *Discourses*. Compare the briefer discussion of the significance of these references for dating in Blair Worden, "The Commonwealth Kidney of Algernon Sidney," *Journal of British Studies* 24 (1985), 38–39. It is possible that Sidney's mean-spirited reference to Danby, when the manuscript was close to completion, was motivated by that habeas corpus appeal in August 1682.

[21] Andrew Marvell, *Complete Works*, ed. A. B. Grosart, 4 vols. (A. B. Grosart, p.p. 1875), 4:331.

Our kings had not wherewithal to corrupt many till these last twenty years, and the treachery of a few is not enough to pass a law. The union of many was not easily wrought, and there was nothing to tempt them to endeavour it; for they could make little advantage during the session, and were to be lost in the mass of the people, and prejudiced by their own laws, as soon as it was ended. They could not in a short time reconcile their various interests or passions, so as to combine together against the public; and the former kings never went about it. We are beholden to Hyde, Clifford and Danby, for all that has been done of that kind. They found a parliament full of lewd young men chosen by a furious people in spite to the puritans, whose severity had distasted them. The weakest of all ministers had wit enough to understand, that such as these might be easily deluded, corrupted, or bribed. Some were fond of their seats in parliament, and delighted to domineer over their neighbours by continuing in them: others preferred the cajoleries of the court before the honour of performing their duty to the country that employed them. Some sought to relieve their ruined fortunes, and were most forward to give the king a vast revenue, that from thence they might receive pensions: others were glad of a temporary protection against their creditors. Many knew not what they did when they annulled the triennial act; voted the militia to be in the king; gave him the excise, customs, and chimney-money; made the act for corporations, by which the greatest part of the nation was brought under the power of the worst men in it; drunk or sober pass'd the five-mile act, and that for uniformity in the church. This embolden'd the court to think of making parliaments to be the instruments of our slavery, which had in all ages past been the firmest pillars of our liberty. (Chapter iii, Section 46, p. 456)

This was the penultimate section of the *Discourses*, and, as it closely matches Marvell's analysis,[22] it also corresponds to the last chapter of Locke's *Second Treatise*, which declares that the magistrate has broken his contract with his subjects "when he either employs the force, treasure, and offices of the society, to corrupt the representatives, and gain them to his purposes: or openly pre-engages the electors, and prescribes to their choice, such, whom he has by solicitations, threats, promises, or otherwise won to his designs; and

---

[22] Compare Sidney's selection of the bad legislation with Marvell's stinging explanation for "the three acts of Corporations, of Militia, and the Five Miles" (*Account*, pp. 305–7, and his diagnosis of the make-up of the Cavalier Parliament that made it susceptible to corruption (pp. 323–31). Of course, Sidney nowhere refers to Marvell's *Account* in the *Discourses*. In one of his letters to Henry Savile, dated 7/17 April 1679, Sidney promises to send him the opposition satire, "The speech of Hodge the clown from the top of the pyramid," otherwise known as "Hodge's Vision from the top of his monument," attributed to Marvell in *Poems in Affairs of State* (1697), and in Hollis's edition of the *Discourses*. "Hodge" was the Whig nickname for Marvell's old enemy, Sir Roger L'Estrange, the Restoration censor.

employs them to bring in such, who have promised beforehand, what to vote, and what to enact."[23] Neither Marvell nor Locke faced the question of what to do with a system vulnerable to such corruption. Sidney did. "But how great soever the danger may be," he concluded, "'tis less than to put all into the hazards of one man, and his ministers . . . 'Tis better to depend upon those who are under a possibility of being again corrupted, than upon one who applies himself to corrupt them, because he cannot otherwise accomplish his designs." Parliament being, "under God, the best anchor we have, it deserves to be preserved with all care, till one of a more unquestionable strength be framed by the consent of the nation" (p. 457).

So now let us reconsider the role of the *Discourses* as witness for the prosecution. There are some unsolved problems here, caused by the fact that the long passage cited in the trial does not appear in the printed text. Blair Worden states that "the passages produced as evidence against Sidney. . . belong to the end of book [Chapter] 2, where we learn from the printed version that 'the rest of this chapter is wanting in the original manuscript.'"[24] He reached this conclusion by comparing the passages cited in evidence, and those around them, with Sidney's general progress through Filmer's *Patriarcha*. The implication is that the passage went missing because it had been extracted from the manuscript for evidentiary purposes. There are, however, two other places where the manuscript was defective that cannot be so explained: the first, in Chapter I, Section 15 (p. 34 in Hollis's edition), where his editors report two pages missing; the second, in Chapter II, Section 3, where, just after Sidney's reference to Jotham's parable, they report another two-page gap. Further, the attorney-general, Sir Robert Sawyer, referred also to "the latter end, the last sheet of all, Section 35" (p. 128), whereupon the Clerk of the Crown quoted the title of Chapter III, Section 36, "The general revolt of a nation cannot be called a rebellion," and Section 38, "The power of calling and dissolving parliaments is not simply in the king." Neither, of course, is "the last sheet of all," if the court were in possession of the complete manuscript. If they were not, it would help to explain why the prosecution did not choose to cite the obviously topical passages, insulting to Charles and James, to be

---

[23] John Locke, *Two Treatises of Government*, ed. Mark Goldie (London, 1993), p. 227.
[24] Worden, "Commonwealth Kidney," p. 39.

found in Sections 42 through 46. This disparity may give some basis to Toland's otherwise unreliable assertion in his preface to the first edition that in his *Last Paper* Sidney informed posterity "that he had left a large and a lesser treatise," the latter unfinished, "and that a small part of the lesser treatise had been produc'd for evidence against him at his Tryal." Sidney said nothing of the sort in his *Last Paper*; but perhaps Toland inherited a tradition that there had been two manuscripts, of which the larger, which he assumed was finished, was now to be made accessible. If so, one could explain this tradition by positing that the latest and most dangerous sections had been secreted by Ducasse, and that what the prosecution confiscated *could* reasonably have been described as Sidney described it, as a purely theoretical answer to Filmer.[25]

But of all the mistakes that Sidney made in his defence, and he made many, the most peculiar error was refusing to do sustained battle with Lord Chief Justice Jeffreys on his notorious new rule that "Scribere est agere" (*Trial*, p. 156). To do so, of course, would have been to own authorship of the *Discourses*, against his lawyers' advice. It was much too early in legal history to win that battle as a free-speech issue, though Sidney could have cited both Throckmorton's case and Lilburne's as to whether words were indeed deeds. In fact, Sidney did refer to "Throgmorton's case" in relation to the overt act distinction (*Trial*, p. 147); but by this time he had lost his grip, his responses were incoherent, and half a sentence later he broke off with the pathetic appeal, "I should have somebody to speak for me, my lord." On the issue of authorship, Sidney prevaricated:

The attorney shews these papers to me, I do not know whether they are my own or no . . . Look upon them, you see they are all old ink. These papers may be writ perhaps these twenty years, the ink is so old. But, my lord, it is a polemical discourse, it seems to be an answer to Filmer, which is not calculated for any particular government in the world. (*Trial*, p. 134)

Meanwhile, Jeffreys in his summing-up had personified the *Discourses* in a skilful and devastating manner, turning them into precisely that speaking witness for whom they were made to substitute:

[25] The modern reader is not helped in her attention to this puzzle by Scott's habit of pasting together quotations from different parts of the *Discourses*. Thus a selective quotation from Chapter III, Section 38 (which does *not* appear to have been read aloud at the trial) is immediately followed by a selective quotation from the passage which was imputed by Worden to Chapter II, Section 32; and the chapter ends thus: "It was these *final* claims that were to attract the crown's most indignant attention at Sidney's trial." See Scott, *Algernon Sidney and the Restoration Crisis*, p. 264; italics added.

And though this book be not brought to that council to be perused, and there debated; yet it will be another, and more than two witnesses against the prisoner: for I would ask any man, suppose a man was in a room, and there were two men, and he talks with both apart . . . And you have heard one witness prove it positively to you, that he consulted to rise in arms against the king, *and here is his own book says*, it is lawful for a man to rise in arms against the king, if he break his trust. (*Trial*, p. 154; italics added)

By fudging the question of his authorship, Sidney gave up the high moral ground, and was forced to rely on points of law that gave him no better foothold. One of his more embarrassing moves was to argue the need for two witnesses from the biblical case of Susanna and the Elders!

There *was* one interesting but extremely brief moment when Sidney appeared, without admitting to authorship, to be about to confront Jeffreys on the principle that writing, at least unpublished writing, is not a political act. "I think 'tis a right of mankind, and 'tis exercised by all studious men, that they write in their own closets what they please for their own memory, and no man can be answerable for it, unless they publish it." The statement was unusual, in that only here during the trial did Sidney use the term "right," and Jeffreys' ears caught it immediately:

Pray don't go away with that *right* of mankind, that it is lawful for me to write what I will in my own closet, unless I publish it. I have been told, curse not the king, not in thy thoughts, not in thy bed-chamber, the birds of the air will carry it. I took it to be the *duty* of mankind, to observe that. (*Trial*, p. 137; italics added)

Between them, they anticipated the absolute difference between Paine and Burke; not to mention the irony expressed in the "New Song of the Times," that what was being posited as material destructive of the state had *not* been circulated by Sidney, but "dispers'd . . . all over his Closet."

Deprived of the defence on principle, Sidney wasted much of his day in court, and all of his witnesses, in trying to damage Lord Howard's already non-existent credibility. Like Vane, he was constantly interrupted by Jeffreys, who in his own frightful way was extremely effective. Sidney made poor use of his legal preparation. As Scott points out, he must have had an incomplete account of Russell's trial, since he did not know that one of the defences he planned to make, that *conspiring* to levy war against the king was not treason under 25 Edward III without some overt act, had already been rendered null by Sir Heneage Finch, solicitor-general, on that occasion. Both Russell and Sidney were relying on Coke's opinion that the two branches of the statute, levying war and imagining the death of the king, were distinct, and could not be used as evidence of each other; but in Russell's case Finch, who had also been attorney-general in Vane's trial, calmly decreed this "an error of my Lord Coke."[26] Even more calmly, in his summing up for the jury, and refuting Sidney's distinction between the two branches of 25 Edw. III, Finch remarked, "Gentlemen, I won't be long in citing authorities: it hath been settled lately by all the judges of England, in the case of my Lord Russel, who hath suffered for this conspiracy." The authority in this redefinition was Finch himself – and reason: "and reason does plainly speak it to be so; for they that conspire to raise war against the king, can't be presumed to stop anywhere till they have dethroned or murdered the king" (*Trial*, p. 148).

Throckmorton would have had a witty retort to such high-handedness, but Sidney was, unfortunately, relying on Throckmorton's case only for its legal substance, not for its style.[27] He had probably discovered it by studying Lilburne's, which had told him where to find it, but not why Throckmorton had succeeded:

If it be not plainly under one of the two branches, that I have endeavoured to kill the king, or levied war, then 'tis matter of construction, and that belongs to no court, but the parliament. Then, my lord, this hath been adjudged already in Throgmorton's case. There are twenty judgements of parliament, the act of 13. Eliz. that say – (p. 147)

Alas, where Throckmorton would have been able to rehearse, if not twenty, the one that counted, Sidney trailed off into incoherence. And when Jeffreys replied, "We are of another opinion," he registered yet again how easily the law could change its shape. Indeed, whenever Sidney raised what he claimed was a point of law, Jeffreys simply told him he was mistaken. According to Burnet, in relation to Jeffreys' overruling Sidney's complaint that his jury was not composed of freeholders, Jeffreys "said on another occasion, why might they not make precedents to the succeeding times, as well as

---

[26] *Tryal of William Lord Russell*, in *State Trials*, 9:629.

[27] An interesting minor instance of Sidney's lack of a sense of humor, and of Jeffreys' consequent ability to control the *tone* of the proceedings, occurred when Jeffreys refused to consider what it would mean if the manuscript were an answer to Filmer: "We have nothing to do with his book; you had as good tell me again, that there was a parcel of people rambling about, pretending to my lord Russel's ghost, and so we may answer all the comedies in England" (p. 136).

those who had gone before them had made precedents for them?"[28]
Yet we should not merely shake our heads at Jeffreys' presumption;
for making precedents for the future was precisely what Throckmorton and Lilburne had intended, by extending the concept of the
jury trial to other unenumerated rights; and that was what Sidney
too was after, in hammering away at his right to see a copy of the
indictment, producing the statute of Edward III and attempting to
hold off pleading guilty or otherwise until the indictment's validity
had been tested. As Jeffreys remarked in the latter case, if they were
to allow that procedure (which Lilburne had used successfully) "all
criminals would say in all cases, I doubt whether the bill be good or
bad, and after I have thus considered of it, I will plead . . . We must
not introduce new methods or forms for anybody. The same case
that is with you, may be with other people" (*Trial*, pp. 109–10).

This business of pre-pleading was, however, a very different
matter from the right to see a copy of the indictment, which was
endorsed, if not by statute, by Reformation ideals of reading for
oneself and other proto-Enlightenment beliefs. On the pre-pleading,
Sidney had been fatally misled by his study of Lilburne's trial,[29] and
had apparently failed to notice that when Vane tried the same
strategy and was driven to plead notwithstanding, he had lost the
early initiative by excepting haphazardly and by self-incrimination.
Writing to Hampden with Vane's trial as published by Sikes open in
front of him, Sidney said that it was there decided that "a man
[may] plead a double plea, and give in his exceptions . . . this you
may find in his triall pg: 29, and if you have not the book I send it to
you."[30] Given what I have described above, this was a serious
instance of misreading legal history, if not the law itself. Sidney also
made a mistake of timing during the arraignment by calling
attention to Vane's trial as a precedent, for Jeffreys then went out
and studied it, to cruel effect when the trial proper began.[31] When
Sidney wrote his *Apology*, he attributed this failure of strategy to his
lack of legal knowledge and the denial of counsel:

Being driven upon theis extremityes by the violence and fraude of the chief

---

[28] Burnet, *History of My Own Time*, 2:401.
[29] See Scott, *Algernon Sidney and the Restoration Crisis*, pp. 311–12.
[30] Sidney's letter to Hamden, No. 6, cited by Scott, p. 312.
[31] "And because you did particularly take notice of the case of Sir Henry Vane last time, I will
shew you the court did indulge more to you, than was done to that person . . . You had the
indictment read to you in latin; which was denied in the case of sir Henry Vane" (p. 113).

justice, whoe threatened, that judgement of treason should be immediately
entered, if I did not come to the generall issue, I was forced to plead not
guilty, and theareby lost the advantage, which was never to be recovered,
unless the judges could have bin changed.[32]

Not until 1751, then, when Richard Baron included the *Apology* in
his new edition of the *Discourses*, could readers see the Sidneian
document that matched, in tone and purpose, the "Reasons for
arrest of judgement" that Vane had written and Sikes had published
a century earlier – that is, the critique of the trial he had received
and the articulation of the principles by which it must be found
unjust. During his trial, Sidney, like Vane, had been prevented from
making a final address to the jury. "Nay, Mr. Sydney," said Jeffreys,
"we must not have vying and revying . . . after the king's counsel
have concluded, we never admit the prisoner to say anything"
(p. 155). That "never," of course, ignored the precedents of Throckmorton and Lilburne. And Sidney replied, "it was a wise man said,
there never could be too much delay in the life of a man." Which
wise man was that, one wonders, Lilburne or Throckmorton? In the
Apology Sidney several times complained of the frequent interruptions
he had suffered, and returned to the injustice of being denied
counsel and a copy of the indictment, in language that made clear
how broadly the issue was to be interpreted. This is a long passage,
but by the same standards Sidney hoped for from his judges and
jurors, it deserves our continued attention:

Mr. Atturney [Sir Robert Sawyer, Knt.] had then so much confidence, and
soe littell charity, as openly to avow, that I should not have councell, lest
they should furnish or teach me the points of lawe that I might insist on.
This appeared strange unto all thoes who have any knowledge of the lawes
of God or man, and that are not equaly deprived of charity and humanity.
*The obtaining of justice is the end of the lawe, and truth the rule of it: hereupon it is
agreed by mankinde, that every man ought to know his accusation, that he may know to
direct his deffence, or receave advice, if he be ignorant in it.* It is an absurd perversion
of all lawe, to say, that I heard it read; when it was rendered soe long and
intricate, that neither I, nor any other man, was, upon reading, able to
comprehend it. One of the worst acts that were imputed unto Caligula, the
worst and basest of men, was, that he caused edicts to be written in a hand,
and set up in a place where no man could read them: hereby turned the
lawe into a snare, and destroyed thoes whoe did not conforme themselves
unto the rule they never knew. They fall under the same condemnation
whoe make accusations obscure, and suffer them not to be examined, least

---

[32] "The Apology of A. Sydney in the day of his death," in *Discourses* (1763), p. 174.

they should be understood. To evade this, my prosecutors falsely pretend, that noe such privilege is allowed to prisoners in England. But, besides that naturall and universal rule of justice, which can be overruled by noe municipall law, I did produce the stat. of 46 Ed. III, which doth plainely enact, that all men, in all cases, wheather they be such as fall out against the king, or any others, shall have coppy of such records as are against them; and shewed, that the parliament, whoes example all other courts ought to followe, had allowed unto the earl of Strafford, the earl of Danby, the lord Stafford, and the popisch lords now in the Tower, coppyes of their indictement: and, if it had bin pretended, that such a priviledge was allowed only unto peeres, I was ready to say, *that though I am not a peere, I am of the wood of which they are made, and doe not find, that our ancestors were lesse carefull of the lives of commoners, then of peeres, or that one lawe is made for them, and another for us.* (pp. 174–75; Hollis's italics)

Of course there are disingenuities here, not the least being Sidney's stress on his ignorance of the law, when he had spent at least three months studying it (however ineffectively). And to say, as he had at the opening of his arraignment, "I never was at a tryal in my life of any body, and never read a law-book" (p. 108) was a bare-faced lie. But the point of this speech, which Sidney had *not* been "ready," or permitted, to deliver at his trial, was to broaden the argument rhetorically, in ways of which Lilburne would have approved. In a single paragraph, which could only be read when the times had changed again, Sidney was able to articulate the old rule of legal intelligibility side by side with an as yet unheard-of principle of equality before the law; to merge natural law theory ("that naturall and universal rule of justice, which can be overruled by noe municipall law") with both statute law and ancient constitutionalism, the latter being implied in that appeal to "our ancestors." And all these supposedly different bases of political thought are further merged in that brilliant use of the first person plural where, given Sidney's arrogance, we might least expect it: "I doe not find . . . that one lawe is made for them, and another for *us*."

Most importantly, however, Sidney was able to return in the *Apology* to the appalling dictum that *scribere est agere.* Cut off as he was by Jeffreys when he attempted to cite the more reasonable policies of even the Spanish Inquisition, Sidney returned to this theme:

That noe tribunall did ever take notice of a man's private, crude, undigested thoughts: that, though the inquisition is the worst and most bloody tribunall that hath bin known in the world, I never feared to writte what I pleased against the religion there professed, when I lived under it. (*Apology*, p. 179).

And in the *Last Paper* also, while maintaining the pretence that the *Discourses* were a treatise written decades earlier in merely theoretical response to Filmer, he made a simple claim for equivalent treatment:

If he might publish to the world his opinion . . . I know not why I might not have published my opinion to the contrary, without the breach of any law I have yet known. I might, *as freely as he, publicly have declared my thoughts, and the reasons upon which they are grounded.*[33]

And he then proceeded to summarize his republican principles.

Eventually, of course, by producing the *Last Paper* and the *Apology*, and with the support of Ducasse, of John Toland, of Richard Baron and Thomas Hollis, Sidney was enabled to publish his political thought and its consequences to himself side by side. And the 1763 edition, for which Hollis was responsible, added a further layer of interpretation; for Sidney's life, letters and *Apology* (though not the *Discourses* themselves, which he left in Baron's format) were richly annotated by Hollis with passages from Milton, Marvell, Ludlow's *Memoirs*, Neville's *Plato redivivus*, Burnet, Temple, Trenchard, etc. In this apparatus Milton's sonnet to Cromwell and Vane and Restoration satires attributed to Marvell stood on equal footing with formal political theory, history and polemical tracts. This was putting ideas in context – in cultural context – with a conviction we might do well to follow.

And one of the most striking insertions, whose importance we will see more clearly at the end of chapter 7, was Hollis's penultimate intervention in the Sidney legend. At the end of the *Apology*, Sidney returned to the theme of justice perverted, using his trial as a prophetic instance of worse to come:

The chiefe justice having performed this exploit, is sayd to have bragged unto the king, that noe man in his place had ever rendered unto any king of England such services as he had done, in making it to passe for lawe, that any man might be now tryed by a jury not consisting of freeholders; and that one witnesse, with any concurrent circumstance (as that of buying the knife), was sufficient to convict him . . . whereby the lawe itself was made a snare, which noe man could avoide, nor having any security for his life or fortune, if one vile wretch could be found to sweare against him such circumstances as he required. (*Apology*, p. 8)

This whole passage was italicized by Hollis, who, after Sidney's recall of Richard II's similar abuses, and his appeal to God to rescue

---

[33] Cited from Hollis's edition, p. 38.

his people from the current ones, also italicized Sidney's distinction between the 1380s and the 1680s:

I dye in the faith that he will doe it, though I know not the time or wayes; and am soe much the more confident he will doe it, that his cause, and his people is more concerned now than it was in former time. The lust of one man and his favyrites was then only to be set up in the exercise of an arbitrary power over persons and states; *but now, the tyranny over consciences is principally affected, and the civill powers are stretched unto this exorbitant height, for the establishment of popery. (pp. 196–97)

And at the asterisk Hollis inserted a huge quotation from the opening of Marvell's *Account of the Growth of Popery and Arbitrary Government in England*; thereby explaining, once again, the binary structure of the Good Old Cause.

Hollis almost certainly sent a copy of Baron's 1751 edition to Harvard, and he certainly sent them a copy of his own edition, which is there still, with his inscription on the flyleaf:

Thomas Hollis, an Englishman, a Lover of Liberty, his Country, and its excellent Constitution, as nobly restored at the happy Revolution, is desirous of having the honour to deposit this book in the public library of Harvard College . . . ap. 14, 1763.[34]

Having ordered twenty copies from Millar for such purposes, he also sent one, and perhaps several, to Jonathan Mayhew, who distributed them "agreeably to your Directions, and my best Discretion."[35] In my last chapter we will see what use John Adams was to make of "reading Sidney." At Winterthur there is a portrait of Adams's friend Benjamin Rush, surgeon-general in Washington's army, and one of the signers of the Declaration of Independence. When Charles Wilson Peale painted the portrait, probably as soon as the war was over, he portrayed him as a philosopher in his study surrounded by his books; and one of those books is Algernon's Sidney's *Discourses concerning Government*.[36]

"It was never more necessary," Blackburne had remarked in his commentary on Hollis's edition, "than it has been within these last seventeen years, to *let such men as Sydney speak for themselves*" (*Memoirs*, 1:188; italics added). Returned to court for his sentencing, Sidney

---

[34] See Chester Noyes Greenough, "Algernon Sidney and the Motto of the Commonwealth of Massachusetts," in *Collected Studies* (Cambridge, Mass., 1940), p. 81.

[35] Greenough, p. 82, citing Hollis Papers, p. 25.

[36] See Wayne Craven, *Colonial American Portraiture: The Economic, Religious, Social, Cultural, Philosophical, Scientific, and Aesthetic Foundations* (Cambridge, 1986), pp. 395–99.

had cried aloud (for once interrupting Jeffreys): "I must appeal to
God and the world. I am not heard"; and Jeffreys had callously
replied, "Appeal to whom you will" (p. 167). That the appeal was, in
fact, successfully made, especially in the American colonies, has
been well established;[37] and in 1791 the American Bill of Rights
suggests that at least on the other side of the Atlantic its legal
implications, particularly, had been heard. The legend of Sidney's
martyrdom came to be seen as part of the *American* national myth,
appearing in one of Herman Melville's novels, *White-Jacket*, as a
weapon against the penal laws of the American navy:

They are an importation from abroad, even from Britain, whose laws we
Americans hurled off as tyrannical, and yet retained the most tyrannical of
all . . . [they] had their congenial origin in a period of the history of Britain
when the Puritan Republic had yielded to a monarchy restored; when a
hangman like Judge Jeffreys sentenced a world's champion like Algernon
Sidney to the block.[38]

---

[37] See Houston, *Algernon Sidney and the Republican Heritage in England and America*, pp. 223–78.
Houston's point, that "to the colonists, the single most important fact about Sidney's life
was the manner of his death," is well taken. But he also carefully documents the fluctuations
in Sidney's reputation in America before 1760, during the Stamp Act crisis, during the
Revolutionary and Constitutionalist periods, and during the slavery debates.

[38] Cited by Houston, p. 274.

CHAPTER 5

Anecdotes

We all know, or think we know, what an anecdote is, and in disciplines that assume or aspire to the scientific use of evidence the value of the anecdote has for two centuries been low. In the late twentieth century, the aspirations of history to scientificity have risen, as witness the respect for statistics in social history, the lost prestige of intellectual history, and the avoidance in political history of large theoretical generalizations. Accordingly the phrase, "only anecdotal," which has always implied unreliable information, has a comforting meaning in history, as it does also in law and medicine, conveying the notion that beyond the anecdotal lies objective and neatly serried fact. As for philosophy, including political philosophy, the invariably *specific* anecdote might be assumed to be completely alien to its generalizing goals and abstracting procedures.

Yet there are signs within these disciplines, at the theoretical or analytical level, that the assumptions demanding the exclusion of the anecdotal from legitimate evidence are again up for interrogation. In *Doctors' Stories*, Kathryn Hunter remarks that whereas physicians today are likely to associate medical anecdotes "with unenlightened, prescientific practice," early modern medicine, like historiography, recognized the importance of single cases. Thus Sir Thomas Syden-ham's case histories in the seventeenth century were themselves a reform of "a practice so tied to theory that physical examination was rarely undertaken and diagnosis by mail was widespread." In the next reform, however, physiological studies and pathological correla-tions took over from single clinical accounts and "ultimately enabled physicians to correct and extend their understanding of disease and its treatment."[1] Medical history, like the history of historiography,

---

[1] Kathryn Hunter, *Doctors' Stories: The Narrative Structure of Medical Knowledge* (Princeton, 1991), pp. 71–72. I owe this reference to Diane Sadoff, who herself encountered it in connection with work on that notorious story-teller, Sigmund Freud.

shows that the relation between individualization and generalization is in constant need of inspection; and it too is perhaps on the verge of a correction in favor of the anecdotal. Apart from their mnemonic value in medical education, anecdotes are useful, Hunter suggests, "not only in locating research problems but also in keeping alive a skepticism about new knowledge claims in a hierarchical, authoritarian discipline. As rough accounts of the unexpected and occasionally the improbable, they are frequently the as-yet-unorganized evidence at the forefront of clinical medicine" (p. 75). And she concludes with a message therapeutic to other disciplines than her own:

Anecdotes represent and preserve the recognition of [the] intractable particularity of the individual . . . the irreducible knot at the center of a discipline of human knowledge . . . (p. 82)

Some of the pressure has been coming, of course, from the various attempts in literary studies to reinflect that discipline with historical knowledge. The so-called New Historicism pioneered by Stephen Greenblatt is perhaps only recognizable as a movement by its reliance on the colorful anecdote, which (precisely because of these new-historical claims) can provoke protests from conservative literary critics. Thus Brian Vickers, after reproaching Greenblatt for misusing the anthropological techniques of Clifford Geertz, remarks: "The dangers of this elevation of the anecdotal to a central status are clear, encouraging as it does the use of interesting little stories not as ornaments to the text but as load-bearing props in the argument, a role to which they are unsuited."[2] While Vickers's complaint is ostensibly procedural ("the New Historicists seldom declare what status they are claiming for the 'cultural samples' on display, an opportunistic silence which leaves their readers unable to know what weight to give this anecdotal material" (p. 228), his language seems infected by the contempt that has attached to the anecdote since its formal existence was recognized.

My own interest in the anecdote differs in principle from the New Historicists, if we may, for heuristic purposes only, imagine them as a collective. Whereas Greenblatt and others tended to choose their anecdotes from widely disparate sources, and to use them as *symptoms* of how early modern society conceived of itself, I am interested rather in how early modern writers chose their own anecdotes, and

---

[2] See Brian Vickers, *Appropriating Shakespeare* (New Haven and London, 1993), p. 229.

used them as *symbols* of their own social analysis and concerns. The theoretical difference resides in the degree of intentionality and self-consciousness attributed to those from the past whom we try to understand; the procedural difference resides in the fact that, while my choice of anecdotes is selective, it is rendered less arbitrary by the fact that those who related them engaged in a prior act of selection.

But there is a further difference between the topic of this chapter and the renewed attention now being paid to the anecdote as a tool or trope of cultural analysis. I focus here exclusively on one kind of anecdote – the historiographical – as distinct, for example, from those imported by New Historicists from anthropology. By "historio-graphical" I mean not only that the original context in which the anecdote appears was, intentionally and formally, a history of some kind; but also that, in its origins, "anecdote" was recognized as a category of historiography, one that became of special importance in early modern England.

In Francis Blackburne's *Memoirs of Thomas Hollis* there appears a provocative allusion to one of Milton's sonnets, the one addressed to Lady Margaret Ley:

A modern retailer of *historical anecdotes* seems desirous to have it thought, upon his own authority, that there was a connection of gallantry between Milton and the Lady Margaret Lee; and he seems willing to have it understood, that Milton's backwardness to receive his repentant wife was owing to an intrigue with that lady. *A man must have a strange appetite for secret history* to advance such a suspicion in the face of so fair an account as has been given of Milton's intercourse with that Lady and her husband by Mr. Philips his nephew.[3]

Today's reader will not necessarily recognize the connection Black-burne makes between "historical anecdotes" and "secret history." Yet in early modern Europe anecdotes were connected to "secret history" both etymologically and by way of certain models of history-writing. In England in the later seventeenth and eighteenth centuries "secret history" became a genre to be reckoned with, one complex enough to subdivide and miscegenate while still remaining recognizable. In one of its branches (the one alluded to by Black-burne) secret history collapsed into sexual scandal for the sake of erotic titillation. In another, it produced scandalous courtly or political *roman à clef*, intended to damage the reputations of the

---

[3] Francis Blackburne, *Memoirs of Thomas Hollis* (London, 1780), p. 518 (italics added).

barely concealed protagonists. In the third, and the one with which this chapter is concerned, secret history became a serious vehicle of alternative or counter-history, dedicated to the revelation of what society as a whole, or at least those responsible for its regulation, would prefer not to have revealed. Blackburne, not incidentally, was addicted to anecdotes; but in this instance he found himself on the other side of the ideological divide, rejecting the "secret history" of Milton's marital life as a slur on the high-minded republicanism of his and Thomas Hollis's ideal. Yet he would certainly have approved of that other kind of secret history whose concerns were national and international politics, and which in England was more frequently deployed by those on the left of center than by their opponents.

The relationship between secret history and the anecdote was originally, as I have said, etymological, rather than structural. Derived from *anecdota*, the Greek word for "things unpublished" (or, interestingly, with respect to women, "not given in marriage") "anecdote" and its cognates entered historiography with the writing, *c.* 550 A.D., of Procopius' *Anecdota*, subsequently known as the *Secret History*. Procopius himself called the work *Anecdota*, indicating that he knew it was unpublishable, though presumably intended for quiet manuscript circulation. First mentioned by Suidas in the tenth century, the *Anecdota* remained in manuscript until discovered early in the seventeenth century in the Vatican Library by Alemanni, the papal librarian, and edited by him in 1623 under the title of *Arcana historia*. One can infer, but not necessarily agree with, its modern reputation from the Loeb edition of 1935, where we are informed that Procopius' "avowed purpose" here:

was to tell the whole unvarnished truth which he had not deemed wise to set down in the seven books of the *Histories*; these had already been published and broadcast throughout the Empire . . . [But here] The interest of Procopius has shifted suddenly from events to persons, and his one purpose comes to be to impugn the motives of Justinian and of the able Belisarius, and to cover with the vilest slander the Empress Theodora and Antonina, the wife of Belisarius.[4]

And, the editor added tartly, "The *Secret History* has been translated into modern languages by several hands, sometimes anonymously and with the manifest purpose of exploiting the salacious tone of

---

[4] *Procopius*, tr. H. B. Dewing, 7 vols. (London, 1928), 1:vi–vii.

some of its passages" (1:xxi). Thus Procopian secret history is dismissed as completely unreliable slander, confirmed by its interest in sex in high places.

The first modern language translation of Procopius occurred in France, a *Histoire secrète*, in 1669, and a whole tradition of French secret history followed. As Erica Harth explained, the classical model immediately merged with the newly fashionable *nouvelles* which replaced the ornate romances of de Scudéry, and which poured from underground presses in the aftermath of the Fronde. What Harth calls French "pseudo-history" was a direct response to the new court style of Louis XIV and his assumption of personal rule. Versailles excluded from the royal councils those nobles who had participated in the Fronde, kept tight ministerial control over state secrets, promoted and regulated the production of official history by court historiographers and gave plenty of scope for prurient speculation about the amours of the king and his entourage. "Excluded from history by the strategies of absolutism," wrote Harth, the public, both nobles and bourgeois, turned to the subversive genre of pseudo-history.[5] By 1685 this trend had actually been theorized by Antoine Varillas, whose *Anecdotes de Florence, ou L'Histoire secrète de la maison de Médicis*, published at the Hague in 1685, explained in its preface both the methods and the dangers incurred by the secret historian. According to Harth, whose term, "pseudo-history," also implies a judgment against Procopianism, the importance of this French version of secret history lay in its transmutation, soon to occur, into the novel. And while she observed that the "newer fiction clearly presented both a moral and a political threat," she implied that its political subversiveness resided exclusively in its sexual charge. "By pretending to peer into the hearts and boudoirs of the great, [it] suggested that history's leaders were just like everyone else, if not worse" (p. 152).

In England, however, the evolution of Procopian history was rather different. The first English translation of the classical model appeared in 1674.[6] The translator remained anonymous; no doubt because of the parallel inevitably suggested at that time between Justinian and Charles II. Here is his rendering of Procopius' original introduction:

[5] Erica Harth, *Ideology and Culture in Seventeenth-Century France* (Ithaca and London, 1983), pp. 147–53.
[6] *The Secret History of the Court of the Emperor Justinian* (London: for John Barkesdale, 1674).

Nothing excited me so strongly to this work, as that such persons who are
desirous to govern in an Arbitrary way, might discover, by the misfortune of
those whom I mention, the destiny that attends them, and the just
recompence they are to expect of their crimes. (Sig. B1)

Two years later the term "anecdote" appeared for the first time in
the English language, in one of Andrew Marvell's polemical pamphlets, *Mr. Smirke, or the Divine in Mode*, itself published anonymously;
the context was Charles II's Declaration of Breda before his return
to England, and what had happened to those early promises once he
was back on the throne.[7]

In 1686 Varillas's *Anecdotes de Florence* were promptly translated for
English readers by Ferrand Spence, just a year after their appearance
in France. Judging by Spence's dedication, this too was apparently to
be understood in terms of contemporary English political history.[8]
But perhaps more importantly, Varillas's preface, also translated,
now offered the first theoretical defence in English of *anecdota* as
alternative history with rules of its own. It spoke of "the sad Destiny
of *Anecdota*, that cannot indure anything mysterious, shou'd be left to
Posterity without explaining it" (Sig. a6). And it provided a distinction between publishable and unpublishable history in terms of the
facts selected for emphasis:

The Historian considers almost ever Men in Publick, whereas the
Anecdoto-grapher only examines 'em in private. Th'one thinks he has
perform'd his duty, when he draws them such as they were in the Army, or
in the tumult of Cities, and th'other endeavours by all means to get open
their Closet-door; th'one sees them in Ceremony, and th'other in
Conversation; th'one fixes principally upon their Actions, and th'other

---

[7] Marvell, *Complete Works*, ed. A. B. Grosart (New York, 1875; repr. 1966), 4:70–71: "For that of
the Savoy, in which he instances, it might almost as well have been in Piedmont. A man
disinteressed either way, might make a pleasant story of the anecdota of that meeting, and
manifest how well his Majesties gracious Declaration, before his return, and his broad seal
afterwards were pursued."

[8] Spence dedicated his translation to Henry, earl of Pembroke, by mistake for Thomas, eighth
earl of Pembroke, who succeeded to the title in 1683, and whose career is alluded to in the
dedication. Created Lord-Lieutenant of Wiltshire at the same time, Pembroke raised the
militia of his county against Monmouth in 1585, in return for which he received a bounty of
£1000 in the late summer. But Pembroke's cooperation with James's government ceased in
1687, when he refused to assist in "regulating" the municipal corporations, and was
dismissed. After the Revolution, to which he promptly transferred his allegiance, he was
reappointed, and carried the sword of justice at the coronation. Spence's dedication had
encouraged Pembroke to note that "these Anecdota may, perchance, by some Gentlemen,
be tax'd with containing Reflections, injurious to a Soveraign House; but . . . what Stem,
however Holy, what Dignities and Offices, however August and Sacred, but have been
tarnish'd by unworthy Members."

wou'd be a Witness of their inward Life, and assist at the most private hours of their leisure. (Sig. a5)

The presence of both "anecdote" and "secret history" in the English historiographical consciousness might now be seen as established; and by the middle of the next century, Chambers' *Cyclopedia* provided the following definition: "*Anecdotes, anecdota,* a term used by some authors, for the titles of Secret Histories; that is, of such as relate the secret affairs and transactions of princes; speaking with too much freedom, or too much sincerity, of the manner and conduct of persons in authority, to allow of their being made public." It is worth noticing, however, that the *Cyclopedia* makes no mention of sexual scandal; responding, no doubt, to the evolution of English political secret history in the late seventeenth and early eighteenth century.

From this sequence of events in the publishing and in the political world came the stigma that now hangs around the *idea* of the anecdote as something unreliable in history as a practice; if not actually scandalous and underhanded, the move that dares not speak its name, then unverifiable, unscientific and self-indulgently gossipy. Hence the pun attributed to John Wilkes, whereby writers entered their "anecdotage." The anecdote, of course, gradually migrated into many other forms of communication, while secret history only occasionally remembered their serendipitous relationship. And yet the two seem to have retained (or developed) a genuine affinity for each other. While not every secret history deploys the anecdote, so many of them do, and in so striking a manner, that we may, after surveying the evidence, begin to speculate about what such an affinity might mean. The first of this pair of chapters will sketch a theory of the anecdote as an item of historiographical practice; and I will then illustrate its presence, or its ghosts, in the liberal secret histories of the early modern period.

THE ANECDOTE IN TUDOR HISTORIOGRAPHY

How far back should the enquiry begin? To rephrase a famous anecdote about what supports the earth (first an elephant, and then tortoises all the way down) it is anecdotes all the way back. While the *term* and its definition appeared in Europe only during the seventeenth century, common sense alone would indicate that the *practice* of anecdotal reporting, especially in a historiographical context, did not have to await the recovery of Procopius. Joel Fineman found it in Thucydides, and, interestingly in the light of *Doctors' Stories*, connected Thucydides' practice as a historian with the medical case histories of Hippocrates.[9]

I choose to begin with the late sixteenth century in England. There is a strong though minor strain of the anecdotal in the major Tudor chronicles (well before the term "anecdote" came into circulation), which is symptomatic of the chroniclers' desire to render the texture of political life as more eccentric and irregular than official policy desires; or, as Fineman would put it more philosophically, to open up a hole in the *grand récit* through which one can actually see history happen.

Tudor chroniclers employed mini-narratives that *we* would now call anecdotes, which had a good deal (but not everything) in common with the "secret history" later derived from Procopius. Read as deliberate insertions, rather than a sign of the chroniclers' lack of discipline or garrulity, these anecotes reveal an agenda which runs, if not exactly counter to the stories of kings and battles, laws and punishments, in energetic counterpoint to it. Though by no means always concerned with the private lives of the powerful – the definition that Varillas gave of *anecdota* – the anecdotes deployed in the chronicles were the symptoms and signals of resistance to the generalizing and ordering impulses, both in historiography and in the societies history tends to monumentalize. They tend to feature those on society's outskirts: rebels, victims, tricksters, women. And one of their most effective strategies is a startling and often (it may seem to us) incongruous display of humor.

---

[9] Joel Fineman, "The History of the Anecdote: Fiction and Friction," in *The New Historicism*, ed. H. Aram Veeser (London, 1989), pp. 49–76. In this characteristically brilliant and chaotic essay, Fineman threw out several insights about the historiographical anecdote, but spoiled them with psychoanalytical and deconstructive jargon. See especially p. 61, where the insight that the anecdote "is the literary form that *lets history happen* by virtue of the way it introduces an opening into the teleological" collapses into the following mixed metaphors:
the opening of history that is effected by the anecdote, the hole and rim – using psychoanalytic language, the orifice – traced out by the anecdote within the totalizing whole of history, is something that is characteristically and ahistorically plugged up by a teleological narration that, though larger than the anecdote itself, is still constitutively inspired by the seductive opening of anecdotal form – thereby opening up the possibility, but again, *only* the possibility, that this new narration, now complete within itself, and thereby rendered formally small – capable therefore, of being anecdotalized – will itself be opened up by a further anecdotal operation, thereby calling forth some yet larger circumcising circumscription, and so, so on and so forth" (italics original). We seem to be back with "Doctors' stories," the doctors being Freud and Lacan.

Fineman emphasized the special status of the anecdote at the intersection of the literary and the real. His remarks are worth quoting, as a point from which to proceed:

The anecdote . . . as the narration of a single event, is the literary form or genre that uniquely refers to the real . . . the anecdote has something literary about it [but] . . . there is something about the anecdote that exceeds its literary status, and this excess is precisely that which gives the anecdote its pointed, referential access to the real . . . These two features . . . allow us to think of the anecdote . . . as a *historeme*, i.e. as the smallest minimal unit of the historiographic fact. And the question that the anecdote thus poses is how, compact of both literature and reference, the anecdote possesses its peculiar and eventful narrative force.[10]

Fineman did not, I think, answer his own question; but reading the Tudor chronicles may be a better route to an answer than those he chose. Anecdotes in the Tudor chronicles are brief, independent narratives about individual human behavior, individual in the sense that the behavior narrated appears to interrogate the system – legal, economic, social, sexual. The story is short enough to be emblematic, independent enough of its surroundings to be portable; that is to say, relocatable from one chronicle to another, from a chronological to an achronological spot, from one style or even one ideological perspective to another. Sometimes the protagonists are "historical" figures in the conventional sense, though caught in an unusual posture, sometimes they are nameless; but their independence of spirit, their refusal to be absorbed into the unifying texture of a grand narrative, is evident nonetheless. The better anecdotes convey character with economical sharpness, and contain snatches of conversation, whose verisimilitude is a key to their memorability, the cause of their having remained in the cultural memory. The best anecdotes function as symbolic paradigms of large and complex issues.

In order to illustrate these claims, I have chosen three anecdotes from different sources, each of which relates directly to the problems released into society by the Reformation. Each bears a certain thematic relationship with major themes of secret history, as these will evolve in the next chapter. The first appears in Edward Hall's chronicle, published in 1548. Hall tells how in 1529/30 Cuthbert Tunstall, bishop of London, was so bent on suppressing William

---

[10] Fineman, "The History of the Anecdote," pp. 56–57; italics original.

Tyndale's translation of the New Testament that he was actually inveigled into financing its second edition. The story is so brilliantly told by Hall that I shall cite it almost in entirety:

the bishop of London . . . debated with himself, how he might compasse and devise, to destroy that false and erronious translation, (as he saide). And so it happened that one Augustine Packington, a Mercer and Merchant of London, and of a great honestie, the same tyme was in Andwarp, where the Bishop then was, and this Packyngton was a man that highly favored William Tindale, but to the bishop utterly shewed himself to the contrary. The bishop desirous to have his purpose brought to passe, commoned of the New Testamentes, and how gladly he would bye them.

Packington then offered to act as an intermediary in such a purchase, adding "if it be your lordshippes pleasure, to pay for them, for otherwise I cannot come by them, but I must disburse money for theim," and promised to buy up every available copy.

The Bishop thinking that he had God by the too, when in deede he had (as he after thought) the Devell by the fist, saied, gentle Master Packington, do your diligence and get them and with all my harte I will paie for them, whatsoever thei cost you, for the bokes are erroneous and naughtes and I entend surely to destroy them all, and to burne theim all at Paules Crosse.[11]

In its first scene, then, the anecdote uncoils as a fable of outfoxing, with the reader's sympathies carefully aligned with the honest Protestant fox who conceals his sympathies. Hall's use of parentheses here is particularly telling, creating irony around the issue of contested biblical exegesis ("that false and erronious translation, (as he saide)"), and folk humor in that proverbial and irreverent vision of "the Bishop thinking that he had God by the too, when in deede he had (as he after thought) the Devell by the fist." There is a wonderful impression of conversational verisimilitude as Packington raises the question of money, it seems apologetically. One would think that the story could hardly get better; but it does:

Augustine Packyngton came to William Tyndale and saied, Willyam I knowe thou are a poor man, and hast a hepe of newe Testamentes, and bokes by thee, for the whiche thou hast both indaungered thy frendes, and beggered thyself, and I have now gotten thee a Merchaunt, whiche with ready money shall dispatche thee of all that thou hast, if you thinke it so proffitable for your self. Whow is the Merchant saide Tindale? The

[11] Edward Hall, *The Union of the Two Noble & Illustre Famelies of Lancastre & Yorke*, ed. Henry Ellis (London, 1809; repr. New York, 1965), pp. 762–63.

bishoppe of London saied Packyngton, O that is because he will burne them saied Tyndale, ye Mary qd Packyngton, I am the gladder said Tyndale, for these two benefites shall come thereof, I shall get money of hym for these bokes, to bring my self out of debt (and the whole world shall cry out upon the burning of Goddes worde). And the overplus of the money, that shall remain to me, shall make me more studious, to correct thesaid New Testament, and so newly to Imprint thesame once again, and I trust the second will much better like you, then ever did the first.

This elegant example of spiritualized capitalism (which Weber would have admired) is successful for the foxes, and even, in a sense, for the wolf. "And so forward went the bargain, the bishop had the bokes, Packyngton had the thankes, and Tyndale had the money." The clever structure of this sentence itself conveys unusual enjoyment. But, as Tyndale had promised, the *new* New Testaments were promptly published, in 1534, and came "thicke and threfold into England." So Tunstall sent for Packington again, and Scene 3 of the comedy begins:

Sir how commeth this, that there are so many New Testamentes abrode, and you promised and assured me, that you had bought al? then saied Packyngton, I promes you I bought all that was then to be had: but I perceive they have made more sence, and it will never be better, as long as they have the letters and stampes, therfore it wer best for your lordeshippe, to bye the stampes to, and then are you sure: the bishop smiled at him and said, well Packyngton well, and so ended this matter.

Within its own frame this anecdote is a comedy of tricksterism in a good cause. It seems to support the modern estimation of Tunstall as a moderate, who hoped by burning bibles to avoid the need for burning heretics. But beyond its narrative frame lie two horrific sequels: Tyndale's execution for heresy in the Low Countries in October 1536, and the murder of Packington's brother in 1537. Were these coincidences? A secret historian would doubt it. Tyndale was betrayed to the Imperial officers by a young Englishman, Henry Phillips, who in May 1535 had insinuated himself into his confidence, much as Packington had dealt with Tunstall, but with graver consequences. No direct evidence that he was the instrument of an ecclesiastical plot against Tyndale has ever been discovered, but his accomplice was an English priest, Gabriel Donne, who was subsequently appointed abbot of Buckfastleigh in Devon.

Robert Packington, who was mysteriously shot to death in London not long after Tyndale's execution, was part of the same family as Augustine, a family noted in Henrician London for their active Protestantism.[12] Hall does not make this suggestion directly, but the way he tells the story of Robert's murder seems related to that of Augustine, at least in the use of circumstantial detail, to an extent that official history would find excessive:

In this yere (1536) one Robert Packyngton, Mercer of London, a man of good substaunce, and yet not so riche as honest and wise, this man dwelled in Chepeside at the signe of the legg, and used daily at foure of the clock Winter and Sommer to rise and go to Masse at a churche then called saint Thomas of Acres (but now named the Mercers chapel) and one mornyng emong all other, beyng a great Mistie morning such as hath seldome be sene, even as he was crossing the strete from his house to the churche, he was sodenly murdered with a gonne, whiche of the neighbors was playnly harde, and by a great nombre of laborers at the same tyme standyng at Soper lane ende, he was both sene go furth of his house, and also the clap of gonne was harde, but the dede doer was never espied nor knowen, many were suspected, but none could be found fauty. (p. 825)

Hall believed that there was an ecclesiastical conspiracy in *this* case at least; for, he continued:

howbeit it is true, that for asmuch as he was knowen to be a man of great courage and one that both could speake & also woulde be harde [heard]: and that thesame tyme he was one of the Burgeses of the parliament, for the Citie of London, and had talked somewhat against the covetousnes and crueltie of the Clergie, he was had in contempt with theim, and therefore mooste lyke by one of theim thus shamefully murdered.[13]

Raphael Holinshed transplanted the story of Robert Packington's murder into his *Chronicles*, carefully rewriting it as he went. When he came to Hall's conspiracy theory, Holinshed was slightly more circumspect. "Albeit," he wrote, "forsomuch as he was one that would speake his mind freelie, and was at the same time one of the burgesses of the parlement for the citie of London, and had talked somewhat against the covetousnesse and crueltie practised by the

---

[12] For the Packingtons, and their connections through the intensely Protestant Mercers' Company with other reformist families like the Lockes, see Susan Brigden, *London and the Reformation* (Oxford, 1989), pp. 116, 182–220. Robert Packington was the younger brother of Sir John Packington, who had a successful legal career, including the position of chorographer of common pleas, which was regranted to him and "Austin Packington" on October 12, 1525. He was a friend and agent of Thomas Cromwell. See *The House of Commons, 1509–1558* (Packington).

[13] Packington's increasing involvement in parliamentary business for the City of London is detailed in S. T. Bindoff, *The House of Commons 1509–1558* (London, 1982), 3:48–49. He replaced William Bowyer for the last two sessions of the 1529 parliament, and was then probably reelected for that of 1536. He was murdered on November 13, 1536.

cleargie; *it was mistrusted least by some of them he came thus to his end."*[14]
But Holinshed's interest in the story did not end here. With his
characteristic focus on legal history, he supplied a supplement:

> At length the murtherer in deed was condemned at Banburie in Oxford-
> shire, to die for a fellonie which he afterwards committed: and when he
> came to the gallowes on which he had suffered, he confessed that he did
> this murther, and till that time he was never had in anie suspicion thereof.

The mystery of Packington's death was not, however, thereby fully
unpacked, especially since Holinshed did not choose to name the
author of this confession. And the relation of this story to secret
history would seem to have been confirmed by another member of
the Protestant mercantile community, Rose [Hickman] Throckmorton, whose autobiography, written "with her hand" *c.* 1610,
looks back to that secret from the previous generation as one of its
defining features:

> My mother in the dayes of King Henry the 8th came to some light of the
> gospell by meanes of some English books sent privately to her by my fathers
> factours from beyond sea: whereupon she used to call me with my 2 sisters
> into her chamber to read to us out of the same good books very privately
> for feare of troble bicause those good books were then accompted
> hereticall, and a merchant named Paginton who used to bring English
> bybles from beyond sea was slaine with a gun as he went in the streete.[15]

Here two conflicting versions of privacy and secrecy show their
causal connection – the very private reading in the maternal
chamber designed to protect the "good" books and their readers
from political conspiracy played out in violence on the streets.

The next anecdote in my series is also a product of the late
Henrician era. It occurs in the 1587 edition of Holinshed's *Chronicles*,
as merely one item in Francis Thynne's long catalogue of the careers
of English archbishops. This was originally inserted into the second
edition under the year 1586, although the chronological moment the
anecdote recalls was actually 1540. The anecdote has laughter within
it, but it is not told facetiously; on the contrary, we can tell
immediately that it is part of the tragedy of church and state set in
motion by Henry VIII's marital barbarism. We can be confident of

---

[14] Raphael Holinshed, *Chronicles of England, Scotland, and Ireland*, 3 vols. (1577, 1587; rep., six vols., London: J. Johnson *et al.*, 1808; New York, 1965), 3:803.

[15] "Religion and Politics in mid Tudor England through the eyes of an English Protestant Woman: The Recollections of Rose Hickman," ed. Maria Dowling and Joy Shakespeare, *Bulletin of the Institute of Historical Research* 55 (1982), p. 97.

the historicality of its protagonists, being Henry himself and archbishop Cranmer; and Thynne was able to translate it verbatim from
an unexceptionable source, the Latin history of the English archbishops by Matthew Parker, himself a holder of that pastoral office.
But despite its impeccable origins, the anecdote shows "official"
policy in a shameful posture, in need of cover-up; an inference surely
confirmed by the fact that Thynne's catalogue of archbishops was
deleted from the second edition of the *Chronicles*, when the work was
called in by the Privy Council in January 1587.

The anecdote belongs to that late stage in the Henrician Reformation, after the death of Thomas Cromwell and the passing of the
fearsome Six Articles in 1539, when counter-Reformation would be a
more appropriate term. "Some of the nobilitie and councell" who
were religious conservatives attempted to persuade Henry to exclude
Cranmer, as a danger to the old religion, from the Privy Council,
and to send him to the Tower:

> For so long as he sat present in the councell, everie one there would be
> afraid to speak what they knew against him. Wherupon rumors were
> spread, that Cranmer by the *secret* judgement of the king should be
> condemned, and loose his hed, as Cromwell had doone . . . wherfore
> Cranmer *secretlie* with tears bewailed the times, though outwardlie he
> shewed a merie countenance. (4:737; italics added)

Henry, therefore, "perceiving whereunto tended this drift of the
pontificals, (which favored the Roman religion) after supper for
recreations cause tooke barge to row up and downe the Thames,"
and to steer towards Lambeth palace. Informed by some of his men
who stood on Lambeth bridge of the king's approach, Cranmer
"speedilie came to the bridge to salute the king either passing by, or
else to receive him on shore, and to lead him to his house":

> But the king commanded him to come into his bote and to sit downe by
> him, with whom he had long and *secret talke*, the watermen stil hovering
> with the bote on the river. (italics added)

This is indeed, in Thynne's translation, secret history, as the three
"secrets" italicized above make clear, only one of which appears in
Parker's Latin. The king himself, in need of privacy for a delicate
negotiation, has had to move onto water for the purpose – a strategy
used for ecclesiastical lobbying at this time.[16] There was "long and

---

[16] See Eamon Duffy, *The Stripping of the Altars: Traditional Religion in England 1400–1580* (New
Haven and London, 1992), p. 400.

secret talke" between them, the "watermen stil hovering with the bote on the river," and Henry pretended to ask Cranmer's advice about how to identify and capture a dangerous archheretic. This is the game of cat and mouse:

Whereunto Cranmer (although he was in great feare) answered with a good countenance that the same counsell pleased him well, being verie glad to hear thereof, because by the punishment of that archheretike the rest of the flocke of heretikes would be bridled. But with this speech he did yet with a certein fatherlie reverence . . . modestlie admonish the king, that he shuld not judge them to be heretickes, who with the word of God strived against mens traditions. Whereunto the king said; It is rightlie spoken by you, for you are declared to us by manie to be that archhereticke of all our kingdome, who in Kent and in all your province doo so withstand us, that the beleefe of the six articles established in parlement be not received of the common people; wherefore openlie declare unto us what you thinke, and what you have doone of and in the same. Cranmer replied, that he was still of the same mind which he openlie professed himselfe to be at the making of that law [i.e. opposed to it], and that yet he had not offended anie thing since the same was made.

This courageous temporizing evidently strikes the right note:

Then the king somewhat leaving this grave talke, merrilie asked of him, whether his inner and privie bed were free from those articles. To which Cranmer (although he knew it dangerous by that law for priests to have wives, and that he certeinlie understood that the king knew that he was maried) answered, that he contracted that marriage before he was archbishop . . . but now because he would not offend so rigorous a law, he had not touched his wife since the making thereof, because he had presentlie sent hir unto hir freends in Germanie. By which plaine answer he wan such favor with the king, that the king incoraged him to be of good comfort. (4:737)

"Hovering" on the river, itself a wonderful locution for negotiation, king and bishop play out the game of mutual understanding and acceptable speech, in the frame of the dangerous politics of the day.

This anecdote is more sardonic than the previous one, at least on the great unspoken subject of what really motivated the Henrician Reformation. Given the king's own marital history, past and future, a corrosive irony exudes from the sexual register in which Henry has chosen to play this particular set of political tennis. Within its own frame it is, like the Tunstall–Packington rally, also a comedy of manners – political manners – which ends with a reconciliation between wit and threat, temerity and authority; but Cranmer's "good comfort" did not last. As Thynne ironically summed up the end of his larger story pages later, in Mary's reign he too, like Tyndale, "was consumed to ashes": "a death not read before to have happened to anie archbishop, who as he was the first that publikelie impugned by established lawes the popes authoritie in England, so was he the first metropolitane that was burned for the same" (4:744). The elegant structure of this sentence mocks the reversals of ecclesiastical fortune in post-Reformation England, perhaps all the more effectively for the historian's[17] withholding of overt expressions of sympathy and regret. And the entire story thematizes the value of indirection, the need to conceal one's true opinions in a climate of political hypocrisy.

For the third example we turn to John Foxe's *Acts and Monuments*, for a splendid anecdote that adds volumes (pun intended) to the history of the Reformation anecdote. It occurs in the second edition of 1570, where Foxe defended his account in the first edition of Sir John Oldcastle, the Lollard knight who was executed for treason in the early years of the reign of Henry V. Foxe had rejected the hostile accounts of Oldcastle provided by the fifteenth-century monastic chroniclers in favor of John Bale's revisionary if hagiographic version; and here he explains how another Elizabethan chronicler was converted to the same revisionary position. Foxe averred that Hall, as the first major Tudor chronicler, had been wooed away from the traditional assessment of Oldcastle by exposure to Bale's *Brief Chronicle*:

The truth hereof is this, that as the said Edward Hall . . . was about the compiling of his story. . . others there were of the same sodality [i.e. liberal Protestants] who be yet alive, and were then in the house of Richard Grafton, he being both the printer of the said book, and also, it is thought, a great helper of the penning of the same . . . It so befell, that as Hall was entering into the story of sir John Oldcastle . . . the book of John Bale, touching the story of the Lord Cobham, was at the same time newly come over: which book was privily conveyed by one of his servants into the study of Hall, so that in turning over his books it must needs come to his hands. At the sight whereof, when he saw the grounds and reasons in that book

---

[17] Presumably the source of the anecdote was Cranmer himself, who had licensed Parker to preach in 1533. Parker's sympathies in this case may be inferred not only from the tone of the anecdote, but from the fact that he was himself married, and virtually in hiding during Mary's reign as a consequence of his support of Lady Jane Grey. Though aspects of his history of the archbishops infuriated the Puritans, it appears that he was a moderate Reformer.

contained, he turned to the authors in the aforesaid book alleged; whereupon, within two nights after, moved by what cause, I know not, but so it was, that he, taking his pen, rased and cancelled all that he had written before against sir John Oldcastle and his fellows, and which was now ready to go to print, containing near to the quantity of three pages. And . . . the very selfsame first copy of Hall, rased and crossed with his own pen, remaineth in my hands to be shown and seen, as need shall require.[18]

This is a well-told story, fulfilling many of the conditions I originally suggested for anecdotal success. It is replete with the aura of the surreptitious book trade (Bale's *Brief Chronicle* was proscribed in 1546), rich in its intimation of the relation between masters and their more radical servants, and astonishingly strong in circumstantial detail. The book that was "privily conveyed" into Hall's study is the formal sign of Reformation secret history – in this instance, quite literally alternative history; and Foxe has added a theme that will become important both to the anecdote and to secret history generally: the claims of the anecdote to historical truthfulness, even as it "relates" material unverifiable by the usual methods. "The truth hereof is this . . . " begins Foxe, and ends by asserting his personal possession of the crucial document, the scratched-out text of Hall's original account of Oldcastle – which Foxe is willing to produce, "to be shown and seen, as need shall require."

For the anecdote, as a genre or a strategy, combines effects that might be thought of as mutually exclusive or contradictory: the aura of personal knowledge and of oral transmission, of details being passed along to the historian from those, at least in this case, "that be yet alive"; and the claim, implied or explicit, that this material is *more* to be trusted than the written accounts of traditional historiography. In this instance Foxe is trying to straddle the breach between oral and documentary history; the human affect of his anecdote depends primarily on the former, with its capacity for human color and emphasis; the historical effect depends on the way ideas are transmitted between persons, but *by* books, in complicated sequences of transmission.

THE RESTORATION ANECDOTE

On the brink of the first English revolution the Caroline cleric and apologist Peter Heylyn disparaged the Tudor chronicles as "full of

---

[18] John Foxe, *Acts and Monuments*, ed. George Townsend, 8 vols. (London, 1913), p. 261.

confusion and commixture of unworthy relations."[19] On the brink
of the second, Spence's translation of Varillas defined the anecdote
in terms that reverse Heylyn's judgement:

The Writer of *Anecdota* . . . stops sometimes, to glean up such matters as
were neglected and flung aside by the Historian . . . willingly do I leave
him in possession of that fine Maxime of Adrianus Marcellinus, *Discurrere
per Negotiorum Celsitudines non humilium minutias indagare Causarum* . . . but I
pretend likewise to be left in my turn, to enjoy, peaceably, the Priviledge of
Anecdota, and to relate with a serious Air, the smallest trifles, when they have
been th'Origine or occasion of the greatest Matters. (Sig. a7)

Entering the new discursive formation of the Restoration – an
inadequate term to describe the dramatic changes that took place as
much *between* 1660 and 1688 as between the "Commonwealth" and
the "Restoration" – it suddenly becomes clear that the "Priviledge"
of the anecdotal, to use Spence's phrase, has been extended. An
occasional gesture has become a minor genre, peculiarly at home in
the memoirs which themselves became a major genre in the later
decades of the century, but also occasionally migrating into other
"serious" communications such as political theory and epistemology. Anecdotes also seem to be used particularly by, or just as
importantly *about*, writers whom retroactively we have come to
recognize as having some reason to be interested in secret history:
those who set themselves athwart of the Restoration governments of
the day, and whose publications were either surreptitious, posthumous, or in some other way unauthorized. As for secret history
proper, its absorption into the mainstream of Whig historiography,
as well as its durability, was defined by the late eighteenth-century
Secret History of Charles II; and as late as 1832, when self-designated
liberals sought to transcend party boundaries for the sake of
parliamentary reform, a *Secret History of the Court of England* drew the
reigns of the second two Georges into the familiar (but still
unrespectable) pattern.

On February 19, 1661, Locke's friend Robert Crosse wrote to
Locke to request the return of his Procopius.[20] It seems most unlikely
that Locke, the most secretive of personalities, whose letters from his

---

[19] Peter Heylyn, *Microcosmus* (London, 1639).
[20] *The Correspondence of John Locke*, ed. E. S. de Beer, 8 vols. (Oxford, 1976), 1:166. De Beer
thought that this was probably *The History of the Warres of the Emperour Justinian*, but it could
equally have been the *Secret History*.

European hideout are full of coded allusions,[21] and who only published his *Two Treatises on Government* when it was safe to do so after the Revolution, would not have observed the arrival of secret history in Restoration culture.

At any rate, he had certainly encountered a work that became canonical in early modern liberal political thought, Sir William Temple's *Memoirs of What Past in Christendom from the War Begun 1672 to the Peace Concluded 1679*. Temple's *Memoirs*, published posthumously and anonymously in 1691,[22] were a rich source of historical information about Charles II's foreign policy and its sinister influence by France. They were also a rich source of memorable anecdotes. We know that Locke knew Temple's *Memoirs*, because he extracted from them the anecdote about a famous talking parrot, and inserted it into the fourth (1700) edition of the *Essay concerning Human Understanding*.

In Book 2, Chapter 27 of the *Essay* Locke was investigating the philosophical nature of identity, person and self. In order to cut the discussion free from abstract debates about substance and from Aristotelian circularity ("a man is a rational animal") Locke introduces the following test case of the permeable boundary between man and the animals, in the form of "a relation we have in an author of great note to countenance the supposition of a rational parrot." Locke then proceeded to quote verbatim the anecdote told by Temple about how he had heard from Prince Maurice of Nassau of the existence of an old parrot in Brazil "that spoke, and ask'd, and answer'd common questions like a reasonable creature."

---

[21] See, for example, Letter No. 913 From Locke to Van Limborch, 26 Feb/8 Mar. 1687:
There is something more I confess: the fact that I dated my letters with your secret numbers, and that you observed it. Beware then, and pardon my silence as soon as you can, lest I prove a greater nuisance to you with my loquacity; you observe that I am penetrating into your secrets. "They want to know the secrets of the house"– and you remember what follows – "and to be feared for that knowledge." De Beer confessed himself unable to decipher the secret numbers, but identified the source of Locke's quotation: "Scire volunt secreta domus atque inde temeri':' Juvenal, III, 113, 2:143–44.

[22] The *Memoirs* were licensed, November 14, 1691, but presented as a "found" text. However, as the publisher, Richard Chiswell, observes in his brief address to the reader, the author's identity should have been immediately evident from the opening pages. The *Memoirs* were dedicated, with an epistle, "To my Son," declaring it intended only for his eyes. From 1681, when Temple was removed from the Privy Council, he had returned to the status of a private man of letters. An edition of his memoirs and letters was in preparation, with the assistance of Jonathan Swift, from 1689 onwards. The *Memoirs of What Past in Christendom* were actually Part 2 of a three-part work, the first of which Temple himself destroyed shortly before his death. The "authorized" edition of Parts 2 and 3 appeared posthumously, in 1709.

The anecdote belongs to the year 1574, to the beginning of the second major stage of Temple's embassy to the States General, his influence being required to settle the Third Dutch War, a point to which we must return:

With the Prince of Orange, return'd most of the General Officers to the Hague; and among the rest, old Prince Maurice of Nassau, who, as the Prince told me, had with the greatest industry that could be, sought all occasions of dying fairly at the Battel of Seneffe without succeeding, which had given him great regrets; and I did not wonder at it, considering his Age, of about Seventy six, and his long habits both of Gout and Stone. When he came to visit me upon his return, and before he went to his Government of Cleve, it came in my head to ask him an idle question, because I thought it not very likely for me to see him again, and I had a mind to know from his own mouth, the account of a common, but much credited story, that I had heard so often from many others, of an old Parrot he had in Brasil during his Government there, that spoke, and ask'd, and answer'd common questions like a reasonable creature; . . . I had heard many particulars of this story, and assever'd by people hard to be discredited, which made me ask Prince Maurice, What there was of it? He said, with his usual plainness, and dryness in talk, There was something true, but a great deal false, of what had been reported. I desir'd to know of him, What there was of the first? He told me shortly and coldly, That he had heard of such an old Parrot when he came to Brasil; and tho he believ'd nothing of it, and 'twas a good way off, yet he had so much curiosity as to send for it; That 'twas a very Great, and a very Old One; and when it came first into the Room where the Prince was, with a great many Dutch-man about him, it said presently, *What a Company of White Men are here?* They ask'd it, What he thought that Man was? pointing at the Prince. It answer'd, *Some General or other.* When they brought it close to him, he ask'd it, *D'ou venes vous?* It answer'd, *De Marinnan.* The Prince, *A qui estes vous?* The Parrot, *A un Portugez.* Prince, *Que fais tu là?* Parrot, *Je garde les Poulles.* The Prince laugh'd, and said, *Vous gardez les Poulles?* The Parrot answered, *Ouy, moy & je scay bien faire;* and made the Chuck four or five times that people use to make to Chickens when they call them. I set down the words of this worthy Dialogue in *French* just as Prince Maurice said them to me. I ask'd him, In what Language the Parrot spoke? And he said, In *Brasilian.* I ask'd, Whether he understood *Brasilian?* He said, No; but he had taken care to have two Interpreters by him, one a *Dutch*-man that spoke *Brasilian,* and t'other a *Brasilian* that spoke *Dutch;* That he ask'd them separately and privately, and both of them agreed in telling him just the same thing that the Parrot said. I could not but tell this odd story, because it is so much out of the way, and from the first hand, and what may pass for a good one; for I dare say this Prince, at least, believ'd himself in all he told me, having ever pass'd for a very honest and pious Man. I leave it to

Naturalists to reason, and to other men to believe as they please upon it; however, it is not, perhaps, amiss to relieve or enliven a busie Scene sometimes with such digressions, *whether to the purpose or no.*[23]

This story comes equipped at the end, evidently, with one of the theoretical justifications of secret history as defined by Varillas – the importance of the seemingly trivial; with a claim for its authenticity such as we have seen produced by John Foxe; and with a special invitation to the reader to decide what it is doing in Temple's account of his diplomatic mission, "whether to the purpose or no."

When transplanted into Locke's *Essay*, the story of the parrot acquires one further qualification of anecdotal significance, the power of portability; and Locke expanded on Temple's claims for its authenticity in a way that actually contradicted his later chapters on historiography in the *Essay*. "I have taken care," he added at the end of this remarkable insertion:

that the Reader should have the Story at large in the Authors own Words, because he seems to me not to have thought it incredible; for it cannot be imagined that so able a Man as he, who had sufficiency enough to warrant all the Testimonies he gives of himself, should take so much pains, *in a place where it had nothing to do*, to pin so close, not only on a Man whom he mentions as his Friend, but on a Prince in whom he acknowledges very great Honesty and Piety, a Story which if he himself thought incredible, he could not but also think ridiculous.[24]

Not only has Locke reopened the issue of the anecdote's mysterious relevance ("in a place where it had nothing to do"); he has also flatly contradicted his statements about degrees of credibility in historical reporting, where the further we get from the source of a story the weaker its powers of reference are taken to be:

A credible Man vouching his Knowledge of it, is a good proof; but if another equally credible, do witness it from his Report, the Testimony is weaker; and a third that attests the Hear-say of an Hear-say, is yet less considerable. *So in traditional Truths, each remove weakens the force of the proof.* And the more hands the Tradition has successively passed through, the less strength and evidence does it receive from them. (p. 664; italics original)

But in regaling his audience in 1700 with the anecdote of the rational parrot, he was only the fifth in a sequence of "Hear-say": Parrot; the interpreters; Prince Maurice; Sir William Temple; John Locke.

---

[23] Sir William Temple, *Memoirs of What Past in Christendom from the War Begun 1672 to the Peace Concluded 1679* (London, 1691), pp. 57–58; final italics added.

[24] Locke, *An Essay concerning Human Understanding*, ed. Peter Nidditch (Oxford, 1975), p. 334.

What Locke thought he was conveying with this anecdote in 1700[25] will perhaps become clear in my penultimate chapter, which is exclusively devoted to him. The issue here is the nature, purpose and texture of Sir William Temple's *Memoirs*, and the meaning of their publication in 1691, just three years after the Williamite revolution. Temple had been Charles II's ambassador in the Low Countries since 1666. He had become close friends with the republican John de Witt, and, when the Second Dutch War was no longer tenable policy for England, became a major player in European diplomacy. He was the immediate agent of the Triple Alliance, the defensive treaty between England, the States General and Sweden, designed, if not to curtail the power of France in its march on the Spanish Netherlands, at least to give the rest of Europe some breathing space. We enter here the territory of secret history, continental style, since secrecy and double-dealing were endemic in Europe in the context of the power shifts of the later seventeenth century. The Triple Alliance was arranged quickly and quietly, to avoid French interference; but it was immediately undermined by Charles II, who on the day of the signing (January 23, 1668) wrote to his sister in France conveying his apology to Louis for this move, as only a temporary expediency. When Louis invaded Lorraine, without any response from England, Temple's credibility was severely damaged. He was recalled from the Hague in September 1670, without being allowed to explain his departure to De Witt or to take his family with him, only to discover to his alarm that the true temper of the court was now leading to the Third Dutch War of 1672–74. Ironically, his diplomatic skills were again called in to negotiate the Treaty of Westminster, whereby that war came to its sorry end; and later in 1674 Temple would successfully negotiate the match between William of Orange and the Princess Mary which ultimately made the Revolution possible.

This mini-history is a necessary condition for understanding the place in Temple's *Memoirs* of the old Brazilian parrot, and the old Dutch warrior prince who negotiated with it through intermediaries. A parrot is not normally supposed to think for itself, but only to repeat what it has been told. This remarkable exception, a parrot whose acuity was a legend in its own time, who takes the initiative in conversation, and whose task was to "gardez les poulles," those

---

[25] The fourth edition was actually published at the end of 1699, though dated 1700.

lesser and sillier birds, acquires the force of political allegory – once the story is retold by an early modern diplomat. What for Prince Maurice himself was merely a curiosity of nature is for Temple a political parable, speaking to the predicament of any intelligent man forced to carry his master's messages abroad. The more independent he becomes in analyzing his surroundings and guarding the chickens from their natural tendency to self-destruction, the less grows the distance between him and this unusual parrot; while the issue of credibility, ostensibly applying only to the truth of the anecdote (though mediated through Prince Maurice's personal credibility, the prince "having ever pass'd for a very honest and pious man"), could easily express Temple's own anxieties about whether his testimony, which was never exclusively his own, should properly have been trusted.[26] And Temple seems to have added an interpretive key to his own anecdote. A few paragraphs earlier in the *Memoirs* he had remarked on the difficulty experienced by the Dutch States General in maintaining a unified position during the war: "And here began those Dissentions," he wrote, "among the chief Captains of the Confederates, that continued to ruin their designs, and prov'd so fatal to them in the whole course of the War; and against all appearances, made good the *Spanish* Proverb, that, *Liga nunca coje grandes poxaras*; the same word signifying a League, and Birdlime; and meaning, That as this never catches great Birds, so t'other never makes great Conquests, though it often does great Defences" (p. 55). The pun establishes a metaphorical level of communication that Temple, as we shall see, found frequently congenial.

As the *Memoirs* progress from 1674 to 1679, they increasingly chronicle Temple's frustration with Charles's seemingly incoherent foreign policy, which fluctuated according to the tidal pull of France. Another salient anecdote made it clear to a Williamite audience that William himself had been quite alert to these currents, especially after he had established a marital connection with England. In January 1679 Temple travelled to Nijmegen for the last time to work

---

[26] Readers who are skeptical of this interpretation might wish to compare two other serious applications of the parrot metaphor to the predicament of the early modern political commentator; the first, John Skelton's early sixteenth-century poem, *Speke Parrot*, in which Skelton bills himself as the learned bird who has picked up a smattering of all the ancient and modern languages and is thereby enabled to converse unintelligibly on the scandals of the Henrician court; the second, Eliza Haywood's mid-eighteenth-century periodical, *The Parrot*, of which both the first and the eighth and final numbers articulate the metaphor of being a parrot in society.

on another treaty, one for his taste far too concessive to France. Shortly after his arrival news was brought from London by Lawrence Hyde of yet another change of English policy, towards war with France, and a new alliance with the Dutch. This is how Temple described William's reaction:

After a short Audience, Mr. Hyde went to the Princess, and left me alone with the Prince, who as soon as he was gone, lift up his hands two or three times, and said, Was ever any thing so hot and so cold as this Court of yours? Will the King that is so often at Sea never learn a word that I shall never forget since my last passage? When in a great Storm the Captain was all night crying out to the Man at the Helm, Steddy, Steddy, Steddy; if this dispatch had come twenty days ago, it had changed the face of Affairs in Christendom, and the War might have been carried on till France had yielded to the Treaty of the Pyrenees, and left the world in quiet for the rest of our lives. As it comes now, it will have no effect at all.

William then asked Temple what was "at the bottom of this new heat in our Court; and what could make it break out so *mal a propos*, after the dissatisfaction they had expressed upon the late Treaty" (pp. 365–66). Temple had no idea, and only later learned that the outbreak of the Popish Plot had motivated Charles to placate his parliament, which had been outspokenly dissatisfied with the pro-French structure of the Treaty of Nijmegen.

The sense of insider trading, so crucial to secret history, coalesces at the end of Temple's *Memoirs* around the disingenuities of the Popish Plot. "We knew very well in Holland," Temple wrote:

That both Houses of Parliament believed the Plot; That the Clergy, the City, the Countrey in general did so too, or at least pursu'd it as if they all believ'd it. We knew the King and some of the Court believ'd nothing of it, and yet thought not fit to own that Opinion: And the Prince told me, He had reason to be confident, that the King was in his heart a *Roman-Catholick*, tho' he durst not profess it. For my own part, I knew not what to believe of one side or t'other, but thought it easie to presage, from such contrary Winds and Tides, such a Storm must rise, as would tear the Ship in pieces, whatever Hand were at the Helm. (p. 388)

In the chaos produced by this situation, Sir William Coventry avowed his Catholicism and resigned as Secretary of State, and Temple was pressed to take on the position. The *Memoirs* describe how Danby wrote him a letter lamenting that the government had "fallen into a cruel Disease, and had need of so Able a Physician." "This put me," wrote Temple, "in mind of a Story of Dr. Prujean (the greatest of that Profession in our time), and which I told my Friends that were with me when these Letters came":

A certain Lady came to the Doctor in great trouble about her Daughter. *Why, what ails she?* Alas, Doctor! I cannot tell; but she has lost her Humour, her Looks, her Stomach; her Strength consumes every day, so as we fear she cannot live. *Why do not you marry her?* Alas, Doctor! *that* we would fain do, and have offer'd her as good a Match as she could ever expect, but she will not hear of marrying. *Is there no other, do you think, that she would be content to marry?* Ah, Doctor! That is it that troubles us; for there is a young gentleman we doubt she loves, that her Father and I can never consent to. *Why, look you Madam,* replies the Doctor gravely (being among all the Books in his Closet) *then the Case is this: Your Daughter would marry one Man, and you would have her marry another: in all my Books I find no Remedy for such a Disease as this.* (pp. 385–86)

So we return once more to the strange connection between historiographical anecdotes and doctors' stories. In this instance the anecdote, humorously yet delicately told, is a political allegory to which Temple himself supplied the key:

I confess, I esteemed the Case as desperate in a Politick as in a Natural Body, and as little to be attempted by a Man who neither ever had his own Fortune at heart (which such Conjunctures are only proper for), nor ever could resolve upon any pursuits of it to go against either the true Interest, or the Laws of his Countrey; One of which is commonly endanger'd upon the fatal misfortune of such Divisions in a Kingdom. (p. 386)

But the story's brilliance exceeds his exposition. "[B]eing among all the Books in his Closet" the man who has himself arranged the most politically astute of marriages has no solution for such parental folly as the anecdote speaks to. "[I]n all my Books I find no Remedy for such a Disease as this." Yet the unauthorized book in which this anecdote appears as part of the final diagnosis itself became part of the solution. Published in 1691/92 for a Williamite audience, it entered the canon of secret histories which early modern liberalism could use to explain its desire for political candor, as a necessary prerequisite to political change.

In H. Trevor Colbourn's analysis of the content of early American libraries, Temple's *Memoirs*, separately or as part of his *Works*, appear with remarkable frequency. Harvard, Yale and Princeton all owned a copy, as did Providence Library, the New York Society Library, the Library Company of Philadelphia, and the Charleston Library Society. John Adams owned the *Works*, as did Robert Carter and

Thomas Jefferson, and the physician Benjamin Rush, who served in the revolutionary army and signed the Declaration of Independence.[27] And Thomas Hollis cited another of Temple's anecdotes revealing Charles II in political undress in his edition of Algernon Sidney's works, in order to justify Sidney's decision to betray his king in 1681.[28]

But in relation to early America, none of Temple's anecdotes had the valence of a story told about Algernon Sidney himself, a story whose plot is directly related to the need for secret history, whose dissemination is a remarkably detailed instance of how secret historians operated, and whose effects and influence is still with us in modern political life. Let us call it "The Guest-book Defaced."

One of the first items that Thomas Hollis included in his *Life* of Sidney was a letter from his father, Robert Sidney, earl of Leicester, in response to several that Sidney had sent him in the summer of 1660 from Denmark, where he had been sent by the Council of State to negotiate a peace between Denmark and Sweden. In August of that year, with the Restoration of Charles II now a certainty, his father replied, warning him not to return to England, for there were rumors that he was to be excluded from the general pardon and act of oblivion. And, added Leicester, although he had tried to intervene in his son's behalf on the grounds "that there was no other exception to [him], than . . . being of the other party," other stories surfaced:

I have heard such things of you, that in the doubtfulness only of their being true, no man will open his mouth for you . . . It is said, that the university of Copenhagen brought their album unto you, desiring you to write something therein; and that you did "scribere in albo" these words,

    . . . .Manus haec inimica tyrannis
    Ense petit placidam sub libertate quietem."

and put your name to it. This cannot chuse but be publicly known, if it be true.[29]

Leicester then proceeded to retail other anecdotes of Sidney's defiant behavior abroad, concluding: "Besides this, it is reported, that you have been heard to say many scornful and contemptuous

[27] H. Trevor Colbourn, *The Lamp of Experience: Whig History and the Intellectual Origins of the American Revolution*, (Chapel Hill, 1965), pp. 200–22; and for Rush, Wayne Craven, *Colonial American Portraiture: The Economic, Religions, Social, Cultural, Philosophical, Scientific, and Aesthetic Foundations*, (Cambridge, 1986), pp. 395–98.

[28] [Thomas Hollis, ed.], Algernon Sidney, *Discourses concerning Government* (London, 1763), p. 30, citing Temple, *Works* (London, 1720), 2:464.

[29] Sidney, *Discourses*, p. 8.

things of the king's person and family, which, unless you can justify yourself, will hardly be forgiven or forgotten; for *such personal offences make deeper impressions, than public actions, either of war or treaty"* (pp. 11–12; italics added). This piece of wisdom is central to the understanding of secret history as I am attempting to define its premises and conditions, for Leicester had grasped that fact that policy is frequently dictated by motives operating at a personal or even subconscious level.

As Hollis certainly knew, a truly memorable anecdote was a blend of personal gesture and larger political issues. He had introduced his edition of Sidney's *Discourses* with an engraved portrait of Sidney in profile (Figure 5), above the version of the anecdote that he had found in Sir Robert Molesworth's *Account of Denmark* (1694). Molesworth's preface to this work is a long disquisition on educational reform in the interests of political freedoms; and it features as honorific the anecdote that had so embarrassed Sidney's father:

That Kingdom [Denmark] has often had the Misfortune to be govern'd by French Counsels. At the Time when Mr. Algernoon [*sic*] Sydney was Ambassador at that Court, Monsier Terlon, the French Ambassador, had the Confidence to tear out of the Book of Motto's in the King's Library, this Verse, which Mr. Sydney (according to the liberty allowed to all noble Strangers) had written in it:
> manus haec inimica tyrannis
> Ense petit placidam sub libertate quietem.

though Monsieur Terlon understood not a word of Latin, he was told by others the Meaning of that Sentence, which he considered as a Libel upon the French Government, and upon such as was then a setting up in Denmark by French Assistance, or Example. (p. xxiii)

Molesworth himself became one of the most revered authorities for the eighteenth-century "commonwealth-men," and his own personal history was thus merged with Sidney's under the auspices of this Latin motto, whose origins remain a mystery.[30]

Translated, the motto reads: "This hand, hostile to tyrants, seeks by the sword peace and quiet under liberty." The anecdote is complex enough, especially in Molesworth's telling, to deserve some exegesis. The alatinity of the French ambassador is opposed to the humanist skills of Sidney, who could wield both sword and word

---

[30] Doubts about the motto, and Molesworth's version of the anecdote, are dutifully rehearsed by Alan Craig Houston, *Algernon Sidney and the Republican Heritage in England and America* (Princeton, 1991), pp. 34–35, n. 76. For our purposes, however, what matters is the Molesworth version and its subsequent transmission.

ALGERNON SYDNEY SECOND SON OF_____ ROBERT EARL OF LEICESTER COLO-
NEL OF A REGIMENT OF HORSE ONE OF THE COVNCIL OF STATE AND COMMISSIONER
TO MEDIATE A PEACE BETWEEN SWEDEN AND DENMARK BEHEADED AFTERWARDS VN-
-IVSTLY FOR HIGH TREASON DEC.VII.MDCLXXXIII.

DRAWN AND ETCHED MDCCLX BY I.B.CIPRIANI A FLORENTINE FROM A PROOF IMPRESSION
OF A SEAL INGRAVED BY THOMAS SIMON IN THE POSSESSION OF THOMAS HOLLIS OF
LINCOLN'S INNE F.R. AND A.SS.

AT THE TIME WHEN MR.ALGERNON SYDNEY WAS AMBASSADOR AT THE COVRT OF DENMARK
MONSIEVR TERLON THE FRENCH AMBASSADOR HAD THE CONFIDENCE TO TEAR OVT OF THE
BOOK OF MOTTOES IN THE KING'S LIBRARY THIS VERSE WHICH MR. SYDNEY ACCORDING
TO THE LIBERTY ALLOWED TO ALL NOBLE STRANGERS HAD WRITTEN IN IT
MANVS HAEC INIMICA TYRANNIS
ENSE PETIT PLACIDAM SVB LIBERTATE QVIETEM
THOVGH MONSIEVR TERLON VNDERSTOOD NOT A WORD OF LATIN HE WAS TOLD BY
OTHERS THE MEANING OF THAT SENTENCE WHICH HE CONSIDERED AS A LIBEL
VPON THE FRENCH GOVERNMENT AND VPON SVCH AS WAS THEN SETTING VP
IN DENMARK BY FRENCH ASSISTANCE OR EXAMPLE. *LORD MOLESWORTH'S*
PREFACE TO HIS ACCOVNT OF DENMARK.

✳ COL. SYDNEY BORE THIS ONLY MOTTO WITHOVT FIGVRE ON THE PARLIAMENT SIDE DVRING THE CIVIL WARS

Figure 5 Portrait of Algernon Sidney. Engraved by I. B. Cipriani for Sidney,
Discourses concerning Government, ed. Thomas Hollis (London, 1763), frontispiece.
Seeley G. Mudd Library, Yale University.

against tyrants. The "liberty" allowed to all noble strangers reverberates with the ideal political liberty under which Sidney sought tranquillity, and condemns that rude French "confidence" which invades the library and commits physical violence against a book.

The anecdote of "The Guest-book Defaced" subsequently crossed the Atlantic, and became permanently incorporated into early American history, as the source of the official motto of the Commonwealth of Massachusetts.[31] Between July 18 and August 5, 1775, as Chester Greenough discovered, the Council adopted a new seal, involving "Instead of an Indian holding a Tomahawk and a Cap of Liberty . . . an English American, holding a Sword in the Right Hand, and Magna Charta in the Left Hand," and beneath it the words "Ense petit placidam sub libertate quietem." Two copies of Molesworth's *Account of Denmark* were acquired by John Adams for his personal library, the first and the sixth edition (Glasgow, 1752). Thomas Jefferson owned a copy. A copy of the edition of 1738 was donated to Harvard College Library by Thomas Hollis. And equally important were the eighteenth-century editions of Sidney's works: John Darby's 1704 edition, which contained the motto alone; the Edinburgh edition of 1750, which contained the anecdote (and was owned by John Adams); and Thomas Hollis's 1763 edition, which was the first to carry the engraved portrait of Sidney above the full text of Molesworth's anecdote (Figure 5) (and was owned by Thomas Jefferson). Finally, in 1770 occurred the first American political tribute to Sidney as a model for the colonists in their struggles with England. In John Adams's famous legal defence of Captain Preston, the defence which most clearly established his reputation as a man who could represent both sides of the question, Sidney's motto appears in the peroration, with the following gloss by Adams as to its current cultural significance:

To use the words of a great and worthy man, a patriot and a hero, an enlightened friend of mankind, and a martyr to liberty – I mean Algernon Sidney – who, from his earliest infancy sought a tranquil requirement under the shadow of the tree of liberty, with his tongue, his pen, and his sword.[32]

---

[31] See Chester Noyes Greenough, "Algernon Sidney and the Motto of the Commonwealth of Massachusetts," in *Collected Studies* (Cambridge, Mass., 1940; repr. from *Massachusetts Historical Society Proceedings*, Vol. 51, 1918), pp. 68–88.

[32] John Adams, *Legal Papers*, ed. L. K. Wroth and H. B. Zobel (Cambridge, Mass., 1965), 3:270.

In Adams's translation, Sidney's motto has expanded to include two instruments (the tongue and the pen) particularly relevant to the history not just of "The Guest-book defaced," but of the anecdote in general, by way of explaining its portability, its remarkable propensity to travel. As Alan Houston has pointed out, the story of the guest-book can no longer be verified; but in Adams's tense court-room it was certainly *bon trouvé*.

CHAPTER 6

Secret history

I might draw too much envy upon myself, if I should take upon me to cite all the examples of this kind that are found in modern histories, or the memoirs that do more precisely shew the temper of princes, and the secret springs by which they were moved.

Algernon Sidney, *Discourses concerning Government*

Having followed the anecdote in liberal historiography from the mid-sixteenth to the later eighteenth century, I will now break the etymological connection between it and secret history, and follow the latter as a separate development. If the rediscovery of Procopius' *Secret History* provided the excuse for and the name of a new genre of political communication in England, it did not, of course, provide the incentive. In 1682, the year of the Popish Plot and the Exclusion crisis, when the Whigs were, like their opponents, looking for new polemical weapons, the anonymous 1674 translation of Procopius was reissued under a more immediately provocative title: *The Debaucht Court. Or, the Lives of the Emperor Justinian, and his Empress Theodora the Comedian*. But it was the phrase "secret history" that apparently touched a nerve or answered a need. How else can we explain its use in so many titles in the last decades of the seventeenth century? Some of these, as I mentioned earlier, developed the idea of erotic scandal in high places into an entire rationale. Others mixed erotic scandal with an appeal to contemporary francophobia, as in *The Cabinet Open'd, or, The Secret History of the Amours of Madame de Maintenon, with the French King* (London: Richard Baldwin, 1690). It is difficult to determine what was the motive behind the revivals of old Roman Catholic propaganda, in *The Secret History of the Duke of Alancon and Q. Elizabeth* (London: Will of the Whisp, 1691), and *The Secret History of . . . Q. Elizabeth and the E. of Essex*, which appeared from the same underground press in 1680,

1681, 1689 and 1695; but the fact that John Darby, Jr. reprinted the latter in 1725 indicates that it was not incompatible with that printer's Whig affiliations.

The second category of secret history, the scandalous political *roman à clef*, seems to have been primarily a feature of Hanoverian party politics, as in Mrs. Delarivière Manly's *The Secret History of Queen Zara and the Zarazians* (Albigion, 1711), an attack on Sarah, duchess of Marlborough, or *The Secret History of Arlus and Odolphus, Chief Ministers of State to the Empress of Grandinsula* (London, three editions in 1710), a transparent attack on Sidney Godolphin and defence of Robert Harley sometimes attributed to Harley himself, sometimes to the indefatigable and protean Daniel Defoe, who changed his party allegiances as often as necessary. This branch of what was now a genre attracted female authors, as in Eliza Haywood's *The Secret History of the Present Intrigues of the Court of Caramania* (1727), which its modern editor describes as "a regular scandal chronicle," representing as if in a French romance the sexual intrigues at the court of George II.[1] To cite Francis Blackburne again, one "must have a strange appetite for secret history" (see p. 155 above) to follow its pulpy intricacies.

It is worth pausing over *The Secret History of Arlus and Odolphus*, however, because its approach to the ethics of reading is related to that of political secret history, the third and most important branch of the new genre. The pamphlet's occasion was the fall of the Whigs in the aftermath of the Sacheverell trial, and the anonymous author supplied everything needed to decode its secrets. A second title-page adds: "In which are discover'd the Laboured Artifices formerly us'd for the Removal of Arlus, and the true Causes of his late Restoration, upon the Dismission of Odolphus and the Quinvirate. Humbly offer'd to those Good People of Grandinsula, who have not yet done wond'ring, why that Princess wou'd Change so Notable a Ministry." The tone of the work is satiric, but on satire's jocular side; and the premise is that its readers should try to rise above party politics, which can only lead to bad behavior all round:

Here is the opening gambit:

'Tis now about seventy Years, since one Half of our Grandfathers first buckl'd on their rusty Armour against t'other, for the Good of their King,

---

[1] See *The Secret History . . . of the Court of Caramania*, ed. Josephine Grieder (New York and London, 1972), p. 5.

and the Country; such was the original Pretence on both sides, but our Histories make no mention (when one of those Sides got uppermost) that either their King or their Country were the better for it: However the same loyal Dispute seems to be intail'd on their Posterity, only with this Difference, that *They* back'd their Arguments with Blows, and *We* that have more Wit, only Rail, and call Names . . . And while there are such unfortunate Words in our Language, as *Hereditary, Limited, Resistance, Passive, Agrarian Laws, High Boys, Low Church, No Church*, &c. I don't see why our Neighbours may not think us a very merry People for t'other thirty Years of the Hundred to come. (p. 5)

This pretence of being above the fray, however, is soon abandoned. Harley's Tories are represented as "Loyalists," the ousted Whigs as "Levellers," and the work ends on an explicit preference for the former.

The subject of this chapter, however, is political secret history proper. This branch of the new genre clearly originated on the leftward or liberal side of the ideological spectrum. At the Revolution of 1688 it became recognizably a Whig genre, and hence spawned some Tory repartee in the first decades of the eighteenth century, but without fulfilling the generic assumptions and protocols outlined below. The most important of these, itself an evolution of the Procopian rationale for *anecdota*, was the structural and ideological connection made between "secret history" as that which reveals what official history would prefer to keep secret and the actual course of early modern political culture. Political secret historians tend to offer, though in fragments, what deserves in the aggregate to be called a theory of secret history. They often claim to be performing a public service, the equivalent of what we now describe as the public's right to know, a demand served today by investigative journalism, but then connected to an ideal of political education. By learning what really happened behind the scenes in relation to the Triple League, or the Popish Plot, or the Exclusion crisis, or James II's "abdication," or, to continue the story into the next century, during the madness of George III, the early modern reader was to be instructed in the politics of suspicion, which should lead not to useless cynicism but to well-informed and responsible activism. Of course there is a good deal of conspiracy theory at work in this kind of secret history; but there was also considerable empirical basis for it. The secret treaty of Dover, for example, between Charles II and Louis XIV, was a cogent proof of the double-dealing that the Whigs attributed to the Stuarts and fully fledged republicans like Sidney believed endemic to monarchy.

Political secret history deals occasionally with scandal, even sexual scandal, but not for scandal's sake. That both Charles II and Louis XIV (and later George IV) happened to be sexual libertines was an ethical advantage for secret historians of a reformist bent; and they often capitalized on sudden deaths by spreading the rumors of poison; but their primary interest was in making available to the reading public those under-the-counter deals that early modern monarchs defined as *arcana*, secrets of state, and the acts of disinformation designed to keep them so. Their target is not the "inner and privy bed," but government behind the scenes.

Unlike the Tory appropriations that developed in Hanoverian England, the examples I have chosen to describe are all, moreover, genuine history as well as polemic; that is to say, sustained analyses of political regimes, often of political crises and what leads up to them. The Tory reaction might claim the name of "secret history" for short tirades like the *Secret History of Arlus and Odolphus* or the *Secret History of the Calves-Head Clubb*, but not its ethical rationale. The second of these, published in 1702, is barely long enough to justify its bludgeoning title: *The Secret History of the Calves-Head Clubb, or the Republican Unmasqu'd: Wherein is fully shewn The Religion of the Calves-Head Heroes, In their Anniversary Thanksgiving Songs on the Thirtieth of January, by them called ANTHEMS; For the Years 1693, 1694, 1695, 1696, 1697. Now published, To demonstrate the Restless, Implacable Spirit of a certain Party still among us, who are never to be satisfied till the present Establishment in Church and State is subverted.* It consists mostly in the texts of republican drinking songs – an odd way, it might seem, to prevent their being sung; and, paradoxically, much of its author's annoyance seems to be generated by the fact that after the Revolution its supporters *no longer* needed to operate in secret. The author of this tract speaks of his informer, "a certain active Whigg, who in all other Respects, was a Man of probity enough," and who attended meetings of the Club as if he were a sympathizer. "He farther told me, that Milton, and some other Creatures of the Commonwealth, had instituted this Clubb, as he was inform'd, in Opposition to Bp. Juxon, Dr. Sanderson, Dr. Hammond, and other Divines of the Church of England, who meet privately every 30th of January; . . . That after the Restauration, the Eyes of the Government being upon the whole Party, they were obliged to meet with a great deal of Precaution; but now, says he, (and this was the Second Year of King William's Reign) they met *almost in a Publick Manner,* and apprehend nothing" (pp. 9–10; italics added).

As political secret history developed a sense of itself as a genre it created a series of models and predecessors, of which Procopius was only the first. Sir William Temple's *Memoirs* were clearly regarded as *anecdota*, not least by the moment and manner of their publication, and were frequently drawn on by subsequent secret historians. One of the true native progenitors of the genre was Andrew Marvell's *An Account of the Growth of Popery and Arbitrary Government*, published in "Amsterdam" in 1677, which not only established some of the premises of the genre, but was so brilliantly written that it soon acquired canonical status. The premise of the *Account*, of course, is that of a grand international conspiracy:

There has now for divers years, a design been carried on to change the lawful Government of England into an absolute Tyranny, and to convert the established Protestant Religion into downright Popery: than both which, nothing can be more destructive or contrary to the interests and happiness, to the constitution and being of the king and kingdom.[2]

And Marvell draws his story to a close with an account of his own historiographical stance and motives:

Thus far hath the conspiracy against our Religion and Government been laid open, which if true, it was more than time that it should be discovered, but if any thing therein have been falsely suggested, the disproving of it in any particular will be a courtesy both to the public and to the relator; who would be glad to have the world convinced of the contrary, though to the prejudice of his own reputation. (p. 411)

Every word of this sentence carefully readjusts the Procopian rationale as it had been somewhat distorted by Spence's translation of Varillas: away from scandalmongering and the determination to "get open the closet door," towards an ideal of probity and integrity;

---

[2] Marvell, *Account*, in *Complete Works*, ed. A. B. Grosart, 4 vols. (1875; privately printed), 4:248. This sentence, and the ideal definition of church and state that follows it, was the last major quotation from the liberal canon that Thomas Hollis imported into his edition of Sidney's *Discourses*, where it became an authority for Sidney's own "Apology," and his final hope, soon to be fulfilled, that God would deliver the nation from the Stuarts. (Hollis added a secret historian's touch, by noting that Marvell died "shortly after" the *Account* appeared, "not without strong suspicion of being poysoned.") See Algernon Sidney, *Discourses concerning Government*, ed. Thomas Hollis (London, 1763), pp. 196–98.

away from the defence of the trivial and back to the attack on "those who are desirous to govern in an Arbitrary way." The notion of the "relator" as he who merely delivers a "naked narrative" (p. 263) of what actually happened, heavily ballasted with the full texts of original documents, is inconsistent with the anti-Catholic polemic with which the *Account* tried to inflame its intended readership; but it was the former rather than the latter that made Marvell (the first, we remember, to use the term *anecdota* in English) so powerful a bridge between classical precedent and early modern English practice.

Marvell's slice of Restoration history was essentially the same as Sir William Temple's in that "unauthorized" segment of his *Memoirs*, from the ending of the Second Dutch War, through the Third Dutch War and its aftermath. Like Temple, Marvell was by this time pro-Dutch and francophobic. Like Temple, he believed that Charles's policy was choreographed by Louis XIV, and vice versa. Noting that the king had reopened parliament after the "Long Prorogation" (which had lasted for thirteen months) on exactly the same day (February 15, 1676) that Louis invaded Flanders, Marvell remarked: "It seemed that his motions were in just cadence, and that, as in a grand balet, he kept time with those that were tuned here to measure" (p. 319). But whereas Temple's perspective was that of the court servant distressed by the terms of his indenture, Marvell's was that of a liberal parliamentarian, who read that "Long Prorogation" and "the three vicious adjournments" (p. 410) that followed as the strongest proofs of the conspiracy, since Charles thereby effectively put the constitution on hold. Much of his account is devoted to the debates in both houses of parliament, where, by Marvell's standards, the story of government ought to be centered: for example, those on the proposed Test Act, which differed from previous loyalty oaths by concluding "And I do sweare that I will not at any time indeavour the alteration of Government either in Church or State." The Test Act was strenuously opposed by a number of peers, among them Shaftesbury, Buckingham, Salisbury, Wharton and Holles; but the public was prevented from reading their objections. "The particular relation in this debate . . . was in the next Session burnt by order of the Lords," wrote Marvell; "but the sparks of it will eternally fly in their adversaries faces" (pp. 309–10). In this way the new English secret historian identifies part of his responsibility: to outsmart the government in its control of information, to make the debates of parliament known outside Westminster, to connect secret history with the venerable liberal issue of freedom of speech and the press. By the same token, he remarks, "it is not without much labour that I have been able to recover a written copy of the Lord Bridgeman's speech [appealing for a supply in the 1670 session], none being printed, but forbidden, doubtless lest so notorious a practice as certainly was never before . . . might remain publick" (p. 267).

The most intensive scrutiny in the entire *Account* was given to the attempt of the Commons to redirect English foreign policy. With meticulous fullness Marvell reported the debates, beginning in March 1577, whereby a majority in the House patiently formulated and reformulated requests to Charles to take unequivocal action against France, and to ally with the United Provinces in the defence of the Spanish Netherlands. The final result, when they made it clear they would not go beyond a supply of two hundred thousand pounds until they saw results, was a severe reprimand from the king for invading his prerogative, followed by an immediate adjournment. "And that which more amazed them afterwards," Marvell added:

was, that while none of their own transactions or addresses for the public good are suffered to be printed, but even all written copies of them with the same care as libels suppressed; yet they found this severe speech published in the next day's news book, to mark them out to their own, and all other nations, as refractory disobedient persons that had lost all respect to his Majesty. (p. 406)

Thus a key aspect of English secret history as pioneered by Marvell was a combination of two liberal premises: that the government of any country ought to be practiced, and seen to be practiced, as the constitution requires; and that the concept of "libel" tends to be deployed as a weapon by those whose administrative conduct will not survive public scrutiny. As Marvell summed up the likely reception of the *Account* (anticipating Roger L'Estrange's desperate campaign to discover the author and printer), "Some will represent this discourse (as they do all books that tend to detect their conspiracy) . . . as if it too were written against the government [which] . . . by being criminal, pretends to be sacred." Such men, wrote Marvell, reversing the compliment, "are the living libels against the government" (p. 414).

A few years too early, perhaps, to call itself a secret history,

Marvell's *Account* nevertheless defined many of the incentives for writing in that genre, whose own premise, paradoxically, is candor. Throughout his *Account* Marvell described the architects of Charles's policy as "conspirators," and stressed the secrecy of their proceedings. Significantly, he reported some in the Commons as saying, in response to the Court party's insistence on the *arcana imperii*, that "they did not much desire secrecy, for let the King take a great resolution, and put himself at the head of his Parliament and people in this weighty and worthy cause of England, and let a flying post carry the news to Paris, and let the French king do his worst" (p. 366).

Algernon Sidney, whose grasp of the principle of alternative history I cited as this chapter's epigraph, understood what Marvell had accomplished. One of the earliest sections of Sidney's *Discourses* is an attack on the theory of *arcana imperii*: "if a prince may have or want the qualities, upon which my faith in him can be rationally grounded, I cannot yield the obedience he requires, unless I search into the secrets relating to his person and commands, which he forbids."[3] The later sections, as we saw in chapter 5, are dominated by the same conspiracy theory, the same obsession with the corruption of parliament, as is the *Account*; and occasionally Sidney attempted a heavy-handed irony that dimly reflects the Marvellian wit.

But if we want secret history that is so designated, and fully explicit as to the reasons for the designation, we have to wait until after the Revolution: for example, for *The Secret History of White-Hall, from the Restoration of Charles II. Down to the Abdication of the late K. James. Writ at the request of a Noble Lord, and conveyed to him in Letters, by —— late Secretary-Interpreter to the Marquess of Louvois, who by that means had the perusal of all the Private Minutes between England and France for many years. The Whole consisting of Secret Memoirs, which have hitherto lain conceal'd, as not being discoverable by any other Hand. Publish'd from the Original Papers.* By D. Jones, Gent. (London: R. Baldwin, 1697). This work was the first production of David Jones, son of a dissenting Welsh minister, who passed up a career in the church in favor of schoolteaching, which led to historical scholarship. Jones spent most of his time in France and was appointed secretary interpreter to the Marquis of Louvois, which certainly gave him inside information. He also wrote a multivolume *Compleat History of Europe*, and many other historical

---

[3] Sidney, *Discourses concerning Government*, Chapter 1, Section 3, p. 10.

works, including *The Wars and Causes of them between England and France from William I to William III* (1698), which suggests that he had, as well he might, a special interest in Anglo-French relations.

The preface to *The Secret History of White-hall* deals directly with the problem of historiographical authority or authenticity. It explains the author's credentials as stemming from his position with Louvois (which was actually as interpreter to Louvois's secretary, who knew no English). It is clear that the writer of the preface, the editor of the volume (who calls himself not the "relator" but the "Methodizer") and the author of the letters are one and the same. We are told that the correspondent remained in France from 1676 until the Revolution of 1688 and then returned to England, "where his stay was not long, but that he was employed by the same Noble Person to return into France again, where the dangerous part he was to Act may be better conceived than now exprest, but concerning which you may hear more hereafter" (A4r). This provocative half-promise, never fulfilled, was presumably for marketing purposes.

What follows, however, is of psychological interest to a theory of secret history. "It is no hard matter to imagine," we are told:

what Qualifications were necessary to recommend our Author to the Imployment afore noted, *and how far his out-side must differ from his in-side* during his aboad there, which together with that part which he has Acted in that Kingdom, since his present Majesty King William's Accession to the Throne, and that he knows not how soon he may still be engaged to return (though he be at present in London) are Reasons of themselves, without superadding any other . . . more than sufficient for the suppression of his Name" (A4r; italics added)

The distinction between outside and inside is a subtle defence of secret history, based on the premise that it takes one person in disguise to unveil another. And if this excuse for anonymity does not set the reader's mind at rest on the subject of the author's veracity, a comparison of the materials included with other secret histories, so-called and not-so-called, should suffice.

[As] the Fate and Address of this Gentleman led him to fetch them out of the Dark, and almost inscrutable Recesses of the *French* Cabinet-minutes, so the *Reader* will find they carry so much Evidence of Truth with them, not only by the Connexion they have with many material Passages in Sir *William Temple's Memoirs*, Mr. Coke's *Detection of the Court and State of* England *during the Four last Reigns*, &c. but by so natural an unfolding of what is obscurely, or but transiently hinted at by those learned Authors, who could not see beyond their light.

The preface continues in this self-congratulatory vein, observing that the author has avoided "those Scurrilities, as well as Inconsistencies, to say no worse, which occur in some other pieces of the same Reigns" (A5v), that is to say, scandalmongering for its own sake; and he adds an interesting procedural claim:

And 'tis hoped nobody will quarrel, that this Piece which is Entituled by the Name of a *Secret History*, &c. should be written in an *Epistolary* way, when it be considered that such a *Form* was indispensably necessary under the Circumstances of the *Author*, and his *Noble Correspondent*, and that there is a very engaging part naturally couched under such a method of bring *State-Arcana's* to light, by way of *Letters*, which, in the very Notion of them carry something of secrecy. (A6r)[4]

The "editor" makes no bones about the fact that the lesson to be learned by all parties is the danger of being "imposed upon by *French emissaries,* and made *Tools* of to serve the Interest of *France"* (A8r). And although the author adopts the pretence of being above party, he is clearly a Williamite, and a supporter of Shaftesbury, "the ablest Statesman we had at the Helm" (May 5, 1681). The letters begin from Paris, January 8, 1676, new style, and end February 27, 1689.

In the *Continuation of the Secret History,* also published in 1697, the "author" reopens his correspondence on May 14, 1689, and closes it again, rather soon, on November 3, 1695, having in January lamented the death of Queen Mary. This takes up only a small part of the volume, which is completed by *The Tragical History of the Stuarts,* from 1068 to Queen Mary's death, indeed a significant terminus. After this deconstruction of a dynasty, whose best member in Jones's view was also its last, the *Tragical History* returns to the anecdotal, which is often (as in the case of Temple's parrot) related to the Aesopian fable:

But if you please, after all this Mournful Entertainment, I'll tell you a Story; "The Lyon, on a time, called to the Sheep, and asked her, If his Breath smelt? she innocently said, Ay; which made him bite off her head for a Fool: then he called to the Wolf, and asked him, who reply'd, No: and his

---

[4] He then explains that the "Methodizer" has sorted out the dates and added prefatory arguments to each letter, "making up some small breaches . . . which are yet grounded upon the most irrefragable *Authorities"* (A7r).

head he bit off for a Flatterer; last of all he put the same Question to the Fox; but the Fox truly for his part desired to be excused; for he had a Cold upon him, and could not Smell." (p. 392)

Jones did not insult the intelligence of his readers by giving the moral of his story; and neither will I.

In distinguishing his own work from the "Scurrilities" of some of his competitors in the field, Jones may have been alluding to the twin works sometimes attributed to John Phillips, the less famous of Milton's two nephews: *The Secret History of the Reigns of K. Charles II and K. James II* and *The Secret History of K. James I. and K. Charles I. Compleating the Reigns of the Four last Monarchs.* These were published separately in 1690, and conjoined as *The Secret History of the Four Last Monarchs of Great Britain* in 1691. The anonymous author, who was careful to claim both works, showed a prurient interest in the duchess of Portsmouth, the French Louise de Kéroualle, and her sexual manipulation of Charles; was particularly vicious in his account of James II; was convinced that Essex was murdered, and so, by Charles's instigation, was Sir Edmund Berry Godfrey. Yet along with this yellow-press attitude goes a long and intense discussion of the trials of Fitzharris, College, Shaftesbury, Russell and Sidney (pp. 123–32). He also delivers a vehement attack (complete with an anecdote about Judge Jeffreys) on the *quo warranto* proceedings of 1681/2 and the changing of the London city charter:

But that this was the Design of getting Court-Sheriffs, Sir G. Jeffries, who well knew the minds of his Superiors at White-hall, was neither afraid nor ashamed to own. For having after the Tryal of Sir Patience Ward, desir'd him to give his Worship a Meeting at Sir Robert Claytons; he there told him after an insulting manner, That he had satisfied his Revenge for the Loss of the Recordership; and besides, that having such Sheriffs as they desir'd, they had now the Law in their hands, and could have the Life of whomsoever they pleas'd. Otherwise it had been impossible, but for the Treachery of the Judges that encouraged the Injustice of a packed Jury, to have found the Lord Russel guilty of death, when the whole of what was villanously sworn against him, was in the opinion of far more honest and equally Learned Lawyers, but Misprision of Treason; or to have convicted Colonel Sydney upon Innuendo's, made out of old Papers found in his Study, and never published. (pp. 131–32)

And whereas David Jones cited Temple's *Memoirs* as one of his authorities, Phillips (in the second volume) cites both an ancient and a recent model. The ancient model is *not* Procopius, but one that makes equal sense:

It is one of the encomiums given to Suetonius, That he made Publick to the World, the Vices and Miscarriages of the Twelve Caesars, with the same freedom with which they were by them Committed. And there is no question, but one of his chief reasons for so doing, was this, Because he would not deceive Posterity; and all agree that he was Contemporary with the Three last. So that the Enormities of Domitian could not but be fresh in his Memory when he wrote his Life; and there might be several Persons Living, as might have the same Partial Affections for Domitian, as there are now Adorers of C.II. and J.II. For which reason there is a wary Caution among some People, That Truth is not always to be spoken. Which perhaps may be sometimes True, but as the Case stands with these Sheets, not at all to be taken notice of; The pains of this short History, being as well to Vindicate, as to Inform. (A2r)

The recent model is Andrew Marvell; not, significantly, as the author of *The Account of the Growth of Popery*, but as the best-known political satirist of the period. In connection with his lurid account of how Portsmouth persuaded Charles to prorogue the parliament during the Popish Plot crisis by putting on a pornographic show, Phillips wrote:

then it was that the King to screen his wicked Ministers from Publick Justice, preferr'd the Caresses of the expanded nakedness of a French Harlot, before the preservation of three Nations. For then it was, as Mr. Andrew Marvel, with a Satyrical Indignation expresses it.

> That Carwell, that Incestuous Punk,
> Made our most Sacred Sovereign drunk;
> And drunk she let him give the Buss,
> Which still the Kingdom's bound to Curse.

This was the Effect of that nights bloudy debauch, which continued till the morning, and all the morning till the Parliament was Dissolv'd, or Orders at least given for the doing it. (p. 85)[5]

Sexual scandal this undoubtedly is; but the point of the secret historian's describing Portsmouth's pornographic show is not finally, a moral one; it is to reveal how sexuality is merely one of the tools of

---

[5] A second instance occurs in connection with the Meal Tub Plot, where the author cries out, in imitation of Marvell's *Advices to the Painter*: "Draw, Painter, here, England's pious Protestant Monarch, Counter-plotting with his Popish Concubine, and her Close-stool Wench, against his Parliament and Kingdom" (pp. 117–18).

political strategy, whose results directly interfere with parliamentary government. In fact, it was not Marvell who wrote these lines. They appear in "The Royal Buss" in a 1697 collection of the *Poems on Affairs of State*,[6] where they are *not* attributed to Marvell, despite the tendency of that collection to use his name as a magnet for anonymous satires. Nor does the context of the poem appear to be the Popish Plot, but rather the parliamentary session of 1676–77. Yet the mistake is useful to my argument, since it reminds us that the two-part 1697 state poems were assimilated into secret history by their editor. As the preface to the first part argues, at a time when England is militarily engaged in trying to restrain the "tyrannic Power" of France, "it cannot be thought unseasonable to publish so just an account of the true Source of all our present Mischiefs: which will be evidently found in the following Poems, for from them we may collect *a just and secret History* of the former times." And the preface to *State-Poems Continued* reiterates and intensifies the claim: "the said State-Poems, and this Continuation, are the best *secret History* of our late Reigns, as being writ by such Great Persons as were near the Helm, knew the Transactions, and were above being brib'd to flatter, or afraid to speak." This link extends the generic connection between secret history, satire, and what governments define as libel.

The role of Marvell in defining secret history becomes clearer in later decades. In 1712 the *Secret History of Europe*, sometimes attributed to John Oldmixon, cites large sections of his *Account of the Growth of Popery* in renewing the liberal attack on French imperial ambitions from the perspective of Anne's reign, and the threat of Jacobite conspiracy:

It was manifest, says Mr. Marvell, in one of his Tracts, that in all these Wars, the French meant [something] less than really to assist us: "[Louis] had first practis'd the same Art at Sea, when he was in League with the Hollanders against us . . . And now he was on the English side, he only studied to sound our Seas, to spie our Ports, to learn our Building, to contemplate our way of Fighting, to consume ours, and preserve his own Navy. . . " (p. 150; cf. *Account*, p. 294)

And again, on the ending of the Third Dutch War in 1674:

---

[6] See *State Poems; Continued from the Time of O. Cromwel, to This Present Year 1697* (London, 1697), pp. 42–43.

how the Ministers manag'd Matters on that Occasion, may be seen in a Book lately Printed, and mention'd before in this Treatise, call'd Peace with France, and War with Holland, suppos'd to be written by Mr. Marvel. He says, "Therefore they were resolv'd . . . to labour that by this Mediation, France might be the only Gainer; and having all quiet about him, might be at perfect Leisure to attend their Project upon England." (p. 154)

"I hope," Oldmixon continued, "we shall never live to see any English administration have such a Dearness for France" (p. 155).

And again, as a prelude to his discussion of the Test Act of 1675, he invoked "Mr. Marvel in his *Growth of Popery*" (p. 160), and included large segments of the *Account*, those that described how "the Great Design came out, in a Bill unexpectedly offer'd one Morning in the House of Lords" (p. 161), and how it was resisted by Shaftesbury, Buckingham, Wharton and other liberal peers. It gradually emerges that what motivated this return both to secret history and to Restoration parliamentary history was the 1710 trial of Sacheverell. Oldmixon wished disingenuously that "the Reader would make the Comparison between the year 1675, and 1710 himself; for I am very little verst in Parallels, and whatever my Imagination may furnish me with for my self, I should certainly want Words to express it; wherefore I shall be content with repeating what this Honest and Witty Author [Marvell] says on the subject" (p. 160). A few pages later the message is fully unveiled:

Never was there shewn since the Restauration, such a Spirit of Liberty, as in the Opposition to this Bill, which would for ever have put an end to any [opposition] in England. Nor has the Debate a little Resemblance with the Vigour that was lately exerted in the same Cause, on the Tryal of the Incendiary. The Temper of the Clergy was the same then, as some hot Men of 'em have shewn in the same Controversy, with this difference only, that there was more Folly in the latter, the Court being against 'em, and more Corruption in the former, the Ministry making a bold Effort to attack our Constitution. (p. 195)

In fact, one fifth of the *Secret History of Europe* is devoted to this parliamentary struggle over freedom of debate; despite the fact that the work's title-page, which lists its supposed preoccupations, never mentions the subject. Instead, we are told it will focus on "the Insincerity of England, Sweden, and Holland, in the Triple League," and on the secret dealings with France that this work attributes not only to Charles II and James II but also to John de Witt. Advertisement of secret history as melodrama is given in the foregrounding of

De Witt's "Murder by the Rabble," inferentially a punishment for his treachery, and "Of the Poisoning of Madam," that is, Charles's youngest sister Henrietta, the go-beween in the secret treaty of Dover.

In what is already seen as a tradition behind *The Secret History of Europe*, the model of Marvell stands side by side with that of Sir William Temple, which was focused not on parliament but on foreign policy as transmitted through diplomacy, more on character than on institutions. In order to contrast the focused policy of France with the fluctuating policies of England, the secret historian recuperates that anecdote in which Temple quoted William to such memorable effect:

Was every any thing so hot and so cold as this Court of Yours? Will the King, that is so often at Sea, never learn a World that I shall never forget since my last Passage? When in a great Storm the Captain was all Night crying out to the Man at the Helm Steddy, Steddy, Steddy. (Biv–iir)

But it is Marvell who seems to be the dominant intellectual and ethical inspiration; and accordingly Oldmixon makes explicit the structural relation between the genre and the fundamental liberal issues, freedom of information, freedom of speech, freedom of the press:

'Tis observable, that wherever the French are concern'd, they are very uneasie at the Liberty of Free States, which will not admit the tying up of the Tongue, and locking up of the Press, as is done where their Tyranny is predominant . . . It will always be so in ill Governments, none being so much averse to Freedom of Speech, as those to whom it can be of no Service, and of whom every true Word that is said, must be a Satyr. (p. 42)

The *Secret History of Europe* was, therefore, an anti-Jacobite work of its moment, with occasional glimpses of a larger liberal vision. The intensity of dislike with which James II is treated here is explicitly turned to a warning against what will happen when Queen Anne dies. " 'Tis ridiculous to say we are in no danger of the Pretender. I defy any one to shew me in History, whether a Twelvemonth before the Restauration, there was any Probability of King Charles's Return to England?" (p. 228). And in the peroration, the author poses two rhetorical questions about the relation between method and message, of which the second, intended to be answered in the affirmative, is the answer to the first: "To Conclude, if it may be askt what's all this History to us . . . ? Are we in any Danger of a Secret

Treaty with France?" The answer to the second is, not while Queen
Anne lives. But "when we have no more Her Piety, Her Goodness
and Her Care to Protect us, if we should be so wicked as to
Countenance those Principles which made the Revolution necessary
. . . we may in vain hope for another Deliverer, having so ill deserv'd
of the last" (pp. 250–51).

THE HISTORY OF HIS OWN TIME

I now want to consider a different model of how secret history
evolved as an instrument of liberal thought and practice. It is
different primarily in the dynamic presence of the first person
singular (as compared, for instance, to Marvell's supposedly detached Relator), and hence in the psychological complexity of the
stance that the secret historian must take. Yet had Gilbert Burnet
himself overseen the publication of his memoirs, he might very well
have called them *The Secret History of the Stuarts*, instead of the *History
of My Own Time*. The first volume of these memoirs, which covered
the reigns of Charles II and James II, was finished by Burnet about
the beginning of the eighteenth century, and published posthumously in 1724 by Burnet's son. Burnet had begun the continuation,
which dealt with the reigns of William and Anne, in 1705, and it was
published in 1734. The continuation, however, excited a great deal
less attention than the first, which was a *succès de scandale*, or so we
are told by M. J. Routh, the editor of the 1803 edition, who had his
own liberal axe to grind. This difference in tone and reception,
wrote Routh, "is by no means to be wondered at, if . . . we consider
the diminished influence of the good or ill qualities of individuals on
the public events and transactions of this later period."[7]

And, he continued, in Charles's reign:

notwithstanding the enormities of courtiers and anti-courtiers, we reflect
with pleasure on the freedom then first securely enjoyed, from every species
of arbitrary taxation, and from extrajudicial imprisonment; on the
provision made for the meeting of parliament once in three years at the
least; in a word, on the possession of a constitution, which King William
admired so much, that he professed himself afraid to improve it.

---

[7] See Burnet, *History of My Own Time*, ed. Osmund Airy, 2 vols. (Oxford, 1897), 1:xxviii.

This rather rosy view of the third Stuart's reign (which does not extend to the fourth) is to be contrasted by the early nineteenth-century reader with what followed:

Times had now passed, which were chequered with great virtues and great vices: but the reigns of William and Anne exhibit to the reader one uniform scene of venality and corruption; and the mind, instead of being interested, is disgusted with the contests of two parties for the government of the country, assuming, as it best suited their selfish purposes, each other's principles. (p. xxviii)

We recognize this stance (of being above the fray of party) from *The Secret History of Arlus and Odolphus*; but here, in a completely different historical context, Routh makes clear what his own principles are. Despite the corrupting effect of party politics, "it ought still however to be remembered what permanent benefits the Revolution had brought":

a solemn recognition was made of the liberties of Englishmen; the power of dispensing with the laws was abrogated in all cases; the judges ceased to be dismissed at the sole pleasure of the crown; a provision was made against the long continuance of parliament; freedom of religious worship was secured to the great body of protestant dissenters; . . . the liberty of the press established; trials for treason better regulated; and a more exact and impartial administration of justice generally introduced in the kingdom. (pp. xxix–xxx)

The modern reader, however, will most likely encounter Burnet's *History*, with Routh's preface, through the medium of Osmund Airy's 1897 Clarendon edition, along with a complex apparatus of notes added to different manuscripts by Jonathan Swift, by Arthur Onslow, by the first earl of Dartmouth and the second earl of Hardwicke – notes that, given the allegiances of their authors, inevitably pull in different ideological directions. Burnet's memoirs therefore become that entity so fashionable in the cultural history of the late twentieth century – a site of contested beliefs and interpretations.[8]

Consider, for example, Burnet's account of the trial of Lord

---

[8] One of the more amusing of such moments occurs when Burnet is expatiating on the reform of preaching style by Tillotson and Lloyd. "It soon appeared that [Charles II] had a true taste. So this helped on the value of these men, when the king approved of the style their discourses generally run in; which was clear, plain, and short" (1:340). And in the apparatus appears Swift's note: "How came Burnet not to learn this style?"

Russell for involvement in the Rye House Plot. Burnet had been a close friend of Russell, and certainly helped him with his scaffold speech, which, Burnet tells us, "was so soon printed, that it was selling about the streets an hour after his death: upon which the court was highly inflamed" (2:384). Here occurs the famous equivocation in which Burnet swore before the Privy Council that Russell had "penned" his speech himself. At this point Swift's note is terse: "Jesuitical." But Arthur Onslow had a very different reaction:

The paper does not seem clear and ingenuous enough for the character of such a man as my Lord Russell, and at such a time with him. He was certainly a very honest man, and truly meant the good of his country in all this transaction, and *that* only. But he was legally convicted, as to the crime, in law, and the evidence of it. It would have been the same with those who engaged in the revolution, if they had not succeeded; and that is his best defence . . . But be all this as it may, what have bad princes, with their instruments, to answer for hereafter, who, by iniquitous acts of pretended government, force unhappy subjects to resist them, for the sake of necessary defence, and who, if they happen to fail, are treated as criminals, and put often to cruel deaths by those very tyrants that provoked them; acting against them (and making it a justification) under the letter and colour of laws, instituted only and avowedly for the protection and security of good government: Is not this murder in the sight of an all-judging God? Would not such princes be safer in this world, and happier in that to come, if, in such cases, they pardoned their miserable subjects, and amended their own future administration of power? (2:385)

Another version of this struggle occurs by way of Burnet's theory of the origin of the term "Whig" in the Pentland rebellion in Scotland: "And this was called the *whiggamors'* inroad: and ever after all that opposed the court came in contempt to be called *whiggs*: and from Scotland the word was brought into England, where it is now one of our unhappy terms of distinction" (1:73). At which point Dartmouth's note seized an opportunity for massive irony:

Which unhappy distinctions no man living was more ready to foment than the good bishop himself: and the first inquiry he made into any body's character was, whether he were a whig or a tory: if the latter, he made it his business to rake all the spiteful stories he could collect together, in order to lessen their esteem in the world, which he was very free to publish, without any regard to decency or modesty.

Burnet's own reputation for candor, which far exceeded prudential concerns, and his lifelong commitment to religious compromise and toleration have, however, been pretty well vindicated; and the persecution he himself suffered, from Lauderdale, from Charles II, and eventually from James II, who had once been his patron, would tend to disconfirm, by explaining, Dartmouth's assessment. The assessment by the *Dictionary of National Biography* has much to recommend it, including its stylishness: "He was . . . a meddler, and yet no intriguer; a lover of secrets, which he was incapable of keeping; a vigorous polemicist, but without either spite or guile; whatever the heart conceived the tongue seemed compelled to utter or the pen to write."

And on this contested site Burnet himself, in his preface of 1702, erected an account of his motives that clearly relates to secret history as a genre. He tells how he "fell into great acquaintance and friendships with several persons who either were or had been ministers of state, from whom, *when the secret of affairs was over,*" he attempted to draw "as many particulars" as they would impart:

I saw a great deal more among the papers of the dukes of Hamilton than was properly a part of their Memoirs, or fit to be told at that time: for when a licence was to be obtained, and a work was to be published fit for the family to own, things foreign to their ministry, or hurtful to any other families, were not to be intermixed with the account I then gave of the late wars. And now for above thirty years I have lived in such intimacy with all who have had the chief conduct of affairs, and have been so much trusted and on so many important occasions employed by them, that I have been able to penetrate *into the true secrets of counsels and designs.* (p. xxxiii; italics added)

Recognizing the privileged position into which he had fallen or insinuated himself, Burnet decided to share his insider knowledge:

This made me twenty years ago write down a relation of all that I had known to that time: where I was in the dark, I past over all, and only opened those transactions that I had particular occasions to know. My chief design in writing was to give a true view of men and of counsels, leaving public transactions to gazettes and the public historians of the times. I write with a design to make both myself and my readers wiser and better, and to lay open the good and the bad of all sides and parties, as clearly and impartially as I my self understood it, concealing nothing that I thought fit to be known, and representing things in their natural colours without art or disguise, without any regard to kindred or friends, to parties or interests. (p. xxxii)

The question of Burnet's impartiality cannot help, however, to continue to be raised; not least because the notes in Airy's edition constantly support or deny it; and because his *History* would soon enter the canon of liberal authorities, as, for example, in the work of Catharine Macaulay.

Burnet claims that he had been "bred up by [his] father to love liberty and moderation," and that (like Locke) he had consolidated these principles by spending most of 1664 in Holland and France:

> I saw much peace and quiet in Holland, notwithstanding the diversity of opinions among them; which was occasioned by the gentleness of the government, and the toleration that made all people easy and happy. An universal industry was spread through the whole country: there was little aspiring to preferment in the state, because little was to be got that way . . . From thence, where every thing was free, I went to France, where nothing was free. (1:371)

But much of his account of the Restoration is colored, not surprisingly given his Scots origins, by observing how Stuart policy was inflected in Scotland. In describing how the Scottish parliament was persuaded to pass the Act of Supremacy and the Militia Act in November, 1669, Burnet not only reveals the backroom politics, but also sharpens his *de facto* definition of himself as a secret historian:

> I had no share in the counsels about this act. I only thought it was designed by lord Tweeddale to justify the Indulgence, which he protested to me was his chief end in it. And nobody could ever tell me how the word *ecclesiastical matters* was put in the act. Leighton thought he was sure it was put in after the draught and form of the act was agreed on: so it was generally charged on lord Lauderdale. And when the duke's religion came to be known, then all people saw how much the legal settlement of our religion was put in his power by this means. Yet the preamble of the act being only concerning the external government of the church, it was thought that *matters* were to be confined to the sense that was limited by the preamble . . . (1:513)

This anecdote belonged to the earlier stage of Burnet's relations with John Lauderdale, before his virtual dictatorship in Scotland and his vicious repression of nonconformity.[9] In hindsight, after they became enemies, Burnet continues:

---

[9] By 1675, however, Lauderdale's repressiveness and Burnet's objections to it were common knowledge. See Andrew Marvell, *Poems and Letters*, ed. H. M. Margoliouth, rev. Pierre Legouis (Oxford, 1971), 2:341–43. This letter, dated July 24, 1675, was written to his nephew William Popple, and describes the maneuvering of the "Episcopal Cavalier Party" to take control of the three kingdoms. In a postscript it addresses Burnet's contest with Lauderdale over the repression of Nonconformists in Scotland, and quotes Burnet as quoting Lauderdale "at the Commons' Bar," to the effect that he hoped the Scottish nonconformists would rebel, so that he could "bring over the Irish Papists to cut their throats."

The earl of Lauderdale valued himself upon these acts, as if he had conquered kingdoms by them. He wrote a letter to the king upon it, in which he said all Scotland was now in his power. The church of Scotland was not more subject to him than the church of England was. This militia was now an army ready upon call: and that every man in Scotland was ready to march whensoever he should order, with several very ill insinuations in it. But so dangerous a thing it is to write such letters to princes, that *this letter fell into duke Hamilton's hands* some years after, and *I had it in my hands for some days*.

Burnet revealed this letter to some members of the Commons during Lauderdale's impeachment;[10] the *History* shows an uneasy conscience about the revelation, which some interpreted as a personal betrayal. It continues at some length to discuss the letter's trajectory, in ways that reveal more than perhaps Burnet intended. Here, indeed, the close relation between secret history and psychology becomes visible; a relation in which the motives behind public policy both converge and conflict with the motives of others for making it public:

The way how it came into *such hands* was this. The king, after he had read the letter, gave it to sir Robert Moray, and when he died it was found among his papers. He had been much trusted in the matter of the king's laboratory, and had several of the chymical processes *in his hands*. So the king after his death did order one to look over all his papers for chymical matters: but all the papers of state were let alone. So this, with many other papers, *fell into the hands of his executors*; and thus this letter came *into hands that would have made an ill use of it*, if greater matters had not been then in agitation. This is not the single instance that I have known of papers of great consequence falling *into the hands of the executors of great ministers, that might have been turned to very bad uses, if they had fallen into ill hands.* It seems of great concern, that when a minister or an ambassador dies, or is recalled, or disgraced, all papers relating to the secrets of their employment should be of right in the power of the government. *But I of all men should complain the least of this, since by this remissness many papers of a high nature have fallen my way.*

Altogether, this complex passage repeats no less than eight times some version of the phrase whereby papers "fall" into "hands," and twice it suggests that such falls are dangerous because the hands into which they fall may be "ill." Since the second set of hands (in the passage, as distinct from actual chronology) into which Lauderdale's

---

[10] At this point one manuscript of the *History* contains the phrase, subsequently crossed out, "to show it to some of the house of commons, and to sound . . . "

deadly letter had fallen was Burnet's own, the "ill hands" from which letters of state *ought* to be protected must include Burnet's – not least because of that other admission, that Lauderdale's letter "came *into hands that would have made an ill use of it,* if greater matters had not been then in agitation." In other words, the Exclusion crisis distracted the attention of the radical members of the Commons who would otherwise have continued to press for Lauderdale's impeachment.

Like the other secret historians already mentioned, Burnet was distressed by the collapse of the Triple Alliance, which like them he probably overvalued. He cites Sir William Temple to the effect that "it was certainly the masterpiece of king Charles's life: and, if he had stuck to it, it would have been both the strength and glory of his reign" (1:456–57). Like Temple, Marvell, and the author of *The Secret History of Europe,* Burnet believed that Charles's sister Henrietta was poisoned by her husband, and in this case Dartmouth's note supports his suspicions.[11] Most importantly, of course, like Temple, he was a Williamite of the first order. When forced abroad by James's accession, he eventually arrived in Utrecht, where he so far gained the confidence of both William and Mary that he was able to give both of them invaluable advice – including on the delicate matter of how the sovereignty of their new kingdom, if they managed to acquire it, should be divided.

Burnet's notoriety in all circles makes him a useful touchstone of early modern historiography. One cannot be sure where he will crop up next, and his activities tend to blur ideological and party lines even more than the complex figures already discussed. But it was the publication and republication of his *History* and its complex annotation – its history of transmission and reception, in other words, that made it more significant than secret history *tout court.* As we see the layers of commentary encrusting Burnet thicken from edition to edition, the work becomes more valuable to cultural history, which feeds on personality, and understands issues all the better by discovering and confronting the conflicting emotions they raise.

---

[11] "Sir William Temple told me, the king employed him in searching into the truth of this report, but finding there was more in it than was fit to be known, unless he had been in a condition to resent it as a great king ought, advised him to drop the inquiry, for fear it should prejudice her daughters, who were afterwards married to the Duke of Savoy and King of Spain" (1:540).

This helps to explain the phenomenon observed by Blair Worden in his introduction to his own edition of part of Ludlow's *Memoirs*, that part that deals with the first two years of the Restoration:

Early in 1698, the opportunity to supply a new genre of Civil War history was taken. It was then . . . that the *Memoirs of Edmund Ludlow*, covering the period from the Accession of Charles I to the Restoration, were published in two volumes. They sold unexpectedly well, and caused a considerable stir. Their vivid narrative provided fresh information which could have only been available to a leading politician who had seen the events of the Puritan Revolution *from the inside*. Those events were presented, for the first time, *through the eyes of a fully rounded personality*. (pp. 18–19; italics added)

But psychological color alone does not explain the phenomenal success of Burnet's *History*, especially transatlantically. Like Ludlow's *Memoirs*, Temple's *Works* and Molesworth's *History of Denmark*, it became a secondary classic. Two thirds of the American public and private libraries listed by Colbourn contained a copy.[12] It was one of the earliest historical works in Harvard's collection. John Adams owned two sets.

Blair Worden drew to our attention, as Caroline Robbins had earlier done, the significance of the *process* by which Ludlow's *Memoirs* entered the public sphere, and what their success led to: the publication of the memoirs of Sir John Berkeley, Denzil Lord Holles, and Thomas Lord Fairfax, all of them self-evidently Whig publications; and how they spawned a Tory counter-attack, in the memoirs of Sir Philip Warwick and Sir Thomas Herbert, and Clarendon's *History of the Rebellion*.[13] Worden's nominations for this new genre, however, do not relate them to secret history, with which they were certainly imbricated, both in terms of a shared methodology (history from the inside) and in the practical terms of the book trade. Worden showed that the Whig memoirs were the product of a radical publishing enterprise, involving the publishers Richard Baldwin and his wife Anne, and John Darby Senior, whose son took over his business in the same spirit. This spirit also generated secret history. It was Richard Baldwin who published Slingsby Bethel's *The Providences of God* (1691 and 1694), but he also published, in addition to David Jones's *The Secret History of White-hall*, three other secret

---

12 See H. Trevor Colbourn, *The Lamp of Experience: Whig History and the Intellectual Origins of the American Revolution* (Chapel Hill, 1965), pp. 200–32.
13 Blair Worden, ed., *A Voyce from the Watch Tower* (London: Camden Society, 1978), pp. 1–2.

histories: *The Cabinet Open'd, or, The Secret History of the Amours of Madam de Maintenon, with the French King*, and *The Secret History of the Dutchess of Portsmouth*, both in 1690,[14] and *The Secret History of the Confederacy between the French King and his Chief Officers* in 1693. It was Anne Baldwin who reprinted Henry Neville's *Plato redivivus* in 1698; but the next year she published David Jones's edition of *Letters Written by Sir William Temple during his being Ambassador at the Hague . . . wherein are Discovered Many Secrets Hitherto Concealed.*[15] It was John Darby Sr. who published the 1698 edition of Sidney's *Discourses*, the 1698 edition of Milton's prose edited by John Toland, and, according to Worden, the version of Ludlow's *Memoirs* produced by Toland in the context of the "standing army" controversy that began in 1697. But John Darby Jr., whose publications are difficult to disentangle from those of his father until the latter's death in 1704, listed in the Stationers' Register in 1698 both Toland's *Life of Milton* and *The Secret History of the Most Famous Plots*, i.e. those of the Pazzi against Lorenzo de Medici and of Piso against Nero, on July 15, 1698. This was a collation of two secret histories published in Paris in 1697 and 1698 respectively, *Histoire secrète des plus fameuses conspirations de la conjuration des Pazzi contre les Médecis*, and *Epicharis, ou histoire secrète de la conjuration des Pisons contre Néron*, both written by Le Noble de Tenneliere.[16]

Worden mentions that Milton's nephews, Edward and John Phillips, were, like Bethel, Jones, and James Tyrrell, the friend of Locke, members of the so-called "Calves-Head" republicans of the 1690s.[17] But he does not note that John Phillips may have written the paired secret histories of the four Stuarts that appeared in 1690 and 1691, nor that part of the Tory reaction to the Whig publishing project was the 1702 *Secret History of the Calves-Head Clubb*. And if we insert secret history into this story, we get a much broader ideological picture of what concerned those on the left of center, whether we call them Calves-Head republicans, classical or Roman Whigs, or any other subset that some political historians seem to need. For the

---

[14] A French translation, *Histoire secrète de la duchesse de Portsmouth*, was also published in London in the same year.

[15] On the Baldwins, see Lena Rostenberg, "English 'Rights and Liberties': Richard & Anne Baldwin, Whig Patriot Publishers," in Rostenberg, *Literary, Political, Scientific, Religious and Legal Publishing, Printing and Bookselling in England, 1551–1780: Twelve Studies*, 2 vols. (New York, 1965), 2:369–431.

[16] See Ralph Coplestone Williams, *Bibliography of the Seventeenth-Century Novel in France* (New York, 1931), p. 64.

[17] Worden, *Voyce*, pp. 18–19.

authors whose works I have described seem unconcerned, even after the Treaty of Ryswick in 1697, by the standing army controversy, and it is not at all clear that their objective was to reveal the 1690s as an era of "apostasy and corruption," so heavily do they bear on these qualities as embodied in the Stuarts, to be washed away in the Revolution. One does not find them saying, at least not in their secret histories, that things have *not* changed for the better, and it is still government as usual. On the contrary, if there is a unifying theme that connects those of the late 1670s with those of the 1690s and beyond, it is the continuing necessity for alertness against the machinations of France, the wellspring of monarchical absolutism.

"THE CRAFTSMAN"

This situation remained intact during the realignment of parties that took place under Robert Walpole, whose Whig government was broadly accused of having sold out the "revolution principles" and brought in an era of governmental corruption. When John Darby Jr. reprinted *The Secret History of . . . Q. Elizabeth and the E. of Essex* in 1725, he was probably using the same principle of historical allusion as that which characterized *The Craftsman*, the most successful political journal of its era. Though sponsored and occasionally written by Bolingbroke, as a liberal Tory, *The Craftsman* owed its energy and wit to Nicholas Amhurst, a rebel Whig. Amhurst had been expelled from St. John's College, Oxford, he explains ironically in the dedication to his *Poems* (1720), for, among other items, "lampooning priestcraft and petticoat craft" and "for prying into secret history."

The Craftsman connected secret history with the danger to England of French interests. The journal began its attacks on Walpole in December, 1726, provoked, Amhurst tells us later, by the signing of the Treaty of Hanover, and "the close Conjunction between France and Us, which ensued upon it . . . [which] We apprehended to be big with fatal Consequences to Great Britain" (No. 278). In one of the early numbers, *The Craftsman* had pretended, with its characteristically heavy irony, to attack earlier Whig francophobia. It drew to its readers' attention *The Secret History of Europe*, written, we are told, "no longer ago than the last Reign, by one of the hot-brain'd Zealots of that Party; which is stuffed, in almost every Page, with the bitterest and most indecent Reflections on that great People [the French], as well as on Those, who were supposed, at that Time, to be in their Interest." And having cited several strong statements from Old-mixon about the dangers of the French interest in England, it broadened the incentive to follow up on secret history: "Nor is He the only Author of this Kind; for it would be an easy Task to produce a Cart-load of Books, Pamphletes and loose Sheets, published by Men of the same Stamp, since the Restoration, in order to inculcate the same malevolent Principles of Aversion to France into the Minds of the People of this Kingdom" (No. 26). This upsidedown gesture, to avoid misunderstanding, is immediately reversed; for what follows is a praise of the Netherlands as a "popular State" which, though providing "excellent Instructions" on government to all "free States," was nearly destroyed, in the reign of Charles II, by France and England in alliance; a position *The Craftsman* supports by citing Sir William Temple.

Amhurst himself and his contributors were not themselves secret historians. On the contrary, they assumed as part of the task of political education the constant recirculation of *standard* English history, especially that of the Stuarts. But their authorities include most of the Whig or liberal canon as we have hitherto defined it: along with Temple's *Memoirs*,[18] *The Craftsman* likes to cite Burnet's histories (Nos. 28, 101, 425), and Sir John Hawles's pamphlets.[19] The case of Algernon Sidney appears often, especially in connection with the liberty of the press (Nos. 2, 4, 117, 467, 478). In No. 281 (November 20, 1731), *The Craftsman* printed Locke's "Reasons why the Commons cannot agree to the Clause . . . which revived the old Printing Act, deliver'd at a Conference with the Lords, 1695," a text retrieved from the Lords' Journals. In No. 151 (May 24, 1729), the attack in Locke's *Two Treatises* on Charles II's or James II's corruption of parliament by bribery is quoted at length (Section 222, 30–50),[20] and reapplied to Walpole. Laslett regards this passage as added in 1689 in order to apply primarily to James. But its "secret history" character, to be discussed in chapter 9, owes much to

---

[18] Temple's *Essay upon the Original and Nature of Government* is also cited at length in No. 111.

[19] See No. 281, where Hawles's *Remarks upon the tryals of Edward Fitzharris, Stephen College . . . the Lord Russel, Collonel Sidney, &cs.* is cited as an authority on the liberty of the press (8.211). See also No. 289, a synopsis of Hawles's *The Englishman's Right, or a Dialogue between a Barrister at Law and a Juryman*.

[20] John Locke, *Two Treatises of Government*, ed. Peter Laslett (Cambridge, 1965), p. 413: "He acts also contrary to his Trust . . . as perfect a Design to subvert the Government, as is possible to be met with."

Marvell's *Account of the Growth of Popery and Arbitrary Government.*[21] In No. 217 (August 29, 1730), sixteen lines from Marvell's Restoration satire, *The Last Instructions to the Painter* (lines 131–46), provide the colorful premise for *The Craftsman*'s attack on a recent proposal for a general Excise tax. No. 449 (February 8, 1745) characterizes its opponents in the polemical press, Walsingham and Frank Osborne, in terms of Marvell's opponent Bayes (Samuel Parker) in the *Rehearsal Transpros'd,* and devotes a long and complex issue to explaining how acute was Marvell's analysis of Parker's misuse of style and argument. It concludes with Marvell's ironic attack on the invention of printing, suggesting that the legend of Cadmus needed to be rewritten; "the Serpent's Teeth, which He sowed, were nothing else but the Letters he invented";[22] a passage "so full of sharp Wit and true Humour" that it recommends both itself and its reappropriation to a later cause. It seems fair to say that *The Craftsman* knew that secret history was a liberal genre, and helped to pass it on as a tradition whose integrity increased over time. Unlike the French versions, which like *nouvelles* were primarily interested in the sexual scandal of the moment, English political secret history was not short-lived. By the very end of the eighteenth century, all of the above propositions were still very much alive.

"THE SECRET HISTORY OF . . . CHARLES THE SECOND"

In 1792 appeared what could be seen as either a curious moment of nostalgia or a grand and pertinent retrospective of alternative history in the early modern period: *The Secret History of the Court and Reign of Charles the Second, by A Member of his Privy Council . . . with . . . a Supplement Continuing the Narrative in a Summary Manner to the Revolution, by the Editor* (London, 1792). The editor of this two-volume work has been identified as Charles McCormick, who withholds not only his own name but also that of the privy councillor whose manuscript has only now seen the light. An "advertisement" to the reader explains that the manuscript was originally in the hands of William Pitt the elder, who entrusted it to Dr. Shebbeare for publication, under the

---

[21] Locke's *Two Treatises* appear again as an authority in No. 441 (December 14, 1734), an essay on the British constitution which cites Locke's Chapter 11 from the Second Treatise.

[22] See *The Rehearsal Transpros'd,* ed. D. I. B. Smith (Oxford, 1971), pp. 4–5. *The Craftsman* desires its readers to "remember that Mr. Marvel was engaged with an Advocate for Ecclesiastical Tyranny, which is not our Case at present, but the Satire will hold equally strong, mutatis mutandis, against all Contenders for civil Oppression."

misapprehension that Shebbeare had liberal opinions. "But Shebbeare was in his heart a Tory; and having had another manuscript
nearly on the same subject, and more agreeable to his own
sentiments, given him a little time after, he resolved to print the
latter, and to prevent, if possible, the appearance of the former"
(d3r). McCormick supplied, however, a powerful ethical preface
further defining secret history as a genre. First, on the question of
authenticity and history from the inside:

> The following work carries with it too great a degree of internal evidence
> to require the aid of argument to demonstrate its genuineness, or to remove
> any doubts of its authenticity. It abounds with information far beyond the
> reach or researches of any writers, who had not a considerable share in the
> events which he relates; and who was not admitted, as it were, behind the
> scenes, to view the machinery of court intrigues, to examine the springs of
> each political measure, and to assist in managing the wires, that put every
> state-puppet in motion. Here alone the materials of history are to be
> collected. Without an easy access to the secrets of government the most
> attentive observer is liable to be dazzled and deceived by the false glare of
> outward appearances. An artificial splendor surrounds the actions, as well
> as the thrones of princes, while their cabinets and their councils are hid in
> almost impenetrable darkness. (a6)

This contrast between the glitter of monarchical rituals and the
backstage darkness of their policy (which the artificial lighting up
front intensifies) adds flair to the already quite complicated theory of
secret history; and this claim to the authenticity of the materials
then, however, modulates into a critique of the original author, who
failed to live up to the true mission of secret history – that of keeping
the public informed:

> When we also consider, that he wrote this history, not for the information
> of his country, but for the use of his own family, out of whose hands he
> declares that it should never pass by his consent, we cannot compliment
> him on the score of public spirit, nor can we feel ourselves under any
> obligation for a favour, which he so selfishly intended to withhold from us.
> (a5r)

But – another twist – such unethical privatization turns out to be an
advantage, elevating this particular secret history into the front rank
of the genre. For "it is a series of the most interesting truths,
extorted, as it were, from the lips of an unwilling evidence":

> It is an undesigned, yet unanswerable satire on the folly of trusting to the
> profession of kings: it is a royalist's dreadful warning to the people of

England never to be betrayed by their affection for any family into a surrender of their inestimable privileges: it is, in short, a full and convincing refutation of all the falsehoods which have been invented, and of all the sophistry which has been devised by prostituted genius in defence of arbitrary power. (a5r)

What in 1792 was the motivation for, as some might say, flogging a dead horse? And to which royal family were the English still in danger of surrendering their privileges? Answer: the House of Hanover, whose current encumbent was George III.

McCormick makes only a few overt references to his own historical context, but they should have been enough to keep his audience alert. On Clarendon's silken dissuasions against calling a parliament in 1663, he noted: "By these remarks we may see, that some of the ministers of Charles II. were almost as well skilled in the arts of *decent corruption*, as Walpole himself, or any of his modern imitators" (2:27). And as he concludes his own "supplement" with two terse pages on James II, McCormick observes:

Tyranny is never more violent than when impelled by religious zeal to break through all the restraints of policy and caution. James's total disregard of both accelerated the REVOLUTION, to which we are indebted for *what still remains* of our civil and religious liberty. (2:130; italics added)

Like the earlier secret histories described above, this one justifies its title (presumably added by McCormick) by dwelling on the secrets of state: Charles's "secret abjuration of the protestant religion," to which Bristol was privy (1:381); the "secret negociation" with France that began even in 1661 (1:399–400) and clearly infected the Second Dutch War, with whose miscarriages the secret history proper concludes. And in his "Supplement" which carries the history from 1669 not, as the title-page promised, to the Revolution, but up to and through the political trials of 1683, McCormick expatiated on the secret Treaty of Dover, "by which one tyrant, immersed in sensuality, betrayed to another, more guided by ambition, the interests of his own kingdom" ("Supplement," p. 2).

In his additions and notes, McCormick reveals that his most important authorities (whereby to expand on and qualify his primary source) were Gilbert Burnet, Catharine Macaulay, Temple's *Memoirs*, Ludlow's *Memoirs*, Marvell's *Account of the Growth of Popery*, and John Milton's poetry! The original writer was himself deeply impressed with Sir William Temple, who becomes a hero of the last phase of the history (2:360ff), for his effective management of the Triple Alliance. Both author and "Editor" express dismay at Charles's sexual libertinism, particularly as expressed by his insistence that his new Portuguese bride should receive Barbara Villiers into her entourage (1:445–50). McCormick shares with almost all secret historians of the previous century the belief that Charles's sister Henrietta was poisoned by her husband, and adds a severe note of his own on the subject of Charles's hypocrisy in permitting a cover-up ("Supplement," p. 26).

The unnamed author had dark views of the Restoration parliament, in agreeing to everything Charles wanted and more, and in establishing such repressive measures as the Act of Uniformity and the Five Mile Act. McCormick's notes are only more colorful expressions of the same disapprovals, developed by way of allusion to the earlier liberal canon. Thus, in a comment on the unprecedented revenue voted the king in 1662, he adds:

The pension-parliament, however, who had carried their compliance with the desires of the court, in this and in many other particulars, to the most criminal length, took care to prevent, as far as they were able, the severity of public reproach. In one act . . . they restrained the right of petitioning; and by another they destroyed the liberty of the press. A licenser was appointed to examine every book and pamphlet, that no bold truths might be disseminated through the kingdom. We may form some idea of the private instructions given to this licenser, as well as of his excessive caution and ignorant zeal, when we are assured that on his taking exception to the following lines in Milton's Paradise Lost, that admirable poem had like to be suppressed. (1:441)

And there follows the notorious simile describing the diminution of Satan's angelic glory in terms of a solar or lunar eclipse, which "with fear of change/Perplexes monarchies."

As for the Five Mile Act, it provokes an unusually long and revealing note – revealing of the late eighteenth-century concerns that have infiltrated and somewhat reshaped this late seventeenth-century narrative. This act, wrote McCormick, "seemed to be the last step in the climax of intolerance":

For to deprive men of the means of subsistence implies more deliberate cruelty, though it does not excite so much horror as fire and faggots . . . Is it not astonishing that so infamous an act, framed and passed by about one hundred of Charles the second's menial servants . . . should be still suffered to disgrace our statute-book! (2:172)

Like his predecessors in this genre, McCormick was obsessed by English parliamentary history from 1672 through 1677, for which he turned to the authority of the *Account of the Growth of Popery and Arbitrary Government*. He cites Marvell *for imaginative color* in relation to the symmetries between English and French affairs:

on the fifteenth of February, the very day the session was to be opened [after the Long Prorogation], the French king appointed his march for Flanders, as if, says Andrew Marvel, his motions were in just cadence, and that, as in a grand ballet, he kept time with those, who were tuned here to his measures. ("Supplement," p. 67)

And again, on the subject of the adjournments of 1677, he cites him because he admires his irony:

his majesty affected to represent [the Commons' advice on foreign policy] as a dangerous encroachment on his prerogative. He made a severe speech on the subject to the commons at Whitehall; and ordered them to be immediately adjourned. The Gazette of the next day contained his reproving speech, being the first which had ever appeared in that paper. Thus, says Marvel, were the commons well rewarded for their itch of perpetual sitting and of acting, the parliament being grown to that height of contempt as to be gazetted among run-away servants, lap dogs, strayed horses, and highway robbers. ("Supplement," p. 73)

Because his source, the unnamed privy councillor, was himself deeply interested in Scotland during the early Restoration, and in the restoration of episcopacy there, long citations from Gilbert Burnet appear, appropriately enough, in the footnotes. But McCormick was particularly concerned by the political trials of Charles II's reign – those of the regicides in 1660–3, and those implicated in the Rye House Plot in 1683, on both of which his source was silent, but which, in his shaping of the story, become the defining opening and closing moments of Charles's reign. The last fifty pages of the "Supplement's" account of that reign are devoted to admiring accounts of Lord Russell and Algernon Sidney; and fifty pages were *inserted* in the first volume to take account of the trials with which the reign began. A reader in 1792 might perhaps overlook this remarkable symmetry; but he could scarcely ignore the following intense rationale, which involves him in a consideration of the historiography of his own day:

[As the writer of the Secret History makes no comment on the trial of the regicides . . . it may be proper to insert here some account of those proceedings for the gratification of the reader's curiosity. This we are the more powerfully incited to from a desire of vindicating the cause of truth, justice, and humanity, which appear to have been equally disregarded by most of our historians in the relation of such plain matters of fact. Some have even thought, that their own loyalty could be displayed only by stabbing the memories of those unfortunate sufferers with more savage cruelty than was exerted against their bodies by a barbarous executioner . . . Is is not rather a libel upon royalty to suppose, that it can be glutted with the blood of freedom; or that the avenues to a throne should resemble the entrance of a giant's cave in romance, and be strewed over with the limbs of slaughtered victims!]. (1:94–95)

Against this picture of a reactionary Georgian historiography, McCormick erected the standard of Catharine Macaulay, whose account of the trials of the regicides he then incorporated into his own narrative. The effect of his editing, then, was to alert his own readers to the role of *party* in history-writing in general; without, of course, doubting the value of the partisanship he himself displays.

For the present argument, the most interesting aspect of this act of retransmission (or double transmission, since the reader is thereby recommended to pursue Macaulay elsewhere) occurs in the finale, where a brief hagiography of Sir Henry Vane provides an opportunity for yet another layering of ethical authorities. "We are irresistibly tempted," wrote McCormick, "by Mrs. Macaulay's example, and by the exquisite beauty of the lines themselves, to introduce here the following extract from Samson Agonistes, in which the divine Milton is supposed to allude to the unexpected turn which the affairs of state had then taken; to the sufferings of the most eminent republicans; and particularly to the unjust execution of sir Henry Vane" (1:142–43). There follow those thirty lines from Milton's closet drama in which the Chorus laments the apparent fickleness of the Lord towards his defenders, abandoning them to "th'unjust tribunal[s], under change of times,/And condemnation of the ungrateful multitude."

Finally, the "Supplement" turned, as I have said, with a dying fall, to the trials and executions of the Rye House plotters, Hampden, Essex, Russell, Sidney. Here too, as in John Phillips's account of these events, enormous indignation is generated by the court attack on city charters and the *quo warranto* proceedings. Here, again, McCormick acknowledged himself indebted to Catharine Macaulay's history, Volume 7, "from which, as being beyond all comparison the best that has yet appeared in the English language, the above supplement is principally taken" (pp. 126–27). McCormick did not explicitly ask his readers the question posed at the end of *The Secret History of Europe*: "what's all this History to us . . . ?" still less rephrase it as chronology might demand, "what's all this old History to us today?" Yet in the last decade of the eighteenth century there was obviously as much need for the combined acts of memory and imagination, thinking backwards in order to think forwards, as there had been exactly a century earlier.

"THE SECRET HISTORY OF THE COURT OF ENGLAND"

The last exhibit in this series will be seen as of questionable credibility; and yet the story of political secret history in the genesis of liberalism would not be complete without it. Not only in its contents but in its own publication history it provides a summary and synthesis of everything that has preceded it in this chapter; and it raises an authorial mystery that, while it can probably never now be solved, has itself some significance for our understanding of the relation between nineteenth-century liberalism, eventually so-called, and the extraordinary mishmash of events, persons, concepts and conventions from which it grew.

In March 1832 appeared *The Authentic Records of the Court of England, for the Last Seventy Years*, supposedly written by Lady Anne Hamilton, and published by John Phillips. A section of that work, dealing with the murder/suicide of the duke of Cumberland's valet, Sellis, became the subject of a libel suit in King's Bench against Phillips. The *Annual Register* for 1833, in recording the libel trial, Phillips's conviction, and the fine of a hundred pounds,[23] remarked that:

the book was composed with no ordinary degree of malice, and the language and facts adduced showed that it was the production of a person with no ordinary talents and powers, the libel itself being introduced in a mode evincing considerable ingenuity. (p. 91)

Sometime between April 19 of that year and, probably, May 18, it

---

[23] A note in the Yale copy of the *Authentic Records* asserts that Phillips broke bail and fled the country to avoid paying the fine.

was followed by a considerably expanded and partially rewritten version of the same book, now published by William Stevenson, of the Strand, and retitled *The Secret History of the Court of England, from the accession of George III to the Death of George the Fourth; including, among other important matters, full particulars of the mysterious death of the Princess Charlotte and the murder of the Duke of Cumberland's valet, Sellis.* We can be so precise about the dating because the *Secret History* alludes twice to the libel case now pending. The first allusion appears in a new preface, which begins: "How far the law of libel (as it now stands) may affect us is best to be ascertained by a reference to the declaration of Lord Abingdon in 1779 . . . " This refers to the long speech by Abingdon in the House of Lords on the case of a libel suit brought against William Parker, printer of the *General Advertiser*, a speech which the revised *Secret History* inserted verbatim. The second allusion to the libel case against Phillips appears in a new legal framework surrounding the Sellis narrative, which now, however, constitutes a rationale for secret history expanding on and updating previous theorizations:

We are the strenuous advocates of the right to promulgate truth – of the right to scrutinize public actions and public men – of the right to expose vice, and castigate mischievous follies, even though they may be found in a palace! The free exercise of this invaluable privilege should always be conceded to the historian, or where will posterity look for impartial information?[24]

And as part of its defensive strategy, the *Secret History* cites a letter to the press by the radical Francis Place, dated April 19, 1932 and listing several mistakes in the coroner's affidavit, one of which involved Place's role as foreman of the 1810 jury which had found that Sellis committed suicide.

Dating is important, since both versions of the work speak specifically to the actual moment of their appearance. The *Authentic Records*, opening in 1761 with George III's enforced marriage to Charlotte of Mecklenburgh (despite the fact that he had previously married Hannah Lightfoot in 1759), concludes in January 1832 with Lord John Russell's bill for parliamentary reform having just been lost in the House of Lords. The *Secret History* was *also* evidently

---

[24] *Secret History*, p. 99. I cite from the single-volume reprint of 1878 (London: Reynolds' Newspaper Office).

produced between the negative vote in the Lords on the Reform Bill and its eventual passage in late May and early June, and even more clearly directs its readers to promote the Bill and threatens those who have hitherto opposed it.[25] As we shall see, therefore, far more was at stake in the revised and expanded version than the struggle for survival of a single printer.

The *Authentic Records* had apparently been promptly disclaimed by Lady Anne Hamilton, as written by a person (gender unspecified) who had abused her confidences. Or so we are told by the *Dictionary of National Biography*, which also circulated the rumor that this "scandalous" work ought to be attributed instead to Olivia Wilmot Serres, a crazy lady who had recently been calling herself the Princess of Cumberland. At least, "there are good reasons," wrote the biographer of Serres without specifying what they were, "for believing that she had a hand in it." But there are also good reasons for thinking that the attribution to poor Mrs. Serres, who was sixty-two in 1832 and died two years later, was as scandalous in its own way as the *Dictionary* declared the *Secret History* to be.[26]

The original spurious attribution to Lady Anne Hamilton was odd by any standards except those of marketing, since she appears only in the third person, while the authors consistently represent themselves as plural: as "editors," whose "'Weapons are Impartiality and Truth" (*AR*, p. vii), and as "honest and fearless historians," (*SH*, p. 142).[27] Perhaps both the strategy of Phillips and that of the *Dictionary* were driven by the assumption, fostered by Mrs. Manley and others, that secret history had become a woman's genre, especially in its more lurid and romantic manifestations. Certainly the contents of the *Authentic Records* are reminiscent of Eliza Haywood's *The Secret History of the Present Intrigues of Court of Caramania* (1727), with its focus on the "inner and privy bed" in the court of George II. Here, however, the lurid plot, which links the forced marriages of both the latter two Georges to their misgovernment (lunacy in the third, profligacy in the fourth) is clearly aimed at more than titillation. The suspected murder of the princess Charlotte is

---

[25] *Ibid.*, pp. 24–27.

[26] Presumably the reasons unspecified by the *Dictionary* for seeing the hand of Serres in the work included its conviction, expressed only in the second, *Secret History* version, that the author of the Junius letters was her uncle, Dr. James Wilmot (pp. 13–14). This was a conviction that Serres had argued in two pamphlets.

[27] While the editorial "we" might have been unremarkable, the grammatical insistence that more than one historian is involved seems to exceed that convention.

only a symptom of a long conspiracy to reenslave the English, which begins when George III is unwillingly married to his German wife, and will end only with a massive reform of the government, its morals, its finances, and the representational system, which in both versions of the work, as the crisis over the Reform Bill intensifies, is seen as a symbolic gesture in the right direction rather than a cure. The cause of the disease is not, however, monarchy itself, but one particular political party. "We do not hesitate to say," the "editors" agree in conclusion, "that the Tories have brought the country to its present degraded state by their misrule for the last seventy years" (p. 394).

The *Authentic Records*, however, is scarcely redeemed by this premise from the stigma of being a scandal chronicle. Its focus is almost exclusively the court, the supposed machinations of Queen Charlotte, the complicity of the younger Pitt in her plans, the supposed poisoning of the younger Charlotte, and above all the miserable and mutually degrading relations between Queen Caroline and her husband, culminating in her defence before the House of Lords against his suit for divorce. One remarkable feature is the inclusion, at length, of that part of Henry Brougham's speech to the University of Glasgow which returned to the theme of the queen's "trial," a term that Brougham violently disavowed (pp. 296–302). Into this melodrama are woven fulminations on the national debt, the wasteful finances of the court, the placeholders in parliament, and especially the "secrets of state." As this Gothic romance draws to its close, the editors ask rhetorically:

What, then, it may be asked, is the cause of the present unhappy state of England? . . . the long concealed secrets of state, which have, alas! led to the commission of crimes – of MURDERS! that must force the tear of pity from the eye of compassionating Humanity. (*AR*, pp. 364–65)

It is easy to dismiss this rhetoric as fatuous and self-defeating. But person or persons in 1832 were apparently capable of making the same observation, and correcting accordingly. For when the work reappeared as the *Secret History* about a month later, the hysterical tone, though still visible in the unchanged sections, had been rendered less noticeable by the greatly enlarged conceptual scope and detailed surface of the work. More important, other perspectives have been added to the editorial or historiographical team. The most striking alterations involve:

1. A new focus on foreign policy, which includes expanded commentary on the war with the American colonies, the partition of Poland, the Irish question, and a huge digression on Napoleon Buonaparte and the wrongfulness of his banishment to St. Helena;

2. A series of insertions that indicate a principled and historically informed commitment to the freedom of the press. These include an expanded account of John Wilkes and the affair of the *North Briton* (p. 6), an allusion to "the glorious acquittal of Hardy, Tooke, and Thelwall" (p. 42) in the treason trials of 1794, and the insertion of the full text of an anti-Canning pamphlet. "The author," remarked these revisers, as a commentary on their own procedure, "was Mr. (now Sir John Cam) Hobhouse, though the fact is little known; but, for some unexplained cause, the book was speedily withdrawn from publication. A few having been sold, however, we were fortunate enough to procure one" (pp. 308–09).

3. A new emphasis on class, with a strong sympathy for "the productive classes" (p. 10). In suggesting that George III when sane shared this sympathy, this phrase is actually *substituted* for the earlier work's conventional references to "the poor and industrious of the realm" (*AR*, p. 12).

4. An inexplicable but nevertheless sustained attempt to render the work more "literary" by the inclusion of quotations from Shakespeare, Cowper, Byron and Milton. This last ambition results in a lengthy attack on Sir Walter Scott for his servile flattery of the court: "Since the art of printing was invented – since that era when Ignorance and Superstition were first driven before the light of Reason, exhibited in the circulation of a free press, – we unhesitatingly affirm that there has never been published an eulogium so totally at variance with fact as that written by the author of 'Waverley' on his Royal Highness of York" (p. 305); and the insertion of all thirty-two stanzas of Byron's *The Irish Avatar* (pp. 227–30), a vicious satire on George IV's triumphal visit to Ireland in the summer of 1821, four days after the death of Queen Caroline, which suggests that the queen and Ireland were equally victims of royal cynicism:

> Ere the daughter of Brunswick is cold in her grave,
> And her ashes still float to their home o'er the tide,
> Lo! George the triumphant speeds over the wave
> To that long-cherish'd isle which he loved like his – bride.

5. Perhaps the most astonishing change, and one which will need

our further analysis outside the *Secret History* itself, is the decision to abandon or at least radically complicate Whig polemic, by substituting for simple anti-Tory invective an attack on party politics generally. This vision (and revision) is worth repeating in (almost) all its distinctive prolixity. Beginning with a sentence inherited from the *Authentic Records*:

According to the pure fabric of the British Constitution, no nation on the surface of the globe ought to have been more happy, . . . more prosperous and contented, than this country.

the revisers suddenly shift the nature of their qualification:

But, from the time of Queen Anne, the State has been gradually retrograding and divided into two aristocratical parties, – Whigs and Tories, – whose watchwords were principles (which might be said to be constitutionally attached to opposition or place), but whose struggles have ever been for power. The spirit of party has been said to furnish aliment to the spirit of liberty; and so perhaps it does, but in this way: by first creating the despotism which it is the office of the spirit of liberty to counteract, and, if possible to overthrow. . . . All party spirit, generally speaking, is injurious. It has been truly denounced by one of the greatest friends of freedom the world has ever seen – the illustrious Washington, – as "the very worst enemy of popular governments." In his farewell address to the American people, he earnestly warns them against it as the thing from which, of all others, they had most to fear. "It serves always," he tells them, "to distract the public councils and enfeeble the public administration. It agitates the community with ill-founded jealousies and false alarms; kindles the animosity of one class against another; foments, occasionally, riots and insurrections; it opens the door to foreign influence and corruption, which find a facilitated access to the Government itself, through the channels of party passions." All party ascendancies have this character in common – that they serve to make the interests of the country subordinate to private ends. It is the established mode with dominant factions to distribute the loaves and fishes among their own adherents exclusively . . . Ever since the Revolution of 1688, England has never been free from the trammels of some such dominant faction or other, and what have been the consequences? One long course of misgovernment, one unceasing heaping of burdens on the people . . . Whether it was Tory or whether it was Whig that was in power, the result to the people was almost always the same. (pp. 339–40)

Thus George Washington is added to the list of liberalism's founding figures. The little vessels carrying the message of early modern liberalism to America start floating back, as it were, to help the country of origin sort out its own problems; oblivious to the irony that the America of the 1830s had avoided none of the disadvantages here fairly if exorbitantly described.

Now, the term used for this congeries of values is, at last, "liberal." In two instances this had been the lexical choice of the "authentic recorders." While his father was alive "the country gave [the Prince Regent] credit for being *liberal* in political principles, and generously disposed for reform. But little of his *real* character was then known" (p. 30). In contrast, Thomas, lord Erskine, was honored as a man whose "sentiments were of too *liberal* a cast for George the Fourth's ideas of subjection and tyranny" (p. 294). But in the revised work, especially in the heavily augmented opening sections, the use of "liberal" begins to look programmatic. In 1771 "various struggles were made . . . to curb the power of the judges, particularly in cases relating to the liberty of the press . . . but the borough-mongers and minions of the Queen were too powerful for the Liberal party in the House of Commons" (pp. 14–15).[28] The Royal Marriage Act of 1772 "was strenuously opposed by the Liberal party" (p. 16). In 1775 "the enlightened and liberal-minded part of the community," as exemplified by Chatham, attempted to avert the war with the American colonists (p. 19). In 1779, yet another libel case against a printer produced a speech by Lord Abingdon in the Lords (a speech now inserted in full) which revealed that "there were a *few* intelligent and liberal-minded men in the House of Lords at that time" (p. 24).

And, as the revisers approached the original scandalous center of the work, the death of Princess Charlotte, they added an unidentified literary quotation that now acquired a startling new pertinence:

We must now, as honest and fearless historians, record the most cold-blooded and horrible crime that ever was perpetrated in this or any other Christian country.

> 'Tis a strange truth. O monstrous act!
> 'Twill out, 'twill out! I hold my peace, sir? No,
> No; I will speak as *liberal* as the air.

These three lines of verse piece together three reactions to one of the

---

[28] The context here was the suit against printers for printing parliamentary speeches, and John Wilkes's intervention on their behalf. "The contest," reported the secret historians, "finally terminated in favor of the printers, who have ever since continued to publish the proceedings of Parliament, and the speeches of the members, without obstacle.

most famous crimes in Shakespeare – the murder of Desdemona by her husband (*Othello*, 5.2.190–91 and 220–21) – in order to transform the courageous testimony of Emilia against *her* husband into a mandate for the secret historian. In this remarkable piece of cultural adaptation, "liberal" has expanded its range of meaning, to incorporate the early seventeenth-century sense of free outspokenness with the early nineteenth-century sense of political reportage.

The presence of this now fully politicized term is significant in itself; but even more remarkable is what, as the work progresses, it has come to mean: not just the classic Whig virtues of ministerial probity and disinterestedness, the liberal insistence on an educated public and a free press, equal justice and religious toleration, but also an implied democratization, or, at the least, an articulated populism. The revised work argues that ordinary people should get – should claim – a decent share of the economic benefits of the system. The demand for change is, implicitly, a demand for self-determination for all; which brings us back to the Reform Bill and its defeat in the Lords. "Why should sensible men give up their judgments to a selfish and hypocritical faction of lords? What better, in the name of heaven, are they than the rest of human creatures?" And here in the argument are placed, without identification, four lines from John Milton; not, as one might have supposed, from the Adamic premise just cited, from *Paradise Lost*, but, more inventively, from *Paradise Regained*, Book 4, ll.343–46:

> Remove their swelling epithets, thick laid
> As varnish on a harlot's cheek; the rest,
> Thin sown with aught of profit or delight,
> Will far be found unworthy. (p. 371)[29]

But what, then, was the real purpose of the revised *Secret History*, produced with so much expedition in the spring of 1832?

Judging from the extensive revisions to the work's conclusion, it

---

[29] The "historians" have adapted to their own purpose Christ's rejection of Greek literature and philosophy in favor of biblical precept. Yet the appropriation is understandable, since Milton's Christ, rejecting temptation, continues:

> Thir Orators thou then extoll'st, as those
> The top of Eloquence, Statists indeed,
> And lovers of their country, as may seem;
> But herein to our Prophets far beneath,
> As men divinely taught, and better teaching
> The solid rules of Civil Government
> In their majestic unaffected style
> Than all the Oratory of Greece and Rome. (lines 353–60)

was to smooth the passing of the Reform Bill by warning the public against violent demonstrations in its favor; or, perhaps, by warning the House of Lords that a second rejection would precipitate more than scattered instances of popular protest. The defeat of the Bill in the Lords in October had been followed by violent rioting in Derby, Nottingham and Bristol.[30]

The *Secret History* appeared, as close as one can judge, while William IV was debating whether he could bring himself to create the necessary number of peers to ensure its passage in May. The secret historians, for all the work's new populism, recommended a constitutional solution to the crisis. They therefore appealed for public restraint, for *strategic* reasons: "Ministers," they warned, "have too long imposed upon the credulity of the timid, by describing every riotous proceeding as the natural consequence of *the progress of liberal opinions*" (p. 348). The people, therefore, must be upon their guard not to give fuel to this fallacy by engaging in popular commotion. "Revolution ought always to be the work of the Government, not of the people, except through the expression of public opinion . . . Physical force ought never to be employed for the correction of social evils, *until* every species of negative resistance has proved to be unavailing" (pp. 373–74; italics added).

But close reading is advisable. Like John Rawls in *Political Liberalism* (cf. Introduction, p. 19), these anonymous historians recall John Locke's canny formulae in the peroration to the *Two Treatises of Government*, which itself, in its turn to conspiracy theory, recalls Marvell's *Account of the Growth of Popery and Arbitrary Government* (cf. chapter 8, pp. 270–1):

For *till* the mischief be grown general, and the ill designs of the Rulers become visible . . . the People, who are more disposed to suffer, than right themselves by Resistance, are not apt to stir. (*Second Treatise*, Section 230)

But if a long train of Abuses, Prevarications, and Artifices, all tending the same way, make the design visible to the People, . . . 'tis not to be wonder'd, that they should then rouze themselves, and endeavour to put the rule into such hands, which may secure to them the ends for which Government was at first erected. (Section 225)

---

[30] For personal contemporary accounts of the pressures and negotiations for and against reform, see E. A. Smith, *Reform or Revolution? A Diary of Reform in England, 1830–2* (Stroud, 1992). The definitive history of the moment is J. R. M. Butler, *The Passing of the Great Reform Bill* (London, 1914, 1964).

And, as Peter Laslett has shown us, these were precisely the sections of Locke's pamphlet that reappeared, as distinct echoes, in the American Declaration of Independence.[31]

The Secret History of the Court of England was reprinted in 1878, with an odd note on the title-page: "This is a faithful reprint of a work which produced an extraordinary sensation on its first appearance forty-four years ago, and was speedily suppressed. It is the same, too, for which the sum of a Thousand Pounds was offered in New York about two years ago." If we are to trust this advertising gimmick, this late secret history was far more important, on both sides of the Atlantic, than our current historiographical practices have registered. It was further reprinted in London in 1883 and 1893, and in Boston in 1901 and 1912. Yet thanks to the disrepute in which *anecdota* as a genre have generally been held, it has subsequently vanished from our view. The *Dictionary of National Biography* assisted its disappearance by attributing the *Authentic Records* to the unfortunate Mrs. Serres.

But even that lurid version deserves to be taken seriously as a formal contribution to the political situation. Its focus has much in common with the views of Brougham, who, while defending Queen Caroline in the Lords in 1820 against George IV's divorce proceedings,[32] was rumored to be holding in reserve proof of George IV's secret and illegal marriage to Mrs. Fitzherbert. Brougham, moreover (who was notorious for his melodramatic behavior, and who quoted *Paradise Lost* in his veiled attack on George IV),[33] believed there was a need for alternative history. In August 19, 1828, he wrote to Lord John Russell:

You know our lives and histories (U.K.) are excellent in many respects – and in one particularly – they inculcate sound and virtuous principles against war, treachery, and slavery. but they do so rather by the reflexions interspersed than by the tone and manner of the narrative. In short, the story is told too much in the ordinary way, and the proper *tone and manner* is

---

[31] Locke, *Two Treatises of Government*, ed. Laslett, pp. 415, 418. The *Declaration* similarly states that "mankind are more disposed to suffer, while evils are sufferable, than to right themselves," and echoes Locke's marking of the point where the worm turns: "But when *a long train of abuses* and usurpations pursuing invariably the same object . . . " (italics added).

[32] See Robert Stewart, *Henry Brougham 1778–1868* (London, 1986), p. 154. Brougham had been the queen's legal advisor since 1812.

[33] Stewart, *Henry Brougham*, p. 158. The astonishing quotation in question was Milton's description of Death, *Paradise Lost*, 2:266–73: "If shape it might be called that shape has none," a passage applied to the obese king also by its final line, "What seemed his head/ The likeness of a kingly crown had on."

wanting . . . What I am above all things anxious to see is such a narrative as may, without *formal observations*, inculcate a hatred of cruelty and perfidy, and to make men feel towards publick delinquents as they do towards common offenders . . . By publick delinquents, I mean tyrants, conquerors, and intriguers. Now, this experiment of writing lives and histories so as to keep up the interest and yet treat the crimes of those vulgarly called great men so as to excite disgust when atrocious, and contempt when mean – and so as, also, to give a proper *relief* to the truly important events and circumstances and sink the less material things to their right [level] is new, and can only be successful by several trying it.

Brougham urged upon Russell the duty of this task, excusing himself on the grounds of ill health and the shortness of the legal vacation. "Otherwise," he concluded, I should certainly take a turn at it, either on a life or a short and famous portion of History."[34]

Did Brougham, as strenuous a reformer as Russell himself, manage to persuade anyone else, perhaps "several," to take up this task, producing the *Authentic Records* of the case in which he himself had been so deeply involved? Could he possibly have written it himself? The style of his quoted address to the University of Glasgow is remarkably consistent with that of the narrative into which it was so oddly thrust. If so, the strategy was altered, with astonishing speed and efficiency, by one or more secret historians with different preoccupations.

One of the most extraordinary aspects of the revised version is the trouble that was taken therein to qualify Brougham's contribution to the defence of Queen Caroline, and to suggest he had been less than fully devoted to her cause. Several paragraphs were introduced (pp. 180–82) detailing Brougham's refusal to meet with the queen in Europe to prepare her case, his attempts to persuade her to remain in France, his declaration at the trial that she "had no intention to recriminate" (p. 194), and his showing one of the incriminatory documents to the prosecution (p. 194). Most striking, however, was the new frame provided for Brougham's speech to the University of Glasgow. The revisers were clearly unhappy with the compliments offered to Brougham (by himself?) on that occasion. The assertion that the speech was delivered "in the following clear and energetic style" (*AR*, p. 296) was removed; and at its end, the revisers added:

---

[34] *Early Correspondence of Lord John Russell*, ed. Rollo Russell, 2 vols. (London, 1913), 1: 278–79; italics original.

"Would that he had performed his own part more consistently with her Majesty's wishes and interests" (p. 290).

Curiosity, though unlikely to be satisfied, demands that we ask who the revisers could have been. The most obvious name to suggest in connection with the new themes of press freedom, sympathy for the "productive classes," and perhaps the complex message about riots, is that of the radical Francis Place, whom the secret historians themselves acknowledge consulting in person on the libel issue (p. 98). Place had not only been a member of the London Corresponding Society, but had helped to secure the acquittal of Hardy, Tooke and Thelwall by monitoring the witnesses for the defence.[35] Place was, of course, a friend of Hobhouse, whose once-anonymous and once-suppressed anti-Canning pamphlet reappeared in the *Secret History*. In 1831 he published his *Letter to a Minister of State, respecting Taxes on Knowledge*, which attacks the hated Stamp Act introduced by Castlereagh and defends the educational value of cheap publications by the same reasoning as does the *Secret History* on the occasion of Joseph Hume's motion for repeal (p. 319). Place himself documented his extraordinary activity as a reform organizer during the late spring of 1832, which included planning a nation-wide insurrection to culminate on May 18, the plans made public for purposes of intimidating the Lords.[36] He would certainly have had energy enough to organize a little editorial activity.

The other person most immediately interested in the passage of Russell's Reform Bill was, of course, Russell himself. The authentic recorders had been scornful of the limited scope of the bill and had described Russell as timid, even frightened, in introducing it. The revised version offers a more generous version of that skepticism. If the necessary reform of the system "may be done by the Russell Reform Bill, it will only be by a circuitous process. But England has no time to wait" (p. 370). Some negotiations on strategy would seem to have intervened. And there are certainly aspects of the *Secret History* which match the contents and emphases of Russell's *Essay . . . on the Constitution*: his use of the Revolution of 1688 as the standard of free constitutional government (compare *Essay*, pp. 130–33, with *Secret History*, p. 317); his repeated emphasis on the importance of a free press; his excursus on what is wrong with current libel law

---

[35] See *The Autobiography of Francis Place*, ed. Mary Thale (Cambridge, 1972), p. 152.
[36] See Butler, *The Passing of the Great Reform Bill*, esp. pp. 294, 310, 396, 411.

(pp. 287–90); his extended attack on what was, in effect, the government budget (the civil list, diplomatic salaries, Crown pensions, military and naval patronage, church properties and revenues, and new peerages or promotions) which for Russell constituted a huge system of bribery (pp. 292–319); his concern about the National Debt and Pitt's responsibility for it (p. 348); and his concluding arguments, that the nation teeters on a precipice, with a collapse into arbitrary power and tyranny as one scenario, and courageous reform as the other. But if we were to imagine that Russell was one of the secret historians, we would also have to acknowledge the contradiction between his strong defence of the party system (*Essay*, pp. 144–53, 329–30) and the *Secret History*'s move to attack *both* Whigs and Tories as equally corrupt.

His involvement with the project in some way is plausible. For his *Life of William Lord Russell*, Russell had inevitably made himself familiar with some of the stepping stones in the evolution of secret history. Despite the scrupulously above-board tone and procedures of his biography, he cited therein several anecdotes from the *Memoirs* of Sir William Temple,[37] and, for details of Russell's trial, Burnet's *History of My Own Time*. He also deferred to Marvell's *Account of the Growth of Popery and Arbitrary Government* (1:77, 84) and *Britannia and Raleigh*, attributed to Marvell in the 1797 *Poems on Affairs of State*.[38] But I would hesitate to attribute to him the brilliantly pertinent quotations from Shakespeare's English histories and tragedies. His *Essay* actually quotes Shakespeare on the defects of Rome's idea of balance of power, by "giving a weight to property against numbers," producing constitutional stalemate:

> . . . When two authorities are up,
> Neither supreme, how soon confusion
> May enter 'twixt the gap of both.
>
> (*Coriolanus*, 3.1.108–10)

This citation, however, derived from David Hume.

And as for the *Secret History*'s invocations of Byron, these too were completely out of character for Russell. Not only did Russell disapprove of Byron, and advise his friend Thomas Moore *not* to

---

[37] Lord John Russell, *Life of William Lord Russell*, 2 vols. (London, 1820), 1:62, 76, 108.
[38] See *Life*, 1:66: "Marvel seems to allude to this story, when he says, 'Till Lee and Garroway shall bribes reject.' "

publish his memoirs, he also does not appear to have known Byron personally. The person who *did* know Byron personally was Moore, who had been in close correspondence with him ever since their meeting in the house of Samuel Rogers in November 1811. In September 1821 Byron sent Moore a fair copy of *The Irish Avatar*, with instructions to get "twenty copies . . . carefully and privately printed off" in Paris. "Send me *six*," Byron wrote, and distribute the rest according to your own pleasure . . . You will take care that there be no printer's name, nor author's . . . at least for the present."[39] These facts, determined by Jerome McGann, though omitted by Moore from his diary for 1821,[40] make a striking fit with the way the poem is introduced into the *Secret History* as a comment on the king's visit to Ireland:

We had the pleasure of his lordship's acquaintance for some years before his lamented death, and he was in the habit of sending us many brilliant effusions of his muse, which he probably never intended for publication. (p. 227)

After Byron's death, the injunction to withhold the name of the author "for the time being" becomes obsolete. The *other* name that acquires a provocative presence in this context, however, is that of Moore himself, with which *The Irish Avatar* concludes:

> Or if aught in my bosom can quench for an hour
> My contempt for a nation so *servile*, tho' sore,
> Which, tho' trod like the worm, will not turn upon power,
> 'Tis the glory of Grattan, the genius of Moore!   (p. 230)

If it were indeed Moore who was responsible for the literary enhancements of the revision, he had selected a witty and self-promoting form of signature.

---

[39] Byron, *The Complete Poetical Works*, ed. Jerome McGann and Barry Weller, 7 vols. (Oxford, 1991), 6:600–01. Twenty copies were accordingly printed by Galignani at Paris in late 1821. Byron also sent a manuscript draft of the poem to Murray. The copy sent to Moore does not survive.

[40] See *Memoirs, Journal, and Correspondence of Thomas Moore*, ed. Lord John Russell, 2 vols. (New York, 1858), 1:395: The *Diary* for November 3 and 4, 1821, merely states: "Received Lord B's tremendous verses against the King and the Irish . . . richly deserved by my servile countrymen, but not on this occasion, by the King, who . . . acted well and wisely. . . Read Byron's verses to Lord and Lady H. and All; much struck by them, but advised me not to have any hand in printing them." See also 1:397, where Moore repeats his disagreement with Byron on the king's conduct, and congratulates himself on his poetry mediating across party lines.

Again, there are aspects of the *Secret History* that seem to point directly to Moore, who had led a double life as a writer, alternating his romantic poetry and Irish lyricism with anonymous or pseudonymous satirical jabs at the Tory government. He too was a friend of Hobhouse. And, though close friends with Russell and Grey, he had, as the Reform debates intensified, increasingly come to regard the Whigs as at least as much at fault as the Tories in England's predicament. In July 1831, he wrote in his diary:

The insight I got into the views and leanings of the [Whig] party during my last visit to town has taken away much of my respect for them as a political body. . . . I am convinced that there is just as much selfishness and as much low party spirit among them generally as among the Tories; without any of that tact in concealing the offensiveness of these qualities which a more mellowed experience of power and its sweets gives to the Tories. There are a few men among them who have the public weal, I believe, most sincerely at heart; and these are easily numbered, – Lord Gray, Lord Althorp, Lord John Russell, and Lord Lansdowne; but even these are carried headlong through a measure, of which in their hearts they must see the danger, by an impulse of party spirit which supersedes too much every other consideration.[41]

In his early letters, Moore was an inveterate quoter of Shakespeare. He would certainly have been capable of grasping and insinuating the relationship between Henry VIII's divorce of Katherine of Aragon and George IV's of Caroline, and of seeing the pertinence of Katherine's farewell, "Would I had never trod this English earth," from *Henry VIII* (3:3:143ff), nine lines of which are inserted in the *Secret History* (p. 202) as though quoted by Caroline herself. Moore was delighted to discover that Scott expressed "liberal" views of Napoleon (2:552), for whom his own admiration was considerable. His anonymous satire on Sir Hudson Lowe, Napoleon's gaoler, was added to the revised version (p. 260) without comment as to its authorship or source.[42] And at least

---

[41] *Diary*, 2:761. It is significant that at this point Russell felt compelled, in a long footnote, to defend the Whigs against the charge of self-interest.

[42] See *Secret History*, p. 260: "This was the kind of conduct in Napoleon's gaoler that gave rise to the following distich:

> Sir Hudson Lowe, Sir Hudson Lowe,
> By name, and ah! by nature so."

Printed as Moore's in *Tom Crib's Address to Congress*, as having first appeared in the *Morning Chronicle*: "The Examiner, indeed, in extracting it from the *Chronicle*, says, 'we think we can guess whose easy and sparkling hand it is.'" Moore acknowledged it rather proudly in his *Diary*, 1:213, and 2:748.

twice Moore acknowledged an interest in secret history or memoirs as a genre.[43]

But again there are aspects of this *Secret History*, such as the attack on his friend Sir Walter Scott, and its late intense democratization,[44] for which Moore could never have been responsible; and if he were responsible for inserting *The Irish Avatar*, Moore would have to have suppressed his own earlier disagreement with Byron on the question of George IV's conduct in Ireland. If the secret of the *Secret History*'s composition is ever to be unlocked, it will surely involve an interesting form of political and literary collaboration, one in which the collaborators agreed, for the larger cause, to participate in a program only parts of which, as independent thinkers, they could ever have approved.[45] Or, to cite Moore himself on the subject of political coalitions, "a compromise and surrender of individual differences of opinion for the attainment of one common object."[46]

This late secret history, the only one of its era, has perhaps imbalanced by the mystery of its genesis the story of the genre as a whole. But in the larger story of early modern liberalism of which it is a part, Thomas Moore's opinions, and his ways of expressing

---

[43] In his comic opera, *The Blue-stocking* (1811), the hero, de Rosier, recommends the French Memoirs to the heroine as alternative history. "While history shews us events and characters, as they appeared on the grand theatre of public affairs, these Memoirs conduct us into the greenroom of politics, where we observe the little intrigues and jealousies of the acts, and witness the rehearsal of those scenes which dazzle and delude in representation." See *Works* (1826), p. 245. And in 1843, Moore wrote to a friend asking him to borrow for him from the London Library Sir Anthony Weldon's *Secret History of the Court of James the First* (1811). See *The Letters of Thomas Moore*, ed. Wilfred S. Dowden, 2 vols. (Oxford, 1964), 2:877.

[44] See Moore's annotation for his diary entry on April 5, 1832: *Diary*, 2:778: "Though the [Reform] bill was quite in consonance with my own political feelings and principles, yet in the view of the consequences to which it must ultimately lead (that of *democratizing* our whole system), I could not but agree with the Tories." Moore too much enjoyed friendship (and dining) with the aristocracy to have concurred in the *Secret History*'s vitriolic attack on the House of Lords.

[45] Moore's interest in literary collaboration was expressed in a letter to Hobhouse of December 21, 1825, in relation to the Byron memoirs. "And now that the word 'cooperate' has escaped me, allow me to ask, my dear Hobhouse, whether it be wholly impossible that we should undertake such a work *jointly*? . . . This sort of Beaumont & Fletcher partnership in Biography is, I believe, new; but with a good understanding between us, it might easily be managed." See *Letters*, 2:544–45. See also Moore's *Diary*, 2:685, for the plan formed in 1829 for a collaborative history of England, Scotland, and Ireland, to be produced by Sir James Mackintosh, Sir Walter Scott and Moore respectively. Mackintosh, himself a strong Whig and religious tolerationist, might well have been a candidate for collaboration on the *Secret History* also, were it not for the fact that from March 1832 he was gradually dying from an inflammation of his throat caused by a chicken bone.

[46] Moore, *Diary*, 1:256. This was but one of several conversations Moore was having with his Whig friends in 1818. See *Diary*, 1:220, 230, 265 (where he observes that the Revolution of 1688 was brought about by a coalition).

them, are both ideologically and rhetorically seductive. I close with his own summary of a speech he delivered on March 1, 1826, to the mayor and corporation of Devizes, to celebrate the election of the Tory Watson Taylor. "Said," wrote Moore proudly that

some years since (staunch Whig as I was) I should have felt myself misplaced in that company; but that at present, under a ministry, who by the liberality of the government at home . . . had conciliated the suffrages of liberal men of all parties, the partition between Whig and Tory, if not removed, was considerably diminished. If there does exist any wall between us, it is like that which of old separated Pyramus and Thisbe; there has been made a *hole* in it, through which we can converse freely, and even sometimes . . . *make love to each other.* (2:571; italics original)

His source for this utopian notion was, of course, irony upon ironies, Shakespeare's *A Midsummer Night's Dream.*

CHAPTER 7

Reading Locke

When Thomas Hollis prepared his beautifully but chastely printed edition of Locke's *Two Treatises of Government*, he chose for its only ornament a portrait of Locke engraved by I. B. Cipriani (Figure 8). This is a very different image of Locke from that which preceded the *Essay concerning Human Understanding* in the second edition of 1694. That portrait, introducing the only one of his major works which Locke acknowledged during his lifetime, is imposing and bewigged (Figure 6)[1] – hardly different in tone from the portrait of Charles II by Van Hove that preceded Filmer's *Patriarcha* in 1680 and to which Locke took sly objection in the opening chapter of the *First Treatise*.[2] The Cipriani engraving derives instead from the late portrait by Sir Godfrey Kneller, painted between 1697 and 1698, when Locke was in his middle seventies (Figure 8). The original head-and-shoulders portrait, now in the Hermitage in Leningrad, shows Locke in an oval frame, with his own grey hair, more plainly dressed than in any of the other representations, his face worn (unsurprisingly for his age) but apparently anxious. It was first engraved by George Vertue for the 1714 edition of Locke's works (Figure 7). Vertue placed Locke, still head-and-shoulders, in a formal frame imitative of an oakleaf wreath, and gave him architectural and heraldic foundations. Cipriani's version moved back in the ethical direction implied by Kneller's portrait,

---

[1] It was based on a tinted plumbago drawing from the life by Sylvester Brounower, Locke's servant, and therefore presumably represents Locke as he wished to be seen. The drawing descended to Francis Cudworth Masham, who gave it to the Speaker Arthur Onslow. It is now in the National Portrait Gallery. For an account of all the known portraits of Locke, see *The Correspondence of John Locke*, ed. E. S. de Beer, 8 vols. (Oxford, 1976–89), 8:444–48.

[2] "I should have taken Sr. Rt. Filmer's *Patriarcha* as any other Treatise, which would perswade all Men, that they are Slaves, and ought to be so, for such another exercise of Wit, as was his who write the Encomium of Nero, rather than for a serious Discourse meant in earnest, had not the Gravity of the Title and Epistle, the Picture in the Front of the Book, and the Applause that followed it, required me to believe, that the Author and Publisher were both in earnest." See *The Two Treatises of Government*, ed. Peter Laslett (Cambridge, 1988), p. 141.

Figure 6 The "Brounower" portrait of John Locke, *c.* 1693. Engraved by P. Vanderbanck, from a drawing by Sylvester Brounower, for the *Essay concerning Human Understanding* (2nd edition, 1694). Beinecke Rare Book and Manuscript Library, Yale University.

Figure 7 The "Kneller" portrait of Locke, *c.* 1697. Engraved by George Vertue, for the 1714 edition of Locke's works. Beinecke Rare Book and Manuscript Library, Yale University.

IOHN LOCKE

Figure 8 The "Kneller" portrait of Locke, *c.* 1697. Engraved by I. B. Cipriani, for Locke, *Two Treatises concerning Government*, ed. Thomas Hollis (London, 1764). Seeley G. Mudd Library, Yale University.

though deepening its aura of mortality and insecurity. The formal frame is replaced by a "real" wreath open at the bottom; and Locke appears now as a lonely unsupported head (as it were decapitated), with only a small liberty cap between him and the empty space below.

This was the image of Locke that Hollis transmitted to America in 1764, when his edition of the *Two Treatises* was published. As Blackburne reported, in 1764:

> Mr. Hollis dispatched a box, inclosing five little parcels, containing chiefly so many copies of the new edition of Locke's treatises on government: one for Dr. Mayhew himself, one for Harvard College, one for the colony of New Haven in Connecticut, one for the college at Prince-town in the province of New Jersey (which, by the way, . . . perished in the flames, along with a noble library, in consequence of military execution inflicted on the *rebellious* colonies so called, by the British troops!!!), and one to the college at Bermuda.[3]

Hollis's image of Locke, undeclarative to the point of austerity, was an apt representation of his authorship of the *Two Treatises*, in relation to which, as Peter Laslett has shown, Locke was secretive to a degree that "can only be called abnormal, obsessive."[4] Despite the fact that his name was frequently mentioned in connection with the *Treatises*, Locke swore his friends to silence, catalogued all copies of the book on his own shelves as anonymous, and only admitted responsibility for it in a codicil to his will, dated September 15, 1704, when it was included in his bequest to the Bodleian Library. This Locke was concerned with his own safety to the point of extreme disingenuity. In 1682 and 1683, the years of crisis for the Whigs in London when the *Treatises* were taking nearly final shape, the Tory spy Humphrey Prideaux reported from Oxford that "John Locke lives a very cunning, unintelligible life here, being two days in town and three out, and no one knows where he goes, or when he goes, or when he returns. Certainly there is some Whig intrigue amanaging, but here not a word of politics comes from him."[5] Apparently Locke so effectively resisted being drawn into political conversation that the Dean of Christ Church believed "there is not in the world such a master of taciturnity."[6]

[3] Francis Blackburne, *Memoirs of Thomas Hollis*, 2 vols. (London, 1780), 1:239.

[4] Locke, *Two Treatises of Government*, ed. Laslett, p. 6.

[5] Maurice Cranston, *John Locke* (New York, 1957), pp. 220–22.

[6] See *An Essay concerning Human Understanding*, ed. Alexander Campbell Fraser, 2 vols. (Oxford, 1894; repub. New York, 1959), pp. xxx–xxxi.

The famous author of the *Essay* and the surreptitious author of the *Two Treatises* were, however, the same person. And so indeed was the author of the *Letter concerning Toleration*, also published anonymously, which Thomas Hollis regarded as equally important for the survival and transmission of early modern liberalism. These three works, along with *The Reasonableness of Christianity* and the follow-up *Letters concerning Toleration*, were identified in that codicil to his will as the Locke canon.[7] Of these three major works it is the *Letter* that fits most comfortably with one of our notions of liberalism, the one which foregrounds the problem of ideological disagreement in society and how and why it must, for society's survival, be subtended by deeper consensual principles; whereas the *Essay* is usually discussed only as epistemology, perhaps with implications for religion, and the *Two Treatises*, especially the second, are fought over exclusively by political philosophers and historians. Thus the tolerationist Locke is conventionally separated from the father of British empiricism, and both tend to be overshadowed by "Locke on Government," who continues to be the center of ideological debate.

Was Locke a bourgeois liberal, obsessed with property, or was he a liberal in the broader and more humane sense? Richard Ashcraft created a stir in 1986 by arguing, on historical grounds, that Locke was a radical, and that his connections were, on religious issues, with the Dissenters, on political issues with the conspiratorial left.[8] Ashcraft believed in an underground resistance movement that operated first around Shaftesbury from 1680 onwards, and then out of an exile community in Holland, in both of which phases Locke was active. Ashcraft's contextualist method, in which all of Locke's major work was seen as instrumental to his political concerns, stressed connections between the known and supposed members of this radical underground and the "canting" or encoded language he believed they used to communicate with each other. A conspiracy theorist myself, I am entranced if not totally convinced by Ashcraft's narrative, which was developed with such richness of historical detail that its value extends far beyond Locke studies. It set the agenda on Locke for the next decade, so that those who follow are compelled to engage with his thesis, and the shape of these engagements has much

---

[7] See *Correspondence*, 8:425–26. The definition of the canon comes in the form of a bequest to the Bodleian Library of late editions of the *Essay concerning Human Understanding* and hitherto unacknowledged publications.

[8] Richard Ashcraft, *Revolutionary Politics & Locke's Two Treatises of Government* (Princeton, 1986).

to tell us about Locke's mysteriousness, his resistance to our full and confident understanding.

For David Wootton, Ashcraft had exaggerated Locke's radicalism. Wootton pointed a severe finger at the Constitutions of Carolina that Locke helped to draw up in 1669, allowed him to have been radicalized by the experiences of 1680–3, but poured doubt on the theory that from 1681 to 1688 Locke was a political activist plotting against the later Stuarts, and concluded that he grew more conservative in later life, having achieved fame and security after the Revolution. Wootton faulted Locke for *not* being socially egalitarian, even in the *Two Treatises* and especially in his contributions to poor law debate.[9]

John Marshall, on the other hand, wrote a scrupulously documented intellectual biography of Locke which attempted to bracket the Ashcraft position between higher-minded concerns.[10] Of the three Rs foregrounded in the subtitle of his study, "Resistance, Religion and Responsibility," Marshall clearly believed that religion was the true center of Locke's concerns. Thus the moment of resistance represented by the *Two Treatises* is relatively brief, and framed by two chapters entitled respectively "Locke's Moral and Social Thought 1660–81: the Ethics of a Gentleman," and "Locke's Moral and Social Thought 1681–1704." Marshall thought that Ashcraft was wrong to link Locke with the Dissenters in the 1670s, placing him instead among the Latitudinarians; and while he partly accepted Ashcraft's conspiratorial Locke, he expressed a "healthy skepticism" about the canting language and the notion that the *Second Treatise* was intended to draw in support from the artisanal classes. For Marshall, Locke "lived and died a gentleman, convinced that . . . it was vital to encourage others to a life of virtue, and that it was most important to influence others of similar status" (p. 455). Thus on both sides of Ashcraft's indefatigably militant if secretive Locke there have subsequently appeared a polite Locke to be admired primarily for his ethical and theological seriousness, and a Locke who was not nearly radical enough.

In this chapter I shall try to bring these various Lockes together, in order to make the claim that the person who gave rise to each of them was indeed a liberal in the sense defined in my Introduction,

---

[9] *Political Writings of John Locke*, ed. David Wootton, (New York, 1993), pp. 41–119.
[10] John Marshall, *John Locke: Resistance, Religion and Responsibility* (Cambridge, 1994).

and that the *Essay*, the *Letter* and the *Two Treatises* are three parts of a coherent vision, perhaps even of a coherent and sustained agenda. Still other Lockes reveal themselves only or primarily in his personal correspondence: the dedicated physician, never too busy, though famous, to write yet another personal letter to Mrs. Mary Clarke about her swollen legs; the belated lover of Damaris Cudworth, incapable of commitment at the crucial moment of her contemplated marriage, yet flirting with her in verse thereafter; the petty and quarrelsome friend exacting penance for slights actual or imagined from James Tyrrell and John Covell. For these a new biography is required that could benefit, as Maurice Cranston's could not, from E. S. de Beer's remarkable scholarship in editing the correspondence. Yet these other Lockes too become intelligible as aspects of this complex personality, a mixture (as most of us are) of basic decency and anxious self-interest, of courage and timidity.

Integrating and demonstrating Locke's liberalism might seem to be much too ambitious a project for a single chapter, or too ambitious altogether. The literature on Locke is so vast and the stakes in deciphering him so great that the options for the newcomer, not to mention the amateur, might seem to be restricted to nibbling round the edges of other people's work or reinventing the wheel. At both extremes, however, there may still be salutary adjustments to be made. And at the end of the chapter I shall return to the fight over "Locke in America" referred to in my Introduction, in order to suggest that Locke's early American readers ought more to be trusted than they recently seem to have been.

"Locke in America" is usually assumed to apply primarily to the influence of the *Two Treatises*. Yet when Thomas Jefferson prepared in 1776 to campaign for the disestablishment of the church in Virginia, he made for himself a commonplace book out of Locke's first and greatest *Letter concerning Toleration*, interwoven with Shaftesbury's *Characteristics*, and supplemented, for his history of episcopacy, with Milton's *Of Reformation* and *The Reason of Church Government*.[11]

In the Introduction, I cited Jefferson's use of Locke's *Letter* to support my contention that in the history of liberalism advances can be made by logical expansion of the claims of one's predecessors. In his notes, Jefferson remarked of Locke, "It was a great thing to go so

---

[11] *Papers of Thomas Jefferson*, ed. Julian P. Boyd *et al.*, 26 vols. (Princeton, 1950), 1:544–53. Jefferson was using Toland's edition of Milton's prose (Amsterdam, 1698).

far (as he himself sais of the parl. who framed the act of tolern.) but where he stopped short, we may go on."[12] This reference to "where he stopped short" applies to the section in Locke's *Letter* where he denies toleration to certain groups whose opinions make them incapable of peaceful cooperation with civil society – atheists who cannot take a binding oath, and (though Locke does not identify them as such) Roman Catholics whose religion requires them to define as heretics and hence disobey all Protestant monarchs. But Jefferson was undeterred in his admiration for Locke by the fact that his thought did not go far enough. What he liked about it was its social and economic import. Jonas Proast, Locke's adversary, had been horrified by how far Locke's theory went, to include non-Christians in the circle of toleration, but Jefferson cited this passage approvingly: "[Locke] sais 'neither Pagan nor Mahamedan nor Jew ought to be excluded from the civil rights of the Commonwealth because of his religion.' Shall we suffer a Pagan to deal with us and not suffer him to pray to his god?" And the other great advantage, to Jefferson, of Locke's *Letter* was its feisty, ironic and often colloquial style – in William Popple's translation. And thereby hangs a tale.

Like all of Locke's three major works, the *Letter* has been the subject of controversy among modern scholars, the central questions being these restrictions within Locke's theory of toleration, the apparent weakness of his logic in arguing that faith cannot be compelled even by persecution (this was the issue on which he was engaged by Jonas Proast), and to what extent he promoted complete toleration as distinct from indulgence or comprehension. At issue here also is whether Popple's translation, which appeared at the end of 1689, was faithful to Locke's intentions, and, more importantly, whether Locke had authorized its appearance. Locke's notorious statement in the codicil to his will, that the translation had been carried out "without my privity" was as ambiguous as his other disclaimers, and the notion that Locke disapproved of it has been effectively demolished.[13] Naturally, those who prefer a sterilized Locke are made uneasy by Popple's dramatic address "To the Reader," which not only broadened the *Letter's* implications for the

---

[12] Jefferson, *Papers*, 1:548.

[13] For Locke's statement, see the codicil to his will in *Correspondence*, 8:426; for discussions of Locke's attitude to the translation, see Raymond Klibansky, ed., and J. W. Gough, *Epistola de Tolerantia* (Oxford, 1968), especially pp. 43–51, where the status of Popple's translation is discussed. Compare Richard Ashcraft's assessment, *Revolutionary Politics*, pp. 498–99, n. 127.

political sphere, but by using the first person plural strongly suggested an English context:

The narrowness of spirit on all sides has undoubtedly been the principal occasion of our miseries and confusions. But whatever have been the occasions, it is now high time to seek for a thorough cure. We have need of more generous remedies than what have yet been made use of in our distemper. It is neither declarations of indulgence, nor acts of comprehension, such as have yet been practised and projected among us, that can do the work. The first will but palliate, the second increase our evil. *Absolute liberty, just and true liberty, equal and impartial liberty, is the thing that we stand in need of.* Now, though this has indeed been much talked of, I doubt it has not been much understood; I am sure not at all practised, either by our governors towards the people in general, or by any dissenting parties of the people towards one another.

This, however, was the version of the *Letter* that Jefferson used (in the 1714 edition of Locke's *Works* that he owned), and this was the English version that Thomas Hollis incorporated into his fine edition of the *Letters* as a group, transmitted to America with that telling quotation from *Paradise Lost* on the title-page (see above, p. 44), and the first identification of Popple as the translator.[14]

Hollis certainly assumed that Locke wrote in a liberal-tolerationist tradition already developed by Milton, as also by Marvell. They are implied, along with others like Vane and Harrington, in the admonitory preface to his edition:

And it should be observed, that though this Nation is greatly obliged to Mr. Locke for defending the cause of religious Liberty in the strongest and clearest manner, yet the old writers are not to be forgotten, as they laid the Foundations; which is the most necessary to be noticed, as many have supposed him to have been the first writer on this subject, when really the argument was well understood and published during the CIVIL WAR . . . as appears by several tracts not unknown among the Curious.[15]

Locke recommended the *Areopagitica* to Shaftesbury in 1670,[16] and

---

[14] [Thomas Hollis], ed., *Letters concerning Toleration by John Locke* (London, 1765), A4v. The identification was made by Richard Baron.

[15] Hollis, unlike Locke, was vehemently anti-Catholic. He used the opportunity of a phrase in one of Algernon Sidney's letters, "Shaftesbury and Halifax are eminent in pleading for indulgence to tender-conscienced protestants, and severity against papists," to assemble a collection of tolerationist statements from Harrington's *Oceana*, Milton's *Areopagitica*, Marvell's *Account*, Temple's *Works* and Locke's *Letter*; but he then balanced them with a set of anti-Catholic statements, including Locke's remarks in the letter about Catholic political subversion! See Hollis, ed., *Discourses concerning Government* (London, 1763), pp. 67–75.

[16] See Nicholas von Maltzahn, "The Whig Milton, 1667–1700," in *Milton and Republicanism*, ed. D. Armitage, A. Himy and Q. Skinner, p. 267 n. 21.

purchased both John Toland's Whig edition of Milton's complete prose when it appeared in 1698 and Toland's separately published *Life of Milton* (1699). He owned not only Marvell's *Account of the Growth of Popery and Arbitrary Government*, but also two copies of the first part of *The Rehearsal Transpros'd* and one of the second part, along with all of the published attacks on it.[17] He also owned Marvell's less well-known defences of the nonconformists, *Mr. Smirke, or The Divine in Mode* (1676), and his 1678 *Remarks* in reply to Thomas Danson.[18] While the Milton acquisitions might have resulted from his uneasy friendship with Toland, this substantial Marvell collection implies a special interest, and one established in the 1670s. It may very well be that Locke's strategy in the *Two Treatises*, whereby a set of satirical animadversions on Filmer's *Patriarcha* is followed by a more profound theoretical argument, derives from the two parts of *The Rehearsal Transpros'd*. And of course the *Letter concerning Toleration* is connected to Marvell by virtue of the fact that its translator, William Popple, was Marvell's beloved nephew and correspondent during the dark days of the 1670s.

As with his other major works, Locke managed to obscure the origins of the *Letter concerning Toleration*. When it was published in Latin in April or May 1689 it was apparently addressed to a European audience. According to Van Limborch, to whom it was enigmatically addressed,[19] it was begun in Amsterdam during the last weeks of 1685, in the context of the final revocation of the Edict

---

[17] See John Harrison and Peter Laslett, *The Library of John Locke* (Oxford, 1965), Nos. 1994, 2938, 1935, 1931–33; the published attacks on *The Rehearsal Transpros'd* were Samuel Parker's own *Reproof to the Rehearsal Transpros'd*, No. 2199; Edmund Hickeringill, *Gregory, Father Greybeard*, No.1447 (in which Locke had marked some page references); and *S'too him Bays*, sometimes attributed to John Dryden, no. 2792. Locke also owned the 5th edition of Buckingham's original *Rehearsal* (1587), No. 2461, which was sent to him by Awnsham Churchill in mid-June 1688, along with Butler's *Hudibras*, Dryden's *The Hind and the Panther* and Charles Cotton's *Scarronides*. See *Correspondence*, 3:476.

[18] Locke, *Library*, Nos. 1935, 1936. Locke also owned a work he attributed to Marvell, *Plain Dealing: or, A ful & particular examination of a late treatise [by M.Clifford] intituled Humane Reason* (Cambridge, 1675) By M.,A. a Countrey Gentleman (No. 1844).

[19] The title-page read: Epistola de Tolerantia ad Clarissumum Virum T.A.R.P.T.O.L.A. Scripta a P.A.P.O.I.L.A. This code was subsequently broken by Le Clerk in his *Eloge de feu Mr. Locke*, who expanded the initials to reveal that the *Letter* was addressed to "Theologia Apus Remonstrantes Professorem Tyrannidis Osoren Limburgium Amstelodamensem," from "Pacis Amico Persecutionis Osore Ioanne Lockio Anglo." See Raymond Klibansky, ed., *Epistola de Tolerantia* (Oxford, 1968), p. xviii. I think it likely that Locke was imitating a famous text of the Marian resistance movement, John Ponet's *Shorte Treatise of Politicke Power*, published in 1556 as written by D.I.P.B.R.W., that is to say, Dr. John Ponet, Bishop of Rochester and Winchester.

of Nantes on October 18 of that year, and the following intensifica-
tion of the persecution of Huguenots in French dominions. Both Van
Limborch and Le Clerc seem to indicate that it was written rapidly
and completed that winter. Yet it was not published until nearly
three and half years later, by which time the *Letter* had acquired a
compelling new set of contexts. The first of these, and one which
surely influenced his decision to publish the *Letter*, was the Declaration of Indulgence issued by James II in 1687, suspending all penal
laws and giving Catholics equality with Protestants. It was the
famous trial of the seven bishops who opposed his order to have the
Declaration read aloud in all English churches that led directly to
the *entente* forged between that other Seven who issued the invitation
to William. Locke could scarcely have failed to note the symmetry
between the circumstances of 1672 (in which he had been embroiled
along with Shaftesbury) and those of 1687, as James repeated his
brother's mistakes. Still more to the point, the *Epistola* appeared just
as the first Williamite parliament was about to pass a compromise
Act of Toleration (that act to which Jefferson referred), conciliating
the Anglican clergy by merely exempting nonconformists from the
penal laws while leaving those laws, and the civil disabilities of the
Test and Corporation Acts, intact.

We cannot now be certain to what extent Locke revised his text or
added to it as its circumstances and most likely audience altered;
although there certainly does seem to have been one substantial
addition towards the end: for after "Vale" ("Farewell") Locke at
some point wrote: "Forsan abs re non fuerit pauca de Haeresi et
Schismate hic subjungere" ("Perhaps it may not be amiss to add a
few things concerning heresy and schism").[20] It also looks as though,
in writing this afterthought, Locke consulted Milton's *Of True
Religion, Haeresie, Schism, Toleration, And What Best Means May Be Us'd
against the Growth of Popery*, which had appeared in March 1673, also in
the wake of Charles's Declaration of Indulgence, which the king had
just been forced by parliament to withdraw.[21] Milton's pamphlet had
attracted some attention. An anonymous letter of 1675 remarked

---

[20] [Thomas Hollis, ed.], *Letters concerning Toleration* (London, 1765), p. 27. All the *Letters* will be
cited from this edition.

[21] See Milton, *Complete Prose Works*, ed. D. M. Wolfe *et al.*, 8 vols. (New Haven, 1953–82),
8:408–30, especially p. 412, where the editor of this tract, Keith Stavely, relates Milton's
title to Charles's royal proclamation of March 13. We might add that Milton's "Haeresie"
and "Schism" reappear in Popple's translation of Locke's postscript, along with several
other apparent allusions to Milton's definitions of these terms.

that "J. Milton has said more for [toleration] in two elegant sheets of true religion, heresy and schism than all the prelates can refute in seven years," and compares him to William Penn and Jeremy Taylor.[22]

I am not, of course, suggesting that Locke made alterations after he left Holland on February 12, 1689, having entrusted his manuscript to Van Limborch with instructions to see it through the press. But on April 12 Locke received from Van Limborch a long letter filled with what amounts to advice as to what he should work for in the toleration debates:

> And it is not only in political affairs but also in ecclesiastical that I hope for the same moderation; that the Anglican Church . . . may afford to all an example of truly Christian toleration, which is well represented under the two heads of Comprehension and Indulgence. But . . . I fear lest that Church of yours may find itself hedged about too narrowly. Popedom is a natural thing to all men, as Luther used to say in his time. Since therefore it is able to recommend itself so plausibly to the multitude we can hardly expect that happiness in human affairs, that those who have the greater power by their votes should all shed their nature; yet I would not deny that recollection of the past might suggest saner counsels. If, however, Comprehension should prove too narrow, then wider Indulgence might offer a way of providing for the security of all, of those whom their conscience, whether wrongly or rightly informed, does not permit to join themselves to the Great Church were allowed to meet together by themselves without fear of punishment.[23]

That same day Locke wrote back, informing Van Limborch that the toleration debates were proceeding very slowly, because of the "disposition of the prelates," but that he still had hopes ("Spero tamen"; 3:597). And on May 6, Van Limborch informed Locke that the *Epistola* had appeared ("non expresso autoris nomine"), and that "in the present state of affairs it could be read with great profit in England." "I shall do my best," he continued, "to induce the booksellers to send some copies to England as soon as possible; but if they are slow I hope to send you some copies of . . . by the first ship sailing from here, on the chance that they may have some mitigating influence on the minds of the more inflexible" (3:607–08). No doubt the books arrived just as the Toleration Act (1 Wm. and M., c. 18) was passed, on May 24. On June 6, Locke announced the arrival of the bound (but not the unbound) copies of his own work, that he and

---

[22] Milton, *Complete Prose*, 8:414, n. 19.   [23] Locke, *Correspondence*, 3:587–88.

Van Limborch continued to refer to as written by some unknown author; and in the same letter he informed his friend that "some Englishman is just now at work" translating the pamphlet. This scenario, along with the failure of a projected Comprehension Act later in 1689, helps to explain not only why and when Popple's translation was conceived, but also the significance of his preface's insistence on "more generous remedies." "It is neither yet Declarations of Indulgence nor Acts of Comprehension, *such as have yet been practised or projected among us*, that can do the work."

To this extent I disagree with Gordon Schochet's view that the *Epistola* was "not intended to be part of this debate," having been published too early and being "too abstract and general to be applied to the Act of Toleration." "There is no need," Schochet continued, to link the *Epistola* to specific circumstances, for Locke had been writing about the relations betwen established religions and members of dissident sects for more than twenty-five years."[24] Indeed he had, from the early *Essay concerning Toleration* of 1667, through his engagement with Shaftesbury's toleration campaign in the early 1670s, to Book IV of the *Essay concerning Human Understanding*, to which we shall shortly come. But the sequence of events outlined above give strong indications that Locke's agenda in the *Epistola*, and subsequently (through Popple's agency) in the *Letter*, had changed and expanded (or perhaps one should say narrowed) to include England and national concerns.

This is not the place to rehearse yet again Locke's famou arguments in the *Letter*, the careful definition of any church as "voluntary society" (which Jefferson copied verbatim into his notes and the even more careful distinction between rules internal to church and those that society, through the civil power, is entitled t enforce. But we should now return to the question of Locke's style i the *Letter*, and the manner in which it was transmitted to the futur by William Popple's translation. For Jefferson, apparently, there wer attractions in the *Letter* which went beyond the purely conceptua He grasped the effectiveness of the aphorisms: "God himself will n save men against their wills," and "Truth will do well enough if le to shift for herself," the latter carrying an allegorical resonanc inherited from Milton's *Areopagitica*. He liked the commonsen:

---

[24] See Gordon Schochet, "John Locke and Religious Toleration," in *The Revolution 1688–1689: Changing Perspectives*, ed. Lois G. Schwoerer (Cambridge, 1992), pp. 158–59. F its coverage of the 1689 toleration contest, however, this essay is indispensable.

negative analogy by which Locke argued for non-interference in religious choices: "No man complains of his neighbor for ill management of his affairs, for an error in sowing his land, or marrying his daughter." He was particularly taken by Locke's condensed version of Bunyan's *Pilgrim's Progress* (which also constituted a critique of Bunyan's exclusionist theology) and he cited it at length:

> If I be marching on with my utmost vigour in that way which according to the sacred geography leads to Jerusalem streight, why am I beaten & ill used by others because my hair is not of the right cut; . . . bec. among several paths I take that which seems shortest & cleanest . . .

In all these instances Popple was faithful, or almost faithful, to Locke's intentions;[25] but his version is more *useful* to an active politician with speeches to make than Locke's elegant Latin could ever have been. "Not of the right cut" is a brilliant substitute for "tonsus"; and leaving Truth to shift for herself deploys the same canny colloquialism as drives the sentence about errors in farming and matrimonial decisions. Popple's translation, in other words, intensifies the air of common sense, the pragmatism, the general lowering of the ideological temperature, that so sharply distinguish Locke's first *Letter* from the polemical rebuttals of Proast that followed it.

The very process of translation, of course, requires attention to nuances – not only to the question of fidelity, but also to those intangibles we call eloquence. But it must also be said that that Popple has increased the propensity to political critique entailed in Locke's broadly liberal argument; a critique that would not have lost its force during the Williamite phase of their mutual experience.[26]

Out of a large number of small adjustments, we will have to make do with two examples. The first is less interesting in terms of style, but crucial in showing how Locke had grasped the principle I outlined in the Introduction: that it was the historical event of the

---

[25] Compare Locke's Latin: "Invitos ne quidem Deus servabit"; "bene profecto cum veritate actum esset, si sibi aliquando permitteretur"; "De vicini sui re familiari male administrata nemo queritur; de semendis agris vel locanda filia erranti nemo irascitur"; "Quod si ego secundum geographiam sacram recta Hierosolymas totis viribus contendo, cur vapulo quod non cothurnatus forsan vel certo modo lotus vel tonsus incedo . . . vel inter varios . . . calles eum seligo qui minime sinuosus coenosusve apparet?"

[26] From late 1691 onwards there are many references in the *Correspondence* to Locke's relationship with Popple, on whom he evidently came to depend for financial and family matters. When Locke became Commissioner of Trade in May 1696, Popple was made secretary of the Commission.

Reformation that had rendered illogical the notion of religious uniformity and a state religion, especially the history of the Reformation in England:

> If [the history of the medieval church] be too remote, our modern English history affords us fresher examples, in the reigns of Henry VIII, Edward VI, Mary, and Elizabeth how easily and smoothly [quam belle, quam prompte] the clergy changed their decrees, their articles of faith, their form of worship, everything according to the inclination of those kings and queens. Yet were those kings and queens of such different minds, in point of religion, and enjoined thereupon such different things, that no man in his wits [nisi amens], I had almost said none but an atheist, will presume to say that any sincere and upright worshipper of God could, with a safe conscience, obey their several decrees.[27]

Thus (and Thomas Jefferson made a note of this point as well) the weathercock religion of the early sixteenth century becomes the rationale for an emergent tolerationist theory, which from narrow beginnings in the late 1570s grows gradually wider in theoretical scope. More precisely, ecclesiastical policy is unveiled as state politics in disguise.

In the passage just cited Popple stuck close to Locke's Latin. Not so in what follows here (though it comes earlier in Locke's argument):

> For, there being one truth, one way to heaven; what hopes is there that more men would be led into it, *if they had no other rule to follow but the religion of the court*, and were put under a necessity to quit the light of their own reason, to oppose the dictates of their own consciences, and blindly to resign up themselves to the will of their governors, and to the religion, *which either ignorance, ambition, or superstition had chanced to establish* in the countries where they were born. In the variety *and contradiction* of opinions in religion, wherein the princes of the world are as much divided *as in their secular interests*, the narrow way would be much straitned; one country alone would be in the right, and *all the rest of the world put under an obligation of following their princes in the ways that lead to destruction*; and that which heightens the absurdity, and very ill suits the notion of a Deity, men would owe their eternal happiness or misery to the places of their nativity. (p. 37)

If one compares this *jeu d'esprit* with Locke's Latin, it becomes evident that Popple has calmly or mischievously added on his own

---

[27] *Letter*, p. 47. Note that Hollis retains Popple's revealing phrase, "our modern history," identifying the writer as an Englishman. Wootton, p. 133 n.21, points out that in the second edition of the *Letter*, which Locke oversaw, that telltale preposition was altered to "*the* modern English history."

authority the phrases italicized above; and in the final sentence, where the translation is faithful ("et quod maxime hac in re absurdem esset et Deo indignum, aeterna felicitas vel cruciatus unice deberetur nascendi sorti") he has nevertheless managed to produce, by choice of diction alone, the Marvellian flair which makes it dance off the page with mockery. Popple had learned from his uncle, apparently, the supreme value in polemic of being amusing; and he certainly helped to bring out the irony inherent in, or dormant in, Locke's Latin, in such a way as to give the *Letter* permanent readability.

BEYOND THE "LETTER": LOCKE'S LATER TOLERATIONISM

Considering the criticisms that have been levelled at Locke for the exclusions to toleration he conceded to conspiracy theory and fears of Louis XIV, it is very worth noting that he subsequently rejected the Miltonic exclusion of Roman Catholics from toleration. There was another important stage of his correspondence about these issues with Van Limborch, initiated by the passing of the Blasphemy Act (9 Wm. III, c. 35) in July 5, 1698, of which Burnet had sent Van Limborch a copy, to his shock and distress. The Blasphemy Act was William's response to the furore caused by the publication of John Toland's *Christianity not mysterious* in 1696, a furore into which Locke had been involuntarily drawn by Stillingfleet's attack on Toland and deism, with its sideswipe at Locke's *Essay concerning Human Understanding*.[28] Van Limborch had, as he told Locke, roundly criticized the Act and Burnet's support of it, and added "I greatly fear that this edict may be the beginning of a new persecution. Cruelty increases little by little from small beginnings."[29] Partly in response to this letter, Locke defined himself as "an Evangelical Christian, not a Papist," and further explained the distinction, in a highly original manner:

Amongst those who profess the name of Christians I recognize only two classes, Evangelicals and Papists: the latter those who, as if infallible, arrogate to themselves dominion over the consciences of others; the former those who, seeking truth alone, desire themselves and others to be convinced of it only by proofs and reasons. (6:495–96).

---

[28] Toland fled to Ireland, where trouble pursued him. On September 9, 1697, the Irish parliament ordered his book burned by the common hangman. See *Correspondence*, 6:192.

[29] Locke, *Correspondence*, 6:461. This letter is dated August 8, 1698.

Thus tolerant Roman Catholics would be classed as Evangelicals, and Anglicans who insisted on conformity as Papists. And at the end of November Van Limborch embraced this new definition, suggesting that "both classes are to be found in every Christian denomination" (6:517).

In 1697 through 1699, then, Locke was far from being the complacent member of the Establishment that Wootton implies. He was concerned about the trial of the boy Thomas Aikenhead in Edinburgh in December 1696 for blasphemy under the Scottish Blasphemy Act, which had been in place since 1661.[30] He was worried about Toland, and even more about insulating himself from Toland's deism. In March 1697 William Molyneux comforted him with the statement that "'tis ridiculous in any man to say in general your book is Dangerous" (6:38), but in October he wrote that "If Men could destroy by a Quil, as they say Porcupines Do, I should think your Death not very far off" (6:237). Samuel Bold expressed anxiety lest his own reputation for having published *A Sermon against Persecution* way back in 1683 (he was imprisoned and fined) should infect his friend (6:68), and later expressed to Awnsham Churchill his suspicions about why so much controversy had arisen about Locke's *Essay* so many years after its publication (6:271). "Sure there is something at the bottom, which they do not yet speak out" (6:271). When the English Blasphemy Act was passed, Locke had some reason to fear that he might share in Toland's disasters. Yet this did not prevent him from purchasing Toland's edition of Milton's prose in 1698, nor other productions of the liberal Whig protest movement, such as Ludlow's *Memoirs* and Algernon Sidney's *Discourses*, both of which appear in his library catalogue. And in February 1698 he received a letter from Johnstoun that (we may reasonably believe) articulated the attitude of Locke and his closest friends to the regime:

I would rather you lived uneasy under disappointments then dyed satisfied that it signifyes nothing to live; which I apprehend is your case. what can a man expect to see who has seen the restauration and Revolution prove disseases instead of remedies! Every thing seems a lincke in the Chain . . . You and many other honest men in this and the last age have made it your work to bring men by knowledge to reason and man no doubt is not

---

[30] Aikenhead was eighteen years old, and executed on January 8, 1697. See the letter from James Johnstoun, *Correspondence*, 6:18–19. His trial appears in *A Complete Collection of State Trials*, Vol. 13.

capable of a greater and better work. You have succeeded in a great measure, but after all where are we now? for Instance in matters of religion . . . Bigottry its true is a declining principle but its evidently a growing Interest almost all over Europe and will be so here too when church recovers which will recover unlesse others prove as bad they. Nou bigottry growing the stronger must grow the principle too in time. what a prospect is this? (6:312)

No doubt it was that prospect that the Locke of Kneller's late portrait (and its offshoots) surveys with such tired and knowing eyes, almost at the end of the seventeenth century. And what of our own prospects for toleration, almost at the end of the twentieth? For the sake of learning from history, Johnstoun's analysis is worth reprinting.

AN ESSAY CONCERNING HUMAN UNDERSTANDING

One of the exceptions to the way in which modern scholarship has tended to carve up the Locke legacy is David Wootton, who argues sensibly that we should treat Locke as a whole, and grounds this opinion in Locke's own theory of identity and responsibility as expressed in the *Essay.* "What makes Locke Locke?" Wootton asks, and proposes that the famous chapter on "Identity and Diversity" (Book II, Chapter 27) sets out, under the sign of "person" as a forensic concept, "a claim not about mind or body, but about moral responsibility." Of course, "person" had been a forensic concept in medieval law and thereafter, but Wootton argues that Locke's argument was novel, and that it still dominates the philosophy of identity, "so that it has recently been said that all later arguments are mere footnotes to it" (p. 30). This concept "has a very simple consequence," wrote Wootton, with Foucault in mind:

Locke was committed to the notion of the author function. He was responsible for the arguments in his works; if they were wrong it was his duty to correct them, if they were right it was his responsibility to defend them. He could not see his life as radically compartmentalized into different functions – natural law theorist, epistemologist, government bureaucrat – because in his view the notion of moral responsibility unified every aspect of an individual's conscious life. Nor would he have wanted to escape responsibility by arguing that the meaning of what he had written was indeterminate: one of the purposes of the *Essay* was to teach people to argue clearly and unambiguously.[31]

---

[31] Wootton, *Political Writings of John Locke*, p. 114.

I agree with Wootton that the *Essay* is the key to an integrated
Locke, but not with his subsequent premise. Attractive as it is in its
own Enlightenment rhetoric, Wootton's emphasis on Locke's emphasis on candor and moral responsibility is dramatically at odds
with the Locke who refused to acknowledge his other works as his.
Wootton mentions, but does not explore, the interesting fact that this
famous definition of identity as a forensic concept was not present in
the first edition of the *Essay* (1690), but added in the second of 1694.
(It received another important supplement in the fourth edition of
1700 – the memorable anecdote of the Brazilian parrot discussed in
chapter 6.) And as a description of the *Essay*, Wootton's emphasis on
unambiguous clarity, an emphasis earlier developed by Neal Wood
in his quest for Baconian elements of Locke's thought,[32] overlooks
certain features of Locke's stylistic procedures that *do* connect his
epistemology with his politics and his mature tolerationist views, but
do so with ingenious indirection.

This indirection is signalled from the start. Like the *Two Treatises*,
approaches to the *Essay* have been bedevilled by arguments about its
genesis, arguments that Locke helped to create by his disingenuous
"Epistle to the Reader," published along with the 1690 edition,
where he was at pains to suggest that the *Essay* had been a very long
time in the works:

Were it fit to trouble thee with the History of this Essay, I should tell thee
that five or six Friends meeting at my Chamber, and discoursing on a
Subject very remote from this, found themselves quickly at a stand, by the
Difficulties that rose on every side. After we had a while puzzled our selves
. . . it came into my Thoughts, that we took a wrong course; and that,
before we set our selves upon Enquiries of that Nature, it was necessary to
examne our own Abilities, and see, what Objects our Understandings were,
or were not fitted to deal with . . . Some hasty and undigested Thoughts,
on a Subject I had never before considered, which I set down against our
next Meeting, gave the first entrance into this Discourse, which having
been thus begun by Chance, was continued by Intreaty; written by

---

[32] Neal Wood, *The Politics of Locke's Philosophy: A Social Study of "An Essay Concerning Human
Understanding,"* (Berkeley, 1983), pp. 50–51: "He quite consciously rejected literary polish
and affectation for simplicity, homeliness and, above all, clarity . . . His views on the
avoidance of figurative language for the sake of clearness and precision, expressed in Book
III, were embodied in the *Essay* itself." Wood also cites the fragmentary and undated letter
to "J.F." written at some stage in Locke's controversy with Stillingfleet in which he rejects
"what . . . looks like a sprinkleing of wit or satyr" in controversy and insists that "a
professor to teach or maintain truth should have noe thing to doe with all that tinsil
trumpery should speake plain and clear" (*Correspondence*, 6:539). Since we do not know the
context of these remarks, it is unwise to put too much weight on them.

incoherent parcels, and, after long intervals of neglect, resum'd again, as my Humour or Occasions permitted; and at last, in a retirement, where an Attendance on my Health gave me leisure, it was brought into that order, thou now seest it.[33]

Rhetorically, almost everything about these statements misleads as much as it assists: the opening *occupatio* ("Were it fit to trouble thee with the History of this Essay . . . ") which calmly ushers in the unfit; the provocatively undefined "Subject" of the meeting between friends; and the emphasis on casualty and contingency, which gives the impression of haphazard construction, a failure to revise, and continues, only half apologetically, further into the Epistle. Like Topsy, the *Essay* "grew insensibly to the bulk it now apears in." "But to confess the Truth, I am now too lazie, or too busie to make it shorter" (p.8).

Locke was not a lazy man; one of the themes of the *Essay* is the duty of intellectual work, the labor of thinking for oneself. Indeed, a few moments earlier the Epistle itself had registered this theme as an incentive to the prospective reader of the *Essay*: "He who has raised himself above the Alms-Basket, and not content to live lazily on scraps of begg'd Opinions, sets his own Thoughts on work, to find and follow Truth, will (whatever he lights on) not miss the Hunter's Satisfaction" (p. 6). There are some odd abrasions here between social theory and epistemology, and between the two sides of Locke's social thought. The gentlemanly sport with which Locke's metaphor opens (the understanding's searches after truth, are a sort of "Hawking and Hunting, wherein the very pursuit makes a great part of the Pleasure") does not lead naturally into the plebeian work-ethic that keeps one from living off charity. But my point here is that this is evidently not the plain speech that, according to Wood and Wootton, Locke both campaigned for and exemplified in the *Essay* as a whole.

I do not mean to imply that Locke's account of the genesis of the *Essay* is entirely fictional, merely that it *could* have been written in a much more straightforward manner. Apparently James Tyrrell was present at the meeting of six friends, and in his marginal notes in his copy of the *Essay* he stated that the "Subject very remote from this" had been "the Principles of morality, and reveald Religion." Taken together with the survival of Locke's very embryonic "drafts" for the

---

[33] Locke, *An Essay concerning Human Understanding*, ed. Peter H. Nidditch (Oxford, 1975), p. 7.

work, which are both dated 1671, this statement was read by Ashcraft to indicate that the *Essay* was originally motivated by tolerationist concerns, begun in the context of Charles II's *Declaration of Indulgence*, and of Samuel Parker's campaign to enforce uniformity of worship on the Dissenters;[34] that is, the same context as inspired Marvell's *Rehearsal Transpros'd*.

In reassessing Ashcraft's thesis, John Marshall doubted that the group of "five or six friends" was most likely to have been made up of Dissenters. He argued that in 1670/71 Locke's closest contacts were with Latitudinarians like John Tillotson, Benjamin Whichcote and Thomas Grigg, husband of Locke's cousin Anne.[35] Yet he agreed with Ashcraft that religious toleration was the original motivation. Locke became involved in Shaftesbury's support of Charles's *Declaration*, which at this stage of events appeared to be the best hope for the tolerationist position. But in November 1672 Shaftesbury was dismissed from the Lord Chancellorship, and Danby became Charles's chief advisor on ecclesiastical affairs. Shaftesbury therefore moved into the opposition and began to build support for religious toleration among both moderate Anglican and nonconformist supporters. Marshall suggested that Locke's continuing interest in the *Essay* was connected to Danby's attempts to introduce an oath in 1675 declaring the government of both church and state to be unalterable – the oath, we should add, about which Marvell wrote the most heroic passsages of his *Account of the Growth of Popery and Arbitrary Government*. This was also the context of the anonymous pamphlet, the *Letter from a Person of Quality*, published in November 1675, which Ashcraft (following some of Locke's contemporaries) had attributed to Locke.[36] This *Letter* was dangerous to its creators. In Marshall's words, "in late 1675 the *Letter* was ordered to be burned by the common hangman; shortly afterwards Locke left England for France, where he stayed for the next three years" (p. 89).

But the project apparently begun in 1670/71 received new impetus at several stages. While in France, Locke translated Pierre Nicole's

---

[34] Ashcraft, *Revolutionary Politics*, pp. 39–74.
[35] John Marshall, *John Locke: Resistance, Religion and Responsibility* (Cambridge, 1994), pp. 79–80.
[36] Ashcraft made a strong claim for Locke's authorship, on the basis of several contemporary attributions, and pointed out that it was only on the basis of Locke's disingenuous letter to Pembroke of December 1684, denying his authorship of any pamphlet, "good, bad or indifferent," that it was removed from the canon of Locke's works (pp. 120–21).

Essais de Morale, especially with relation to what we know of God (proofs for his existence, of God and the immortality of the soul, etc.)[37] His letters of 1678 to Denis Grenville are absorbed by the problem of what it is to be human (Nos. 374 and 426). Those written from the spring of 1686 onwards are frequently concerned with the *Essay*, which sounds near to completion. In December 1686, Locke sent Edward Clarke the fourth book of the *Essay*, with much self-deprecatory statement about its disorderliness and repetitiveness, showing that his apologies as published in the Epistle were not merely a disclaimer. In his letter to Clarke (No. 886), Locke wrote, "Of what use it may be to any other I cannot tell, but, if I flatter not myself, it has been of great help to [our first inquiry], and the search of knowledge ever since has been in my thoughts, which is now five or six years."[38]

In late December 1687 Locke wrote Clarke a manipulative letter, which despite its small-mindedness holds important news about the stage the *Essay* had reached:

You will perceive by the inclosed that my Lord Pembroke is soe well satisfied with the designe of my Essay Concerning Human Understanding by the Abrigment of some parts of it that I have sent him that he desires to see the whole discourse at large. I must therfor beg the favour of you to send him that Copy that you have and this inclosed letter together by a safe hand on the first opportunity . . . If I should set Syl [Locke's servant] on worke to Copy it for him it would bee too long before I should be able to satisfie him. I must therefor desire you to send the Copy in your hands you will have noe great losse by it, for it is at best but a trifle and if you desire anouther you shall not fail to have one if it be not printed which I am apt to expect it will now be ere long. But before you send it away you must be sure carefully to teare out all that is writt particularly to you at the beginning or ending of any of those litle books it is bound up in. For it would be a litle ungracefull that a copy which I send him should cary the marks of being intended for anybody else.(3:322–23).

But the *Essay* was evidently still not yet in its 1690 form. Consider its unique internal dating: "Thus, seeing water at this instant, it is an unquestionable truth to me that water doth exist; and remembering that I saw it yesterday, it will also be always true and, as long as my memory retains it, always an undoubted proposition to me that water did exist 10 July, 1688" (Book IV, Chapter 11, Section 11). "This

---

[37] Marshall, *Locke*, pp. 134–36.
[38] De Beer notes that Rand may have mistranscribed this letter, since if the 1671 date on Drafts A and B is correct, by 1686 this should have read "fifteen or sixteen years."

instant" has a force entirely different from the "long intervals of neglect" that were emphasized in the Epistle; and when brought into conjunction with the revolutionary significance of 1688 as a date to be thankful for "as long as my memory retains it," substitutes for the idea of slow and uncertain gestation the urgency of very recent and momentous events. On June 30, 1688 the invitation to William was agreed on, and dispatched in the hands of Admiral Arthur Herbert, who crossed the channel disguised as a common sailor. On July 6, in fact, the French ambassador to the Netherlands, D'Avaux, reported to Louis XIV that William's friend and agent Dijkvelt had arrived in Amsterdam to sound out the burgomaster on the possibility of supporting the invasion.

Even in its first edition, then, the *Essay* implied almost up-to-the-minute revision and expansion. In the second edition Locke altered and expanded the chapter on "Power," and added the new chapter "On Identity," at the suggestion of William Molyneux. Molyneux, perhaps his most congenial sounding board, did not live to see the fourth edition of 1700, to which Locke added not only "Of the Association of Ideas," but also the peculiar "Of Enthusiasm," which became the penultimate chapter.[39] We have, therefore, to consider not only what the genesis of the *Essay* might have been, but what its purpose was by the mid-1680s when it was nearing final form, the agenda implied by its 1690 publication, with that crucial date flying like a flag in the center, and what difference, if any, Locke thought was made by the chapters added in 1700. Did the *Essay*, as Peter Nidditch stated, though originating in discussions about religious toleration, relegate "the Principles of morality, and reveal'd Religion" to the status of a vestigial subtext (p. xviii)? Is it best understood, as John Yolton believed, by focusing on Locke's idea of ideas, including his opening attack on innateness?[40] Was it, as Neal Wood argued, so driven by Baconian practical idealism – the recognition and control of what Bacon called "idols" of the mind and we call ideology – that it deserves to be called a political treatise?[41] Was it intended to be, as David Wootton claimed, a purely theoretical contribution to the intellectual revolution that Ian Hacking has named "the emergence of probability"? Was it, while inflected with Locke's Latitudinarian

---

[39] Technically, the prepenultimate, but the last chapter is a fragment.
[40] John Yolton, ed. *An Essay Concerning Human Understanding* (London, 1993), pp. xx–xlii. See also his *John Locke and the Way of Ideas* (London, 1956).
[41] Wood, *The Politics of Locke's Philosophy.*

principles, primarily devoted, as Marshall argues, to a set of problems in theology (the existence of an immortal soul, for instance) that Locke was unable to solve? Or was it part of some larger agenda of which the *Two Treatises* and the *Letter concerning Toleration* were, at least from the late 1680s, complementary instruments?

In fact, Locke signals his intentions in the *Essay* rather clearly, and in such a way as to explain its structure. In the second paragraph of the opening chapter, he wrote:

> This, therefore, being my Purpose to enquire into the Original, Certainty, and Extent of humane Knowledge; together, with the Grounds and Degrees of Belief, Opinion, and Assent . . . he that shall take a view of the Opinions of Mankind, observe their Opposition, and at the same time, consider the Fondness, and Devotion wherewith they are embrac'd; the Resolution, and Eagerness with which they are maintain'd, may perhaps have Reason to suspect, That either there is no such thing as Truth at all; or that Mankind hath no sufficient Means to attain a certain Knowledge of it. (pp. 43–44)

This statement existed almost as it now stands in Draft B of the *Essay*,[42] and therefore registers both Locke's earliest and latest understandings of his purpose. By this Rawlsian standard, however, we can now see that everything in the *Essay* moves inexorably towards those later chapters of Book iv of which no traces exist in the drafts, where Locke lays out his conclusions: that, given the multifarious factors that intervene between men and a genuinely rational, objective inquiry into truth, there are no grounds for anyone to impose his beliefs on others. Among these factors are misuse of language, the insidious power of custom, self-interest and "party," and an undue reliance on scriptural revelation. This, we eventually learn, was his motive for writing Book iii, that long excursus on language and the importance of precise denotation, some of which is predicated in Draft B:

> Some confused or obscure notions have served their turns; and many who talk very much of religion and conscience, of church and faith, of power and right, of obstructions and humours, melancholy and choler would perhaps have little left in their thoughts and meditations if one should desire them to think only of the things themselves and lay by those words with which they so often confound others, and not seldom themselves also. (Book iv, Chapter 5)

---

[42] Locke, *Drafts for the Essay Concerning Human Understanding* . . . , ed. Peter H. Niddith and G. A. J. Rogers, 3 vols. (Oxford, 1990), 1:101–02.

Book IV, Chapter 15, whose topic is "Probability," ends as follows:

And if the opinions and persuasions of others whom we know and think well of be a ground of assent, men have reason to be Heathens in Japan, Mahometans in Turkey, Papists in Spain, Protestants in England, and Lutherans in Sueden. But *of this wrong ground of assent, I shall have occasion to speak more at large in another place.* (p. 657; italics added)

We can be sure that other place is the *Letter concerning Toleration* when we turn to that text and follow Locke's arguments for a clear separation of church and state – that is, the argument about geographical destiny as a wrong ground of assent, enlivened by William Popple's translation (see p. 247 above). And in the next chapter, "Degrees of Assent," Locke lays out his proto-Rawlsian position with an eloquent appeal for an agreement to disagree, inflected by a sense of the pathos of the human condition:

Since therefore it is unavoidable to the greatest part of Men, if not all, to have several Opinions, without certain and indubitable Proofs of their Truths; . . . it would, methinks, become all Men to maintain Peace, and the common Offices of Humanity, and Friendship, in the diversity of Opinions, since we cannot reasonably expect, that any one should readily and obsequiously quit his own Opinion, and embrace ours, with a blind resignation to an Authority, which the Understanding of Man acknowledges not . . . We should do well to commiserate our mutual Ignorance, and endeavour to remove it in all the gentle and fair ways of Information; and not instantly treat others ill, as obstinate and perverse, because they will not renounce their own, and receive our Opinions, or at least those we would force upon them . . . The necessity of believing, without Knowledge, nay, often upon very slight grounds, in this fleeting state of Action and Blindness we are in, should make us more busy and careful to inform our selves, than constrain others. (pp. 659–60; italics added)

That "since therefore," the sign of an argument coming to its logical conclusion, is the strongest rhetorical evidence that Book IV is the end to which the whole epistemological inquiry has, over nearly two decades, tended. Whatever its basis in an actual compositional experience, then, Locke's opening apology for the *Essay*'s diffuseness and "incoherent parcels" is eventually revealed as an authorial trope of haphazardness designed to disarm if not actually to mislead his readers. The disclaimer intimated that an "essay" was just that – was a well-established genre for *exploring* problems (as distinct from a treatise, which assumed systematic demonstration), and that it descended from Montaigne and Bacon as much as from Pierre

Nicole. Later in his life Locke was to complain that his readers had forgotten this generic premise.

Despite this disclaimer, Locke had evidently *built* the *Essay* carefully, as a theoretical foundation for toleration by intellectual default and geopolitical relativism. But its last stage is an argument from economic inequality. This seems to address directly the disagreement between Ashcraft (in the middle) and Wootton and Marshall on each side of him, with respect to Locke's social theory and conscience. Like Milton in *The Reason of Church Government*, who goaded himself with the reminder that "ease and leasure was given thee for thy retired thoughts out of the sweat of other men,"[43] Locke opened the last chapter of the *Essay*, "Of wrong Assent, or Errour," with an acknowledgment of the difference between the scholarly life and that of "the greatest part of Mankind." On the principle used by other "transmitters" of early modern liberalism, including Thomas Hollis, I shall quote this passage at what may seem excessive length, since not only does it not seem to have registered strongly on any of Locke's recent commentators, but it also articulates perhaps the greatest dilemma for higher education today:

Men want Proofs, who have not the Convenience, or Opportunity to make Experiments and Observations themselves, tending to the Proof of any Proposition; nor likewise the Convenience to enquire into, and collect the Testimonies of others: And in this State are the greatest part of Mankind, who are given up to Labour, and enslaved to the Necessity of their mean Condition; . . . These Men's Opportunity of Knowledge and Enquiry, are commonly as narrow as their Fortunes; and their Understandings are but little instructed, when all their whole Time and Pains is laid out, to still the Croaking of their own Bellies, or the Cries of their Children. 'Tis not to be expected . . . that he who wants Leisure, Books, and Languages . . . should be in a Condition . . . to find out Grounds of Assurance so great, as the Belief of the points he would build on them, is thought necessary. So that a great part of Mankind are, by the natural and unalterable State of Things in this World . . . unavoidably given over to invincible Ignorance of those Proofs, on which others build, and which are necessary to establish those Opinions: The greatest part of Men, having much to do to get the Means of Living, are not in a Condition to look after those of learned and laborious Enquiries.

What shall we say then? . . . Are the current Opinions, and licensed Guides of every Country sufficient Evidence and Security to every Man, to venture his greatest Concernments on; nay, his everlasting Happiness, or

---

[43] Milton, *Complete Prose Works*, 1:804.

Misery? Or can those be the certain and infallible Oracles and Standards of Truth, which teach one Thing in Christendom, and another in Turkey? Or shall a poor Country-man be eternally happy, for having the Chance to be born in Italy; or a Day-Labourer be unavoidably lost, because he had the ill Luck to be born in England? (Book IV, Chapter 20, pp. 707–08)

Geopolitical relativism, inflected with the same spirited irony that William Popple had built into his translation of the *Letter*, is now intensified by a dry compassion for the irremediably poor and uneducated.[44] True, Locke adds, "No Man is so wholly taken up with the Attendance on the Means of Living, as to have no spare Time at all to think of his Soul" (p. 708). But the "enslavement" to which he refers both at the beginning and end of this passage is more than metaphorically connected with the discourse of slavery that opens the *Two Treatises*, with their sardonic summary of Filmerism:

Slavery is so vile and miserable an Estate of Man, and so directly opposite to the generous Temper and Courage of our Nation; that 'tis hardly to be conceived, that an Englishman, much less a Gentleman, should plead for't.[45]

And still Locke has not finished tying together his major concerns; he sets beside this economic deprivation another form of constraint that afflicts the more socially privileged: those "whose largeness of Fortune would plentifully enough supply Books, and other Requisites for . . . discovering of Truth." This more fortunate class are, however, themselves imprisoned:

cooped in close, by the Laws of their countries, and the strict guards of those, whose Interest it is to keep them ignorant, lest, knowing more, they should believe the less in them. These are as far, nay farther *from the Liberty and Opportunities of a fair Enquiry*, than those poor and wretched Labourers, we before spoke of. And, however they may seem high and great, are confined to narrowness of Thought, and enslaved in that which should be the freest part of Man, their Understandings. This is generally the Case of all those, who live in Places where Care is taken to propagate Truth, without Knowledge; where Men are forced, at a venture, to be of the Religion of the Country; and must therefore swallow down Opinions, as

---

[44] One should not over-sentimentalize this passage, however. Wood and Wootton are probably more right than Ashcraft on Locke's limited sympathy toward the working classes, or worse still the idle poor, whose conditions of life appeared to him to be inevitable and related to their inferiority. See Wood, *Politics of Locke's Philosophy*, p. 35, and Wootton, *Political Writings*, p. 116.

[45] Locke, *Two Treatises of Government*, ed. Laslett, p. 141.

silly People do Empiricks Pills, without knowing what they are made of . . .
but in this, are much more miserable than they, in that they are not at
liberty to refuse swallowing, what perhaps they had rather let alone; or to
chuse the Physician, to whose Conduct they would trust themselves. (pp.
708–09; italics original)

Here Locke, whose brilliant cure of Shaftesbury's hydatid abcess
of the liver had reshaped his career and redirected his intellectual
commitments, uses for his peroration the venerable metaphor of
doctoring that had functioned in political discourse since Plato.
Milton had used it in *The Reason of Church Government*, which itself
looked back to Plato's *Gorgias*;[46] and Locke used it twice against
Filmer, in ways that lock the *Essay* to his overtly political writing.
Cheerfully observing in the *First Treatise*, "'Tis in vain then to talk of
Subjection and Obedience, without telling us whom we are to obey,"
Locke adds a touch of comic absurdity: "Men too might as often and
as innocently change their Governours, as they do their Physicians,
if the Person cannot be known, who has a right to direct me, and
whose Prescriptions [a nice pun] I am bound to follow" (Chapter 9,
pp. 202–03). And in the saucily entitled chapter, "Who Heir?" Locke
shows how the metaphor of doctoring connects church and state,
even as he will argue in the *Letter* for their separation:

In the State the world now is, irrecoverably ignorant who is Adam's heir,
this Fatherhood, this Monarchical Power of Adam descending to his Heirs,
would be of no more Use to the Government of Mankind, than it would be
to the quieting of Men's Consciences, or securing their Healths, if our A.
had assured them, that Adam had a Power to forgive Sins or cure Diseases,
which by Divine Institution descended to his Heir . . . And should not he
do as rationally, who upon this assurance of our A. went and confessed his
Sins, and expected a good Absolution, or took Physick with expectation of
Health from any one who had taken on himself the Name of Priest or
Physician. (Chapter 11, Section 125, pp. 232–33).

LOCKE'S LOCKS: THE MEANING OF METAPHOR IN THE "ESSAY"

The story of *how* Locke wrote the *Essay*, as distinct from why, has, as I
intimated earlier, been differently told according to how its modern
readers have been trained. At one end of the scale are those who
believe that the end of the seventeenth century witnessed a massive

---

[46] Milton, *Complete Prose*, 1:835–37, 845–48, the second passage reflecting *Gorgias*, pp. 524–25.

cultural reaction against rhetoric in favor of the scientific or philosophical plain style; within Locke studies, such convictions result in assertions that Locke practiced what he preached in his Baconian chapters on language in the *Essay*, eschewing nuance and metaphorical language in favor of a precisely denotative style. At the other end of the scale are a group of suspicious readers, some of whom have been influenced by Jacques Derrida's critique of philosophical writing as revelatory of unsound premises, who realized that Locke frequently depended for persuasion on figurative speech while denying that philosophers should do so. In his *Locke, Literary Criticism and Philosophy* William Walker claimed to take his place in a lengthy tradition:

> identifying and interpreting metaphors of mind in *An Essay Concerning Human Understanding* are standard practices in mainstream philosophical commentary on this work from Leibnitz to Rorty.[47]

According to Walker, Locke's metaphors sometimes obstruct and distort his thinking, thereby paradoxically *revealing* that thought's structure, its incomplete solutions and self-contradictions. Obviously this approach – discovering philosophical cracks in Locke's argument by paying close attention to its surface – derives from the Derridean form of Deconstruction.

Evidently, these positions are incompatible; and it is possible that neither is correct, in part because of deep confusions as to what constitutes figurative language, and whether its use can be obscured by a general plainness of tone and a seeming procedural innocence. Walker remarks "the obvious figurative profusion" of the *Essay* (p. 134). But despite his quarrel with Paul de Man as to what counts as a metaphor, he never himself addressed that analytical question head on. What, for example, in Locke's practice in the *Essay* is the difference between a metaphor such as "force" one might be forced, if only by linguistic habit, to use, and a vivid philosophical example (a worm shut up in the drawer of a cabinet)? How alive or dead were Locke's metaphors at the time? Was he always conscious of using them, always unconscious, or (the most testing situation theoretically) sometimes one, sometimes the other? I shall here use Walker's avoidance of these procedural questions to address them myself, and suggest some guidelines for what counts as a metaphor in the *Essay* and elsewhere, including the *Two Treatises*.

---

[47] William Walker, *Locke, Literary Criticism and Philosophy* (Baltimore, 1994), p. xiii.

Walker decided that the most revealing clusters of figurative writing in the *Essay* were as follows: of printing and impression, which Locke is said to reject as the discourse of innatism; of the mind as a room "furnished," which Walker literalizes as filled with furniture, moveable property; of work, which Walker takes to be gendered as male; of "acquaintance," which Walker connects through sexual *double-entendre* with women as objects of seduction; and of light, of course a deeply conventional trope in relation to truth and knowledge. Locke's practice here, however, is complicated by the late arrival of the chapter on "Enthusiasm" in which those who claim to see the Light most clearly are attacked as purveyors of disinformation.

I suspect that the figurative clusters Walker observed were recommended to his attention by one of our standard images of Locke: as the apostle of bourgeois acquisitiveness, with women being added to the property category in the light of recent feminist criticism. But it would be equally possible to recognize, by looking at the figurative evidence, the textual shadow of Ashcraft's Locke, the nervous political conspirator. As a subset of his discussion of images of force and weight, Walker alludes to clusters of words which represent knowing in political or juridical terms.[48] Though following James Tully and others in seeing the juridical discourse of the *Essay* as a cultural phenomenon of the late seventeenth century and particularly entailed by probability theory, Walker deemphasizes it in

---

[48] For an earlier discussion of juridical discourse in the *Essay*, see James Tully, "Governing Conduct," in *Conscience and Casuistry in Early Modern Europe*, ed. Edmund Leites (Cambridge, 1988), pp. 12–71. Influenced by Foucault, Tully aimed to describe "the ensemble of power, knowledge, and habitual behaviour at the point, 1660–1700, when its relatively enduring features consolidated, and from the perspective of one person who described, evaluated, and partly constructed it: John Locke" (p. 12). For Tully, the presence of juridical language in the *Essay* was determined purely by Locke's philosophical analysis, gradually deepening over the various stages of its composition, of the role in governing belief of the three juridical spheres of church, state and what he calls "the humanist juridical apparatus," but which I would call more simply peer pressure, that with which John Stuart Mill was most deeply concerned. See Tully, pp. 41–43. This accounts, as Tully argues, for Locke's emphasis in "Power" on divine law and punishments. The concept of "uneasiness" that Locke introduced in the second edition was a "little penal mechanism" (p. 49) implanted in the mind by God. But at the very end of his essay, he wonders whether the penalized self that Locke assumes, and intensified by adding his chapter on "Identity," was not itself an instance of the dire effects of habit and custom, an instance inscrutable to Locke himself:

Locke could assume that this penalized self was constituted prior to the juridical apparatus that governs and subjects it. We should ask, rather, if this self, so familiar to us in its relative regularity and law-abidingness, is not a product of centuries of subjection to juridical governance? (p. 71)

favor of the language he himself has declared symptomatic of Locke's concerns. Thus terms like "liberty," "govern," "authority," "usurp," and "tyrannize" are designated "remnants" of what Gilbert Ryle had named the "para-political myth" of mind, which Ryle had believed displaced, in Descartes and Locke, by a "para-mechanical myth."[49] Yet in Locke's chapter on "Of Power," whose most powerful term is probably "Liberty," images of accident or mechanics – "a Man falling into the Water, (a Bridge breaking under him,)" or "a Tennis-ball struck with a Racket" (pp. 238, 239) – *compete* for our attention with those of imprisonment and torture.

It would theoretically be possible to have read "Of Power" in 1690, when it first appeared, or in 1694, when Locke drew attention to its revision, as a remarkable act of linguistic reclamation, as neutralizing the term "liberty" by restraining it within the science of mind. Thus "trial," "wrong judgments," "punishment," "the enforcements of . . . law," not to mention "power" itself, might be said in Locke's theory of mental choice to be removed from the literally juridical sphere where they operated in the *Two Treatises* and the *Letter concerning Toleration* to the terrain of epistemology and theology. The revisions that Locke made to this chapter in the second edition might then be seen as further emasculating the ideologeme "liberty" by equating it more clearly with *suspension* of choice, which renders negative liberty (the absence of external constraint) even more passive by its nearness to procrastination.

But what happens to the reader who is taught to understand this eccentric version of voluntarism in terms of the following illustrations?

[s]uppose a Man be carried, while fast asleep, into a Room, where is a Person he longs to see and speak with; and be there *locked* fast in, beyond his Power to get out: he awakes, and is glad to find himself in so desirable Company . . . I ask, Is not this stay voluntary? . . . and yet being *locked* fast in, 'tis evident he is not at liberty not to stay, he has not freedom to be gone. (p. 238; italics added)

And again:

He that is a close Prisoner, in a Room twenty-foot square, being at the North-side of his Chamber, is at liberty to walk twenty foot Southward, because he can walk, or not walk it: But is not, at the same time, at liberty, to do the contrary; ie. to walk twenty foot Northward. (p. 248)

---

[49] Gilbert Ryle, *The Concept of Mind* (London, 1978), pp. 24–25.

And again:

> He that has his Chains knocked off, and the Prison-doors set open to him, is perfectly at liberty, because he may either go or stay, as he best likes; though his preference be determined to stay, by the darkness of the Night, or illness of the Weather, or want of other Lodging. He ceases not to be free; though the desire of some convenience to be had there, absolutely determines his preference, and makes him stay in his Prison. (p. 266)

Three major (that is, narratively extended) images of literal incarceration are adduced to explain the concept of intellectual or psychological freedom (Locke, of course, does not make that distinction). Such repetitiveness requires accounting for, especially since none of these images appears in either of Locke's early drafts.[50] But what sort of interpretation is the most plausible? Was Locke signifying to his readers, in Foucaultian terms, that they lived in a carceral society? If so, why did that emphasis not appear in the *Two Treatises* as one of the symptoms of despotism? In fact, Locke cites as his proofs that a government has dissolved itself taxation without consent, the obstruction of parliament and the underhand favoring of "that Religion" which is most likely to support absolutism (*Second Treatise*, Chapter 18, "Of Tyranny," p.405). He uses the same proofs, that is, that Marvell selected to document "the growth of popery and arbitrary government" in the late 1670s. But where Marvell includes among his charges the parliamentary struggle of February 1676, which ended in Shaftesbury, Buckingham, Salisbury and Wharton being sent to the Tower, "under the notion of contempt,"[51] Locke remarkably never mentions illegal imprisonment. One might even wonder whether in some perverse way Locke was comfortable with a carceral society, since his three images of imprisonment seem relatively harmless, almost domesticated. Did he notice the presence of that emblematic "lock" in the first and most benign example, where the prisoner finds himself exactly where and with whom he

---

[50] Locke did include in Draft B an example of imprisonment as mental deprivation: "Suppose a man bread constantly in a darke dungeon without seeing sun or moone or observeing any motion at all . . . " See *Drafts*, p. 236. This long example exploring how we create our complex ideas of duration is strikingly *not* political, but instead fantastic in conception, with its protagonist "bred" in a dark dungeon from birth and possessed of perfectly regular sleeping habits!

[51] Marvell, *Account of the Growth of Popery and Arbitrary Government*, in *Complete Prose Works*, 4 vols., ed. A. B. Grosart (privately printed, 1875), 3:322. "Thus," concluded Marvell, "a prorogation without precedent was to be waranted by an imprisonment without example. A sad instance! and whereby the dignity of Parliaments, and especially the House of Peers, did at present much suffer, and may probably more for the future."

wants to be? How could he not, given in 1660 he had written a tiny poem on the theme of voluntary confinement:

> How hate full is a Locke to some
> confineing them within a Roome
> But plesant is a Locke to me
> it keepes me from bad company.[52]

Yet this jingle, written in 1660 on the back of a letter he had received from Thomas Westrowe, must have been in some sense a response to the contents of that letter, in which Westrowe had informed him from London that "this day is pased the house that all those of the Kings judges that came not in shall be guilty as well for life as for estate." The Restoration began by acting out the juridical basis of society with a vengeance, and all of Locke's career, at least after 1681, was conditioned by his not unreasonable fear that such could happen to him. And, of course, Locke had visited Shaftesbury in the Tower on August 18 and September 16, 1681,[53] and probably on several other occasions.

The rack (as an instrument of torture) is also *three* times mentioned in this chapter (pp. 239, 267, 271), the second also being added in 1694. In "Of Power," the rack is mentioned ostensibly as an instance of strong forces which deter men from exercising their mental freedom; but in what becomes the third occurrence, Locke makes another of his rare allusions to contemporary events: "A neighbour Country has been of late a Tragical Theatre, from which we might fetch instances, if there needed any" (p. 272.) In 1894 Alexander Fraser assumed that Locke here referred to France, and to the recent persecution of Protestants following the abrogation of the Edict of Nantes.[54] But in the late stages of the *Second Treatise*, as he was marshalling his arguments for resistance, Locke used a matching phrase, "a Neighbour Kingdom has showed the World an odd Example" (Section 205, p. 402), in describing what can happen when a monarch puts himself in a state of war with his people.

I conclude, therefore, that Locke did not intend this chapter to depoliticize (by philosophical appropriation) his images of torture and imprisonment, but rather to suggest that they were a part of everyday life in England under the later Stuarts, and causally a part

---

[52] *Correspondence*, 1:149;
[53] Ms. c. 1, fol. 132, cited by Ashcraft, *Revolutionary Politics*, p. 345 n. 25.
[54] *Essay*, ed. Fraser, 1:354.

of the pressure that ideology (and "party") exerted on the mind. Moreover, the exchange between ethical and political registers is clearly indicated, in a passage added in 1694 to substantiate the argument for the rational suspension of choice: "Nor let any one say, he cannot govern his Passions, nor hinder them from breaking out, and carrying him into action; for what he can do before a Prince, or a great Man, he can do alone, or in the presence of God, if he will" (p. 268). Nor did Locke lose sight of his penal imagery in later life. A *fourth* instance of the rack as metaphor for unbearable pain was added in 1700, in the new chapter "Of the Association of Ideas," in relation to the affecting example of the mother who cannot stop grieving for her dead child. "Use the Consolations of Reason in this case," wrote Locke, "and you were as good preach Ease to one on the Rack, and hope to allay, by rational Discourses, the Pain of his Joints tearing asunder" (Book II, Chapter 23, Section 13, p. 398). The qualifying phrase, "the Pain of his Joints tearing asunder" makes it clear that Locke is using the image literally and consciously, rather than as a dead metaphor or habit of speech.

TWO TREATISES ON GOVERNMENT

At the end of his argument for Locke's Baconian program in the *Essay*, Neal Wood asks himself the question: "If the *Essay* is a political work, what is its relationship to the *Second Treatise*?"[55] Like Wootton, he rejects the notion that Locke "was a highly pluralistic thinker who tended to compartmentalize and keep his various intellectual endeavours distinct and separate." But he answers his own question in terms that privilege the Locke of conventional American political philosophy. "One common denominator between the two books is a single conception of human nature: of partial, corrupt, selfish, and ambitious man" (p. 180). Both books, in Wood's view, are characterized by a "fundamental individualism," with the *Essay* establishing the primary philosophical grounds for "the self-directed individual pursuing his own interest in an enlightened, industrious, and disciplined manner" (pp. 180–81). But Wood also observed that the *Essay*'s primary ideal (learning to think, carefully, for yourself) could not be fulfilled except in what we would now call a liberal society, where "men could freely and securely assemble, speak, write,

---

[55] Wood, *The Politics of Locke's Philosophy*, p. 180.

publish their opinions, and worship as they please" (p. 119). This insight ought to override the partially conflicting hypothesis of a Locke devoted to individualism (Wood), to possessions (Walker), or to the gentlemanly status quo (Marshall), despite the fact that Locke was not innocent of providing these hypotheses with data.

The task of the *Essay*, then, was to establish not the grounds of belief but, with a holistic skepticism, the multiple barriers in the way of such a project, and hence the need for mutual tolerance. The task of the *Letter* was to develop a *means* for instituting that mutual tolerance in the one arena where it mattered most – religious belief – by arguing pragmatically for the separation of church and state. And the task of the *Two Treatises* was, both in 1681–3 and in 1689, to set out according to the demands of the moment the political conditions for wider freedoms than those governing religious worship alone. The *effect* of the *Two Treatises*, however, was to open a logical space not only for resistance when the contract between subject and sovereign appeared to have been broken or undermined by the latter (that is to say, Lockean resistance meant *restoring* a benign but imaginary status quo), but also for radical innovation and constitutional change.

The most dramatic extension of "Locke on Government" occurred, of course, in the American colonies. But even in England it was the respectability Locke conferred on himself, by default and from timidity, in offering the *Two Treatises* as a work of 1689, that increased its elasticity. The fiction created by Locke himself in the preface of 1689, that the work was intended to "establish the Throne of our Great Restorer, Our present King William," may or may not have been believed at the time. But it was certainly useful, for example, in 1794, in defending Thomas Hardy against the charge of treason for organizing a working-class convention with parliamentary reform as its agenda. The defence attorney, Thomas Erskine (who would appear as one of the heroes of the *Secret History* of the Reform Bill campaign), discovered to his delight that one of the prosecution's main pieces of evidence was a speech delivered at Sheffield by Henry Yorke that cited the *Second Treatise*. Erskine said:

Let us not broach the dangerous doctrine that the Rights of Kings and of Men are incompatible: Our Government at the Revolution began upon their harmonious incorporation; and Mr. Locke defended King William's title upon no other principle than the Rights of Man. It is from the revered work of Mr. Locke, and not from the Revolution in France, that one of the papers in the evidence, the most stigmatised, most evidently flowed; for it is proved that Mr. Yorke held in his hand Mr. Locke upon Government, when he delivered his speech . . . and that he expatiated largely upon it; – well, indeed, might the witness say he expatiated largely, for there are many well selected passages taken verbatim from the book.

And, following Yorke's example, Erskine proceeded to argue that the chief aim of the London Corresponding Society – universal male franchise – had been included by Locke in the *Second Treatise* (Chapter 13, Sections 157 and 158) as "such an inherent part of the Constitution as that the King himself might grant it by his prerogative"; so that the supposedly revolutionary demands of Hardy, Tooke and Thelwall stood "upon the authority of Mr. Locke, the man, next to Sir Isaac Newton, perhaps of the greatest strengh of understanding which England, perhaps, ever had; high too in the favour of King William, and enjoying one of the most exalted offices in the state."[56]

Even more than the *Letter* and the *Essay*, the *Two Treatises* therefore illustrate the tension in scholarly understanding between original intention and subsequent appropriation, between political philosophy in the abstract and what happens when we look at an argument as roughly shaped, if not absolutely constrained, by the historical circumstances to which it originally spoke. And as with the *Letter* and the *Essay*, Locke and his friends (early modern and modern) have made the genesis and evolution of the *Two Treatises* into an oversized mystery. The fiction of 1689 had a long life, until it was decisively challenged by Peter Laslett, who first proposed that the *Two Treatises* were produced in the context of the Exclusion crisis, with the *Second Treatise* having been written in 1679, and the *First* later, after the publication of Filmer's *Patriarcha* in 1680. And so intriguing did the contextualist exercise become that Laslett's dating was subsequently further challenged and refined by Ashcraft, Marshall and Wootton.[57] The disadvantage of this debate is that the

---

[56] *The Trial of Thomas Hardy for High Treason . . . taken in short-hand by Joseph Gurney*, 3 vols. (London, 1795), 3:241–45.

[57] In Ashcraft's view, the *First Treatise* was written in 1680–1, and the *Second* in 1681–3, after the trial and execution of Stephen College revealed the lengths to which the crown was prepared to go. Wootton, focusing on its relationship to Tyrrell's *Patriarcha non monarcha*, thought the *Second Treatise* to have been written more or less in its entirety in 1681. Marshall preferred 1682/83, when the Whigs lost control of the London juries, and recognized that extralegal action was the last resource. The volume published in 1689 thus combined a *First Treatise* which was an Exclusion tract and a *Second Treatise* which was either a Rye House tract (Ashcraft and Marshall), or merely a theoretical exercise written before any rebellion was planned. Mark Knights, in *Politics and Opinion in Crisis, 1678–81* (Cambridge, 1994),

arguments are circular, since the writer's conviction about dating is influenced by what he thinks Locke's motivations were likely to have been; and the initial provocation may be less important to our understanding of the work than the defensive energies it developed (even, perhaps, as it lay hidden in a trunk or under the title *De Morbo Gallico*) as circumstances changed and became more threatening. Whenever he began to rebut Filmer and Hobbes, there are clear traces of the impact on Locke of the discovery of the Rye House Plot of 1683; for he inserted into the *First Treatise* a scathing reference to Judge Jeffreys who "pronounced Sentence of Death in the late Times" (Chapter 11, Section 129, p. 236), comparing his authority to that of Absalom, who pronounced the death sentence against his Brother Amnon, "and much upon a like occasion, and had it executed too."[58] The execution of Algernon Sidney for material found among his private papers must have remained for Locke a cogent example of the penalties writers faced for expressing their opinions, even if, as was true of Sidney, they steadfastly refused to take responsibility for them until actually brought to the scaffold. So here, in the *First Treatise*, stands the red flag of immediacy, matching that provocative date in the center of the *Essay*. As it had for Milton in his sonnets, the word "late" for Locke carried a historical charge disproportionate to its lexical modesty.[59] And as with Milton's sonnets, the *Two Treatises* probably contain the traces of Locke's political experience over at least two decades.

Peter Laslett scrutinized the text of the *Second Treatise* to determine what parts of it, if any, postdated the débâcle of the Rye House plot. There is one section, indeed, that appears only in the second state of

pp. 250–57, favored Laslett's earlier dating, on the grounds that Locke, he thought, was replying specifically to loyalist tracts published between September 1679 and February 1680.

[58] The reference is to 2 Samuel 13. Laslett observes that the reference to Jeffreys "must have been inserted after the end of James II's reign and is the only sentence in *Two Treatises* which dates itself, in 1689" (p. 236). I do not follow this logic. It must have been written after Algernon Sidney's execution, but it could have been inserted at any time before publication. Locke's phrase, "much upon a like occasion" almost certainly governs the relationship between Jeffreys and Absalom, (that is, two participants in a civil war) rather than the intervening story of Judah and his sister Thamar, which had been introduced by Filmer. Nor would a 1689 insertion make sense if Locke was still, as Laslett also argues, so nervous about the consequences of his authorship of the *Two Treatises* that he refused to acknowledge them.

[59] Compare *Letters concerning Toleration*: p. 195, "The horrid cruelties that in all ages, and *of late in our view*, have been committed under the name . . . of religion"; p. 210, "whither at last must it come, but to the *late* methods of procuring Conformity . . . in France, or severities like them"; p. 369, "the *late* barbarous usage of the Protestants in France."

the first edition, which might seem to apply to the executions of Sidney and Russell, or, for that matter, Fitzharris and College, but which Laslett imagines might have been added in 1689, so as to provide immediate justification for the Revolution:

nay where an appeal to the Law, and constituted Judges lies open, but the remedy is deny'd by a manifest perverting of Justice, and a barefaced wresting of the Laws, to protect or idemnifie the violence of injuries of some Men, or Party of Men, there it is hard to imagine anything but a State of War. For wherever violence is used, and injury done, though by hands appointed to administer Justice, it is still violence and injury, however colour'd with the Name, Pretences, or Forms of Law. (p. 281)

It is worth remembering, however, that when he annotated the 1698 edition of the *Treatises*, in the famous copy that Thomas Hollis donated to Christ's College, Cambridge, Locke added on the title-page a quotation from Livy (9.c.1) that extended both backwards and forwards the historical life of his appeal against violent injustice, ending with the statement that the powerful "will not be placated unless we yield to them our blood to drink and our entrails to tear out" ("placari nequeant, nisi hauriendum sanguinem laniandaque viscera nostra praebuerimus").

And whatever the order in which the two *Treatises* were written, the last sections of the *Second* (like the last sections of the *Essay*) have the feel of finality; that is, if considered at all from the perspective of style, the logical conclusion of the argument (that resistance is justified in certain circumstances) coincides with the rhetorical heightening that used to be called a peroration. This is one problem with Laslett's thesis that the close (and costive) refutation of Filmer was written later. In what Locke *published* as his latest thoughts on sovereignty, he develops a Marvellian irony worthy of the *Account of the Growth of Popery*. He wrote in Chapter 19, "Of the Dissolution of Government":

Who would not think it an admirable Peace betwixt the Mighty and the Mean, when the Lamb, without resistance, yielded his Throat to be torn by the imperious Wolf?[60] Polyphemus' Den gives us a perfect Pattern of such a Peace . . . wherein Ulysses and his Companions had nothing to do, but quietly to suffer themselves to be devour'd. And no doubt Ulysses, who was a prudent Man, preach'd up Passive Obedience, and exhorted them to a quiet

---

[60] Locke's devotion to Aesop's fables is evidence by his six copies of Aesop (including John Ogilby's verse translation of 1683–84) and his four copies of Phaedrus. See *Library*, Nos. 31–35a, 2290–93.

Submission . . . by shewing the inconveniencies might happen, if they should offer to resist Polyphemus, who had now the power over them. (p. 417)

The most brilliant example of style, however, occurs at the moment when Locke engages, like Marvell, in secret history *avant la lettre*, producing not only a flexible conspiracy theory for the reigns of *both* Charles II and James II (it is impossible to decide the chronology of the passage) but also an original twist to the venerable metaphor of the ship of state, which by cultural standards must now have been dead in the water:

But if all the World shall observe Pretences of one kind, and Actions of another; Arts used to elude the Law, and the Trust of Prerogative (which is an Arbitrary Power in some things left in the Prince's hand to do good, not harm to the People) employed contrary to the end, for which it was given: If the People shall find the Ministers, and subordinate Magistrates chosen suitable to such ends, and favoured, or laid by proportionably, as they promote, or oppose them: If they see . . . that Religion underhand favoured (though publickly proclaimed against) which is readiest to introduce it . . . if *a long Train of Actings shew the Councils* all tending that Way, how can a Man any more hinder himself from being perswaded in his own Mind, which way things are going: or from casting about how to save himself, than he could from believing the Captain of the Ship he was in, was carrying him, and the rest of the Company to Algiers, when he found him always steering that Course, though cross Winds, Leaks in his Ship, and want of Men and Provisions did often force him to turn his Course another way for some time, which he steadily returned to again, as soon as the Wind, Weather and other Circumstances would let him? (p. 405)

How perverse an imagination Locke possessed, how devious he was himself, can be perhaps best understood by following the diversionary tactics he has introduced into this ancient political metaphor. Since at some level of cultural memory we wish for the ship to come safely to shore, cross winds and leaks notwithstanding, it takes considerable intellectual discipline to follow the metaphor through its stacked conditionals to its unexpected conclusion. The fact that Algiers was the site of a slave market for Christians captured by Moorish pirates, as Laslett's note is now needed to explain, is only the most elegant and reticent detail of Locke's figure, which requires the reader to think for herself, and not to be carried along as an ignorant passenger on the route to captivity. If she is not to be sold into slavery, the metaphor further implies, the captain will have to be disposed of; as indeed, during the civil war period, a broadside had graphically envisaged (Figure 9).

Figure 9 "The captain overboard." Civil war broadside. British Library, 193.3.11.

And, as it turns out, this metaphor of the ship of state which is secretly a slave ship tacking its way to Algiers is a subtle reworking of a much longer figure that Locke had developed at the earliest stage of his thoughts on toleration. In *An Essay concerning Toleration*, written, though of course not published in 1667 (the year of Milton's *Paradise Lost*), the slave ship appears as a warning to those who would now, via the Clarendon Code, enforce conformity on the Dissenters. "I ask those," wrote Locke, "who in the late times so firmly stood the ineffectual force of persecution themselves . . . and yet are now so forward to try it upon others" (that is to say, the Anglican clergy) "whether all the severity in the world could have drawn them one step nearer to a hearty and sincere embracing the opinions that were then uppermost." And he then cited as another example galley slaves who have returned from Turkey, who "though they have endured all manner of miseries rather than part with their religion," yet have none of the characteristics – patience and cheek-turning – one associates with Christianity. Such men, Locke imagines, would readily have cut their captors' throats had they had the opportunity:

Whereby we may see it would be an hazardous attempt, if any should design it, to bring this island to the condition of a galley where the greater part shall be reduced to the condition of slaves, be forced with blows to row the vessel, but share in none of the lading, nor have any privilege or protection unless they will make chains for all those who are to be used like Turks, and persuade them to stand still while they put them on.[61]

Almost every phrase in this passage exfoliates into a political theoretical premise. The Lockean irony is present here too; and the connection between the two metaphors grapples the different parts of Locke's work together in a way that no conceptual restatement can do. But if one had to guess their chronological relationship, bereft of any hard information about when and why they were written, I would wager that the masterly inclusiveness of the "sailing to Algiers" metaphor would seem to be (as indeed it was) the product of longer and larger experience.

---

[61] See *An Essay* in *Political Writings of John Locke*, ed. Wootton, pp. 204–05. I cite from this edition in order to draw attention to Wootton's fine treatment of the *Essay*, which he calls "a founding text in the liberal tradition" (p. 38), but which has been overshadowed by the first *Letter concerning Toleration*, including in my own treatment.

LOCKE IN AMERICA

At the end of the *Two Treatises* Locke anticipated the vogue for secret history that would take hold in England in the 1690s, as the "designs" of the later Stuarts were explained by the Whig historians. Twice in the *Essay concerning Human Understanding*, in his new chapter on "Identity," (pp. 344, 347) and once in his *Second Letter concerning Toleration* (p. 95) Locke mentions "the great day, when the secrets of all hearts shall be laid open," alluding to I Corinthians 14.25 and 2 Corinthians 5.10. That revelatory moment will presumably explain which of the Lockes recognized by modern scholarship was master of the others at the time – was, if not the "true" early modern Locke, the one that Locke himself most respected and cherished.

In the meantime, because it has consequences for education and beyond that for the civil society, we must continue to address the question of "Locke in America." In his book of that title, Jerome Huyler himself uses the pun "unlocking" (p. 32) to describe the duties and difficulties of the Locke scholar today, forced to decide between different conceptions of what such scholarship should do.[62] Huyler rejects the "culturally specific" analysis of Richard Ashcraft, "reaching no farther than the 'social life world' inhabited by the author, his audience, and his adversaries" (p. 30). Influenced by the Straussian Thomas Pangle, Huyler wishes to return to the possibility "that political debate or argument is not simply or entirely reducible to 'ideology'," and that "some past statesmen, historians, and theorists may at times have been capable of liberating themselves" from the constraints of their own historical moment (p. 31). In his search for what is fundamentally and permanently "Lockean," however, Huyler virtually ignores such old-fashioned evidence as what Jefferson, Adams, James Otis and others actually said about Locke and the relation of his thought to their own.[63] My own sense is that they would have been both shocked and amused by the revisionist arguments of the last two decades, which set Locke (or rather, the property-conscious and invididualistic Locke) on one side

---

[62] Jerome Huyler, *Locke in America* (Lawrence, Kansas, 1995), p. 31.
[63] However, one valuable feature of this book is its introductory summary (pp. 1–41) of the revisionist debates of the last two decades over Locke's status as a founding father of American liberalism.

and Milton, Sidney, Harrington, Gordon and Trenchard on the other.[64]

Although Thomas Jefferson carefully studied the *Letter concerning Toleration* and Benjamin Franklin was deeply influenced by the *Essay concerning Human Understanding*,[65] it was undoubtedly "Locke on Government" who had standing in colonial and revolutionary America. For Jefferson, "Locke on government" was one of the "elementary books of public right," not in contradistinction to, but along with, Algernon Sidney's *Discourses*. In looking back at his work on the Declaration of Independence, he wrote:

> I did not consider it as any part of my charge to invent new ideas altogether . . . My aim was simply to place before mankind the common sense of the subject . . . It was intended to be an expression of the American mind . . . the harmonizing sentiments of the day, whether expressed in conversation, in letters, printed essays, or the elementary books of public right, As Aristotle, Cicero, Locke, Sidney, etc.[66]

In March 1825 he wrote a resolution for the Board of Visitors of the University of Virginia, in order to provide that no principles should be inculcated at the University which were incompatible with the Virginia and U. S. Constitutions:

> For this purpose it may be necessary to point out specially where these principles are to be found legitimately developed . . .
> Resolved, that it is the opinion of this Board that as to the general principles of liberty and the rights of man, in nature and society, the doctrines of Locke, in his "Essay concerning the true original extent and end of civil government," [i.e. the *Second Treatise*] and of Sidney in his "Discourses on government," may be considered as those generally approved by our fellow citizens . . .[67]

John Adams, as we shall see in the next chapter, agreed whole-heartedly with Jefferson in grouping *together* those same liberal thinkers that Thomas Hollis regarded as the basis of the early modern liberal canon. And in 1769 *The Political Register* celebrated the defeat of Archbishop Secker's campaign to introduce episcopacy to America in a print which shows the colonists waving books at the

---

[64] For a similarly counter-revisionary view, see Alan Craig Houston, *Algernon Sidney and the Republican Heritage in England and America* (Princeton, 1991), pp. 223–31.

[65] On Franklin's commitment to the *Essay*, see Wood, *The Politics of Locke's Philosophy*, p. 63.

[66] See Carl Becker, *The Declaration of Independence: A Study in the History of Political Ideas* (New York, 1942), pp. 25–26.

[67] See *The Complete Jefferson*, ed. Saul K. Padover (New York, 1943), p. 1112.

Figure 10 Satirical print from *The Political Register* (1769). Reproduced in John Wingate Thornton, *The Pulpit of the American Revolution* (1860), opposite p. xxx.

departing cleric, with "Locke" printed on one cover and "Sydney on Government" on the other (Figure 10).[68]

But in some respects Locke was *more* useful as an authority precisely because of his inveterate habits of caution and secrecy. He may have purchased the Whig editions of republican writers and the polemical works of Marvell, but he never cites them as authorities; with the exception, that is, of his posthumously published *Some Thoughts Concerning Reading and Study for a Gentleman*, in which he recommended Sidney's *Discourses*, while claiming never to have read them himself.[69] His alliances with Milton, Sidney and Harrington can scarcely ever be more than a matter of inference. This made Locke respectable in America when the republican tradition was not.

On April 5, 1818, John Adams wrote a long letter (it was actually only the first of a long series on the same subject) to William Tudor, once his law-clerk, now a judge. "I have now before me," wrote Adams:

a pamphlet, printed in 1762 . . . entitled *A Vindication of the Conduct of the House of Representatives of the Province of Massachusetts Bay* . . . by James Otis, Esq., a member of said House . . . I wish I could transcribe the whole of this pamphlet, because it is a document of importance in the early history of the Revolution, which ought never to be forgotten. It shows, in a strong light, the heaves and throes of the burning mountain, three years, at least, before the explosion of the volcano in Massachusetts or Virginia.[70]

Adams considered Otis to have at least as strong a claim as Patrick Henry to be a founder of American independence (10:311), and to have preempted, in this one pamphlet, the Declaration of Independence, and the works of Richard Price, Joseph Priestley and Thomas Paine. And Adams especially noted the long citations from "Locke on Government" that Otis had deployed in his attacks on the British acts of trade; and despite complaints about his aged eyes and fingers, Adams respectfully transcribed the whole of Otis's assessment of Locke as the best authority for the purpose:

It is possible there are a few . . . that cannot bear the names of liberty and

---

[68] Reproduced from John Wingate Thornton, *The Pulpit of the American Revolution* (1860), opposite p. xxx.

[69] *The Educational Writings of John Locke*, ed. James L. Axtell (Cambridge, 1968), p. 400. In these notes, first published by Pierre Desmaiseux in 1720, Locke paired Sidney with Hooker as guides to political theory, and also recommended Tyrrell's *History of England*.

[70] John Adams, *Works*, ed. Charles Francis Adams, 10 vols. (Boston, 1856), 10:300.

property, much less that the things signified by those terms should be enjoyed by the vulgar. These may be inclined to brand some of the principles advanced in the Vindication of the House, with the odious epithets, *seditious* and *levelling*. Had any thing to justify them been quoted from Colonel Algernon Sidney, or other British martyrs to the liberty of their country, an outcry of rebellion would not be surprising. The authority of Mr. Locke has therefore been preferred to all others, for these further reasons. 1. He was not only one of the most wise as well as most honest, but the most impartial man that ever lived. 2. He professedly wrote his discourses on government, as he himself expresses it, "to establish the throne of the great restorer, King William" . . . By this title, our illustrious sovereign, George 3d (whom God long preserve), now holds. 3. Mr. Locke was as great an ornament, under a crowned head, as the Church of England ever had to boast of. Had all her sons been of his wise, moderate, tolerant principles, we should probably never have heard of those civil dissensions that have so often brought the nation to the borders of perdition . . . (10:312–13)

If Locke was, as I have claimed, a master of taciturnity; if he "professedly" (Otis's term shows that he was not deceived) constructed his political theory exclusively on natural law principles that did not exclude the possibility of constitutional monarchy; if his commitment to religious toleration was indeed the substratum of all his major work (Otis was one of those who received from Thomas Hollis a copy of the *Letters concerning Toleration*);[71] then one can certainly understand why Otis and political reformers, adopting Locke's own strategies, could claim his work, in Jefferson's words, as "the expression of the American mind."

[71] See W. H. Bond, *Thomas Hollis of Lincoln's Inn: A Whig and his Books* (Cambridge, 1990), p. 121.

CHAPTER 8

John Adams: reader extraordinary

These are what are called revolution principles. They are the principles of Aristotle and Plato, of Livy and Cicero, and Sydney, Harrington and Locke. The principles of nature and eternal reason. The principles on which the whole government over us, now stands.

In the first of his famous *Novanglus* essays, written in the aftermath of the Boston Tea-Party and published in the *Boston Gazette* of 1774, a man who would become president of the United States defined his political principles, giving a list of authorities whose names, taken in the aggregate, explained the creative muddle that he was: a "new Englishman," basing his political thought on the first principles of Aristotle and Plato (however those founding figures in the history of political philosophy pull in different directions), on the classical republicanism of Livy and Cicero, on the radical antimonarchism of Algernon Sidney, the senatorial utopianism of John Harrington, and the natural-law anti-Filmerism of John Locke. At other moments his liberal canon would include Sir Edward Coke, John Milton, Sir Henry Vane, Henry Neville, Marchamont Nedham, Edward Hyde, earl of Clarendon, the *State Trials*, Gilbert Burnet. This confident syncretism, so alien to certain traditions in the modern history of the United States and to political philosophy more generally, should be more intelligible at the end of this study. It reveals Adams as a liberal, and not only strategically: a product of his reading and, by his writing, a further definer of the liberal canon. Given the extraordinary intellectual, legal and rhetorical contributions Adams made to the American Revolution, it is worth reconsidering how he came by this syncretism. I propose to round off this book, which began with the Anglo-American republic of letters, with another instructive example of transatlantic communication or, as an early modern thinker might put it, another *translatio studii*. This chapter, too, returns for its form to humanist biography; and as the opening chapter on Thomas Hollis introduced most of the themes and writers covered in this study, so the closing one on John Adams will, it is to be hoped, reiterate them in such a way as to show that the web has been honestly woven.

Procedurally, and in keeping with my wish to honor the translators and the process of transmission itself, John Adams will be featured here through the mediation of Charles Francis Adams, his grandson, editor of the great mid-nineteenth-century edition of Adams's *Works*.[1] Rather than move to the supposedly neutral territory of modern editions, I encourage readers to explore Adams's thought with the assistance of this subtle yet strongly interventionist editor, whose project, it seems to me, was not unlike that of Thomas Hollis and Francis Blackburne. One symbol of that project I discovered by chance: that the Yale University library copy of the *Works* was donated by Charles Francis Adams himself, in the year of its publication. And because so much of my argument throughout has depended on persons – not on extracting thought from its context but on putting it back into the heads of real thinkers and into the causal webs of real lives – this chapter relies heavily on Adams's *Diary*, again in the composite text produced by Charles Francis Adams (with insertions from the much later *Autobiography*), rather than on L. H. Butterfield's modern edition.[2] As a fully rounded personality (in the physical as well as the metaphysical sense) Adams is a wholesome encounter for a reader of the late twentieth century, not least because we have become so accustomed to thrusting the names of the past into ideological compartments. And especially as a lawyer, and an ethical theorist of the law, Adams adds a dimension to this study that seems appropriate both to the time and place in which it is written.

The second president of the United States did not always sound as he did in the first of the *Novanglus* letters. In later life he fell into the habit of distinguishing between the sacred texts of the liberal tradition, and even of citing them against each other. In the late 1780s, in response to the criticism of the new American constitution by Turgot, the French minister, Adams reread Milton, Locke,

[1] *The Works of John Adams, Second President of the United States*, ed. Charles Francis Adams, 10 vols. (Boston, 1851). The quotation above is from 4:15.
[2] L. H. Butterfield *et al.*, eds., *The Diary and Autobiography of John Adams*, 4 vols. (Cambridge, Mass., 1961).

Sidney, Nedham and Harrington. He delivered a hilarious attack, in the Miltonic high style, on Milton's *Readie and Easie Way* as a plan for a new republic,[3] and in another chapter of his *Defence of the Constitutions of America* remarked that "Americans in this age are too enlightened to be bubbled out of their liberties, even by such mighty names as Locke, Milton, Turgot or Hume" (4:466). But although he had nothing but scorn for the idea of a permanent unicameral senate, the evolution of his political thought (and the intricacy of his personality) greatly resembled Milton's. Both began as monarchists, with a powerful commitment to proto-enlightenment ideals of education. Both were catapulted into a maelstrom of events that required them to rethink their political premises. Both were auto-didacts to an extreme, and acquired extraordinary control over language and its use in the public sphere. Both were obsessed with self-description, an art or a need in which candor was well seasoned with disingenuity. Both had a phase of extreme radicalism to match the revolutionary moment of their countries; but like Milton, Adams was (with a few rare moments of populist fervor or sympathy) opposed to "a constitutional structure in which the popular branch dominated."[4]

Adams, who in his early twenties seems actually to have set himself Milton as a model, has been subjected to similar debates in the modern academy as to just how radical or revolutionary he was in his formative years;[5] and, with more justice than Milton, has been accused of becoming conservative as he aged. It is certainly proper to ask how I can apply the term "liberal" to a man who led the

---

[3] *Works*, ed. Charles Francis Adams, 4:465–66.
Can one read, without shuddering, this wild reverie of the divine, immortal Milton? . . . What! a single assembly to govern England? an assembly of senators for life too? What! did Milton's ideas of liberty and free government extend no further than exchanging one house of lords for another, and making it supreme and perpetual? What! Cromwell, Ireton, Lambert, Ludlow, Waller, and five hundred others of all sects and parties, one quarter of them mad with enthusiasm, another with ambition, a third with avarice, and a fourth of them honest men, a perpetual council to govern such a country! It would have been an oligarchy of decemvirs on the first day of its sitting; . . . John Milton was as honest a man as his nation ever bred, and as great a friend of liberty; but his greatness most certainly did not consist in the knowledge of the nature of man and of government, if we are to judge from this performance.

[4] See Trevor Colbourn, *The Lamp of Experience: Whig History and the Intellectual Origins of the American Revolution* (Chapel Hill, 1965), p. 105: "History had showed [Adams] that the people never succeeded in maintaining their liberties; only a balanced, aristocratically inclined republic would do that."

[5] For a summary of the views of his biographers on this point, see John Ferling, *John Adams: A Life* (Knoxville, 1992), pp. 81–82.

Federalist party against Jefferson's Republicans, who so hated the French Revolution that he abandoned many of his earlier liberal heroes, and who became so embroiled in electoral politics that he passed the Sedition Act of July 1798, thereby undoing every word he had spoken earlier in defence of freedom of the press.[6] I imply no apology for the later Adams, however, in exploring the significance of the early Adams – the one whose acquaintance with early modern liberalism, *combined with his first-hand experience* of political conditions not vastly dissimilar to those that produced Milton, Sidney or Locke, makes a highly instructive coda to earlier arguments. And the very late Adams – the one who corresponded with William Tudor about the origins of the American Revolution – was, as we saw at the end of the last chapter, engaged in retrospective analysis that partly reconstituted him as the liberal idealist he had been in the 1760s and 1770s.

In the process of following Adams through his formative years, many of the themes of this book recur in surprising rearrangements: the importance of Milton in America; the significance of the state trial in crystallizing political resistance; the relation between liberal thought and the anecdote; the idea of secret history itself as a weapon in the campaign for political openness; and above all the dynamic interplay between memory and imagination in converting the past into a better future. All of these can be found, as if by chance or destiny, in the pages of Adams's *Diary* and its surrounding texts.

Adams, therefore, was actually exactly the sort of liberal of whom Thomas Hollis would have approved – a complex figure whose political profile was sufficiently labile to permit of appropriation to different historical circumstances, but not so structurally ambiguous as to become an effective weapon in the hands of one's opponents, either to be dismissed as a radical or claimed as an apostate. In fact, as Adams became a friend and correspondent of Brand Hollis in the 1790s, so too he had been, without knowing it, coopted a quarter of a century earlier into the Hollis program. As Blackburne pointed out in his *Memoirs* of Hollis:

---

[6] Ferling, *John Adams*, p.367, dissents from Page Smith's whitewashing of this event, which was motivated by electoral fear of Jefferson and the Republicans. He points out that the administration secured at least fourteen indictments under the Sedition Act, including suits against five of the six most important Republican newspapers. For an important account of the role of the Sedition Act in the history of First Amendment interpretation, see Anthony Lewis, *Make No Law* (New York, 1991), pp. 55–66.

Mr. Hollis procured to be printed in the London Chronicle, "A Dissertation on the Canon and Feudal Law," during the ferment occasioned by the stamp-act. This excellent performance passed for a long time for the work of Jeremy Gridley, Esq., attorney general . . . This Dr. Hollis had noted at the end of Dr. Chauncey's Sermon on the repeal of the stamp-act. But he was afterwards better informed; and accordingly wrote at the end of his copy of this Dissertation, printed by Almon, 1768: " . . . written by John Adams, Esq. a young gentleman of the law, who lately removed from the country to Boston."[7]

The person who set Hollis right on this was Andrew Eliot, who at the end of a long letter of October 17, 1768, describing the political and ecclesiastical climate, added:

I have now authority to inform you that the Dissertation on the canon and feudal law, was written by John Adams Esq., a young gentleman of the law, who lately removed from the country into Boston. As I have the pleasure of an acquaintance with this gentleman, I presented him one of the copies you was so good as to send me, and let him know how favorably it was received in Great Britain. He also wrote the piece signed, *Sui Juris*: but though he seemed in that to promise more, he has not written anything further. He has a large practice, and I am mistaken if he will not soon be at the head of his profession. This information is not designed to be kept secret.[8]

Blackburne's account slightly obscures the stages of Hollis's interventions. Adams's *Dissertation* had been originally published in the *Boston Gazette* in August 1765, in serial form. Immediately it came to Hollis's attention he arranged to have it published in the *London Chronicle*. It was reprinted, again thanks to Hollis, by John Almon in 1768 in a collection of pamphlets entitled *The True Sentiments of America*, which was Hollis's major contribution to putting the case of the colonists fairly before the English public. Towards the end of his life Adams recorded an ever-so-slightly churlish account of the matter. Writing to F. A. Vanderkemp on March 3, 1804, Adams was both querulous and disingenuous:

Almost forty years ago, that is in 1765, I wrote a few thoughts in Edes and Gill's Gazette. Mr. Hollis of London printed them in a pamphlet and imputed them to Mr. Gridley. He gave them the title of a Dissertation on the Canon and Feudal Law. A lamentable bagatelle it is. I have no copy of it, and know not where to get one.[9]

---

[7] Francis Blackburne, *Memoirs of Thomas Hollis, Esq.*, 2 vols. (London, 1780), 1:291.

[8] *Letters from Andrew Eliot to Thomas Hollis*, in *Massachusetts Historical Society Collections*, 4th series, vol. 4 (Boston, 1858), p. 434.

[9] John Adams, *Correspondence*, in *Works*, 9:589.

He fails to mention his communications with either Andrew Eliot or Brand Hollis, or the fact that his famous library contained a copy of Blackburne's *Memoirs*. This late letter introduces that side of Adams that continues to puzzle historians. As he became a pillar of the institutions he had helped to found, he sometimes (depending on his audience) wished to underemphasize his earlier, more radical positions and influences.

But in the *Dissertation*, at the age of thirty, Adams had effectively argued for the binary structure of the Good Old Cause as Sir Henry Vane had defined it in the middle of the seventeenth-century revolution: as principled resistance to injustice and oppression of the many by the few in both church and state: "Since the promulgation of Christianity, the two greatest systems of tyranny, that have sprung from this original, are the canon and the feudal law" (3:449). Catholicism was particularly to blame, by reducing the minds of people all over Europe "to a state of sordid ignorance and staring timidity; and by infusing into them a religious horror of letters and knowledge" (3:450). "One age of darkness succeeded another" until the Reformation, which led, by a proto-Enlightenment, to the struggles between the English and their Stuart monarchs. Like John Rawls, Adams thought back to the Reformation as the distinctive moment when liberalism became thinkable, indeed, unavoidable; and like the Whig historian that he was at this stage, he developed a "cause" for the American settlements that was in fact more broad-reaching than Puritan escape from the regime of Archbishop Laud:

> It was this great struggle that peopled America. – It was not religion alone, as is commonly supposed; but *it was a love of universal liberty* . . . It was a resolution formed by a sensible people, – I mean the Puritans – almost in despair. They had become intelligent in general, and many of them learned . . . This people had been so vexed and tortured by the powers of those days, for no other crime than their knowledge and their freedom of enquiry and examination, and they had so much reason to despair of deliverance from those miseries on that side the ocean, that they at last resolved to fly to the wilderness for refuge . . .
>
> After their arrival here, they began their settlement, and formed *their plan both of ecclesiastical and civil government, in direct opposition to the canon and the feudal systems.* (3:451; italics added)

Crucial to this escape, in Adams's historiography, was an ideal of education:

> The leading men among them, both of the clergy and the laity, were men

of sense and learning: To many of them, the historians, orators, poets, and philosophers of Greece and Rome were quite familiar; and some of them have left libraries that are still in being, consisting chiefly of volumes, in which the wisdom of the most enlightened ages and nations is deposited – written, however, in languages, which their great grandsons, *though educated in European Universities*, can scarcely read. (3:451–52)

It was the civil and religious principles of the Puritan settlers, Adams argued, that gave them such a commitment to education:

For this purpose they laid very early the foundations of colleges, and invested them with ample privileges and emoluments; and it is remarkable that they have left among their posterity so universal an affection and veneration for those seminaries, *and for liberal education*, that the meanest of the people contribute cheerfully to the support and maintenance of them every year, and that nothing is more generally popular than projections for the honor, reputation and advantage of those seats of learning. (3:455; italics added)

They also made provision for grammar schools, thereby establishing an unrivalled system of public education and public expense. And the consequence of this commitment, Adams added, is that "a native of America who cannot read and write is as rare an appearance as a Jacobite or a Roman Catholic, that is, as rare as a comet or an earthquake" (3:456).

It begins to come clear that Adams's *Dissertation* is primarily an argument for a liberal education, broadly reconceived in the light of the Puritan migration, and far more egalitarian in its sense of a general need for, and entitlement to, education, than anything he could have found in Milton's *Of Education*. Adams warns his readers that:

there has been among us a party for some years, consisting chiefly not of the descendants of the first settlers of this country, but of high churchmen and high statesmen imported since, who affect to censure this provision for the education of our youth as a needless expence, and an imposition upon the rich in favor of the poor, and as an institution productive of idleness and vain speculation among the people, whose time and attention it is said ought to be devoted to labour, and not to public affairs, or to examination into the conduct of their superiors. (3:456)

It is this class-selective anti-intellectualism that, by revealing its own economic motives, should generate a counter-movement – a liberal intellectualism capable of exploiting the analogies between Enlightenment theories of knowledge, Protestant theology and responsible government:

And liberty cannot be preserved without a general knowledge among the people, *who have a right*, from the frame of their nature, *to knowledge*, as their great Creator, who does nothing in vain, has given them understandings, and a desire to know; and besides this they have *a right, an indisputable, unalienable, indefeasible, divine right to that most dreaded and envied kind of knowledge, I mean, of the characters and conduct of their rulers.* Rulers are no more than attorneys, agents and trustees, for the people: and if the cause, the interest and trust is insidiously betrayed, or wantonly trifled away, the people have a right to revoke the authority that they themselves deputed, and constitute abler and better agents, attorneys and trustees. And the preservation of the means of knowledge, among the lowest ranks, is of more importance to the public than all the property of all the rich men in the country. . . The only question is, whether it is a public emolument? and if it is, the rich ought undoubtedly to contribute, in the same proportion as to all other public burdens, – that is, in proportion to their wealth which is secured by public expenses. (3:456–57; italics added)

Thus a proto-Enlightenment belief in education as the basis of responsible citizenship, and of the public's right to know what its government is up to, is supported by a still more radical notion – that the wealthy ought to pay for the education of the poor through taxation. Adams then proceeded to connect this "American" idea of education to a venerable liberal theme, freedom of the press, to which, he argued, the American colonists have been and should be particularly dedicated. "Care has been taken that the art of printing should be encouraged, and that it should be easy and cheap and safe for any person to communicate his thoughts to the public" (3:457). And he urged the printers, in particular, not to be intimidated, identifying timidity as a colonial problem, even as he had a moment before been praising the settlers for their courage:

The cause of this timidity is perhaps hereditary, and to be traced back in history as far as the cruel treatment the first settlers of this country received, before their embarkation for America, from the government at home. Everybody knows how dangerous it was to speak or write in favor of any thing, in those days, but the triumphant system of religion and politics. And our fathers were particularly the objects of the persecutions and proscriptions of the times. It is not unlikely therefore, that, although they were inflexibly steady in refusing their positive assent to any thing against their principles, they might have contracted habits of reserve, and a cautious diffidence of asserting their opinions publicly. These habits they probably brought with them to America, and have transmitted them down to us. (3:459)

But Adams then reversed himself once again, on the cultural effects of persecution, and ended his tract with a ringing peroration, whose antecedents will finally be named:

Let the pulpit resound with the doctrine and sentiments of religious liberty . . . Let the bar proclaim, "the laws, the rights, the generous plan of power," delivered down from remote antiquity; – inform the world of the mighty struggles, and numberless sacrifices, made by our ancestors, in defence of freedom. Let it be known, that British liberties are not the grants of princes or parliaments, but original rights, conditions of original contracts, coequal with prerogative, and coeval with government; that many of our rights are inherent and essential, agreed on as maxims and established as preliminaries, even before a parliament existed. Let them search for the foundations of British laws and government in the frame of human nature, in the constitution of the intellectual and moral world . . . Let the colleges join their harmony, in the same delightful concert . . . Let the public disputations become researches into the grounds and nature and ends of government . . . Let the dialogues and all the exercises become the instruments of impressing on the tender mind . . . the ideas of right and the sensations of freedom.

In a word, let every sluice of knowledge be opened and set a-flowing. The encroachments upon liberty, in the reigns of the first James and the first Charles, by turning the general attention of learned men to government, are said to have produced the greatest number of consummate statesmen which has ever been seen in any age or nation. *The Brookes, Hamdens, Vanes, Seldens, Miltons, Nedhams, Harringtons, Nevilles, Sydneys, Lockes, are all said to have owed their eminence in political knowledge, to the tyrannies of those reigns.* (3:462–63)

In other words, what drives political thought is not earlier political thought alone, but negative – appalling – political experience. The political repression imposed by the Stuarts, Adams proposes, created its own opposition. By its self-evident unfairness, it galvanized men (who might otherwise have led more ordinary lives) to become political thinkers and crusaders; and between them the lawyers and the academics share the responsibility of carrying on that tradition, of constitutional historical knowledge informing courageous political critique.

AUTODIDACTISM

John Adams had graduated from Harvard in 1755, too early to profit from any of the Hollis benefactions in terms of books. But he determined to acquire "at any sacrifice . . . a proper library," suitable for the study of law.[10] In April 1756, at age twenty, as is frequently noted, he recorded his admiration in his *Diary* for Milton, as follows:

Reading Milton. The man's soul, it seems to me, was distended as wide as creation. His power over the human mind was absolute and unlimited. His genius was great beyond conception, and his learning without bounds.[11]

Less noticed by subsequent researchers, perhaps because it does not show up in the index of Adams's works under the heading "Milton," is a remarkable letter he wrote to his friend Webb still earlier than this diary entry, in the September after he graduated from Harvard:

Dear Sir:

I promised to write you an account of the situation of my mind. The natural strength of my faculties is quite insufficient for the task. Attend, therefore, to the invocation. O thou goddess, muse, or whatever is thy name, who inspired immortal Milton's pen with a confusion ten thousand times confounded, when describing Satan's voyage through chaos, help me, in the same cragged strains, to sing things unattempted yet in prose or rhyme.[12]

Ten years before he published his ringing attack on the canon and feudal laws, therefore, Adams was giving off signs of having found a model for his own intellectual development – a model who had carefully recorded *his* intellectual development in the autobiographical passages of *Reason of Church Government* and elsewhere.

At the same time as he was reading Milton, Adams was reading *The Independent Whig*, produced by Thomas Gordon, the author of *Cato's Letters*. Gordon's works, Charles Francis Adams noted, "have passed into oblivion, but at this period they were much read on account of their free and independent spirit" (2:5). Two years later, in 1758, Adams recorded his admiration of a young friend, Peter Chardon, whom he had met in Boston, and who "quotes Locke's Conduct of the Understanding" (2:39). Apparently he had not yet read it himself; but by 1760, still berating himself for his inadequacies as a scholar, he vowed: "Let me remember to keep my chamber, not run abroad; my books, – Naval Trade, Coke, Andrews, Locke, Homer . . . Law, and not poetry, is to be the business of my life." By 1790, his library

---

[10] *Autobiography*, in *Works*, 2.50n.   [11] *Works*, 2:14.

[12] Adams, *Works*, 1:27. In the *Diary* he complained, on March 23, 1756, at the age of twenty, that his study plan was not working: "My brains seem constantly in as great confusion and wild disorder as Milton's chaos; they are numb, dead. I have never any bright, refulgent ideas" (2:13).

contained a three-volume edition of Locke's works, and "Locke on Government," in the 1694 edition.[13] He was also reading Montesquieu's *Spirit of the Laws* (2:93), and beginning to figure out what *kind* of lawyer he would be. For on November 5, 1760, he inserted in his diary a rough draft of an article on "the spirit of the laws" as he now understood them. Significantly, the occasion was the death of the Chief Justice Sewall, and Adams, in the fourth year of his legal studies,[14] felt prepared to outline the qualifications of his successor:

> Such persons know that the rules of the common law are extremely numerous; the acts of parliament are numerous; . . . such persons know that the histories of cases and resolutions of judges have been preserved from a very great antiquity; and they know also, that every possible case being thus preserved in writing and settled in a precedent, leaves nothing, or but little, to the arbitrary will or uninformed reason of prince or judge. And it will be easy for any man to conclude what opportunities, industry, and genius employed from early youth, will be necessary to gain a knowledge from all these sources sufficient to decide the lives, liberties, and fortunes of mankind with safety to the people's liberties as well as the king's prerogative; that happy union in which the excellence of the British government consists, and which has often been preserved by the deep discernment and noble spirit of English judges. (pp. 99–100)

This definition of the lawyer's mission was motivated by the candidacy for Chief Justice of Thomas Hutchinson, whose selection by the British governor, Adams's grandson reminds us in a footnote, "largely contributed to bring on the Revolution." This was a purely political appointment, since Hutchinson, as John Ferling observes, "was bereft of legal training."[15]

In the summer of 1761, Adams was still struggling with Coke's *Institutes*; but he was a long way advanced in his social and political theory of the law. In relation to a case where an apprentice sued his master for non-performance of his covenant, which included teaching him to read and write, Adams wrote a speech in which he fully articulated all the major branches of early modern liberalism, and their interconnection:

> the English law greatly favors education. In every English country, some

---

[13] At this time (1760), Locke is triangulated with Bacon and Newton, which suggests that Adams had read the *Essay concerning Human Understanding*, rather than the *Two Treatises* (2:105, 109).

[14] A few days later he lists all the lawbooks he has read, and those he has mastered! Coke's *Institutes* fell into the previous category (2:103–04).

[15] Ferling, *John Adams*, p. 42.

sort of education, some acquaintance with letters is necessary, that a man may fill any station whatever. In the countries of slavery and Romish superstition, the laity must not learn to read, lest they should shake off the yoke of bondage. But in Protestant countries, and especially in England and its colonies, freedom of inquiry is allowed to be not only the privilege, but the duty of every individual. We know it to be our duty to read, examine, and judge for ourselves, even of ourselves, what is right . . . Now, how can I judge what my Bible justifies unless I can read my Bible?

The English constitution is founded, 'tis bottomed and grounded, on the knowledge and good sense of the people. The very ground of our liberties is the freedom of elections. Every man has in politics as well as religion, a right to think and speak and act for himself. No man, either king or subject, clergyman or layman, has any right to dictate to me the person I shall choose for my legislator and ruler. I must judge for myself. But how can I judge, how can any man judge, unless his mind has been opened and enlarged by reading . . . (2:131)

Here, clearly, was the Lockean embryo of the arguments that emerged in his *Dissertation on the Canon and Feudal Laws*, the first instalment of which appeared in August 1765. But in the shorter version it is perhaps even more striking how clearly Adams had intuited the binary structure of the Good Old Cause, the relation between self-determination in religion and in politics, and the relation between both the first two and education.

Nevertheless, at this stage in his self-education, Adams, unlike his cousin Samuel Adams, not only saw no contradiction between his ideals and the British constitution, but saw the latter as the guarantor of the former. The first instalment of the *Dissertation* appeared before Adams had grasped the significance of the Stamp Act of that autumn. In fact, Adams responded only mildly to the furor over the Stamp Act. He drew up a petition to the selectmen of Braintree, and called a meeting to discuss the issue, which resulted in the drafting and publication of a resolution against the tax in a local paper. Later, in the *Autobiography*, Adams rather exaggerated the impact of this local protest, compared to the dramatic demonstrations managed by Samuel Adams; and he did not see the Act, as did his cousin, as the first sign of a plot to enslave the colonies, but rather, when he finally mentioned it towards the end of the *Dissertation*, as a temporary aberration by a basically acceptable government. The plot John Adams saw was the one that had engaged Jonathan Mayhew, to impose an Anglican episcopate on America.[16]

[16] Ferling, *John Adams*, p. 47.

But the cessation of all legal business after November 1765 was a powerful lever to move Adams further in the direction that his broader principles already demanded. Not only was he temporarily out of a job. Not only did he have plenty of time to think. On December 20, he was appointed by the town of Boston to assist Jeremiah Gridley and James Otis in appealing to Governor Bernard to reopen the courts. The appeal was unsuccessful. But in preparing for it, Adams wrote as follows in his *Diary*:

> Shall we contend that the Stamp Act is void – that the Parliament have no legal authority to impose internal taxes on us, because we are not represented in it – and therefore, that the Stamp Act ought to be waived by the judges as against natural equity and the constitution? . . . or shall we ground ourselves on necessity only? (2:157)

Having chosen the former argument, Adams went home to think some more:

> Are not protection and allegiance reciprocal? and if we are out of the King's protection, are we not discharged from our allegiance? Are not the ligaments of government dissolved? Is it not an abdication of the throne? In short, where will such a horrid doctrine terminate? It would run us into treason. (2:162)

These transitional years, as recorded in Adams's *Diary*, seem powerfully to illustrate Adams's own contention that thought is driven by events, a process which in his own case he increasingly felt to be fateful. But the medium through which he *experienced* events was frequently early modern writing. It cannot be entirely coincidence that at this time Adams analyzed the character of his four political friends, James Otis, his cousin Samuel Adams, Harrison Gray and Thomas Cushing, as all versions of "Il Penseroso," Milton's thinking person; nor that he was intensifying his legal research on taxation without consent, and citing Coke on 11 Henry VII and the fate of Dudley and Empson (2:164–65). This research was put to use in the first of his January 1766 "Clarendon" letters to the *Boston Gazette*, in response to the English polemicist against the colonists who wrote under the name of "William Pym." This device required the premise that both protagonists had changed sides (3:473), and that Clarendon now repented of his *History* of the seventeenth-century revolution, which he would no longer call a "rebellion." Yet the very choice of Clarendon as a persona speaks volumes about the stance – statesmanlike and barely to the left of center – that Adams was attempting to take. In May 1766 parliament repealed the Stamp Act, and Adams, who had done comparatively little to bring that about, was wary and skeptical in his responses. He welcomed the political calm that the repeal inaugurated, and fulminated against Hutchinson for the provocative nature of his speech to the two houses in early December (2:204). By the beginning of 1768 he was still puzzling over what direction his life should take, admitting that his chief concern was the building of his library, without knowing to what ends such an expensive and time-consuming project would be the means (2:208).

"READING SYDNEY" AND THE STATE TRIALS

But during 1768 events again gave his reluctant political instincts a shove. Just after he had moved to Boston, the affair of the *Liberty*, John Hancock's vessel, and the riots caused by its impounding, increased the tensions between the English government and Massachusetts Bay. English troops landed in Boston, clearly representing, in Adams's view, "the determination in Great Britain to subjugate us" (2:214). He was drawn in to the conflict to the extent of helping the town of Boston to instruct their representatives to vote against appropriations for the maintenance of the British troops in Massachusetts Bay; and in the fall he defended John Hancock in his trial for smuggling. Looking back on this trial from the perspective of retirement, Adams declared that it had been "painful drudgery" and that it was an "odious cause" (2:215–16). But we should not be misled by this elderly rancor.[17] Charles Francis Adams wisely included in his notes a long paragraph from that defence itself, in which it is clear how deeply and broadly Adams had chosen to construe that somewhat ambiguous test case of British financial control of the colonies:

among the group of hardships which attend this statute, the first that . . . ought never to be forgotten, is . . . That it was made without our consent . . . The patrons of these laws allow that consent is necessary; they only contend for a consent by construction, by interpretation, a virtual consent. But this is only deluding men with shadows instead of substances.

---

[17] As was Ferling, *John Adams*, p. 59, who emphasizes Adams's reluctance to take the case, and speculates rather meanly on why he did so: "In all likelihood, he agreed to represent the defendant both because of the handsome fee that he could expect and from fear of the consequences of refusing the entreaties of someone as popular and powerful as Hancock."

Construction has made treason where the law has made none . . . whenever we leave principles and clear, positive laws, and wander after constructions . . . we get at an immense distance from fact and truth and nature, lost in the wild regions of imagination and possibility, where arbitrary power sits upon her brazen throne, and governs with an iron sceptre. (2:115)

The Hancock trial may, however, have been less significant in Adams's development than an earlier one, in June of the same year, that is not even mentioned in John Ferling's biography. This too was a symbolic test case of the British customs regulations. Four American soldiers were tried for murder and piracy on the high seas before a specially convened Admiralty court, on the grounds that they had killed a British customs officer, Lieutenant Panton, who entered the frigate *Rose* by force, both to search for uncustomed goods and as the leader of a press gang. Adams had successfully defended them, in the sense that he was so well prepared that the court, which included the British governors Bernard and Wentworth and Chief Justice Hutchinson, had not dared let him present his case, but decided themselves on a verdict of not guilty because the violence occurred in self-defence. Just before Christmas 1769, Adams recorded "reading Sydney" in his office, which almost certainly referred to the 1750 edition of the *Discourses concerning Government*, in two volumes, which he had purchased in 1766[18] (although he had apparently first read the *Discourses* at the age of twenty-four). Why was he reading, or rather rereading, Sidney at this moment? In his reflections on that case after the event, Adams was considering publishing an account of the trial that would serve the same purposes as did the editions of the four trials-in-context described in chapters 3 and 4:

A publication only of the record, (I mean the articles, plea to the jurisdiction, testimonies of witnesses, &c.) would be of great utility. The arguments that were used are scarcely worth publishing; those which might be used, would be well worth the perusal of the public. A great variety of useful learning might be brought into a history of that case, and the great

---

[18] This was identified by Chester Noyes Greenough in the Boston Public Library as Adams, 292.17. This edition did not contain the trial or the *Apology*. See "Algernon Sidney and the Motto of the Commonwealth of Massachusetts," in his *Collected Studies* (Cambridge, Mass. 1940), p. 77. On the flyleaf of this volume Adams had dated its purchase. See *ibid.*, p. 78. The Adams library also contained a copy of the 1772 edition, a reprint of Hollis's 1763 edition, containing Sidney's trial.

curiosity of the world after the case, would make it sell. I have half a mind to undertake it. (2:224–25)

The whole mind necessary to the undertaking was apparently never produced. But almost fifty years later, in December 1816, Adams had not forgotten the case. Thanks to Charles Francis Adams, we can connect this entry in the *Diary* with his letter to William Tudor, who had become his law clerk in August 1769 and was now himself a judge. In this letter, Adams told the story of the arguments that "might [have been] used" on that occasion, and so, via his grandson, the case of Michael Corbet and his companions entered the territory (and the style) of secret history:

You must remember it. A volume would be necessary to relate this cause as it ought to be, but never will be related . . . I had taken more pains in that case than in any other, before or since; I had appealed to Heaven and earth; I had investigated all laws, human and divine; I had searched all the authorities in the civil law, the law of nature and nations, the common law, history, practice, and every thing that could have any relation to the subject. All my books were on the table before me, and I vainly felt as if I could shake the town and the world.

Adams then proceeded to describe how, after he had merely stated the basis of his defence, justifiable homicide, and cited a single authority, Hutchinson jumped up and moved adjournment to the council chamber:

No reason was given; not a word was said; the Pope's bull was implicitly and unanimously obeyed . . . Dismal was the anxiety of the town, dreading a sentence of death the next morning. Alas, for me, my glass bubble was burst! my *boule de savon* was dissolved! All the inflammable gas was escaped from my balloon, and down I dropt like Pilatre des Rosiers.

But the next morning, as soon as the court reconvened, the President astonishingly announced that the unanimous decision of the court was justifiable homicide in necessary self-defence. "You may say," continued Adams to Tudor, "I write romance and satire":

I say that true history, in this case, is the most surprising romance and the keenest satire. *But I have not yet explained the secret.* First and last, it was FEAR. Hutchinson dreaded . . . the public investigation, before the people, of the law applicable to that case. They dared not pronounce judgment in favor of impressment in any possible case. Such a judgment would, at that time, have been condemned, reprobated, and execrated, not only in New England and all the other Colonies, but throughout the three kingdoms. It would have accelerated the revolution more than even the impeachment of the judges, or Hutchinson's foolish controversy about the omniscience and omnipotence and infinite goodness of Parliament did afterwards.

But there is a secret behind, that has never been hinted in public, and that Hutchinson dreaded should be produced before the public. You know, Mr. Tudor, that I had imported from London, and then possessed, the only complete set of the British Statutes at Large, that then existed in Boston, and, as I believe, in all the Colonies. In that work is a statute which expressly prohibits impressments in America; almost the only statute in which the word or idea of impressment is admitted.[19] The volume which contains that statute, doubled down in dog's ears, I had before me, on the table, with a heap of other books . . . (2:224–26; italics added)

In terms of what his defence of Captain Preston did for his reputation, Adams's defence of the American sailors in 1768 has been overshadowed by his defence of the British soldiers who fired on a riotous Boston crowd in 1770, the so-called "Boston Massacre." But the two cases are connected by the theme, and fact, of Adams "reading Sydney." For this was the occasion on which the famous Sidney motto, "*Manus haec inimica Tyrannis / Ense petit placidam sub libertate quietem*," which has featured at length in my chapter on the anecdote, was first brought into direct contact with American politics and juridical history. The reasons for Adams having taken on this case for the "other side" were discussed by Ferling with character-istic ungenerosity, for he assumed that Adams "was encouraged to take the case in exchange for political office," a move encouraged by Samuel Adams, who had other discreditable agendas to forward thereby.[20] John Adams knew that he took considerable risks in defending Preston, and he began with a high-minded self-justification from Beccaria's *Essay on Crime and Punishments*, subsequently imported into the *Diary*:

If, by supporting the rights of mankind, and of invincible truth, I shall contribute to save from the agonies of death one unfortunate victim of tyranny, or of ignorance equally fatal, the blessing and tears of transport will be a sufficient consolation to me for the contempt of all mankind. (2:238)

But if this seems self-serving, the same cannot be said of Adams's peroration. "To use the words of a great and worthy man, a patriot and a hero, an enlightened friend to mankind, and a martyr to

---

[19] In the notes for his Admiralty cases, which his grandson appended to his edition of the *Diary*, this statute is identified as 6 Anne, c. 37.

[20] Ferling, *John Adams*, p.68.

liberty – I mean Algernon Sidney – who, from his earliest infancy sought a tranquil retirement under the shadow of the tree of liberty, with his tongue, his pen, and his sword." And he then cited (and supplemented) Sidney's *Discourses* on the nature of law:

The law no passion can disturb. 'Tis void of desire and fear, lust and anger. 'Tis *mens sine affectu*, written reason, retaining some measure of the divine perfection. It does not enjoin that which pleases a weak, frail man, but, without any regard to persons, commends that which is good, and punishes evil in all, whether rich or poor, high or low. 'Tis deaf, inexorable, inflexible. *On the one hand, it is inexorable to the cries and lamentations of the prisoner; on the other, it is deaf, deaf as an adder, to the clamors of the populace.* (1:114)[21]

The italicized sentence was Adams's addition to Sidney, unnoticed by Charles Francis Adams, our only source for Adams's peroration. And what goes unmentioned is that Sidney's own ringing sentences are merely a flourish in his central claim, that "it is not upon the uncertain will or understanding of a prince, that the safety of a nation ought to depend." Adams thus translates an early modern argument that monarchs, given their human failings, must be subordinate to the law into a modern claim for law's impartiality, a far more abstract idea. Both the citation and the addition were typical, we can say with hindsight, of his attempts to keep himself above the fray; but that odd phrase, "deaf, deaf as an adder," was operative at another level, one of the small surprises by which a great speaker hammers tacks into the attention of his audience.

Still to come was the issue on which Adams's legal training was most effectively merged with his politics – the crisis caused by the affair of the judges. In 1773 a rumor developed that the colonial judges might be put on salary by the crown, an event that would obviously affect their independence. Governor Hutchinson had taken it upon himself, in January 1773, to deliver a speech in the Massachusetts legislature asserting the sovereignty over the colony of the British parliament, an incendiary move that once again catapulted Adams into political action, not least because he was challenged to do so by William Brattle, who defended the new policy in the public press. Adams responded with not one but eight letters to the *Boston Gazette*, helped Samuel Adams and Joseph Hawley to

[21] See Algernon Sidney, *Discourses concerning Government*, Chapter 2, Section 15: "A general presumption, that kings will govern well, is not a sufficient security to the people." In Thomas Hollis's 1763 edition, the passage occurs on p. 316.

draft a response from the Massachusetts House, and eventually became so convinced of the seriousness of the issue that he developed a plan to impeach those judges who accepted such salary, especially the Chief Justice, Hutchinson himself. Adams's *Autobiography*, inserted by Charles Francis Adams into the structure of the *Diary*, is particularly interesting here in terms of acknowledging the influence on Adams's thought of the Whig collections of state trials:

> Major Hawley came to my house, and told me he heard I had broached a strange doctrine. He hardly knew what an impeachment was; he had never read any one, and never had a thought on the subject. I told him he might read as many of them as he please; there stood the State Trials on the shelf, which was full of them, of all sorts, good and bad. I showed him Selden's works, in which is a treatise of judicature in Parliament, and gave it him to read. I added, that judicature in Parliament was as ancient as common law and as Parliament itself; that without this high jurisdiction it was thought impossible to defend the constitution against princes, and nobles, and great ministers, who might commit high crimes and misdemeanors which no other authority would be powerful enough to prevent or punish; that our constitution was a miniature of the British; that the charter had given us every power, jurisdiction, and right within our limits which could be claimed by the people or government of England. (2:330)

Thus the great paradox of Adams's life and thought came to full development; that his reading of English constitutional law and legal history provided the artillery by which America would separate itself from everything English in terms of government, retaining only the common law. In this evolution, the *State Trials* that Thomas Salmon had begun to publish in 1719 are revealed as dragon's teeth, sown abroad and soon to metamorphose into armed men. In Adams's famous library, but more importantly as a result of Adams's self-education, the *State Trials* became an agent of much broader changes than Salmon presumably envisaged.[22] Although the Council refused to act on the House's recommendations for impeachment, the courts were in fact brought to a standstill nevertheless, because the grand and petit jurors refused to sit while the accusations against the Chief Justice were pending. And this stalemate, Adams recorded dramatically, continued. "The court never sat again until a new one was appointed by the Council exercising the powers of a Governor under

---

[22] Adams could have owned either the 1719 *State Trials*, edited by Thomas Salmon (in five volumes), or the six-volume 1730 edition which carried the series up to the end of the reign of George I.

the charter, after the battle of Lexington on the 19th of April, 1775"
(2:332).

The trial of Michael Corbett, as I have suggested, initiated Adams
into the world of secret history, the world in which governments and
courts have two faces. By 1774, Adams had acknowledged the formal
existence of the genre. In one of the *Novanglus* letters, written to
defend the colonists' act of resistance to the Tea Act, Adams paused
to take exception to the claims of "Massachusettensis" that smuggling was a Whig characteristic. One of the reasons he paused was
that his eye had been caught by his opponent's style:

There is one passage so pretty, that I cannot refuse myself the pleasure of
transcribing it. "A smuggler and a whig are cousin germans, the offspring
of two sisters, avarice and ambition. They have been playing into each
other's hands a long time. The smuggler received protection from the whig;
and he in his turn received support from the smuggler . . . (4:88)

"The wit and beauty of the style in this place," remarked Adams
with truly Marvellian irony, "seem to have quite enraptured the
lively juvenile imagination of this writer." But the facts were against
him:

Some years ago, the smugglers might be pretty equally divided between the
whigs and the tories. Since that time, they have almost all married into the
tory families, for the sake of dispensations and indulgences. *If I were to let
myself into secret history*, I could tell very diverting stories of smuggling tories
in New York and Boston. Massachusettensis is quarrelling with some of his
best friends. Let him learn more discretion. (4:88; italics added)

But Adams himself was far from eschewing the techniques of
secret history, especially its use of the telling anecdote. Flushed with
the enthusiasm of his legal victory in the Preston case, he accepted
nomination to the Massachusetts House of Representatives, a position to which he was easily elected. What remained in his memory of
his first session, when he came eventually to write his memoirs, is
very much history from behind the scenes. Referring his readers to
the official journals of the House "if they are not lost," for all details
of its struggles with the Lieutenant-Governor, and the strong role
that the Boston seat took in them, Adams preferred to encapsulate
the tenor of the proceedings by way of anecdote:

Among other things will be found a labored controversy, between the House and the Governor, concerning these words: "In General Court assembled, and by the authority of the same." I mention this merely on account of an anecdote, which the friends of government circulated with diligence, of Governor Shirley, who then lived in retirement in his seat in Roxbury. Having read this dispute, in the public prints, he asked, "Who has revived those old words? They were expunged during my administration." He was answered, "The Boston seat." "And who are the Boston seat?" "Mr. Cushing, Mr. Hancock, Mr. Samuel Adams, and Mr. John Adams." "Mr. Cushing I knew, and Mr. Hancock I knew," replied the old Governor, "but where the devil this brace of Adamses came from, I know not." This was archly circulated by the ministerialists, to impress the people with the obscurity of the *par nobile fratrum*, as the friends of the country used to call us, by way of retaliation. (2:233)

Indeed, this anecdote does more work in conveying the political import of this session than could any selection or summary of the debates. The constitutional significance of "those old words" (which matched for their intransigence, but not their fatality, Sir Henry Vane's reference at his arraignment to "the sovereign Court of Parliament") is more elegantly displayed through the social snobbery and pique of the "old Governor" than it could possibly be by yet another declaration of ancient liberties; while the *function* of the anecdote as political currency, whose mobility and memorability renders it valuable in transactions on both sides of the ideological divide, is itself an important theme in Adams's retelling.

To return to a theme contracted for in my Introduction, one of the central points continuously in dispute about the intellectual origins of the American Revolution concerns the respective influences of the property-based version of liberalism attributed to Locke, versus the self-righteous critique of acquisitiveness attributed to Sidney, and later to Gordon and Trenchard. One cannot attribute to Adams either of these versions exclusively. He was definitely interested in acquiring property (his *Diary* often reveals a Pepysian satisfaction in his growing prosperity), and was both in his own time and ours accused of putting legal fees ahead of principle. Yet no one could sound more like Sidney on the topic of the financial corruption of government than Adams. In August 1770 the *Diary* contains a fragment of an essay he was writing in response to the newspaper debates, in which Jonathan Sewall, with whom he had once been on friendly terms, was defending Governor Bernard under the pseudonym of "Philanthropos." The claim of philanthropy by the Tories

seems to have particularly irritated him; and it drove him back to
Shakespeare. Citing Falstaff's joke from Shakespeare's *The Merry
Wives of Windsor*, "If I would but go to hell, for an eternal moment or
so, I might be knighted," Adams adopted a very un-Falstaffian moral
high ground. "In times of simplicity and innocence," he wrote,
"ability and integrity will be the principal recommendation to the
public service . . . but when elegance, luxury, and effeminacy begin
to be established, these rewards will begin to be distributed to vanity
and folly." Eventually corruption will so take over that real crimes
will be rewarded:

In such times you will see a Governor of a Province, for unwearied industry
in his endeavors to ruin and destroy the people, whose welfare he was
under every moral obligation to study and promote, knighted and
ennobled. You will see a "Philanthrop," for propagating as many lies and
slanders against his country as ever fell from the pen of a sycophant,
rewarded with the places of Solicitor-General, Advocate-General, and
Judge of Admiralty, with six thousands a year. (2:250–51).

It was perhaps just as well that Adams never published this essay;[23]
its own tone sounds scarcely disinterested. At this point the *Diary*
breaks off, and when it reassumes, Adams claims to have put politics
behind him (2:257). He had moved back to Braintree in the spring of
1771, regretting his inability to continue to represent the people of
Boston and frequently complaining of the ill will that seemed to have
been his only reward for public service. Yet shortly afterwards he
recorded an anecdote, one that means a great deal more than it says.
His friends were exchanging proverbs one evening, and Dr. Cooper
repeated one from his Negro Glasgow:

And then told us another instance of Glasgow's intellect, of which I had
before thought him entirely destitute. The Doctor was speaking to Glasgow
about Adam's Fall, and the introduction of natural and moral evil into the
world, and Glasgow said, they had in his country a different account of this
matter. The tradition was, that a dog and a toad were to run a race, and if
the dog reached the goal first, the world was to continue innocent and
happy; but if the toad should outstrip the dog, the world was to become
sinful and miserable. Everybody thought there could be no danger; but in
the midst of the career the dog found a bone by the way, and stopped to

---

[23] He returned to this theme, *and* the Shakespeare quotation, in February 1772, remarking that
"there is sentiment enough in these few words to fill a volume" (2:294). It was a lesson
Adams had difficulty remembering. He had then just been reading Burnet's translation of
"Utopia, or the Happy Republic; a philosophical romance, by Sir Thomas More" (2:292).

gnaw it; and while he was interrupted by his bone, the toad, constant in his malevolance, hopped on, reached the mark, and spoiled the world. (2:262–63).

Unlike his unfinished essay on political integrity, this story, as retold yet once more by Adams, persuades. It is (literally) a fable, not a harangue. Its own simplicity and restraint does the ethical and political work that polemic and character assassination, even or especially without naming names, can never do. And in the context of Adams's personal story, it goes inside the *teller*, psychologically, in a way that extends the theory of the anecdote yet further. It encapsulates all the ambivalence and anxiety that biographers have seen as marking the years 1771–73. Adams had been attacked by James Otis for caring for nothing "but to get money enough to carry you smoothly through this world" (2:301). At thirty-seven, he felt a Miltonic panic as to how he was using his talents, "ere half my days, in this dark world and wide."[24] Like the dog in the fable, he had perhaps "in the midst of the career . . . found a bone by the way," and meanwhile the toad hopped on.

In August 1772, Adams was still vacillating. He moved his family back to Boston, but "with a fixed resolution to meddle not with public affairs" (2:298). Yet at the end of this statement of resolution he inserted a verse epitaph for Algernon Sidney, derived from the 1697 *Poems of Affairs of State*,[25] in which what appears to be satire is really veneration:

> Algernon Sidney fills this tomb,
> An Atheist, for disdaining Rome;
> A rebel bold, for striving still
> To keep the laws above the will.　　　　　　(2:299)

He looked back at the start of his personal record-keeping eleven years previously, and reflected on the distance that had grown between himself and Jonathan Sewall, since it was their correspondence with which the *Diary* had begun. He turned down a request to speak at the anniversary of the Boston Massacre. And then came the

---

[24] See Milton, Sonnet 19, "When I consider how my light is spent." Adams's version of this was as follows: "Thirty-seven years, more than half the life of man, are run out. What an atom, an animalcule I am! The remainder of my days I shall rather decline in sense, spirit, and activity. My season for acquiring knowledge is past and yet I have my own and my children's fortunes to make" (2:299).

[25] See *Poems on Affairs of State from The Time of Oliver Cromwell, to the Abdication of K. James Second* (London, 1697), p. 175.

return, with a vengeance, of secret history – the story of the "purloined letters."

The purloined letters were a private correspondence between Hutchinson, his brother-in-law, Andrew Oliver, and others, on the American side, and Thomas Whately, an undersecretary in the British Treasury department. The letters had been written between 1767 and 1769, so they were now out of date, and in fact contained hardly anything more sinister than what had been said in public. They came from Benjamin Franklin in London to Thomas Cushing, Speaker of the House, and Adams believed they had been given to Franklin by Sir John Temple, with perhaps a further intermediary in the British parliament. "They came," wrote Adams, "under such injunctions of secrecy – as to the person to whom they were written, by whom and to whom they are sent here, and as to the contents of them, no copies of the whole or any part to be taken, – that it is difficult to make any public use of them" (2:318). Used they were, however, after Samuel Adams and the radicals had announced the existence of a conspiracy to subvert the Constitution, and had carefully built up the suspense in newspaper articles.[26] From this moment Adams seems to have been converted to conspiracy theory, much as Marvell was converted to suspicion of the secret Treaty of Dover in 1670 and the subsequent undermining of Parliament; and all his vocational confusion disappeared.

REREADING THE PAST

From a cultural (and psychological) perspective, it is intriguing to see him at this moment returning imaginatively to Milton. One of his earliest responses to news of the secret correspondence was as follows: "Bone of our bone, born and educated among us! . . . The subtlety of this serpent is equal to the old one" (2:318). The next day he heard a sermon by Dr. Cooper on Revelations, 12:9, "And the great dragon was cast out, that old serpent called the Devil and Satan, which deceiveth the whole world," and asked himself "whether the Doctor had not some political allusions in the choice of this text?" (2:319). In January 1775, when the North ministry had been reelected in Britain, and Dartmouth was about to order General Gage to proceed by force, Adams was still thinking in these

---

[26] See Ferling, *John Adams*, pp. 80–81.

terms. Writing to James Warren, he said that he always thought of that "junto there, immured as they are," in terms of Milton's fallen angels: "after they had recovered from their first astonishment arising from their fall from the battlements of heaven to the sulphurous lake, not subdued, though confounded, and plotting a fresh assault on the skies." He then quoted *Paradise Lost* 1:105–08, 158–60; and concluded, "Is not this rather too frolicsome and triumphant for the times, which are dull enough, and as bad as they can be?"[27] Unconscious, then, of the hermeneutical problems that result from applying Milton's poem to one's own times, Adams placed himself and his now fully rebellious colleagues on the side of Heaven and its obedient, not its rebellious, angels.[28]

In fact, Adams was continually rereading the texts of his youthful idealism, and appropriating them to new and urgent uses. In 1776 he was asked by representatives of both Virginia and North Carolina to suggest what form of government the colonies should adopt if the conflict pushed them towards independence. His response to Virginia was subsequently published as *Thoughts on Government*; and as is frequently noted, he there claimed that his seventeenth-century heroes alone – Sidney, Harrington, Locke, Milton, Nedham, Neville, Burnet and Hoadley – "will convince any candid mind, that there is no good government but what is republican" (4:194). Writing to John Penn shortly afterwards, John Adams again repeated this list of authorities, and their meaning for the colonies at this time. What is not mentioned, however, is Adams's suggestion that these names constitute, if not quite forbidden reading, an eccentric and even dangerous library. To mention these names, Adams observes in both these documents (for the second is close adaptation of the first), "a man must be indifferent to the sneers of modern Englishmen." "No small fortitude is necessary to confess that one has read them" (4:194). And, oddly enough, he takes this opportunity to identify himself with Milton in the early years of the seventeenth-century revolution, by quoting Milton's Sonnet 12 on the hostile reception of his divorce pamphlets:

---

[27] *Works*, 9:354.

[28] For Miltonic quotations in the political discourse of Adams and also Thomas Jefferson, see also Tony Davies, "Borrowed Language: Milton, Jefferson, Mirabeau," in *Milton and Republicanism*, ed. David Armitage, Armand Himy and Quentin Skinner (Cambridge, 1995), pp. 254–62.

> I did but prompt the age to quit their clogs
> By the known rules of ancient liberty,
> When straight a barbarous noise environs me
> Of owls and cuckoos, asses, apes and dogs.[29]

The sense of isolation, of being surrounded by people less informed and far-seeing than oneself, is efficiently conveyed by Milton's mid-seventeenth-century complaint; one cannot tell whether Adams recognized the further similarity, that he too was advocating an unprecedented divorce – of the colonies from the parental country.

RETROSPECTIVES

When he wrote his *Defence of the Constitutions of Government* in the late 1780s, as I have said, Adams went back to Milton, Sidney, Locke and, as a new enthusiasm, Marchamont Nedham, whose *Excellency of a Free State* had been republished by Thomas Hollis in 1767. Ten years later, just in time for the *Defence* against Turgot, Adams received a copy of this edition as a gift from Brand Hollis; and not only did it energize him to include a massive commentary on Nedham's work in his *Defence*, where it serves as the conclusion; it also inspired him to write a brief history of liberal political thought, divided into three periods. The first of these periods, in Adams's view from the 1780s, was the Reformation, whose political thought was characterized by Machiavelli, but more importantly by John Ponet's *Short Treatise of Politicke Power* (1556). According to Adams, this work "contains all the essential principles of liberty, which were after dilated on by Sidney and Locke" (5:4). The second period was the Interregnum, as Adams calls it. "In the course of those twenty years, not only Ponnet [*sic*] and others were reprinted, but Harrington, Milton, the *Vindiciae contra Tyrannos*, and a multitude of others, came upon the stage." The third period was the Revolution in 1688, "which produced Sidney, Locke, Hoadley, Trenchard, Gordon, Plato Redivivus," a concept of "production" that is ambiguous, with respect to whether it is the thought, or published versions of the thought, that historical experience produces. Half-noticing the ambiguity, Adams added, "The discourses of Sidney were indeed written before, but the same causes produced his writings and the

---

[29] In the *Thoughts on Government* Adams used the quotation as a coda, to strengthen his request for anonymity. In the letter to Penn, he absorbed it back into the argument that his liberal authorities would be widely disapproved of. See *Works*, 4:200, 204.

Revolution," a qualification which rather increases than dispels the confusion!

Nevertheless, this passage is admirably pertinent to the story I have tried to tell, and the methods I have tried to use in telling it; not least because Adams continues, in a missionary vein:

Americans should make collections of all these speculations, to be preserved as the most precious relics of antiquity, both for curiosity and use. There is one indispensable rule to be observed in the perusal of all of them; and that is, to *consider the period in which they were written, the circumstances of the times, and the personal character as well as the political situation of the writer.* (5:4–5; italics added)

It would be hard to find a better definition, in its avoidance of theoretical legerdermain, of how to do cultural history.

And long after his retirement, when Adams really had put politics behind him, he went back to reading Sidney's *Discourses*, in a spirit of respect for the material *book*, for the medium of transmission, which would have deeply gratified Thomas Hollis. Writing to Thomas Jefferson, his old political rival, from the perspective of their very old age and new philosophical friendship, he informed him on September 17, 1823, that he had been rereading "Algernon Sidney on Government," with, as it were, new eyes:

There is a great difference in reading a book at four-and-twenty and at eighty-eight. As often as I have read it and fumbled it over, it now excites fresh admiration that this work has excited so little interest in the literary world. As splendid an edition of it as the art of printing can produce, as well for the intrinsic merits of the work, as for the proof it brings of the bitter sufferings of the advocates of liberty from that time to this, and to show the slow progress of moral, philosophical, political illumination in the world, ought to be now published in America. (10:410)

Only the "splendid" edition produced by Thomas Hollis in 1763 and reissued in 1772, the latter of which Adams owned, could fit this description; not least because, for evidence of the "bitter sufferings of the advocates of liberty from that time to this" Adams must have been reading both the texts of Sidney's trial and his *Apology*, and Hollis's elaborate notes. Hollis had packed into those notes, as I showed in earlier chapters, a mini-history of early modern liberalism. And although going back to this text reminded John Adams of the slow progress of liberalism in the world (not to mention its reverses) "on the whole," he thought, "the prospect is cheering." That seems a good note on which to end.

Index

306

IDEAS IN CONTEXT

Edited by QUENTIN SKINNER (*General Editor*),
LORRAINE DASTON, WOLF LEPENIES,
J. B. SCHNEEWIND and JAMES TULLY

Titles marked with an asterisk are also available in paperback